Formatting Toolbar Buttons

B	Bold	$	Currency Style
I	Italic	%	Percent Style
U	Underline	,	Comma Style
	Align Left		Numbering
	Center		Bullets
	Align Right		Properties
	Justify		Decrease Indent
	Center Across Columns		Increase Indent

Mail's Button Bar Buttons

Compose	New Message	Delete	Delete Message
Reply	Reply to Sender	Previous	View Previous Message
ReplyAll	Reply to All	Next	View Next Message
Forward	Forward Message		
Move	Move Message		

FOR EVERY COMPUTER QUESTION, THERE IS A SYBEX BOOK THAT HAS THE ANSWER

Each computer user learns in a different way. Some need thorough, methodical explanations, while others are too busy for details. At Sybex we bring nearly 20 years of experience to developing the book that's right for you. Whatever your needs, we can help you get the most from your software and hardware, at a pace that's comfortable for you.

We start beginners out right. You will learn by seeing and doing with our **Quick & Easy** series: friendly, colorful guidebooks with screen-by-screen illustrations. For hardware novices, the **Your First** series offers valuable purchasing advice and installation support.

Often recognized for excellence in national book reviews, our **Mastering** and **Understanding** titles are designed for the intermediate to advanced user, without leaving the beginner behind. A **Mastering** or **Understanding** book provides the most detailed reference available. Add one of our pocket-sized **Instant Reference** titles for a complete guidance system. Programmers will find that the new **Developer's Handbook** series provides a higher-end user's perspective on developing innovative and original code.

With the breathtaking advances common in computing today comes an ever increasing demand to remain technologically up-to-date. In many of our books, we provide the added value of software, on disks or CDs. Sybex remains your source for information on software development, operating systems, networking, and every kind of desktop application. We even have books for kids. Sybex can help smooth your travels on the **Internet** and provide **Strategies and Secrets** to your favorite computer games.

As you read this book, take note of its quality. Sybex publishes books written by experts—authors chosen for their extensive topical knowledge. In fact, many are professionals working in the computer software field. In addition, each manuscript is thoroughly reviewed by our technical, editorial, and production personnel for accuracy and ease-of-use before you ever see it—our guarantee that you'll buy a quality Sybex book every time.

To manage your hardware headaches and optimize your software potential, ask for a Sybex book.

FOR MORE INFORMATION, PLEASE CONTACT:

Sybex Inc.
2021 Challenger Drive
Alameda, CA 94501
Tel: (510) 523-8233 • (800) 227-2346
Fax: (510) 523-2373

Sybex is committed to using natural resources wisely to preserve and improve our environment. As a leader in the computer books publishing industry, we are aware that over 40% of America's solid waste is paper. This is why we have been printing books on recycled paper since 1982.
This year our use of recycled paper will result in the saving of more than 153,000 trees. We will lower air pollution effluents by 54,000 pounds, save 6,300,000 gallons of water, and reduce landfill by 27,000 cubic yards.

In choosing a Sybex book you are not only making a choice for the best in skills and information, you are also choosing to enhance the quality of life for all of us.

TALK TO SYBEX ONLINE.

JOIN THE SYBEX FORUM ON COMPUSERVE

- Talk to SYBEX authors, editors and fellow forum members.
- Get tips, hints, and advice online.
- Download shareware and the source code from SYBEX books.

If you're already a CompuServe user, just enter GO SYBEX to join the SYBEX Forum. If you're not, try CompuServe free by calling 1-800-848-8199 and ask for Representative 560. You'll get one free month of basic service and a $15 credit for CompuServe extended services—a $23.95 value. Your personal ID number and password will be activated when you sign up.

Join us online today. Enter GO SYBEX on CompuServe. If you're not a CompuServe member, call Representative 560 at 1-800-848-8199

(outside U.S./Canada call 614-457-0802)

CompuServe

SYBEX
Shortcuts to Understanding

The SYBEX Instant Reference Series

Instant References are available on these topics:

1-2-3 Release 2.3 & 2.4 for DOS

1-2-3 Release 4 for Windows

1-2-3 Release 5 for Windows

AutoCAD Release 12 for DOS

AutoCAD Release 12 for Windows

AutoCAD 13

CorelDRAW 4

dBASE IV 2.0 for Programmers

DOS 6.2

Excel 5 for Windows

Harvard Graphics 3

Internet

Microsoft Access 2

Microsoft Office Professional

Norton Desktop for Windows 2.0

Norton Utilities 7

OS/2 2.1

Paradox 4.5 for DOS Users

Paradox 4.5 for Windows Users

PC Tools 8

Quattro Pro 5 for Windows

SQL

Windows 3.1

Word 6 for Windows

Word for Windows, Version 2.0

WordPerfect 5.1 for DOS

WordPerfect 6 for DOS

WordPerfect 6 for Windows

WordPerfect 6.1 for Windows

MICROSOFT® OFFICE PROFESSIONAL

INSTANT REFERENCE

Sheila S. Dienes

SYBEX®

San Francisco • Paris • Düsseldorf • Soest

Acquisitions Editor: Kristine Plachy

Developmental Editor: Brenda Kienan

Editor: Abby Azrael

Technical Editor: Beth Shannon

Book Designer and Compositor: Seventeenth Street Studios

Production Assistant: Marc Duro

Indexer: Matthew Spence

Cover Designer: Design Site

Cover Photographer: David Bishop

Screen reproductions produced with Collage Plus.

Collage Plus is a trademark of Inner Media Inc.

SYBEX is a registered trademark of SYBEX Inc.

TRADEMARKS: SYBEX has attempted throughout this book to distinguish proprietary trademarks from descriptive terms by following the capitalization style used by the manufacturer.

Every effort has been made to supply complete and accurate information. However, SYBEX assumes no responsibility for its use, nor for any infringement of the intellectual property rights of third parties which would result from such use.

Copyright © 1995 SYBEX Inc., 2021 Challenger Drive, Alameda, CA 94501. World rights reserved. No part of this publication may be stored in a retrieval system, transmitted, or reproduced in any way, including but not limited to photocopy, photograph, magnetic or other record, without the prior agreement and written permission of the publisher.

Library of Congress Card Number: 94-69703

ISBN: 0-7821-1657-4

Manufactured in the United States of America

10 9 8 7 6 5 4 3 2

To Debbie, Rick, Mike, Matt, and Alex James

Acknowledgments

Every book is a group effort. I would like to take this opportunity to thank some of the people who were involved in the production of this book.

Many thanks to the people at SYBEX who made this book possible, including Dr. Rudolph Langer, Barbara Gordon, and Kristine Plachy. In addition, I want to thank Brenda Kienan, developmental editor, for the overall concept for this book and for her original ideas. A special thank you to editor Abby Azrael, for her super editing skills and her eternal patience. Abby's insights are a wonderful addition to any book.

My deepest appreciation to technical editor Beth Shannon for her invaluable assistance, and to book designer and desktop publisher Lorrie Fink, production assistant Marc Duro, and indexer Matthew Spence.

Last, but not least, a huge thank you to Barry J. Schlossberg, M.D., my first computer mentor.

Contents

Introduction xxi

PART I
An Orientation to Microsoft Office Professional xxvi

Working with Microsoft Office Manager 1

An Overview of the Opening Screens 2

Access 3

Excel 5

Mail 8

PowerPoint 9

Word for Windows 11

Getting Started 13

PART II
Command and Feature Reference 14

Address Book 15

Adding Names to the Address Book 15

Creating a Personal Group 16

Alignment 17

Annotation 19

Inserting an Annotation 20

Listening to or Viewing an Annotation 21

Auditing 22

Tracing Dependents 23

Tracing Errors in a Worksheet 24

Tracing Precedents 25

AutoCorrect 25

Changing an AutoCorrect Entry 26

Creating an AutoCorrect Entry 26

AutoFormat 28

Using AutoFormat in Excel 28

Using AutoFormat in Word 29

AutoLayout 32

Creating a Slide with AutoLayout 32

Editing the Layout of a Slide 33

Inserting a Placeholder on a Slide 34

AutoText 35

Creating an AutoText Entry 35

Editing the Contents of an AutoText Entry 36

Inserting AutoText Entries 37

Renaming AutoText Entries 37

CONTENTS

Bookmark 38
Creating a Bookmark 39
Displaying Bookmarks 40
Editing a Marked Item 40

Borders and Shading 42
Applying Borders and Colors in Excel 42
Applying Borders and Shading in PowerPoint 44
Applying Borders and Shading in Word 47

Bound Object 49

Bullets and Numbering 49
Adding Bullets to Presentation Text 49
Adding Bullets and Numbering in a Word Document 49

Captions 52
Adding a Caption to a Graphic 52
Automatically Inserting Captions 53
Changing the Caption Numbering Format 55

Cell 56
Selecting a Cell 56

Change Case 57

Chart 58
Creating a Chart 58
Editing a Chart 60

Clip Art 62
Using the ClipArt Gallery 62

Close 65

Columns 65
Adding Columns to a Document 65
Editing Columns 67

Control 67
Creating a Bound Control 69
Creating a Calculated Control 69
Creating an Unbound Control 70
Editing Control Labels 71
Moving Controls 72
Selecting Controls 73
Sizing a Control 74

Control Properties 76
Changing a Control's Properties 76
Changing the Default Properties for a Form or Report 78

Cross-Reference 79
Creating Cross-References 79
Editing a Cross-Reference 81

Crosstab Query 82
Creating a Crosstab Query 82

Cue Cards 84

Cut, Copy, and Paste 84
Cutting or Copying an Item to the Clipboard 85

Pasting the Contents of the Clipboard 85

Database 86
Creating an Access Database 86
Creating an Excel Database 88
Entering Records in a Database 89
Inserting a Database in a Word Document 89

Date and Time 93
Inserting the Date and Time in Access 93
Inserting the Date and Time in Excel 94
Inserting the Date and Time in PowerPoint 95
Inserting the Date and Time in Word 96

Drag and Drop 97
Moving or Copying with Drag and Drop 97

Draw 97
Displaying the Drawing Tools 98
Using the Drawing Tools 98

Drop Cap 103
Creating Dropped Capitals 104

Duplicate 105
Duplicating a Selection 105

Envelopes 106
Addressing and Printing an Envelope 106
Including Graphics on an Envelope 108

Exit 109
Exiting an Application 109
Exiting Microsoft Office 110

Field 110
Defining a Field 111
Naming a Field 112

Field Code 112
Displaying Field Codes in a Document 112
Inserting a Field Code 113
Toggling between Field Codes and Results 114
Updating Fields 114

File Management 115
Backing Up a Message File 115
Closing an Open File 116
Creating a New File 117
Inserting a File 118
Opening a File 119
Saving a File 120

Filter 123
Filtering a List with AutoFilter 124
Filtering a List Using Compound Criteria 125

Find File 128
Defining the Search Criteria 128
Displaying File Information 131
Managing Files in the List 132

CONTENTS

Find and Replace 134
Finding Items 134
Replacing Items 137

Folder 138
Creating a Folder 139
Editing a Folder 140
Moving or Copying a Private Folder 140

Font 141
Applying Fonts to Characters 142
Changing the Character Spacing 144
Changing the Default Font 145

Footnotes and Endnotes 146
Adding a Note 146
Displaying Notes 148
Editing Notes 149
Editing Note Separators 150

Form 151
Creating Forms in Access 151
Creating Forms in Excel 154
Creating Forms in Word 155
Editing an Access Form 159
Filling In a Word Form 161

Format 163
Changing the Format of a Number in Excel 164

Format Painter 166
Copying Formats to Characters 166

Formula 167
Entering Expressions in Access 167
Entering Formulas in Excel 168
Entering Formulas in Word 170

Frame 170
Creating a Frame in a Word Document 170
Editing a Frame 171

Function 174
Entering Functions 174
Using AutoSum in Excel 175
Using the Function Wizard 175

Goal Seek 177

Go To 178
Going to a Location in an Access Database 178
Going to a Location in an Excel Worksheet 179
Going to a Location in a Word Document 181

Graphic 182
Editing a Graphic 182
Inserting a Graphic File 185
Linking a Graphic File 186

Guides 187
Aligning Objects with the Guides 187

Header and Footer 188
Creating a Header or Footer in Access 188

Creating a Header or Footer in Excel 191

Creating or Editing a Header or Footer in Word 192

Creating Different Headers and Footers in Word 194

Help 195

Getting Context-Sensitive Help 196

Getting "How To" Help 197

Using Cue Cards 197

Import/Export Data 198

Attaching a Table 198

Exporting Data 200

Importing Data 201

Setting Import/Export Specifications 203

Indent 205

Indenting a Paragraph 205

Indenting a Paragraph with Exact Measurements 205

Labels 206

Creating Labels in Access 206

Creating Labels in Word 208

Line Spacing 212

Changing the Line Spacing in a Paragraph 212

Link 213

Linking Data 214

Linking a File 216

Modifying a Link 217

Macro 220

Adding Conditions to Macros in Access 220

Creating and Running an Access Macro 221

Creating a Macro Group in Access 225

Creating and Running a Macro in an Access Form or Report 226

Recording and Running an Excel Macro 227

Recording and Running a Word Macro 232

Mail 236

Creating a Mail Message 236

Receiving a Mail Message 238

Sending an Online Document 239

Merging Revisions Made to a Word Document 241

Mail Merge 242

Creating a Main Document 242

Designating a Data Source 243

Editing a Data File 245

Editing the Main Document 246

Inserting Fields in a Word Data Source 247

Merging the Data File and the Main Document 248

CONTENTS

Margins 250

Setting the Margins for an Access Form or Report 251

Setting the Margins for an Excel Worksheet 251

Setting the Margins in a Word Document 252

Master Document 254

Changing a Document into a Master Document 255

Creating a New Master Document 256

Editing a Subdocument 257

Inserting a Subdocument into a Master Document 257

Locking a Subdocument 258

Merging and Splitting Subdocuments 259

Moving or Renaming a Subdocument File 259

Master View 260

Applying a Slide Master Format 260

Using the Other Master Views 262

Message Finder 263

Microsoft Office Manager 264

Customizing Microsoft Office 264

Module 267

Creating an Event Procedure 268

MS Query 269

Creating a Query 269

Working with a Query 272

New File 273

Note 274

Creating a Note 274

Object Linking and Embedding 276

Creating and Embedding a New Object 277

Editing an Embedded Object 278

Embedding an Existing File 278

Embedding Part of a File 280

Modifying the File Format of an Object 280

Open 281

Outline 282

Using Outline View in Excel 282

Using Outline View in PowerPoint and Word 284

Numbering Word's Outline Headings 287

Page Break 288

Inserting Hard Page Breaks 288

Page Numbers 289

Numbering Pages in Access 290

Numbering Pages in Excel 291

Numbering Pages in Word 291

Page Setup 293
Setting Up the Page 294

Paragraph 299
Setting Paragraph Spacing 300

Password 301
Assigning a Password to an Access User Account 301

Assigning a Password to an Excel or Word File 302

Permissions 305
Changing Ownership 305

Creating a Group or User Account 306

Granting Permissions 309

Pivot Table 312
Creating a Pivot Table 312

Customizing a Pivot Table 315

Customizing the Way the Table Is Displayed 319

Postoffice Manager 321
Managing the WGPO 321

Presentation 323
Creating a Presentation 323

Editing a Presentation 326

Print 328
Printing a File 328

Setting Up the Printer 331

Setting Word's Default Print Options 332

Print Preview 334
Changing to Print Preview 334

Print Report 338
Creating a Report 338

Print Security 341

Protection 341
Protecting Data in Excel 342

Protecting the Text of a Word Document 346

Query 348
Creating a Query 348

Range 352
Naming Cells or Ranges 352

Record 356
Adding Records to a Database 356

Adding Records in a Datasheet 356

Adding Records in a Form 357

Editing Records 357

Reference 358
Defining Reference Types in Formulas 358

Using Reference Operators 359

Moving and Copying References and Formulas 361

Relationship 362
Creating and Defining a Relationship 362

CONTENTS

Rename 366

Repeat 366

Repeating the Last Command or Action 366

Report 367

Creating a Report 367

Revision 369

Comparing Versions of a Document 369

Marking and Reviewing Revisions in a Document 370

Merging Revisions 372

Ruler 373

Using the Ruler 374

Scenario 375

Creating a Scenario 376

Section 378

Adding Sections to an Access Form or Report 378

Adding Sections to a Word Document 380

Sequence 382

Entering a Sequence with AutoFill 382

Shortcut Menus 385

Slide Show 386

Creating a Slide Show 386

Hiding a Slide 388

Inserting Special Effects 388

Setting a Timing for Each Slide 391

Solver 392

Solving a Problem 392

Specifying Solver's Options 396

Sort 399

Sorting Data in Access 399

Sorting Data in Excel and Word 403

Spelling 406

Checking Spelling 407

Creating a Dictionary of Excluded Words 409

Creating a Custom Dictionary 410

Style 412

Applying a Style in an Excel Worksheet 413

Applying a Style in a Word Document 413

Copying Styles in Excel 415

Copying Styles in Word 415

Creating or Modifying a Style in Excel 417

Creating or Modifying a Style in Word 418

Style Gallery 420

Copying Styles from a Template 421

Summary Info 422

Entering Summary Information 422

Table 424
Creating a Table 424
Creating Table Headings 426
Editing the Table 427
Modifying the Table Format 433
Numbering Table Cells 434

Tabs 435
Setting Tab Stops 435
Templates 437
Creating a Document Based on a Template 437
Creating a New Template 438
Managing Templates 439

Thesaurus 441
Using the Thesaurus 441

Toolbars 442
Creating or Editing Toolbars 443
Customizing a Toolbar 444

Undo/Redo 445
Using Undo and Redo 445

View 446
Changing the View in Access 446
Changing the View in Excel and Word 447
Changing the View in PowerPoint 449

Viewer 450
Copying PowerPoint Viewer 450
Running a Slide Show with Viewer 451

View Manager 452
Creating a View 452

Window 454
Managing Open Windows 454

Wizards 456

Workbook 457
Managing Worksheets 457
Selecting Worksheets in the Active Workbook 459

Worksheet 460
Changing the Column Width and Row Height 460
Hiding a Column or Row 462

Workgroup 463
Creating a Unique Workgroup 463
Joining a Different Workgroup 464

Zoom 465
Adjusting the Magnification 465

Index 467

Introduction

Microsoft Corporation has created a package of Windows applications, called Microsoft Office Professional, that probably contains all the computing power you need. You can use each application in the package to perform most of the tasks necessary to keep your office running smoothly. Together, the Microsoft Office Professional applications form a winning team for producing professional-looking forms and reports, spreadsheets, presentations, and documents.

What Is Microsoft Office?

Microsoft Office Professional is a package containing five of the most useful, popular, and powerful Windows applications on the market. The Microsoft Office Professional package allows you to accomplish just about any computing task. For example, perform all your word processing with Word; use Access to manage database files; create electronic spreadsheets with Excel; and present information graphically with PowerPoint. Last but not least, you can electronically communicate with others in your workgroup using Mail.

The Microsoft Office Professional package offers you even more than the use of its individual applications. Microsoft Office Professional lets you integrate your data into any of its applications. For example, the data you enter into a file in one program can easily be copied, inserted, or imported into another. Or, you can link or embed your data into a different file with Object Linking and Embedding (OLE).

Who Needs This Book?

The *Microsoft Office Professional Instant Reference* is designed to be used by beginners, intermediate

INTRODUCTION

users, and upgraders of any of the Microsoft Office Professional applications. Whether you are familiar with all the applications or none of them, this book will help you accomplish virtually all your computing tasks. The book assumes you have some experience using Windows.

Beginners can skim an entry for general information about performing a task, and then follow the specific steps necessary to produce the desired results. Both intermediate users and upgraders will find some entries useful as reminders of how to perform specific tasks requiring seldom-used features. In addition, upgraders can scan the appropriate entries to find out what new features are included in each Microsoft Office Professional application. All readers will find suggestions that will make their work easier.

In addition, the *Microsoft Office Professional Instant Reference* is small enough to leave out on your desk so you can find information quickly. Or, pack it in your briefcase or laptop computer case to take it with you when you are out of your office.

How This Book Is Arranged

This book is designed to be both concise and useful, so it contains two parts. Part One contains a short introduction to each of the Microsoft Office Professional applications. Part Two contains an alphabetical reference to the commands and features available in Microsoft Office Professional.

Part One: An Orientation to Microsoft Office is aimed especially at new users and upgraders. If you have not yet used one of the Microsoft Office Professional applications, read this section to learn enough to get started.

INTRODUCTION

In Part Two: Command and Feature Reference, you will find that many of the commands and features appear in more than one application. When they are truly different or require the use of different steps, each application is listed alphabetically within the entry. When the features are very similar, glance at the steps or list to find the options that are applicable to the action you wish to perform. You can glance below an entry's title to see the icon of each application that is discussed in the entry.

At the end of each entry in the reference section, you will find a list of related entries. Check the list to find out where additional information can be found, or to find commands and features that perform a similar task.

Conventions Used in This Book

There are some conventions you will find as you examine an entry or glance at a topic. For example, Notes, Tips, Warnings, and Troubleshooting tips are sprinkled throughout the book to help you better understand how to perform the task at hand.

NOTE: *Notes provide you with information that is important for the command or feature, but that does not appear in the associated steps.*

TIP: *Tips provide you with information that will make the task easier. Tips include shortcuts and alternative ways to perform a task.*

WARNING: *Read any Warnings, so you can avert a possible disaster. The Warnings will help you avoid losing important data.*

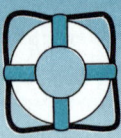

INTRODUCTION

> ### TROUBLESHOOTING
>
> ### Troubleshooting Boxes
>
> Some entries contain troubleshooting tips—boxes in which common mistakes or improper results are described and explained. You will discover lots of useful information in each Troubleshooting box.

In addition, each time a toolbar or button bar button is suggested as a method to be used to carry out a command or to perform some action, a picture of the button appears to the left of the step or paragraph. Click on the button on the toolbar indicated to carry out the command or action associated with the button.

When a command on one of the pull-down menus is specified, it appears as *Menu Name* ➤ *Command Name*. For example, if you see File ➤ Open, you should select File on the menu bar, and then choose Open in the drop-down menu that appears to display the Open dialog box. The underlined letters indicate the *hotkeys* you can press as an alternative method of performing your task. If there is also a shortcut key sequence that can be used to carry out the command, it appears in parentheses after the command. For example, if File ➤ Open (Ctrl+O) is specified, you can also hold down Ctrl while pressing O to display the Open dialog box.

Terms Used in This Book

There are several terms used in this book to describe actions you can perform:

Click Point to an item with your mouse, and then quickly press and release the left mouse button.

INTRODUCTION

Double-click Point to an item, and then quickly click twice on it.

Right-click Point to an item with your mouse, and then quickly press and release the right mouse button.

Drag Hold down the left mouse button, and then move the mouse to a different location on your screen.

Select Choose an item so it is *highlighted*, or appears in reverse video. An item must be selected before you can perform any action on it.

Toggle Many commands have only two choices–on or off. These are called toggle switches. Select the command once to toggle it on. Select the command again to toggle it off.

Check box Many dialog boxes contain check boxes, which are options that you can turn on or off. Select, or click on, a check box (place an X in it) to turn on its option. Clear a check box that contains an X (again, click on it) to turn off its corresponding option.

Spin wheel Many dialog boxes also contain text boxes into which you can either type a number or measurement, or click on the spin wheels– the ↑ or ↓ button beside the text box–to adjust the measurement.

Preview Some dialog boxes contain a Preview area, where the results of the options you select in the dialog box are displayed.

PART ONE

AN ORIENTATION TO MICROSOFT OFFICE PROFESSIONAL

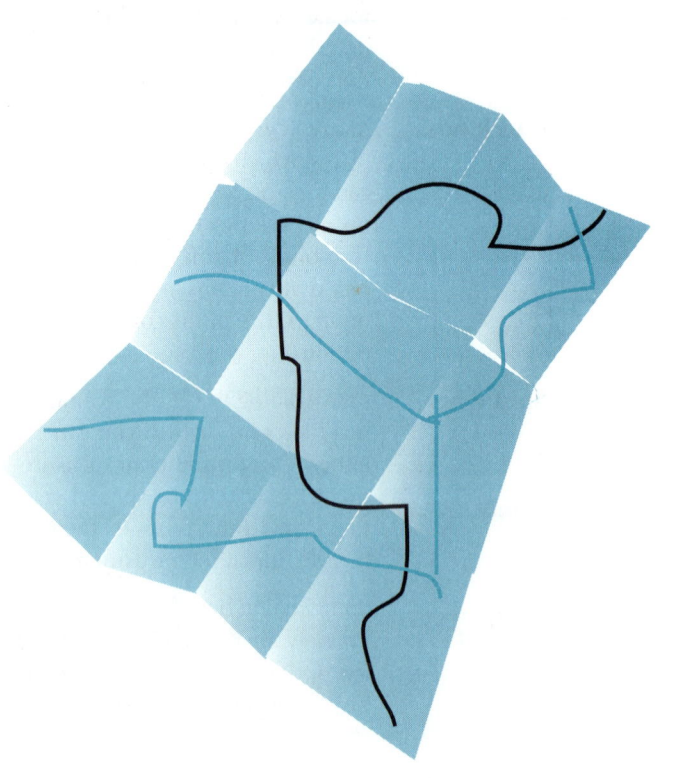

WORKING WITH MICROSOFT OFFICE MANAGER

icrosoft Office Professional is a group of five of the most popular and widely-used Windows applications. Included in Microsoft Office Professional are Access, a relational database program; Excel, an electronic spreadsheet; Mail, an electronic mail application; PowerPoint, a program used to create presentations; and Word for Windows, a word-processing application.

Each of the Microsoft Office applications can be used in conjunction with any of the others. For example, you can create a database of customer names and addresses in Access and then use Word's Mail Merge feature to create a form letter addressed to everyone in the database. You can add a chart created in Excel to a PowerPoint presentation. Or, you can use Mail to electronically send the text of a Word document to several people for review. With Word's revision marking and annotation features, each person can add notes or suggest revisions to the document, which can later be accepted or rejected.

Working with Microsoft Office Manager

Microsoft Office is designed to let you easily work with data in several programs. Use the buttons on the Microsoft Office Manager toolbar, which is always displayed (by default) in the top-right corner of your screen, no matter what Windows

AN ORIENTATION TO MS OFFICE PROFESSIONAL

application is active. It appears on the title bar of the maximized, active application.

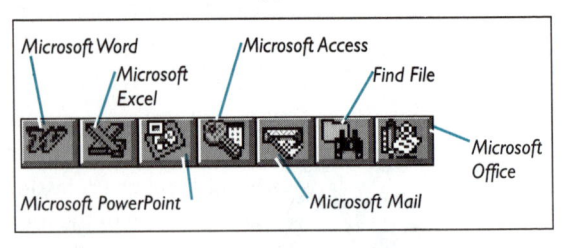

Microsoft Word — Microsoft Excel — Microsoft PowerPoint — Microsoft Access — Find File — Microsoft Mail — Microsoft Office

The Microsoft Office Manager toolbar buttons work in the same way as do the buttons on any toolbar in the individual Microsoft Office applications. To immediately open or switch to one of the Microsoft Office applications, just click on the appropriate button on the Microsoft Office Manager toolbar.

You can also click on the Find File button on the Microsoft Office Manager toolbar to display the Find File dialog box. See the Find File entry for information on searching for a file using specific criteria.

Click on the Microsoft Office button on the Microsoft Office Manager toolbar to display a drop-down menu. Select the corresponding menu item to open or switch to any of the Microsoft Office applications, Windows Program Manager and File Manager, the Find File dialog box, and Microsoft Office Setup. Or, display the Microsoft Office Help Contents window or Cue Cards to find help or instructions on specific topics. Select E_x_it to close Microsoft Office Manager and remove its toolbar.

An Overview of the Opening Screens

One of the most useful features of Microsoft Office is that each of its individual applications uses the same (or a very similar) environment. Each of the applications' windows contains similar items, such as the title bar, menu bar, toolbars, and status bar.

AN OVERVIEW OF THE OPENING SCREENS

Once you learn how to carry out a command or perform a specific action in one program, you can apply your knowledge and experience to carry out a similar command or perform a similar action in another Microsoft Office application.

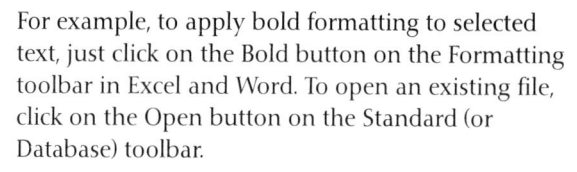

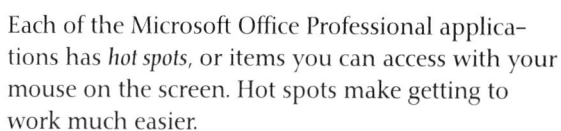

For example, to apply bold formatting to selected text, just click on the Bold button on the Formatting toolbar in Excel and Word. To open an existing file, click on the Open button on the Standard (or Database) toolbar.

Each of the Microsoft Office Professional applications has *hot spots*, or items you can access with your mouse on the screen. Hot spots make getting to work much easier.

Access

Access is a relational database application. Use Access's features to create the structure of a database in a table. Access comes with Wizards that allow you to quickly create forms based on the fields in the structure of the database. You can enter data in the database in either a form or a table.

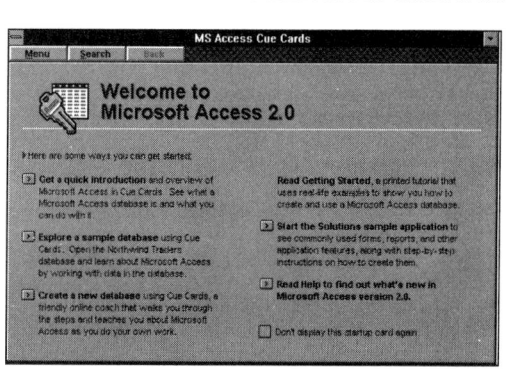

When you first start Access, the MS Access Cue Cards window appears to help you get started.

To close the Cue Cards, double-click on the window's Control menu box, or click on it and choose Close (Alt+F4).

AN ORIENTATION TO MS OFFICE PROFESSIONAL

TIP: *To permanently remove the opening Cue Cards window, select the Don't Display This Startup Card Again check box before you close Access's opening Cue Cards. When you need to see the Cue Cards, click on the Cue Cards button on the Database toolbar to display the Cue Cards that are relevant to the action being performed.*

For the Access screen (and most of the toolbar buttons) to be active, you must create or open a database file. Click on the New Database button on the Database toolbar or select File → New Database (Ctrl+N) to create a new file. Click on the Open Database button on the Database toolbar or choose File → Open Database (Ctrl+O) to open an existing file. Once a file is open, the Database window appears.

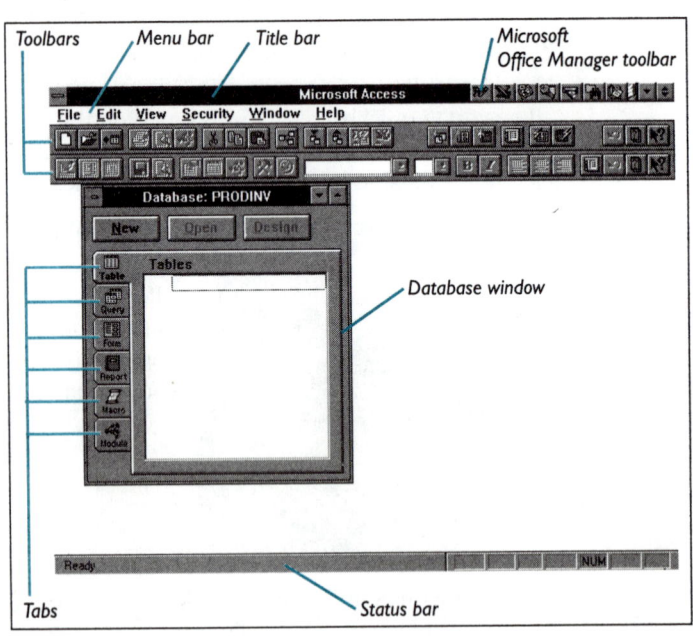

AN OVERVIEW OF THE OPENING SCREENS

There are several active areas on the Access screen:

- The *Database window* is Access's *control center*—it allows you to manipulate the database. Click on the tab of the type of database item you want to create or activate and then create the new item or select an existing item.

- The *Microsoft Office Manager toolbar* appears on Access's title bar.

- The *menu bar* appears just below the title bar. The menus that are available change, depending on the current action in Access.

- The *toolbars* appear below the menu bar. The toolbars that are displayed also change, depending on the current action being performed. For example, the Database and Form Design toolbars are displayed when the Database window is active. If a table in the database is active, the Table Datasheet toolbar replaces the Database toolbar.

- The *status bar* displays information about the current view, property, toolbar button, Toolbox button, or command.

Excel

Excel is an electronic spreadsheet application. The basic file in Excel is a *workbook*—a collection of worksheets saved in a single file. By default, each new Excel file contains 16 worksheets, although Excel files can contain up to 255 worksheets.

Excel's opening screen contains many of the same kinds of features as those in Access—a title bar with the Microsoft Office Manager toolbar, a menu bar, the Standard and Formatting toolbars, and a status bar.

AN ORIENTATION TO MS OFFICE PROFESSIONAL

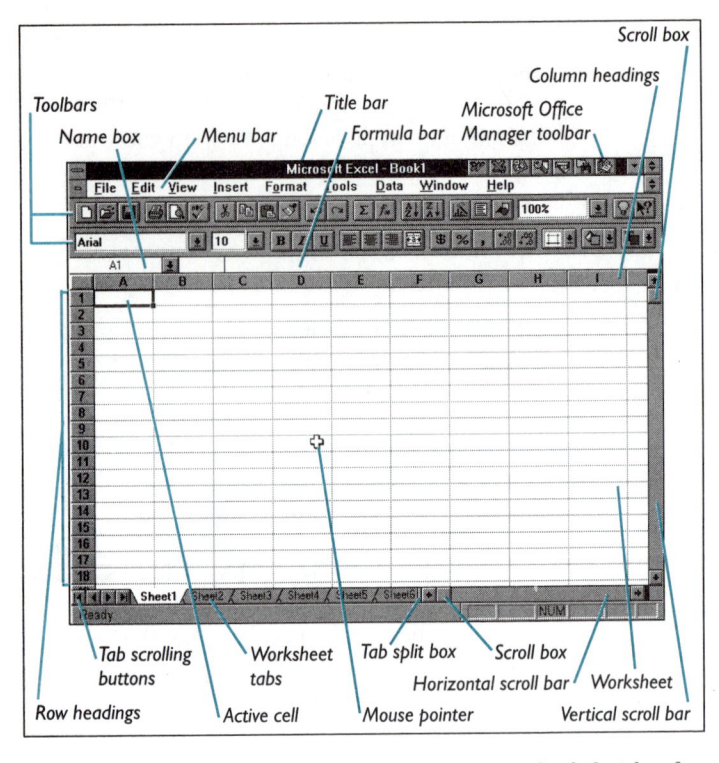

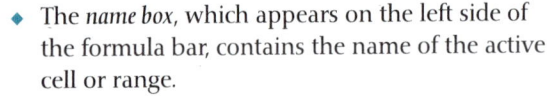

- The *name box*, which appears on the left side of the formula bar, contains the name of the active cell or range.

- The *formula bar*, just below the Formatting tool bar, displays the contents of the active cell. Click in the entry area of the formula bar to activate it and then edit the cell contents. When the formula bar is active, the insertion point appears in it, and the Cancel box, Enter box, and Function Wizard button appear.

- The *active cell* appears with a heavy border. Data that you enter is placed in the active cell.

AN OVERVIEW OF THE OPENING SCREENS

- The *worksheet* is the grid that appears in Excel. The grid is a table, composed of rows and columns of cells.

- The rows in the worksheet are numbered on the left side of the screen. Each row's number is a *row heading*. Click on the heading of a row to select the entire row.

- The column letters appear in the *column heading*, just above the worksheet. To select an entire column, click on the column heading.

- The *mouse pointer* appears as a three-dimensional plus sign when it is positioned in the worksheet, or over the column or row headings.

- To move up and down through the displayed worksheet, click on the ↑ or ↓ button or drag the *scroll box* on the *vertical scroll bar*.

- To move the displayed portion of the worksheet to the left or right, click on the ← or → button or drag the scroll box on the *horizontal scroll bar*.

- The *worksheet tabs* appear just above the status bar. To activate a worksheet and display its contents, click on its tab.

- Click on the First or Last *tab scrolling button* to display the first or last worksheet tab. To move through the worksheet tabs one sheet at a time, click on the Next or Previous tab scrolling button.

- To display additional worksheet tabs, drag the *tab split box* to the right. To display a larger horizontal scroll bar, drag the tab split box to the left.

TIP: *To reset the display of the worksheet tabs back to the default, double-click on the tab split box.*

AN ORIENTATION TO MS OFFICE PROFESSIONAL

Mail

Each time you start Microsoft Mail, the Mail Sign In dialog box appears.

Type your password in the Password text box and then choose OK to display Mail's screen.

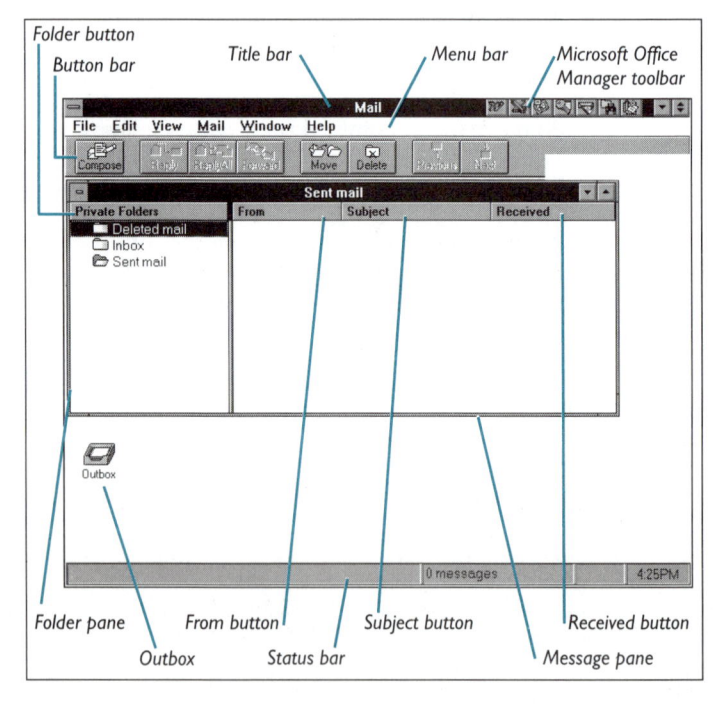

Click on the Maximize button to make the Microsoft Office Manager toolbar appear on Mail's title bar. The items that appear on Mail's opening screen include the following:

- Mail has a *button bar* rather than the toolbars in each of the other Microsoft Office applications.

AN OVERVIEW OF THE OPENING SCREENS

To access the buttons on Mail's button bar, click on the button that corresponds to the task you want to perform.

- The *folder pane* contains a list of the current folders. Click on the *Folder button* to switch between the list of Private Folders and Shared Folders.

- The *message pane* displays the list of mail messages in the folder that is highlighted in the folder pane. To change the order in which the list is displayed, click on the *From button* to sort the list by the name of the sender, the *Subject button* to sort the list by the subject indicated, or the *Received button* to sort the list by the date and time it was received.

- To forward messages, drag them from the message pane to the *Outbox*, where they are held until Mail can send them.

PowerPoint

Use PowerPoint to quickly create professional-looking presentations. Each time you start PowerPoint, the Tip Of The Day dialog box appears. Read the tip, and then choose OK to remove that dialog box and display the PowerPoint dialog box.

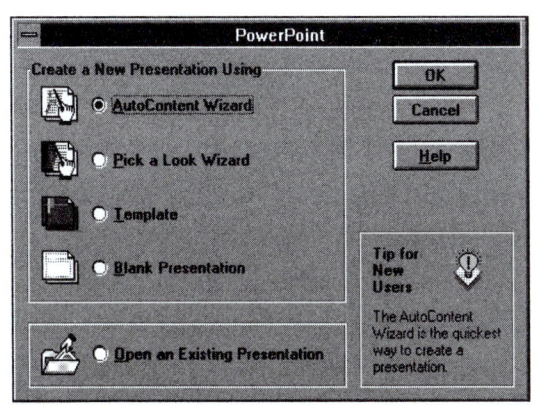

The selection that you make in the PowerPoint dialog box determines how the PowerPoint screen will appear. If you choose Blank Presentation and then

AN ORIENTATION TO MS OFFICE PROFESSIONAL

choose OK, the New Slide dialog box appears. Select one of the layouts in the Choose An AutoLayout list box and then select OK to display the opening screen. The following items appear on PowerPoint's screen:

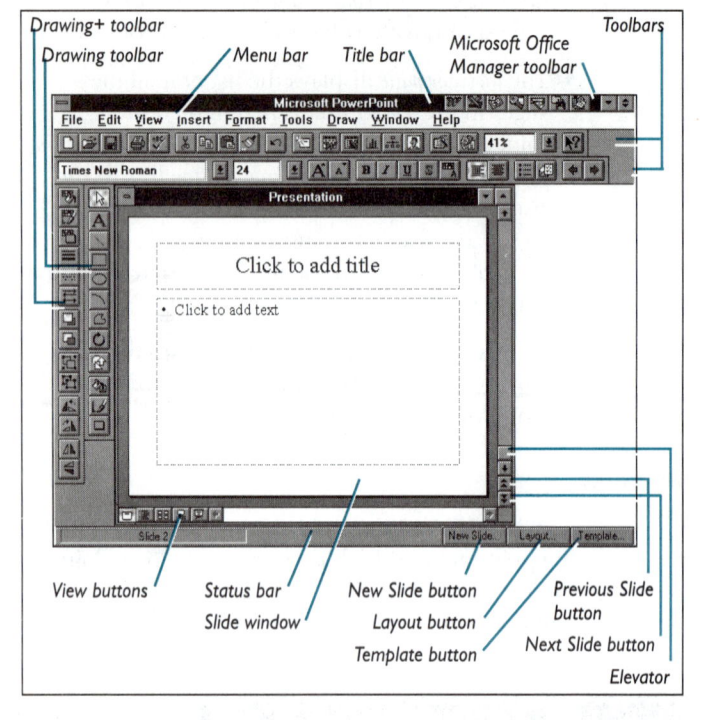

Screen diagram with labels: Drawing+ toolbar, Drawing toolbar, Menu bar, Title bar, Microsoft Office Manager toolbar, Toolbars, View buttons, Status bar, Slide window, New Slide button, Layout button, Template button, Previous Slide button, Next Slide button, Elevator

- In addition to PowerPoint's Standard and Formatting toolbars, the *Drawing* and *Drawing+ toolbars* are displayed when a presentation appears in Slide view.

- All the work being performed on the presentation is done in the *slide window* when the presentation appears in Slide view.

AN OVERVIEW OF THE OPENING SCREENS

- To change the view, click on the appropriate *View button* on the left side of the Slide window's horizontal scroll bar. You can switch between Slide view, Outline view, Slide Sorter view, Notes Pages view, or run a Slide Show with the View buttons.

- Glance at the *status bar* to see which slide or page is active, or in which view the presentation is displayed. Or, click on the *New Slide* button to insert a new slide after the current slide, click on the *Layout* button to select a new page layout for the current slide, and click on the *Template* button to select a different background for the presentation.

- PowerPoint's vertical scroll bar allows you to move through the pages of a presentation while it is displayed in Slide or Notes Pages view. Drag the *Elevator* to move to a different presentation page. The number of the slide or page that will appear when you release the mouse button is displayed as you drag. Or, click on the *Next Slide button* or the *Previous Slide button* to move to the next or previous slide or page.

Word for Windows

Word's Tip Of The Day dialog box also appears each time you start Word. After you read the tip, choose OK to remove it and display Word's opening screen. Then use any of the following items in the Word window to create and edit all your documents:

TIP: *To permanently prevent the display of the Tip Of The Day dialog box in PowerPoint and Word, clear the Show Tips At Startup check box before you choose OK.*

AN ORIENTATION TO MS OFFICE PROFESSIONAL

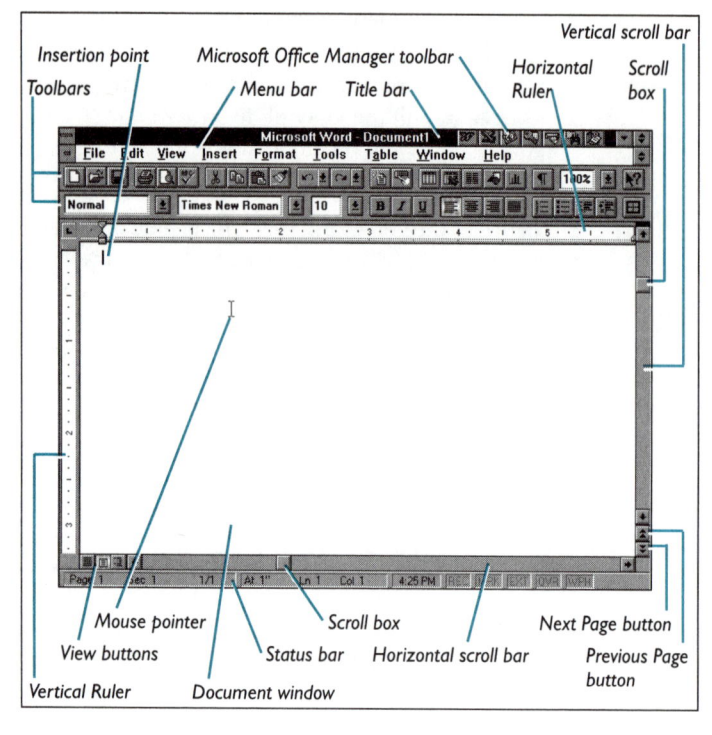

Figure labels: Insertion point, Toolbars, Microsoft Office Manager toolbar, Menu bar, Title bar, Vertical scroll bar, Horizontal Ruler, Scroll box, Mouse pointer, View buttons, Vertical Ruler, Document window, Status bar, Scroll box, Horizontal scroll bar, Next Page button, Previous Page button

- Both a *Horizontal* and a *Vertical Ruler* appear in Page Layout view. Use the Rulers to change the margins in the current section, to change the indentation of the current paragraph, to change the tab stops in the current paragraph, or to help position framed items in a document.

- The *insertion point* is located in the *document window* where the next character you type will appear. Each character or other document item is placed within the document window as the document is created or edited.

- The *mouse pointer* appears as an I-beam in the document window. To move the insertion point, click in the position in which it is to be placed.

12

AN OVERVIEW OF THE OPENING SCREENS

- The *status bar* displays the page and section number of the currently displayed page in the document, the position of the insertion point on the page, and the system time. Double-click on one of the mode areas on the right side of the status bar to quickly change to Record Macro, Revision Marking, Extend Selection, Overtype, or WordPerfect Help mode.

- Drag the *scroll box* on the *vertical scroll bar* to scroll up or down in a document, or click on the *Next Page button* or *Previous Page button* to scroll one page (or screen) down or up. Drag the scroll box on the *horizontal scroll bar* to move the portion of the document that is displayed to the left or right. Click on the appropriate *View button* on the horizontal scroll bar to change the way the document is displayed on your screen to Normal, Page Layout, or Outline view.

Getting Started

Now that you've mastered the basics, you can get started using any of the Microsoft Office applications. Don't worry about making a mistake—one of the nicest things about using a computer is that you can undo almost everything!

PART TWO

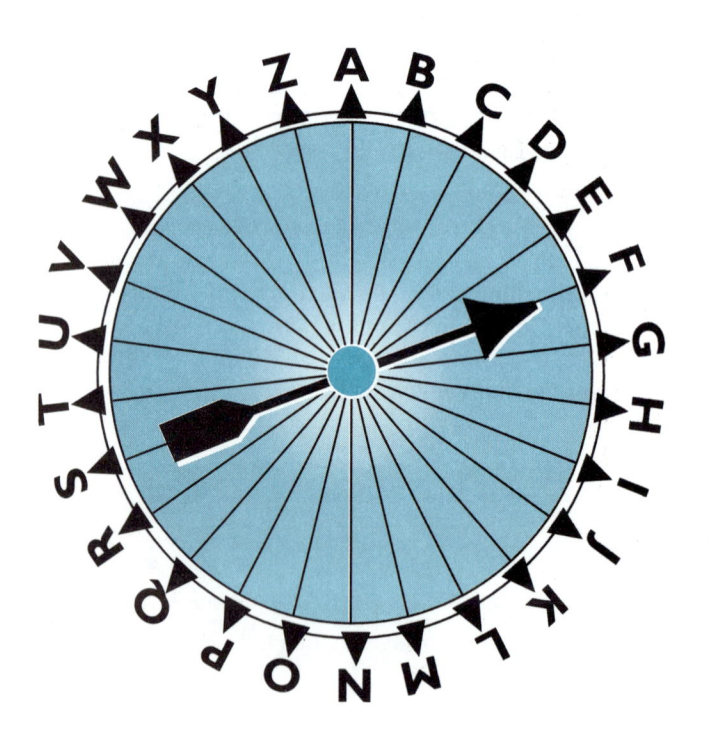

COMMAND AND FEATURE REFERENCE A-Z

Address Book

You can use Mail's address book to create a list of the names and e-mail addresses of the people with whom you correspond. Then, select the names of people in the address book when you create a message instead of retyping the name for each message.

Adding Names to the Address Book

The address book contains the names of the people in your Work Group Post Office, which is stored on the computer that contains the WINDOWS\WGPO subdirectory (usually the computer that belongs to the network administrator). You can add individual or group names to your Personal Address book.

To add names to the address book:

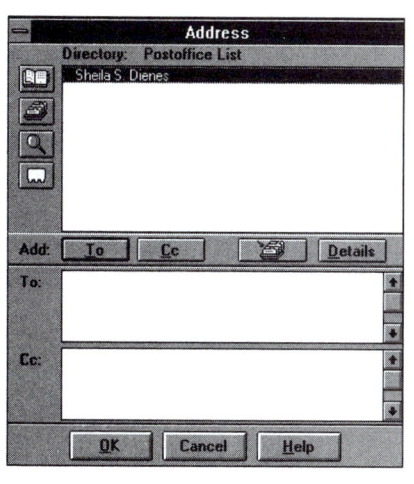

1. Click on Mail's Compose button to display the Send Note dialog box, and then choose A_ddress. Or, select _Mail ➤ A_ddress Book to display the Address dialog box.

2. Click on the Personal Address Book button to display a list of people and Personal Groups in the Directory list box.

COMMAND AND FEATURE REFERENCE

3. Click on the New button to display the New dialog box.

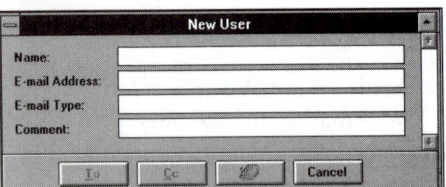

4. Because Custom Address is already selected, choose OK to display the New User dialog box.

5. Type the person's name in the Name text box, the address in the E-mail Address text box, and the type of address for this person (Microsoft Mail or another e-mail application) in the E-mail Type text box. Type any comments in the Comment text box.

6. Click on the Add button to add the name and address to your Personal Address Book.

7. Click on Cancel to close.

To remove a name from the Personal or Post Office Address Book, highlight the name in the Directory list box in the Address dialog box, choose Remove, and then choose Yes.

Creating a Personal Group

Create a personal group if you regularly send several people the same Mail message. The name of a personal group appears in bold in the Directory list box of your Personal Address Book.

To create a personal group:

1. Select Mail ➤ Personal Groups, and then select New in the Personal Groups dialog box.

2. Type a name for the group in the New Group Name text box, and then choose Create. The Personal Groups dialog box appears.

3. Select a name in the Directory list box, and then choose Add to add it to the group. The name appears in the Group Members text box.

NOTE: *To remove a name from the group, highlight the name in the Group Members text box, and then press Del.*

4. Repeat step 3 for each name you want to include in the group.

5. Choose OK to add the group to your list of personal groups.

6. Select Close to return to Mail.

While the Personal Groups dialog box is displayed, select Edit to add or remove members of the group, or choose Remove to delete the group that is high-lighted in the list box.

SEE ALSO: *Mail; Postoffice Manager*

Alignment

Alignment refers to the position of text or data within a cell, between margins, or within a frame or text box. Use the buttons described below, found on the Formatting toolbar in Excel, PowerPoint, and Word, to align your data.

Click on the Align Left button to align the data in selected cells in an Excel worksheet along the left edges of the cells, selected text within a text box along the left edge of the text box in PowerPoint, or the selected paragraph along the left margin in a Word document.

Click on the Center button to center the selection within selected cells, within a text box, or between the left and right margins.

COMMAND AND FEATURE REFERENCE

Click on the Align Right button to align the selection along the right edges of cells, within a text box, or along the right margin.

Click on the Justify button to align selected data evenly between the cell edges, sides of a text box, or left and right margins.

Alternatively, use the following commands to align a selection:

- In Excel, select Format ➤ Cells (Ctrl+1), select the Alignment tab, choose Left, Center, Right, or Justify in the Horizontal area, and then choose OK.

Excel's other alignment options include:

General (The default) aligns values to the right and text to the left.

Fill Repeats the characters in a selected cell until the cell is filled.

Center across Selection Centers the data in the first cell in a selection across adjacent selected cells in the same row.

TIP: *Click on the Center Across Columns button on the Formatting toolbar to quickly center the data in the first cell of a selection across several adjacent cells in the same row.*

Top Aligns the data in selected cells along the top edges of the cells.

Center Centers the data in selected cells between the top and bottom edges of the cells.

Bottom (The default), aligns data in selected cells along the bottom edges of the cells.

ANNOTATION

> **J<u>u</u>stify**   Aligns data in selected cells evenly along the top and bottom edges of the cells.
>
> **Orie<u>n</u>tation**   Changes the rotation of the data in selected cells.
>
> **<u>W</u>rap Text**   Wraps text in selected cells to the next line in the cells when the check box is selected.

- In PowerPoint, select F<u>o</u>rmat ➤ <u>A</u>lignment, and then choose <u>L</u>eft (Ctrl+L), <u>C</u>enter (Ctrl+E), <u>R</u>ight (Ctrl+R), or <u>J</u>ustify (Ctrl+J).

- In Word, select F<u>o</u>rmat ➤ <u>P</u>aragraph, select the Indents And Spacing tab, highlight Left (Ctrl+L), Centered (Ctrl+E), Right (Ctrl+R), or Justified (Ctrl+J) in the Alignment drop-down list, and then select OK.

SEE ALSO: *Indent; Line Spacing; Margins; Tabs*

Annotation

Use Word's Annotation feature to add text or sound objects as notes to a document. Annotations can be used by the reviewers of a document to insert notes that do not affect the appearance of the document or the way it will appear when it is printed.

Annotations are represented in a document by annotation marks, which contain the user's initials and the number of the note. Annotation marks are inserted by default in hidden text format.

COMMAND AND FEATURE REFERENCE

> ### TROUBLESHOOTING
>
> ## *Displaying Annotations*
>
> What if you cannot see the annotation marks or the annotation pane in a document? Annotation marks are formatted as hidden text—they will not print when you print the document. To see the annotation marks, click on the Show/Hide ¶ button on the Standard toolbar to toggle on the display of nonprinting characters.
>
> To display the annotation pane as well, which contains the text of annotations in the document, select View ➤ Annotations.

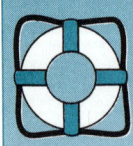

Inserting an Annotation

Annotations are created in the annotation pane, which appears at the bottom of your screen when you select Insert ➤ Annotation or View ➤ Annotations. Use Word's regular editing methods to create or edit a text note in the annotation pane.

TIP: *If you have a pen system, you can insert pen annotations in a document.*

To insert an annotation:

1. Select the text or other item to annotate, or position the insertion point where you want to place a note.

2. Choose Insert ➤ Annotation (Alt+Ctrl+A) to place a hidden annotation mark in the document window and to simultaneously display the Annotation pane. The insertion point appears in the Annotation pane.

ANNOTATION

> **NOTE:** *You must have a sound board and a microphone installed on your computer to insert a voice annotation into a document.*

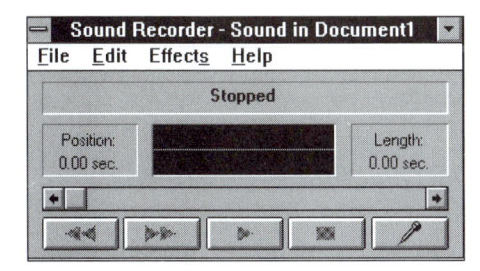

3. Type the text of the note. Or, click on the Insert Sound Object button at the top of the Annotation pane to display the Sound Recorder dialog box.

> **NOTE:** *To combine a sound note with a text note, type the text note in the annotation pane first, and then create the sound object or open a sound file.*

4. To record a note up to 60 seconds long, click on the Record button in the Sound recorder dialog box, and then speak into your microphone. Click on the Stop button when you have finished recording.

5. If necessary, click in the document or press F6 to move the insertion point into the document, and then repeat steps 1 through 3 to place additional notes in the document.

> **NOTE:** *To delete an annotation, select the annotation mark in the document window and press Del or Backspace.*

6. When you are finished, click on the Close button at the top of the Annotation pane or press Alt+Shift+C to close the Annotation pane.

Listening to or Viewing an Annotation

Annotations that correspond to the part of the document that is displayed on your screen appear in the annotation pane. You must display the annotation pane to see or hear an annotation.

COMMAND AND FEATURE REFERENCE

To display the text of an annotation:

- Double-click on its annotation mark in the document window.

OR

- Select <u>V</u>iew ➤ <u>A</u>nnotations to display the annotation pane.

By default, the annotations created by all reviewers are displayed in the annotation pane. To view the annotations created by a specific reviewer, select the name of the reviewer in the F<u>r</u>om drop-down list at the top of the annotation pane.

Once the annotation pane is displayed, double-click on a sound object symbol to listen to the annotation.

TIP: *If an annotation was created for selected text in a document, that text is highlighted (but not selected) in the document when the insertion point is positioned in the corresponding annotation in the annotation pane. Press Alt+F11 to select the highlighted text in the document when you want to edit the text.*

SEE ALSO: *Go To; Print; Protection; Revision*

Auditing

Use buttons on Excel's Auditing toolbar to trace cell dependents, cell precedents, and errors in a worksheet. The Auditing tools display *tracer arrows* from the active cell to any cells containing related data.

Tracer arrows point in the direction of the data flow (always toward the formula). The dot at the end of a tracer arrow indicates a value that is a direct dependent or precedent. Tracer arrows appear in blue on a color monitor, and with a worksheet icon attached if a dependent or precedent is in a different worksheet.

To display the Auditing toolbar:

- Right-click on one of the displayed toolbars, and then select Auditing in the toolbar list.
- Choose Tools ➤ Auditing ➤ Show Auditing Toolbar.

Tracing Dependents

Cells that contain formulas referring to other cells are called *dependents*. A cell that contains a formula that refers to the active cell is called a *direct dependent*. An *indirect dependent* is a cell that refers to a direct dependent or another indirect dependent.

To trace all the dependents of the active cell:

1. Click on the Trace Dependents button on the Auditing toolbar or select Tools ➤ Auditing ➤ Trace Dependents to display tracer arrows to all direct dependents.

2. Click on the Trace Dependents button or select Tools ➤ Auditing ➤ Trace Dependents again to display the first level of indirect dependents.

3. Repeat step 2 for each subsequent level of indirect dependents you want to trace.

Click on the Remove Dependent Arrows button to remove the arrows that are farthest away from the active cell. Click again to remove each subsequent level of arrows.

NOTE: *Click on the Remove All Arrows button on the Auditing toolbar or select Tools ➤ Auditing ➤ Remove All Arrows to remove all the arrows from the worksheet.*

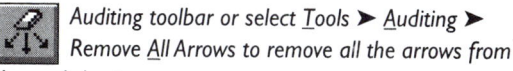

COMMAND AND FEATURE REFERENCE

> **TROUBLESHOOTING**
>
> ## Correcting an Error Value
>
> When a formula cannot be calculated, Excel produces an error value as its result, to indicate that there is a problem. For example, if a formula tries to divide a value by 0, Excel returns #DIV/0! to indicate the error. You can either change the formula to conform to the values in dependent cells, or change the value that is the source of the error to remove the error value and display the correct result of the formula.
>
> Error values always begin with a # (number sign), followed by uppercase letters. The other error values are #N/A (value not available), #NAME? (unrecognized name), #NULL! (reference to an intersection that does not intersect), #NUM! (a problem with a number), #REF! (a nonvalid cell reference), and #VALUE! (the wrong type of argument or operand).

Tracing Errors in a Worksheet

When the formula in a cell displays an error message, trace the error to discover the source of the first error value (displayed with a red arrow on a color monitor) and the cell that contains the value that caused the first error value (displayed with a blue arrow).

To trace errors in a worksheet:

1. Select a cell that contains an error value.

2. Click on the Trace Error button on the Auditing toolbar, or select Tools ➤ Auditing ➤ Trace Error. A red arrow is drawn to the original error, and a blue arrow is drawn to the cell that contains the value that produced the original error.

Tracing Precedents

Cells to which a formula refers are called *precedents*. A cell that is referred to by the formula in the active cell is called a *direct precedent*. An *indirect precedent* is a cell that is referred to by a direct precedent or another indirect precedent.

To trace all the precedents of the active cell:

1. Click on the Trace Precedents button on the Auditing toolbar or select Tools ➤ Auditing ➤ Trace Precedents to display tracer arrows to all direct precedents.

2. Click on the Trace Precedents button or select Tools ➤ Auditing ➤ Trace Precedents again to display the first level of indirect precedents.

3. Repeat step 2 for each subsequent level of indirect precedents you want to trace.

Click on the Remove Precedent Arrows button to remove the farthest set of precedent arrows from the active cell. Each additional click removes the subsequent level of tracer arrows.

SEE ALSO: *Note*

AutoCorrect

With Word's AutoCorrect feature, you can save an abbreviation for often-used text or a graphic, and then type the abbreviation followed by a space to insert the text or graphic in a document. For example, create AutoCorrect entries to insert a company name or logo, words you often misspell, or boilerplate phrases or text in a document.

COMMAND AND FEATURE REFERENCE

Word comes with a few AutoCorrect entries already defined.

Changing an AutoCorrect Entry

There are several ways to change an AutoCorrect entry:

- To add the same entry with a different name, choose Tools ➤ AutoCorrect, select the entry in the list box, type the new name for the entry in the Replace text box, and then select Add.

- To change a plain text entry's contents, select the entry in the AutoCorrect dialog box, type the new contents for the entry in the With text box, and then choose Replace.

- To edit a formatted text entry, make the necessary changes in the document, select the entire entry, and then display the AutoCorrect dialog box. Type the name of the entry in the Replace text box, and then choose Replace. Choose Yes to confirm that you want to redefine the entry, and then choose OK.

- To delete an AutoCorrect entry, select the entry in the AutoCorrect dialog box's list box and choose Delete.

Creating an AutoCorrect Entry

Each AutoCorrect entry must be defined with a name you create. The name can contain as many as 31 characters, but it cannot contain any spaces. Do not use a real word as an AutoCorrect entry's name, because when you type the word in a document followed by a space, the AutoCorrect entry will be inserted rather than the word.

AUTOCORRECT

To create an AutoCorrect entry:

1. If necessary, select the text (for a paragraph or long entry) or the graphic for which you want to create a name.

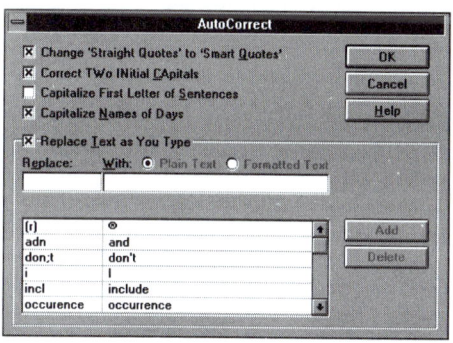

2. Choose Tools ➤ AutoCorrect to display the AutoCorrect dialog box.

3. If necessary, select the Replace Text As You Type check box.

4. Type the name (an abbreviation) of the entry in the Replace text box.

5. If you did not select text in step 1, type the text you want to enter each time the AutoCorrect entry name is typed in the With text box.

6. If you selected text in step 1, choose either the Plain Text or the Formatted Text option. Plain text has no formatting, and the entry can contain up to 255 characters. Formatted text is saved with the formatting applied in the document and can be as long as you wish, depending on the memory available in your computer.

7. Choose Add to insert the entry in the list box.

8. If necessary, repeat steps 4 through 7 to create additional AutoCorrect entries.

9. Select OK in the AutoCorrect dialog box.

TIP: *To turn off the AutoCorrect feature, clear the Replace Text As You Type check box, and then choose OK in the AutoCorrect dialog box.*

COMMAND AND FEATURE REFERENCE

SEE ALSO: AutoText; Find and Replace

AutoFormat

Both Excel and Word have an AutoFormat feature. Excel's AutoFormat allows you to select one of the built-in formats for the data in a worksheet. Word's AutoFormat can analyze your document and select one of the built-in formats for you.

Using AutoFormat in Excel

Excel's AutoFormat feature automatically applies number formats, data alignments, fonts, and borders and patterns, and changes the row height and column width as necessary in a selected table.

To use AutoFormat in Excel:

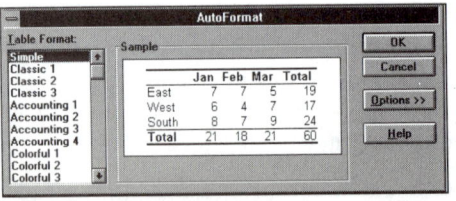

1. Select one cell in a table of data, and then choose Format ➤ AutoFormat. Excel automatically selects the entire table and displays the AutoFormat dialog box.

NOTE: *If the data you are formatting contains any blank rows or columns, you must select all the cells in the range before you choose Format ➤ AutoFormat.*

2. Select the name of a format in the Table Format list box. An example of the format appears in the Sample area.

28

3. If necessary, select Options to display the Options dialog box, and then clear the check boxes of any of the types of formatting you do not want to change in the Formats To Apply area.

4. Choose OK in the AutoFormat dialog box.

Using AutoFormat in Word

Use Word's AutoFormat feature to apply consistent formatting to a document. With AutoFormat, you type the text, and then Word analyzes the document and suggests styles to apply to each part of the document. Word uses any formatting you have already applied to help in the analysis. If you accept Word's formatting suggestions, the corresponding styles are applied to the document text.

TIP: AutoFormat applies only Word's built-in styles. To have AutoFormat apply your own styles, redefine Word's built-in styles with your own formats.

To have Word quickly analyze and format the current document or selected text, click on the AutoFormat button on the Standard toolbar.

To have Word analyze and suggest appropriate formatting for a document or selected text:

1. Place the insertion point anywhere in the document or select the text you want to format.

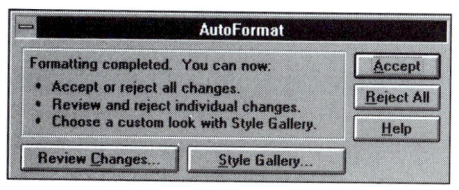

2. Select Format ➤ AutoFormat, and then choose OK to have Word analyze the document or selection. The AutoFormat dialog box appears.

COMMAND AND FEATURE REFERENCE

> **TROUBLESHOOTING**
>
> ## What If AutoFormat Doesn't Apply Any Formats to the Document?
>
> By default, AutoFormat only applies formats to text that is formatted with the Normal or Body Text style, so that any formats you have applied will remain in the document. To have AutoFormat apply styles to all document text, choose Tools ➤ Options, and then select the AutoFormat tab. In the Preserve area, clear the Previously Applied Styles check box, and then choose OK.

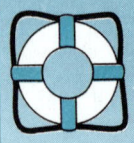

3. Choose any of the following options:

Accept To agree to all the changes Word has proposed, or to agree to all the changes after any changes already accepted or rejected, select this button.

Reject All Choose this option to discard all the remaining formatting changes.

Review Changes Choose this option to display revision marks (in color on a color monitor) and the Review AutoFormat Changes dialog box.

Style Gallery Select this option to display the Style Gallery dialog box.

AUTOFORMAT

If you choose Review Changes in the AutoFormat dialog box, Word inserts the following revision marks in the document:

- A blue ¶ at the end of the paragraph indicates that Word applied a style.
- A red ¶ indicates a deleted paragraph mark.
- Deleted characters appear with a red – (strikethrough character).
- Inserted characters appear with a blue _ (underline character).

The following items and options are available in the Review AutoFormat Changes dialog box:

Description	Each time you find a revision, a short description of the revision appears in this area.
Hide/Show Marks	Select Hide Marks to display the document as it will appear if all the revisions are accepted. Select Show Marks to display the revision marks in the document.
Undo Last	Choose this option to reverse the last rejected revision.
← Find	To return to the previous AutoFormat revision, select this option.
→ Find	To proceed to the next AutoFormat revision, choose this option.
Reject	This option returns the AutoFormat revision to its original format.

COMMAND AND FEATURE REFERENCE

Find Next   Select this check box to have
After Reject   Word automatically move to the next AutoFormat revision after you have selected Reject.

SEE ALSO: *Format; Format Painter; Style; Style Gallery; Table*

AutoLayout

PowerPoint's AutoLayouts are predefined slide layouts that you can use to create your presentation slides. The AutoLayouts contain placeholders (graphics and text boxes) into which you can insert various aspects of your presentation, such as the title, a chart, a bulleted list, a symbol, or some clip art.

Creating a Slide with AutoLayout

Each time you create a new presentation, you must begin by creating a slide. You can insert a new slide into an existing presentation at any time, and in any view. The new slide is placed after the current slide in an existing presentation.

NOTE: *If you insert a new slide while you are in Outline view, the new slide has the same layout as the slide that precedes it.*

To create a slide with AutoLayout:

1. Click on the New button on the Standard toolbar to create a new presentation. Or, make the slide that will precede the new slide current, and then

AUTOLAYOUT A

click on the Insert New Slide button on the Standard toolbar or the New Slide button the statusbar, or select <u>I</u>nsert ➤ New <u>S</u>lide (Ctrl+M).

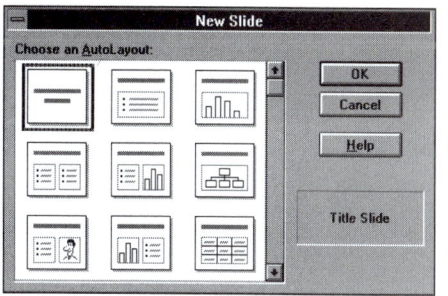

The New Slide dialog box appears (unless you are in Outline view).

2. If necessary, scroll through the Choose An <u>A</u>uto-Layout list box, and then select the layout for the new slide. The name of the selected layout is displayed under the command buttons.

3. Select OK to insert the new slide in the presentation.

TIP: *To enter data on a slide, double-click on a graphics box to insert a graphic, or click on a text box, and then type the presentation text.*

Editing the Layout of a Slide

As you are working on a presentation, you may wish to change the layout of an existing slide. Any text and graphics on the slide remain when you change the layout.

To edit the layout of a slide:

1. If necessary, click on the Slide View button on the horizontal scroll bar to change an existing presentation to Slide view.

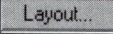

2. Activate the slide whose layout you want to change, and then click on the Layout button on the status bar, or select F<u>o</u>rmat ➤ Slide Lay<u>o</u>ut to display the Slide Layout dialog box.

33

COMMAND AND FEATURE REFERENCE

> **TIP:** *To activate the previous slide in a presentation, click on the Previous Slide button on the vertical scroll bar or press PgUp. To activate the next slide in a presentation, click on the Next Slide button on the vertical scroll bar or press PgDn.*

3. If necessary, scroll through the Reapply The Current Master Styles list box, and then select the layout for the new slide.

4. Select Apply to apply the new layout to the current slide.

Inserting a Placeholder on a Slide

To insert a placeholder on the active slide, insert a new object for the placeholder.

Click on the Insert Microsoft Word Table button on the Standard toolbar, and then drag through the number of rows and columns to insert the placeholder for a Word table.

Click on the Insert Microsoft Excel Worksheet button on the Standard toolbar, and then drag through the number of rows and columns to insert the placeholder for an Excel worksheet.

Click on the Insert Graph button on the Standard toolbar to insert the placeholder for a Microsoft Graph object.

Click on the Insert Org Chart button on the Standard toolbar to insert an organizational chart.

Click on the Insert Clip Art button on the Standard toolbar to insert a picture on the slide.

In addition, you can select Insert ➤ Object, select one of the objects in the Object Type list box, and then choose OK to insert the object on the current slide.

SEE ALSO: *Chart; Clip Art; Graphic; Object Linking and Embedding; Slide Show*

AutoText

Use Word's AutoText feature to insert recurring text or graphics in your documents. AutoText entries are similar to glossary entries, which were used in previous versions of Word.

AutoText entries are stored in the template on which the document is based. To make AutoText entries available to all documents, store them in the NORMAL.DOT template.

Creating an AutoText Entry

Use names that are descriptive and easy to remember for your AutoText entries. If you select text in a document as an AutoText entry, Word suggests a short name for it using the first word in the selection.

TIP: *To easily access the AutoText entries you often use, assign them to a toolbar button, a menu, or a shortcut key combination.*

Click on the Show/Hide ¶ button on the Standard toolbar to display paragraph marks when you are creating or editing the contents of an AutoText entry. If you include the paragraph mark in a selection, the formats applied to the selection are stored in the entry.

COMMAND AND FEATURE REFERENCE

To create an AutoText entry:

1. Select the text or graphic you want to use as an AutoText entry.

2. Click on the Edit AutoText button on the Standard toolbar to display the AutoText dialog box.

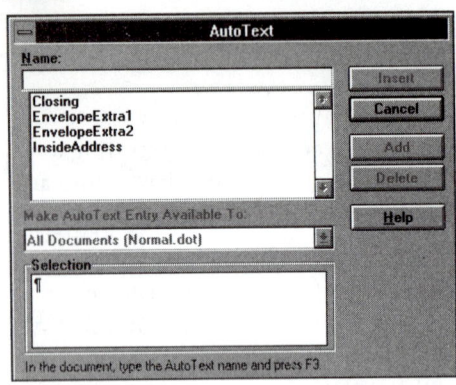

3. If necessary, type a new name for the entry in the Name text box.

4. Choose Add to insert the name of the entry in the Name list box in alphabetical order.

NOTE: *To delete an AutoText entry, select Edit ➤ AutoText, highlight the name of the entry in the Name list box, choose Delete, and then choose Close.*

Editing the Contents of an AutoText Entry

To edit the contents of an AutoText entry:

1. Insert the entry into a document, and make any changes you want to the entry.

2. Select the edited entry, and then click on the Edit AutoText button on the Standard toolbar to display the AutoText dialog box.

3. Select the entry's name in the Name list box.

4. Select Add, and then choose Yes to confirm that you want to redefine the entry.

AUTOTEXT

Inserting AutoText Entries

There are several ways to insert an AutoText entry into a document at the position of the insertion point:

- Type either the entry's name or several of the letters at the beginning of the entry's name surrounded by spaces, and then click on the Insert AutoText button on the Standard toolbar. The contents of the entry replace the characters you typed.

- Type either the entry's name or several of the letters at the beginning of the entry's name surrounded by spaces, and then press F3, Alt+Ctrl+V, or the shortcut key combination assigned to the entry. The contents of the entry replace the characters you typed.

- Position the insertion point where you want to insert the entry, and then select Edit ➤ AutoText, highlight the name of the entry in the Name list box, and choose Insert.

Renaming AutoText Entries

To change the name of an AutoText entry:

1. Select Format ➤ Style to display the Style dialog box.

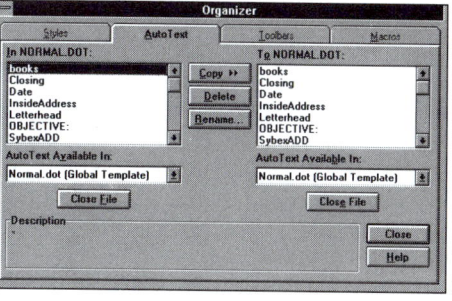

2. Choose Organizer to display the Organizer dialog box, and then select the AutoText tab.

3. Select the entry whose name you want to change, and then choose Rename.

37

COMMAND AND FEATURE REFERENCE

> **TROUBLESHOOTING**
>
> ### If an AutoText Entry Doesn't Appear in the List...
>
> Only the AutoText entries for the NORMAL.DOT template, any other templates that are loaded as global templates, and the current document template appear in the list box in the AutoText dialog box. If an entry you want to insert is not in the list box, it is stored in another template. You can copy the AutoText entry from the template in which it is stored into the NORMAL.DOT template. Open a file based on the template that contains the AutoText entry, select File ➤ Templates, and choose Organizer. Select the AutoText tab and highlight the name of the AutoText entry in the In *Template* list box. Then choose Copy to copy the entry to the To *Template* list box, and choose Close.

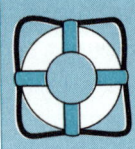

4. Type a different name in the New Name text box, and then choose OK.

5. Select Close to return to your document.

NOTE: *You can copy AutoText entries from one template to another in the Organizer dialog box using the same methods as those used to copy styles.*

SEE ALSO: *AutoCorrect; Field; Print; Style; Templates; Toolbars*

Bookmark

In Word documents, bookmarks can be used to mark places, or to mark an index or cross-reference entry. Once a bookmark is placed in a document,

BOOKMARK B

you can quickly move to the bookmark or use bookmark names in a formula.

Each bookmark in a document must begin with a letter and have a unique name. Bookmark names can contain up to 40 characters, but cannot contain any spaces. Use the underline character to indicate a space in a bookmark name.

Creating a Bookmark

To create a bookmark:

1. Position the insertion point in the location or select the text or graphic you want to mark.

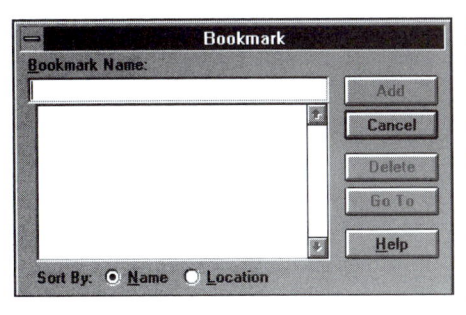

2. Choose Edit ➤ Bookmark (Ctrl+ Shift+ F5) to display the Bookmark dialog box.

3. Type a name for the bookmark in the Bookmark Name text box.

4. Select Add to mark the location or selection.

There are several other options available in the Bookmark dialog box:

- Select Delete to remove the bookmark highlighted in the Bookmark Name list box, without deleting the text that was marked in the document.

- Select Go To to move to the location or select the marked text or graphic of the bookmark highlighted in the Bookmark Name list box, and then choose Close to remove the Bookmark dialog box from your screen.

- To choose how the bookmarks are sorted in the Bookmark Name list box, select the Name option

COMMAND AND FEATURE REFERENCE

button to list the names alphabetically, or the Location option button to list the names in the order in which they appear in the document.

Displaying Bookmarks

By default, bookmarks are not displayed in your documents. However, you can display bookmarks when you want to edit the document or the bookmark. When you display bookmarks, they are displayed in all your documents, not just the active document.

To display bookmarks:

1. Select Tools ➤ Options to display the Options dialog box.

2. If necessary, select the View tab.

3. Select the Bookmarks check box in the Show area.

4. Choose OK.

The bookmark for selected text appears in a document as bold brackets surrounding the text. A bookmark that defines a location appears as a bold I-beam.

Editing a Marked Item

If you have marked selected text, display bookmarks in your documents so you see each bookmark's brackets. Then you can:

- Delete text within the brackets to change the contents of the bookmark.

TIP: *To delete both a bookmark and the associated marked text, select the text along with the bookmark brackets, and then press Del or Backspace.*

BORDERS AND SHADING

- Add text at the beginning of the marked item or between any two characters within a marked item to change the contents of the bookmark.

- Add text at the end of the marked item, select the bookmark and the inserted text, choose Edit ➤ Bookmark, and then select Add to redefine the bookmark.

Or, you can use the Cut, Copy, and Paste buttons on the Standard toolbar to copy or move a bookmark or its contents. When you do, one of the following events will occur:

- If a marked item is copied to a different location in the same document, only the contents of the bookmark are copied. The bookmark remains with the original item.

- If a marked item is copied to a different document, both the bookmark and the contents are copied to the document. If there is already a bookmark with the same name in the new document, only the bookmark's contents are copied. The original bookmark and item remain in the original document.

- If a marked item is cut to a different location in the same document or to a different document, both the bookmark and the item are moved to the new location. If there is already a bookmark with the same name in the new document, only the bookmark's contents are copied, and the bookmark remains in the original document.

SEE ALSO: *Captions; Cross-reference; Cut, Copy, and Paste; Field*

COMMAND AND FEATURE REFERENCE

Borders and Shading

You can add *borders* and *shading* to selected paragraphs in a Word document, selected cells in an Excel worksheet, or to a selected text box or graphic in PowerPoint. Borders are lines that surround the cells, paragraphs, or graphics boxes. Shading is the amount, color, and pattern of the fill inside the borders.

Applying Borders and Colors in Excel

There are two ways to apply borders and colors to a selected cell or range in an Excel worksheet. Use either the Borders and Color buttons on the Formatting toolbar or the options on the Border and Patterns tabs in the Format Cells dialog box. If you display the Patterns tab in the Format Cells dialog box, you can also select a pattern to apply to the selection.

To apply borders and colors using the Border and Color buttons:

1. Select the cell or range to which you want to apply a border and color.

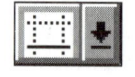

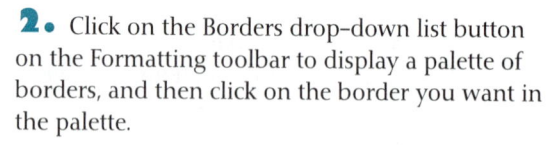

2. Click on the Borders drop-down list button on the Formatting toolbar to display a palette of borders, and then click on the border you want in the palette.

3. Click on the Color drop-down list button on the Formatting toolbar to display a color palette, and then click on the color in the palette.

Or, follow these steps to apply a border and color using the options in the Format Cells dialog box:

1. Select the cell or range to which you want to apply a border and color.

BORDERS AND SHADING

2. Select F<u>o</u>rmat ➤ C<u>e</u>lls (Ctrl+1) to display the Format Cells dialog box.

3. Select the Border tab.

4. In the Border area of the tab, choose one of the options described below:

<u>**Outline**</u> Places a border along the outer edges of the selection.

<u>Left</u> Places a border along the left edge of each selected cell.

<u>R</u>ight Places a border along the right edge of each selected cell.

<u>T</u>op Places a border along the upper edge of each cell in the selection.

<u>B</u>ottom Places a border along the lower edge of each cell in the selection.

5. Choose a style for the line in the Styl<u>e</u> area of the Border tab.

6. If necessary, click on the <u>C</u>olor drop-down list button, and then select a color for the border in the palette.

7. If necessary, repeat steps 4 through 6 for each edge.

8. Select the Patterns tab.

9. Select a color for the background of the selection in the <u>C</u>olor palette.

10. If necessary, click on the <u>P</u>attern drop-down list button to display a Pattern palette, and then select a pattern.

11. Choose OK to apply the border and color.

COMMAND AND FEATURE REFERENCE

Applying Borders and Shading in PowerPoint

Because PowerPoint is primarily a graphics program, there are several things you can do to change the border and fill of a selected graphics object, graphics box, or text box.

To apply borders and shading in PowerPoint:

1. Click on the Slide View or Notes Pages View button to change to either view.

2. Select the object to which you want to apply a border and color.

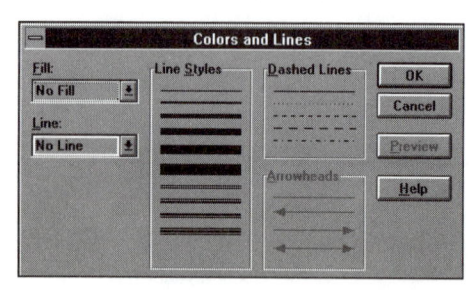

3. Select Format ➤ Colors And Lines to display the Colors And Lines dialog box.

4. Select the style of the border in the Line Styles list box.

5. If necessary, select a pattern for the line in the Dashed Lines list box.

6. To apply a color to the border, click on the Line drop-down list button and select a color in the palette that appears. Or, select Other Color to display the Other Color dialog box, click on the color you want in the Color Palette area, and then choose OK.

7. To apply a fill to the object, click on the Fill drop-down list button to display a palette of fill options and colors, and then select the color you want for the background of the object.

8. If necessary, click on the Fill drop-down list button again, and select Shaded to display the Shaded Fill dialog box.

BORDERS AND SHADING

9. Choose any of the following shading options:

Vertical	Places the shading in a variety of vertical positions.
Horizontal	Places the shading in a variety of horizontal positions.
Diagonal Right	Places the shading in a variety of diagonal positions from right to left.
Diagonal Left	Places the shading in a variety of diagonal positions from left to right.
From Corner	Places the shading in one of the four corners.
From Center	Begins the shading in the center of the selection.
Color	Select the color you want for the fill in the drop-down list.
Dark/Light	Drag the scroll box to the left to make the fill darker, or to the right to make the fill lighter. Or, press Alt+D, and then press ← to make the fill darker or → to make the fill lighter.

10. Select the fill design in the Variants area.

11. Select OK to apply the fill to the selected object.

12. Click on the Fill drop-down list button, and then select Pattern to display the Pattern Fill dialog box.

13. Click on the pattern you want for the fill in the Pattern area.

COMMAND AND FEATURE REFERENCE

14. If necessary, select a color for the foreground or the background in the Foreground or Background drop-down list.

15. Choose OK in the Pattern Fill dialog box.

16. Choose OK again in the Colors And Lines dialog box to apply the selected border, colors, and fill.

NOTE: *To delete a border or fill from a selected object in PowerPoint, click on the Line Color or the Fill Color button on the Drawing+ toolbar, and then select No Line or No Fill.*

You can also bypass the Colors And Lines dialog box when you want to apply borders, colors, and fill. Use the following buttons on the Drawing+ toolbar to display various portions of the Colors And Lines dialog box. Then follow the corresponding steps above to apply borders and colors to the selected object.

TIP: *To add a shadow to a selected graphics box, click on the Shadow Color button on the Drawing+ toolbar, and then select a color in the palette or Embossed in the list.*

Click on the Line Color button to display a list box with the same options as those in the Line drop-down list.

Click on the Line Style button to display the list of line styles that appears in the Line Styles area.

Click on the Dashed Lines button to display the list of dashed line styles that appears in the Dashed Lines area.

Click on the Fill Color button to display a list box with the same options as those in the Fill drop-down list.

BORDERS AND SHADING

> **NOTE:** *To return the line, fill, or shadow of a selected PowerPoint object to the layout's default, click on the Line On/Off, Fill On/Off, and Shadow On/Off buttons on the Drawing toolbar.*

Applying Borders and Shading in Word

Use either the buttons on the Borders toolbar or the options in the Paragraph Borders And Shading dialog box to apply borders and shading to a selected paragraph in a Word document.

To apply borders and shading using the Borders toolbar:

1. Select the paragraph or position the insertion point in the paragraph to which you want to apply a border or shading.

2. Click on the Borders button on the Formatting toolbar to display the Borders toolbar.

3. If necessary, click on the Line Style drop-down list button, and then select a style for the border.

4. Click on the button whose picture resembles the border you want. You can choose the Top, Bottom, Left, Right, Inside, or Outside Border buttons.

5. Click on the Shading drop-down button and select the fill or pattern.

To apply borders and shading using the options in the Paragraph Borders And Shading dialog box:

1. Position the insertion point in the paragraph to which you want to apply borders and shading, and then select Format ➤ Borders And Shading.

2. If necessary, select the Borders tab.

COMMAND AND FEATURE REFERENCE

3. In the Presets area, choose Box to place a box around the selection, or Shadow to place a drop-shadow border around the selection.

4. If necessary, click on any of the edges on which you want to place borders (or remove existing borders) in the Border area.

5. In the Line area of the tab, select one of the line styles for the border in the Style list box. A sample of the border appears in the Border area.

6. If necessary, select the color you want for the border in the Color drop-down list.

7. Select the Shading tab.

8. Highlight the fill or pattern in the Shading list box.

9. Choose OK to apply the border and shading to the selected paragraph.

To delete a border in a selected paragraph in a Word document, click on the No Border button on the Borders toolbar. Or, choose Format ➤ Borders And Shading, select None in the Presets area of the Border tab, and then choose OK.

To delete the shading in a selected paragraph, choose Clear in the Shading drop-down list on the Borders toolbar, or choose Format ➤ Borders And Shading, choose the Shading tab, select Clear in the Shading drop-down list, and then choose OK.

SEE ALSO: *Cell; Font; Frame; Graphic; Paragraph; Range*

BULLETS AND NUMBERING

Bound Object

SEE: *Control; Control Properties*

Bullets and Numbering

Use bullets to indicate list items in PowerPoint or Word. In Word, you can also automatically number paragraphs or display them in a multilevel list.

Adding Bullets to Presentation Text

The easiest way to add bullets to text in a presentation is to change the layout of the slide. Select one of the AutoLayouts that contains a bulleted list. You can also select the text box of an unbulleted item, and then click on the Bullet On/Off button on the Formatting toolbar.

You cannot select the bullets or numbers you insert into a presentation or document because they are automatic. However, you can remove automatic bullets or numbers by toggling the feature off in selected paragraphs.

Adding Bullets and Numbering in a Word Document

Bullets and numbers are automatically added to and updated in the paragraphs you create after you insert a bullet or number into the current paragraph.

To insert a bullet or number before the paragraph that contains the insertion point, toggle the Bullets

COMMAND AND FEATURE REFERENCE

or Numbering button on the Formatting toolbar. Or, click on the Bullets or Numbering button to remove a bullet or number from the current paragraph.

You could also follow these steps to specify the type and format of bullets and numbers for your document:

1. Select the paragraphs for which you want to insert bullets or numbers, or position the insertion point where you want to begin a bulleted or numbered list.

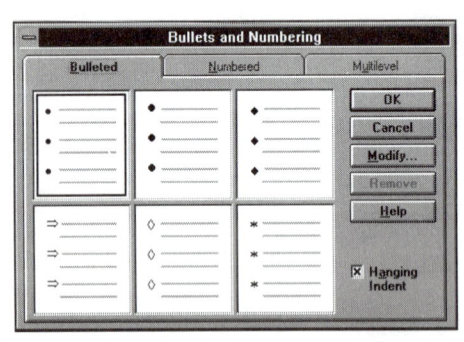

2. Select Format ➤ Bullets And Numbering to display the Bullets And Numbering dialog box.

3. Select the format for the bullets or numbers on the Bulleted, Numbered, or Multilevel tab.

4. To change the format of the bullet, numbers, or multilevel list, select Modify to display the Modify dialog box for the selected tab. The following options are available on the corresponding tab:

Bullet Character Select the symbol you want for the bullets in the list.

Point Size Select the size in points for the bullets in the list.

Color Select a color for the bullets in the list.

Bullet Choose a different symbol to use as the bullet character from the Symbol dialog box.

BULLETS AND NUMBERING

Text Before	Type any text you want to appear before each number in the text box.
Number/ Bullet or Number	Select the type of bullets or numbers you want in the drop-down list.
Text After	Type any characters you want to appear after each number in the text box.
Font	From the Font dialog box, choose a different font, size, attribute, and color for the bullets or numbers and the characters you entered in the Text Before and Text After text boxes.
Start At	Type the starting number for the items in the list.
Include from Previous Level	Select Nothing (the default), Numbers, or Numbers And Position as the format from the previous level to be used for the level displayed in the Level N list box.
Level N	To change the number format of a level in a multilevel list, scroll through the list until the number of the level is displayed, and then choose one of the options in the Include From Previous Level drop-down list.
Alignment of List Text	Select Left, Centered, or Right as the alignment of the text in the list.

COMMAND AND FEATURE REFERENCE

Distance from Indent to Text Specify the distance between the left indent and the text in a first-level paragraph.

Distance from Bullet/ Number to Text Specify the distance between the bullet or number and the text in the first line of the paragraph.

Hanging Indent Select the check box to have each bulleted or numbered-paragraph appear with a hanging indent.

5. Select OK to insert a bulleted, numbered, or multilevel list in the selected format.

SEE ALSO: *AutoLayout; Font; Indent; Outline*

Captions

Word's caption feature allows you to easily add a caption as a field code to a selected item or to all items of the same type in your document. Captions are formatted in the Caption style, and are automatically updated in your document when you add or delete a captioned item.

Adding a Caption to a Graphic

To insert a caption for a selected graphic or table:

1. Select the graphic or table to which you want to add a caption.

2. Choose Insert ➤ Caption to display the Caption dialog box.

CAPTIONS

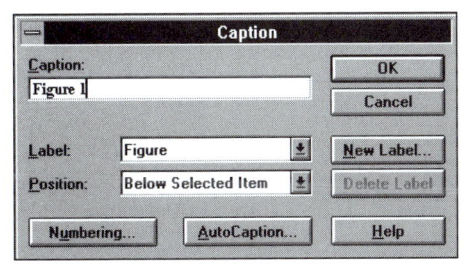

3. Type the text for the caption in the Caption text box. You cannot type over the label and caption number that automatically appear in the text box.

4. To change the label that appears in the Caption text box, select Equation, Figure, or Table in the Label drop-down list. Or, select New Label, type the label in the Label text box, and then select OK in the New Label dialog box.

5. In the Position drop-down list, select Above Selected Item or Below Selected Item as the location for the caption.

6. Choose OK to insert the caption.

NOTE: *To edit the text of an automatic or manual caption, use the regular editing methods to delete, insert, or replace characters.*

To delete a caption label you have defined, display the Caption dialog box, select the label in the drop-down list, and then choose Delete Label. Select Close to return to your document. The label will not be deleted from items to which it is assigned in your document, but it will no longer be available for additional items to which you want to add a caption.

Automatically Inserting Captions

Use Word's AutoCaption feature to create caption labels that are uniformly formatted and correctly numbered for each graphic in a document. You can add more than one type of graphic caption to your document. For each type of caption you add automatically, select a specific label and caption position.

COMMAND AND FEATURE REFERENCE

> **TIP:** *To update the numbers of all the captions in a document, choose Edit ➤ Select All (Ctrl+A), and then press F9.*

Once the caption label is inserted in your document, place the insertion point after the caption label and type the text directly in the caption.

To automatically insert a caption:

1. Position the insertion point in your document where you want to begin automatically adding captions, and then select Insert ➤ Caption.

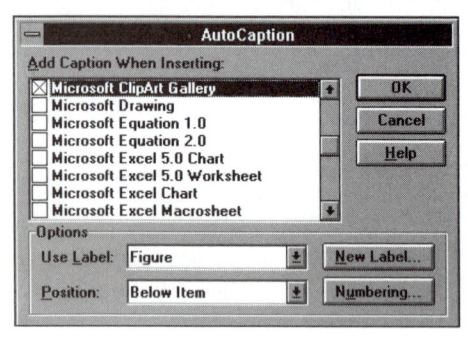

2. Select AutoCaption to display the AutoCaption dialog box.

3. Select the check box beside an item to which you want to add a caption in the Add Caption When Inserting list box.

4. Select the label for the item in the Use Label drop-down list. Or, select New Label, type a name for the label in the Label text box, and choose OK in the New Label dialog box.

5. Choose Above Item or Below Item in the Position drop-down list box.

6. Repeat steps 3 through 5 for each item to which you want to automatically add a caption.

7. Choose OK in the AutoCaption dialog box.

Once you have made AutoCaption selections for a document, Word automatically saves the selections to the template on which the document was based. The AutoCaption selections are available for all new documents based on that template.

CAPTIONS

TIP: *To change the format of the text you type for each caption, change the style of a caption, and then apply the new caption style to each caption in a document.*

Changing the Caption Numbering Format

To change the number format of a selected caption:

Caption Numbering

Format:	I, II, III, ...
☒ Include Chapter Number	
Chapter Starts with Style	Heading 1
Use Separator:	— [em-dash]

Examples: Figure II-1, Table 1-A

1. Choose Insert ➤ Caption, and then select Numbering to display the Caption Numbering dialog box.

2. Highlight the format you want in the Format drop-down list. If you are using AutoCaption, the formats of all caption numbers of the same type as the one selected are changed.

3. To include the chapter number in the label, select the Include Chapter Number check box, and then select a style from the Chapter Starts With Style drop-down list. Choose the separator character to place between the number of the graphic and the chapter number in the Use Separator drop-down list.

4. Choose OK in the Caption Numbering dialog box.

5. Choose OK again in the Caption dialog box.

SEE ALSO: *Control; Draw; Field Code; Graphic; Style; Table; Templates*

COMMAND AND FEATURE REFERENCE

Cell

A cell is the rectangle that appears at the intersection of a row and a column in a table, and is the basic unit for data entry. Tables can be found in an Access database and an Excel worksheet, and can be created in a PowerPoint presentation and a Word document.

The active cell is the cell in which the cursor is positioned. A heavy border appears around the active cell in Excel to show that it is currently selected. In Access, PowerPoint, and Word, the insertion point appears in the active cell, or the data in the cell is selected. Any data that you enter will appear in the active cell.

Selecting a Cell

Use any of the following methods to select a cell in a table:

- Click on the cell you want to select.
- Press ↑, ↓, ←, or → to select an adjacent cell in Excel.
- Press ↵ to enter data into the active cell and then select (activate) the cell below it in Excel.
- In Access, PowerPoint, and Word, press Tab to move the insertion point to the next cell in the row, and Shift+Tab to move the insertion point to the previous cell.

> **TIP:** In Excel, double-click on the cell to enter or edit the data directly in the cell. You can also click on the edit line, which appears just above the column headings in a worksheet, to edit the data in the active cell. Then press ↵ or click on the Confirm button on the edit line to enter your changes.

CHANGE CASE

SEE ALSO: *Table; Worksheet*

Change Case

To change the case of selected text in PowerPoint and Word:

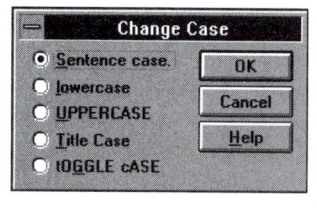

1. Select the text whose case you want to change, and then select Format ➤ Change Case to display the Change Case dialog box.

2. Select one of the following options:

Sentence case Capitalizes the first word of a sentence or the first word after a sentence.

lowercase Changes all the text to lower-case letters.

UPPERCASE Changes all the text to upper-case letters.

Title Case Capitalizes each word.

tOGGLE cASE Changes all uppercase letters to lowercase, and all lowercase letters to uppercase.

3. Choose OK.

To change the format of selected text in a Word document to small caps or all caps, choose Format ➤ Font, select the Small Caps or All Caps option in the Effects area on the Font tab, and then choose OK.

COMMAND AND FEATURE REFERENCE

SEE ALSO: *Font; Format Painter*

Chart

Each application in Microsoft Office (except Mail) allows you to create a chart. Charts are embedded objects, and are saved in the file in which they were created. Excel and Word charts can be linked to Access forms or tables, and to PowerPoint presentations.

Creating a Chart

In Access and in Excel, use the Graph Wizard and Chart Wizard to create a chart using data entered in a file. In PowerPoint and Word, use the Microsoft Graph application that comes with Microsoft Office to enter the data you want to chart into the datasheet.

In Access, you can insert a chart while you are in Form or Report view. The chart you create will appear on each form in the database.

To create a chart:

1. Open the Access or Excel file that contains the data you want to plot. Or, open the PowerPoint or Word file in which you want to create a chart.

2. In Access, click on the Design View button on the Form Design or Report Design toolbar, and then click on the Toolbox button on the Form Design or Report Design toolbar to display the Toolbox.

3. Click on the ChartWizard or Chart button on the Standard toolbar in Excel, PowerPoint, and

CHART

Word, and in Access's Toolbox. Click in the location in Access's form or report, or in the Excel worksheet where you want to place the chart. The Graph Wizard dialog box appears in Access, and the Chart-Wizard dialog box appears in Excel. In PowerPoint and Word, both a Chart window and a Datasheet window appear with a sample chart and data.

4. Answer the question in the Graph Wizard or ChartWizard dialog box, and then select Next. Continue until each of the questions is answered, and then select Finish. Or, select the data in any cell in the datasheet window, and then type the data you want to plot. The chart window reflects any changes you make.

There are several different items that are either used to create a chart or that appear in the chart, depending on the type of chart you create:

- The *data series* is the row, column, or field of data used to plot the chart.

- The *chart* is the area inside the Chart window, including all the items that make up the graph.

- The chart's *axes* are the lines used to plot data on the chart.

- The *plot area* is the region of the chart in which the data is plotted. The axes and data markers used to plot the data are located in the plot area.

- A *data marker* is the symbol in the chart that marks a data point or value.

- *Gridlines*, which often make the chart easier to read, begin at tick-marks and continue through the chart either horizontally or vertically.

COMMAND AND FEATURE REFERENCE

- The *chart text* describes the data or chart items.
- The *legend* is an inset in the chart that identifies the colors, patterns, or symbols assigned to the markers in the data series.

Editing a Chart

You can change virtually every element of the chart, including the chart's size and type, the chart text, and the data that is used to plot the chart.

To make any changes to a chart in Access, you must be in Design view. To make any changes to an Excel chart, click on the chart to select it, or double-click on it to activate the chart.

TIP: *You can use various commands on the shortcut menus for selected chart items to change the font, size, or format of chart text, the colors of the text or data markers, and the format of values along the y-axis.*

Use any of the following methods to edit a chart:

- In Access, PowerPoint, or Word, double-click on the chart to display Microsoft Graph's Datasheet and Chart windows. Select the cell that contains the value you want to change, and then type the new value to be plotted in the chart. The chart is automatically updated in the chart window.

- In Excel, select the cell that contains the value you want to change, and then enter the new value. The chart is automatically updated to reflect your change.

- To move a chart, click just inside the frame that surrounds the chart to select the chart. Then drag the chart to a different location.

- Double-click on the chart text you want to change to activate its text box, and then select

CHART

> **TROUBLESHOOTING**
>
> ### Changing the Chart Type of an Existing Chart
>
> Suppose you don't like the way the data is presented in an existing chart? You can easily change the chart's type. Double-click on the chart to activate it, and then right-click just outside the plot area of the chart to display its shortcut menu. Select Chart Type in the shortcut menu to display the Chart Type dialog box, choose a different type of chart, and then choose OK. The same data that was used to compile the original chart is used to draw a new chart of the selected type.

the text and type the new text to replace the selection.

- Select one of the axes, right-click on it, and then select Insert Gridlines to display the Gridlines dialog box. Select the check boxes of any gridlines you want to appear in the chart, and choose OK.

- To insert a chart title or axis title in a chart, right-click on an axis, and then select Insert Titles to display the Titles dialog box. Select the check box of any chart item for which you want a title, and then choose OK. A text box appears in the chart with some text in it describing the chart item. Edit the text as described above.

SEE ALSO: *Shortcut Menus*

COMMAND AND FEATURE REFERENCE

Clip Art

Microsoft Office comes with a ClipArt Gallery, which contains all the clip art files from each of the Office applications. There are more than 1000 clip art files included with Microsoft Office, so the ClipArt Gallery makes it easy for you to insert a picture that came with Access into a Word document.

Using the ClipArt Gallery

To insert a clip art file into one of the Microsoft Office applications:

1. Open the database file and then display the form or report in Design view, or open the worksheet, presentation, or document into which you want to insert a picture.

2. Choose one of the following options, depending on which application is active, to display the Insert Object dialog box:

- In an Access form or report in Design view, click on the Object Frame button in the Toolbox, and then click in the position where you want to place the picture. Or, select Edit ➤ Insert Object.

- In Excel, select the cell in which you want to insert a picture, and then select Insert ➤ Object.

- In PowerPoint, activate the slide on which you want to insert a picture, and then click on the Insert Clip Art button on the Standard toolbar or select Insert ➤ Object.

- In Word, position the insertion point where you want to insert a picture, and then select Insert ➤ Object.

CLIP ART

3. If necessary, select the Create New option button or tab.

4. Select Microsoft ClipArt Gallery in the Object Type list box, and then choose OK to display the Microsoft ClipArt Gallery dialog box.

5. If necessary, select a clip art category to display in the preview list box in the Choose A Category To View Below list box.

6. Click on a picture in the preview list box. The category and name of the selection are displayed on buttons below the preview list box.

7. Choose OK to insert the selected picture in the form or report, worksheet, slide, or document.

The following options are also available in the Microsoft ClipArt Gallery dialog box:

◆ Select Options to display the Options dialog box, and then select one of the following options:

> Select Refresh to add any clip art files on your computer to the ClipArt Gallery, and to remove any pictures from the preview list box whose files are not available.

> Select Add to choose specific clip art files to be added to the ClipArt Gallery.

> Select Change A Category to change the name of or delete an existing clip art category. These are the same options that appear

COMMAND AND FEATURE REFERENCE

when you click on the Category button below the preview list box.

Select <u>E</u>dit Picture Information to change the description of or move the picture selected in the preview list box. These are the same options that appear when you click on the Name button below the preview list box.

◆ To search for a particular picture in the ClipArt Gallery, select <u>F</u>ind to display the Find Picture dialog box. Select one of the following options, and then choose OK to display all the pictures that meet the search criteria in the preview list box:

With the <u>C</u>ategory   Select the name of the clip art category you want to preview.

With a <u>D</u>escription containing   Type the characters for which you want to search to preview all the clip art that contains those characters in their descriptions.

With a <u>F</u>ilename containing   Type the characters for which you want to search to preview all the clip art that contains those characters in their file names.

Of this <u>T</u>ype of File   Select the type of graphic file you want to preview.

TIP: *To insert one of the clip art files that came with a Microsoft Office application, select <u>I</u>nsert ➤ <u>P</u>icture, select the name of the clip art file in the File <u>N</u>ame list box, and then choose OK.*

SEE ALSO: *Frame; Graphic*

Close

SEE: *File Management*

Columns

By default, Word documents that are based on the NORMAL.DOT template have only one column. You can insert columns into a section in a document, or change existing text into columnar format. Columns are created as newspaper columns, in which the text from the bottom of one column flows to begin the top of the next column.

TIP: *To create side-by-side paragraphs in a document, such as a fax cover sheet, insert a table.*

Columns can be of equal or unequal widths. To view columns in your document, you must be in Page Layout or Print Preview mode.

Adding Columns to a Document

To quickly create columns of equal width in a document, position the insertion point where you want columns to begin or select the text to be changed into columns, click on the Columns button on the Standard toolbar, and then drag through the number of columns in the column palette that appears.

COMMAND AND FEATURE REFERENCE

To simultaneously add and format columns in a document, follow these steps:

1. Position the insertion point in the location where you want to insert columns, or select the text you want to change into columns.

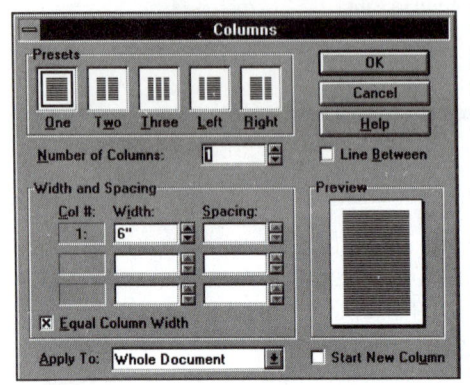

2. Select Format ➤ Columns to display the Columns dialog box.

3. Select One, Two, Three, Left, or Right as the column definition in the Presets area of the dialog box.

4. If necessary, enter a different number in the Number Of Columns text box.

5. If necessary, clear the Equal Column Width check box. Then, for each column specified in the Col # box, enter a measurement to define the width of the column in the Width text box, and the amount of space between the column and the next column in the Spacing text box.

6. Highlight the portion of the document that you want to be columnar in the Apply To drop-down list.

7. To insert a vertical line between the columns, select the Line Between check box.

8. Choose OK in the Columns dialog box.

NOTE: *You can add graphics to columnar text. A graphic in a frame can be positioned so that it is in one column, part of a column, or is placed across several columns.*

Editing Columns

In Page Layout view, you can also edit some column features using the following methods:

- Drag the left or right column marker on the horizontal ruler to change the widths of all columns of equal width, or to change only the active column in columns of unequal width.

- Drag the indent marker on the horizontal ruler to indent the paragraph that contains the insertion point. Or, select an indented paragraph in columnar text, choose Format ➤ Paragraph, and change the options in the Indentation area of the Indents And Spacing tab.

- To insert a column break in a column, position the insertion point where the column is to break and press Ctrl+Shift+ ↵. Alternatively, choose Format ➤ Columns, select the Start New Column check box, and then choose OK, or select Insert ➤ Break, choose Column Break, and then select OK.

- To balance the lengths of columns on a page, move the insertion point to the end of the column you want to balance and choose Insert ➤ Break. Select Continuous, and then choose OK in the Break dialog box.

SEE ALSO: *Frame; Graphic; Paragraph; Ruler; Table; Worksheet*

Control

Controls are graphic objects that contain all the information on an Access form or report. For example, the text that describes the data in a

COMMAND AND FEATURE REFERENCE

corresponding text box is a *control label*, and the text box itself is a control. A picture on a form is also a control (contained in an object frame), based on a graphic. In a report, even the lines and rectangles used to enhance the appearance of the report are controls.

TIP: *Use the Form Wizard to automatically create a form and its controls with the fields in the underlying table when you select Form Wizards in the New Form dialog box.*

There are three different types of controls, each of which contains a specific type of information. You define the controls on a form or report by the type of information displayed in the control.

◆ A bound control displays data from the table that contains the database (or a query based on the database) on which the form or report is based. Often a bound control is a text box, into which you can enter text, values, a date, etc.

◆ An unbound control does not have a source of data in the underlying database. Unbound controls are often informational or descriptive, such as a control label.

◆ A calculated control is a control that displays data based on an expression (a formula). The expression contains operators, such as = (equal to), + (plus), – (minus), / (division), or * (multiplication), and can contain values from the fields in an underlying table or query. For example, to calculate a six percent sales tax on the total amount of a sale in a query, a calculated control will contain the expression **=[Total]*.06.** The expression can begin with an = (equal sign) or + (plus sign). The above expression contains the name of a field (a variable) enclosed in brackets. Finally, the variable is multiplied by six percent (a constant). The results of the expression are displayed in the calculated control.

CONTROL

Creating a Bound Control

Follow these steps to create a bound control:

1. Select the Form or Report tab in the Database window of an open database file. Or, select View ➤ Forms or View ➤ Reports to display the list of existing forms or reports for the open database.

2. Select the name of the form or report in which you want to create a bound control in the Forms or Reports pane, and then select Design.

3. Click on the Field List button on the Form Design toolbar to display the list of fields in the database.

4. Select the name of the field in the field list, and then drag it onto the form. When you release the mouse button, a new control has been created that is bound to the field, and the control label has been created to indicate the name or number of the control.

To select multiple names simultaneously in the field list box, hold down the Ctrl key while you click on the names. To select all the field names, double-click on the field list box's title bar. When you drag the selected field names into the form, they are placed in the order in which they appear in the field list box below the first control that is created.

Creating a Calculated Control

A calculated control uses an expression as the source of the data it displays. Calculated controls are usually entered in text box controls.

Follow these steps to place a calculated control in a form or report:

1. Select the Form or Report tab in the Database window of an open database file. Or, select

COMMAND AND FEATURE REFERENCE

View ➤ Forms or View ➤ Reports to display the list of existing forms or reports for the open database.

2. Select the name of the form or report in which you want to create a calculated control, and then select Design.

3. Click on the Text Box button in the Toolbox.

4. Click on the position in the form or report where you want to place the text box control. The control appears, already selected.

5. Click in the text box control to place the cursor in it, and then type the expression in the text box and press ↵.

6. Click on the Form View button on the Form Design toolbar to return to Form view. The results of the calculated expression appear in the text box control on the form.

Save the form before you close it to save the changes made to it.

Creating an Unbound Control

Use tools in the Toolbox when you are in Form Design or Report Design view to create an unbound text box or label control in a form or report. Label controls are always unbound because they are a description of the data in an attached text box control, or other information helpful to the user of the form or report, and do not depend on the underlying table or query for the information they display.

To create an unbound control:

1. Select the Form or Report tab in the Database window of an open database file. Or, select View ➤ Forms or View ➤Reports to display the list of existing forms or reports for the open database.

CONTROL

2. Select the name of the form or report in which you want to create an unbound control, and then select Design.

3. Click on the Text Box button in the Toolbox, and then move the mouse pointer into the Detail pane of the form and click in the position where you want the text box control. Leave enough room for a label control for the text box, because the text box control appears with an attached label control.

4. To create an unattached control label, click on the Label button in the Toolbox, and then click on the position in the Detail pane where you want to place the label control.

5. Type the text you want in the label control. As you type, the label control is automatically resized to accommodate the label.

6. Click on the Form View button on the Form Design toolbar to return to Form view so you can enter data in the form.

To delete a selected control in Form Design or Report Design view, press Del.

Editing Control Labels

Control labels can be attached to a different control, or unattached. For example, an attached control label may contain a description of the contents of the text box control to which it is attached. An unattached control label may display information to the user of the form or the reader of the report.

To edit an attached or unattached control label:

- Click on the label to select it, and then click again to place the cursor in the control label. Drag through the characters you want to replace, and then type the new characters to replace text in the label.

COMMAND AND FEATURE REFERENCE

- Or, position the insertion point where you want to insert characters, and then type the characters.

To attach an unattached label to a control that does not have a label:

1. Select the unattached label, and then choose Edit ➤ Copy (Ctrl+C).

2. Select the control to which you want to attach the label, and then choose Edit ➤ Paste (Ctrl+V).

The following steps allow you to detach an attached label from a control:

1. Select the label, and then choose Edit ➤ Cut (Ctrl+X).

2. Click in the position on the form in which you want to place the label, and then select Edit ➤ Paste (Ctrl+V).

Moving Controls

While you are in Design view, you can move a selected control on a form or report, or move a group of selected controls.

To move a control and its attached label:

1. Select the control or the label, and then position the mouse pointer over the border of the selection until it appears as a hand. Do not position the mouse pointer over any of the selection's handles.

2. Drag the control or the label to a different position.

To move an attached label without moving its control, or a control without moving its attached label:

1. Select the label or the control, and then move the mouse pointer over the selection's move handle–the large handle in the top-left corner of the selected control. The mouse pointer will look like a pointing hand.

CONTROL

2. Drag the label or control to a different location.

To move a group of controls that is enclosed within another control:

1. Select View ➤ Options to display the Options dialog box.

2. In the Category list box, select Form & Report Design to change the Items list box.

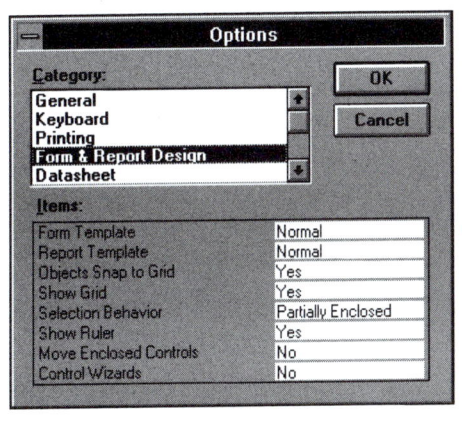

3. Click in the Move Enclosed Controls area to select it, and then click on the ↓ button and select Yes.

4. Choose OK in the Options dialog box.

5. Select the outer most control (the one that is enclosing the group), and then move the mouse pointer over one of its borders until it appears as a hand. Do not position the mouse pointer over the move handle.

6. Drag the control and the enclosed group to a new location.

To move only the control that encloses a group when Moved Enclosed Controls is set to Yes, position the mouse pointer over the move handle of the selected control, and then drag the move handle to a different location.

Selecting Controls

A control must be selected before any changes can be made to it. To select specific controls:

◆ To select a control, click in the control. If you select a text box control with an attached label, it

COMMAND AND FEATURE REFERENCE

appears surrounded by a large square move handle and seven smaller *size handles*. The attached label appears with only a move handle. If you select a label with an attached text box control, the label appears with a large move handle and seven smaller size handles, and the text box appears with only a move handle.

- To select multiple controls, hold down the Shift key while you click on each control.

- To select adjacent multiple controls, press and hold down the left mouse button outside the first control, and then drag just beyond the last adjacent control.

- To select all the controls in a column, click in the horizontal ruler directly above the column.

- To select all the controls in a row, click in the vertical ruler directly to the left of the row.

- To select all the controls in an area that includes both rows and columns, click on the ruler just above or to the left of the first control, and then drag down or to the right on the ruler until all the controls you want to select are outlined and release the mouse button.

To deselect selected controls:

- Click in an empty area of the form to deselect all selected controls.

- To deselect a control in a selected group, hold down the Shift key while you click on the control.

Sizing a Control

To change the size of a selected control:

1. Select the control, and then position the mouse pointer over one of the seven small size handles surrounding the control until it appears as a two-headed arrow.

2. Drag the handle away from the control to make it larger, or toward the control to make it smaller.

To change the size of selected controls relative to each other:

1. Select the controls.

2. Choose Format ➤ Size, and then select one of the following options:

to Fit	Resizes the selected controls so the height and width of the control can accommodate the characters entered in the font and size selected.
to Grid	Changes the size of the sides of selected controls so each of their corners snap to the nearest grid point.
to Tallest	Resizes the selected controls so they are the same height as the tallest control in the selection.
to Shortest	Resizes the selected controls so they are the same height as the shortest control in the selection.
to Widest	Changes the size of selected controls so they are the same width as the widest control in the selection.
to Narrowest	Changes the size of selected controls so they are the same width as the narrowest control in the selection.

COMMAND AND FEATURE REFERENCE

> **SEE ALSO:** Captions; Control Properties; Cut, Copy, and Paste; Field; Form; Frame; Graphic; Report

Control Properties

Control properties define the appearance of the control on a form or report, and the appearance of the information it contains. For example, the size of a control text box and the format of the characters in it are defined by its control properties.

If a control is bound to data in the underlying table or query, its properties are the same as those in the corresponding field in the table or query. You can change the property of a control in a selected form or report without changing the property in the table or query upon which it is based.

> **TIP:** To make bound controls consistent in the forms and reports created for the underlying table or query, set the properties in the table or query.

You must set the properties for calculated controls that are not based on a query in the form or report that contains the calculated control.

Changing a Control's Properties

To customize an existing control in a form or report, change the properties of the control in the control properties sheet. You must be in Form Design or Report Design view to change control properties.

CONTROL PROPERTIES

To change a control's properties:

1. Double-click the control whose properties you want to change. Or, select the control, and then click on the Properties button on the Form Design or Report Design toolbar. The properties sheet for the selected control appears.

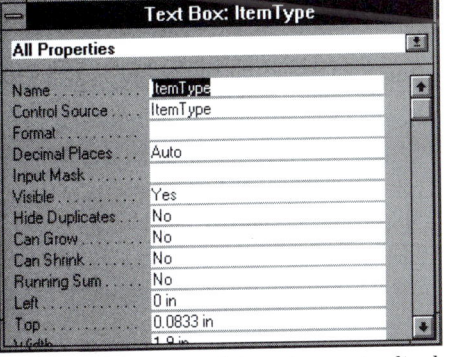

2. Click on the drop-down list button to display the following list of property categories, and then select the appropriate category to display:

All Properties	All the properties of the selected control are displayed.
Data Properties	The properties that determine the format of the data in the selected control, such as the number of decimal places, are displayed.
Layout Properties	The settings that define the appearance of the control are displayed.
Event Properties	The settings that define where and when an event will take place, such as when a macro will run, are displayed.
Other Properties	Displays other properties of the control, such as its name and any information that is to be displayed in the status bar.

3. Select the property whose setting you want to change. If a drop-down list button appears, click on

77

it to display the list of available settings for the property, and then select the setting you want in the list. Otherwise, type the setting for the property into its option area.

4. Repeat steps 2 and 3 for each property you want to change.

5. Double-click on the property sheet's Control menu box to return to Form Design or Report Design view.

To change a property for several controls simultaneously, select one control and display its property sheet, and then select the other controls whose property you want to change. Display the appropriate property categories list, and then change the setting of the property.

Changing the Default Properties for a Form or Report

The default properties of controls you add to a form or report can also be changed. For example, you may want to change the format of the text that appears on all the macro buttons you create in a form.

Once you change the default properties of controls, all succeeding controls that you create for that form or report are created with the new defaults.

To change the default properties for a form or report:

1. Display the property sheet for any existing control.

2. Click on the button in the Toolbox for the tool whose defaults you want to change.

3. Select the category that contains the property you want to change.

4. Select or type the new default property in the property's option area.

SEE ALSO: Control; Form; Report

Cross-Reference

Cross-references are used to refer the reader to additional or related information placed in a different location in the same or in a different document. In Word, you can create cross-references to heading text formatted with one of the built-in heading styles, footnotes and endnotes created with Insert ➤ Footnote, captions created with Insert ➤ Caption, and bookmarks.

Cross-references are especially useful in long documents such as a master document.

Creating Cross-References

Cross-references are inserted as field codes in your document. To create cross-references:

1. Position the insertion point in your document where you want to create a cross-reference, and

---

TROUBLESHOOTING

Section and Chapter Cross-References

Do you want to include section or chapter cross-references in a header or footer? Apply one of Word's built-in Heading styles to the section heading or chapter title in the document. Then insert the heading text as a cross-reference in the Header or Footer text.

COMMAND AND FEATURE REFERENCE

then type any introductory text, such as "See Page." Be sure to insert a space after the introductory text.

2. Select Insert ➤ Cross-reference to display the Cross-Reference dialog box.

3. Highlight Heading, Bookmark, Footnote, Endnote, Equation, Figure, Table, or a caption label you created as the type of item you want to cite in the Reference Type list box.

4. Highlight the type of information to place in your document in the Insert Reference To list box. The following types of information are available, depending on the selected Reference Type:

Heading Text   Inserts the text you have specified if it is formatted as a Heading style.

Heading Number   Inserts a heading number applied with Format ➤ Heading Numbering.

Page Number   Inserts the number of the page on which the cross-reference item is located.

Paragraph Number   Inserts the number of a paragraph, applied with Format ➤ Bullets And Numbering, in which a bookmark is located.

Bookmark Text   Inserts the text of a defined bookmark.

Footnote Number   Inserts the reference number of a footnote.

Endnote Number   Inserts the reference number of an endnote.

Entire Caption   Inserts the label, number, and optional text of a caption.

CROSS-REFERENCE

Only Label and Number Inserts the caption's label and number, but not the optional text.

Only Caption Text Inserts the optional text of a caption, but not the caption's label and number.

5. Select the specific item to reference in the For Which list box.

6. Choose Insert.

7. Click in the document window to activate it, and then insert any optional text or the new introductory text for the next cross-reference.

8. Repeat steps 3 through 7 for each cross-reference.

9. Choose Close to return to your document.

To insert cross-references to items in a document into a different document, make sure both documents are included in a master document.

Editing a Cross-Reference

You can change or delete cross-references you have inserted in your document. To edit a cross-reference:

- To replace selected text in a cross-reference, type the new text.

- To delete a reference placed in the document by Word, select the reference and press Backspace or Del. An error message will appear the next time you update the cross-reference.

- To change a reference placed in the document by Word to a different type of reference, select the reference and choose Insert ➤ Cross-reference. Select a different item in the Insert Reference To list box, choose Insert, and then choose Close.

COMMAND AND FEATURE REFERENCE

SEE ALSO: Bookmark; Captions; Field Code; Footnotes and Endnotes; Master Document; Style

Crosstab Query

Create a crosstab query in Access to compare data or see trends in the data in a database. The results of the crosstab query appear as a summary in tabular format, which cannot be updated.

Creating a Crosstab Query

The easiest way to create a crosstab query is to use the Crosstab Wizard. However, you can also design your own crosstab query:

1. Open the database file or activate the Database window of the file in which you want to create a crosstab query.

2. Select the Query tab in the Database window and choose New, or click on the New Query button on the Database toolbar to display the New Query dialog box.

3. Choose New Query to create a new query and display the Add Table dialog box with a list of existing tables for the database (if a table was not selected in the Database window).

4. If necessary, select Tables, Queries, or Both in the View area to display the corresponding list in the Table/Query list box.

5. Select the table or query that contains the fields you want to place in the crosstab query in the Table/Query list box, and then choose Add to place

CROSSTAB QUERY

a list of the field names in the top pane of the Select Query window.

6. Repeat step 5 for each table or query that contains fields you want to summarize. When you are finished, select Close in the Add Table dialog box.

7. Drag the first field you want to analyze to the first cell in the Field row in the query-by-example grid in the bottom pane of the Select Query dialog box.

8. Specify the criteria for the field in the Criteria row. If necessary, define the sort order for the field.

9. Repeat steps 6 and 7 for each field you want to analyze in the crosstab query.

10. Click on the Crosstab Query button on the Query Design toolbar or select Query ➤ Crosstab. The Crosstab and Total rows appear in the query-by-example grid.

11. Select the Crosstab cell in a column that contains a field name you want to use as a row heading in the crosstab query, and then select Row Heading in the drop-down list.

12. Repeat step 11 for each row heading in the crosstab query.

NOTE: *To eliminate a field you used for sorting, grouping, or setting criteria from the crosstab query datasheet, select (Not Shown) in the drop-down list in the Crosstab cell.*

13. Select the Crosstab cell in the column that contains the field name you want to use as a column heading in the crosstab query, and then select Column Heading in the drop-down list.

14. Select the Crosstab cell in the column that contains the field you want to use as a summary value in the crosstab query, and then select Value in the drop-down list.

COMMAND AND FEATURE REFERENCE

15. Select the Total cell in the column that contains the field that will be the summary value, and then select how the value will be calculated in the drop-down list.

16. Click on the Datasheet View button on the Query Design toolbar, or select View ➤ Datasheet to display the crosstab query.

When you are creating a crosstab query, only one field can be used as a column heading although you can have multiple row headings. The Total cell for both the column heading and the row headings must be set to Group By.

Also, you can have only one summary field (the one set to Value in step 14). The Total cell for the Value field must not be set to Group By. Instead, it must be set to a specific type of value, such as Count, Sum, Max, or Min.

SEE ALSO: *Pivot Table*

Cue Cards

SEE: *Help*

Cut, Copy, and Paste

Use the Cut or Copy commands or buttons on the Standard toolbar in any of the Microsoft Office applications to cut or copy text, tables, graphics,

CUT, COPY, AND PASTE

charts, or any item in your database, worksheet, mail message, presentation, or document to the Clipboard. You can then use the Paste command or button to paste the item into the same file or another file.

Cutting or Copying an Item to the Clipboard

When you cut or move a selected item, you remove the selected item from the active file and place a copy of it on the Clipboard. When you copy a selected item, the selection remains in its original position and a copy is placed on the Clipboard.

Follow these steps to move or copy a selection:

1. Select the item to be moved or copied.

2. Choose Edit ➤ Cut (Ctrl+X) or click on the Cut button on the Standard toolbar to move the selection. Or, choose Edit ➤ Copy (Ctrl+C) or click on the Copy button to copy the selection to the Clipboard.

Pasting the Contents of the Clipboard

Once you have copied an item to the Clipboard, paste it in the location in which you want it in your file.

TIP: *The contents of the Clipboard can be pasted into a document as many times as you wish. However, each time you use the Cut or Copy command, the Clipboard contents are replaced with the new selection.*

To paste the contents of the Clipboard:

1. Position the insertion point where you want to place the Clipboard contents.

2. Select Edit ➤ Paste (Ctrl+V) or click on the Paste button on the Standard toolbar.

SEE ALSO: *Drag and Drop*

COMMAND AND FEATURE REFERENCE

Database

You can create a database in either Access or Excel, and then insert the database into a Word document or create a report using the data in the database. You can also filter and insert records from a Word database, such as a merge data source file, into a Word document.

A database consists of *records* that contain all the information about a specific person or item. Records are composed of *fields*, which define each individual type of information in a record.

Creating an Access Database

To create a new database in Access:

1. Select File ➤ New Database (Ctrl+N) or click on the New Database button on the Database toolbar to display the New Database dialog box.

2. Type a name for the database in the File Name text box, and then choose OK. Access automatically adds the .MDB file extension.

3. The Database window appears, with the Tables pane displayed. Select New to display the New Table dialog box.

4. Choose Table Wizards to have Access create a database from a template. The Table Wizard dialog box appears. Select Business or Personal as the type of template you want to appear in the Sample Tables list box.

DATABASE

5. In the Sample Tables list box, select the name of a table that contains field definitions similar to the type you want.

6. Highlight the name of one field in the Sample Fields list box, and then click on the > button to add it to the Fields In My New Table list box. Or, to add all the fields in the selected table template, click on the >> button.

7. If necessary, highlight the name of a field in the Fields In My New Table list box, and then click on the < button to remove it from the list. Or, click on the << button to remove all the field names from the list box.

NOTE: *If you choose Set The Primary Key Myself, select the field you want as the primary key in the drip-down list in the Table Wizard dialog box that appears when you choose Next.*

8. Select Next to display the next Table Wizard dialog box. Type a name for the table in the corresponding text box, and then select either Let Microsoft Access Set A Primary Key For Me or Set The Primary Key Myself.

9. Select Next, and then choose Modify The Table Design, Enter Data Directly Into The Table, or Enter Data Into The Table Using A Form The Wizard Creates For Me.

10. Select Finish to display the table in the design you created.

You can enter data for each record in the cells of the table, or into the field boxes in a form.

If you select New Table in step 4 to create a new, blank table, you must name and define the fields yourself, and specify the type of data each field will contain.

COMMAND AND FEATURE REFERENCE

Creating an Excel Database

Use an Excel worksheet to organize associated data by rows into labeled columns in a *list*. Excel automatically identifies a list as a simple database, with the rows of data as records and the columns of data as fields. The column labels in the first row, called the *header row*, are part of the list, even though they are not items in the list.

There are several points to keep in mind when you create a list:

- Place each list in a separate worksheet. However, you can store many lists on different sheets of a workbook.

- Position a list in a worksheet so there is at least one blank column and row between it and other data in the worksheet.

- Do not leave any blank rows between the header row and the items in the list. Instead, format the text in the header row so it appears different from the formatting of the items in the list, or add a solid border to the bottom edge of the cells that contain the labels to divide the column labels from the list items.

- Do not place essential data to the left or right of a list, because it may be hidden when you filter the list.

To create a list:

1. Select a new worksheet tab in a workbook.

2. Enter the column labels in the first row of the list, and then apply a format to the labels that is different from the format for the data.

3. Apply the same format to each cell in a column of the list. For example, in a Date field, format each cell in the column except the cell in the header row with a date format.

DATABASE

4. Optionally, select the range of cells that contains the list, including the column labels, and choose Insert ➤ Name ➤ Define to display the Define Name dialog box. Type a name for the list in the Names In Workbook text box, and then choose OK.

Entering Records in a Database

In both Access and Excel, you can enter data directly into each cell of a table or list:

- Select the cell in an Access table or an Excel worksheet into which you want to enter data, and then type the data. Press Tab to enter the data and move to the next table cell. To move to the previous cell, press Shift+Tab.

- Enter the data in the list without blank spaces at the beginning of each cell.

- Use uniform capitalization so you can sort the list later.

Inserting a Database in a Word Document

Once you have created a database and entered records into it, you can select which fields of data you want from the data source and filter the selection of records to be inserted into a table in a Word document. You can also format the table to meet your needs, and have Word update the table if the data source changes.

TIP: *Click on the Find File button on the Microsoft Office toolbar to perform a search for the database file you want.*

To insert a database in a Word document:

1. Open the document into which you want to insert the database, and then place the insertion point where you want the database to appear.

COMMAND AND FEATURE REFERENCE

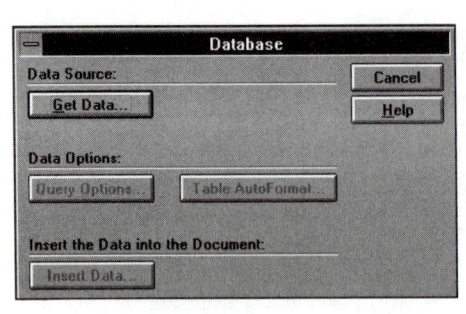

2. Select Insert ➤ Database to display the Database dialog box.

3. In the Data Source area, select Get Data to display the Open Data Source dialog box.

4. If necessary, change to the directory that contains the database file, and then select the type of the database file in the List Files Of Type drop-down list.

5. Highlight the name of the file in the File Name list box and choose OK. Or, if necessary, select MS Query to insert and sort specific information from the data source.

6. If you chose OK in step 5, select the name of a table or query in the dialog box that appears, and then choose OK to return to the Database dialog box.

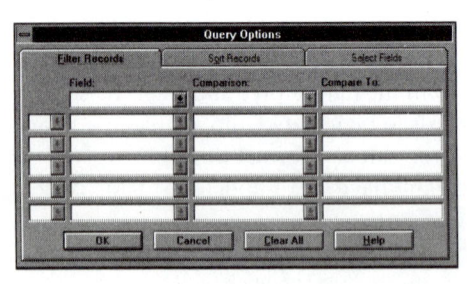

7. To filter and sort the data in the file, select Query Options to display the Query Options dialog box.

8. Choose the query options on the appropriate tab, and then select OK. Choose the **Filter Records tab** to define which records to insert in the document.

- Select the data source field to be used in a comparison in the Field drop-down list, and then select the operator to be used for alphabetical and numerical data in the Comparison drop-down list.

DATABASE

- Type the alphabetical or numerical value you want to compare with the selected field in the Compare To text box.

- To include additional fields, operators, and comparison values, select the And/Or drop-down list. Choose And if additional criteria must be met in the filter, or choose Or if only one of the criteria should be met.

- To erase all the selection criteria and insert all the data source records, select Clear All.

Select the **Sort Records tab** to define the order in which the records will appear in your document.

- Highlight the field that you want as your first data selection in the Sort By drop-down list, and then select Ascending (a–z) or Descending (z–a) to define the alphabetical or numerical order of the items in the table.

- If necessary, choose the second field on which to define the sort in the Then By drop-down list, and the third field in the Then By drop-down list, and select Ascending or Descending as the sort order for each field.

- To remove all the sorting criteria, choose Clear All.

Choose the **Select Fields tab** to define which records will be included in the table.

- Fields that will be included in the table are listed in the Selected Fields list box. To eliminate a field in the table, highlight the field in the Selected Fields list box and choose Remove. Choose Remove All to prevent all the fields from appearing in the table.

- Highlight a field in the Fields In Data Source list box and choose Select to add the

COMMAND AND FEATURE REFERENCE

> **TROUBLESHOOTING**
>
> ### Updating a Database Inserted as a Field
>
> Do you want to update a database inserted in a Word document? If a database is inserted as a field, each time you update the database records any table and text formatting you have applied to the table in the Word document will be lost. To update a database with a selected table format, you must reinsert the database and the table format in your document. If you edit a table inserted as a database field in a Word document, your changes will be lost when the field is next updated.

field to the Selected Fields list box. Choose Select All to include all the data source fields in the table.

- Select the Include Field Names check box to use the field names as column names in the table.

- To remove all the field selection criteria, choose Clear All.

9. Select Table AutoFormat to display the Table AutoFormat dialog box. Select the name of the table format you want to use in the Formats list box, and then choose OK.

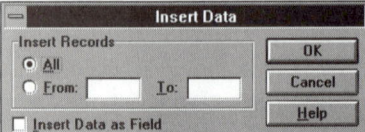

10. Select Insert Data to display the Insert Data dialog box.

11. Choose any of the following options, and then select OK to insert the database table into your document:

- Select All to insert all the records that meet the selection criteria. If no selection criteria

DATE AND TIME

are specified, all the data source records are inserted.

- Or, select From, and then specify the beginning record number in the text box and the last record in the range in the To text box.

- Select the Insert Data As Field check box to insert the specified source data as a database field so the changes made to the data source can be updated in your Word document.

SEE ALSO: *Field Code; Find File; Form; Mail Merge; MS Query; Query; Table; Worksheet*

Date and Time

You can insert your system's date and time as either text or a field code. If you insert the date or time as text, it will stay the same as when it was inserted in your document. If you insert the date or time as a field code, you can update the field to reflect the current system date and time.

TIP: *To enter the date or time as text, just type it in the location in which you want it to appear.*

Inserting the Date and Time in Access

To insert the system date and time into the active Access form or report:

1. If necessary, click on the Design View button on the Form Design toolbar to change to Design view.

COMMAND AND FEATURE REFERENCE

> **NOTE:** *A report can be displayed only in Design view or in the Print Preview window. Click on the Close Window button on the Print Preview toolbar to display the report in Design view.*

2. Click on the Text Box button in the Toolbox, and then click in the location on the form or report in which you want to place the text box.

3. Click on the Properties button on the Form Design or Report Design toolbar to display the property sheet dialog box for the new text box.

4. If necessary, select Data Properties in the drop-down list.

5. Click in the Control Source options area, and then type **=Date( )** to display the system date or **=Now( )** to display the system time in the text box.

6. Click in the Format options area, and then select one of the date or time formats in the drop-down list.

7. Double-click on the property sheet dialog box's Control menu box to close it.

8. Click on the Save button on the Form Design or Report Design toolbar, or select File ➤ Save (Ctrl+S) to save the changed design of the form or report.

9. Click on the Form View button on the Form Design or Report Design toolbar to change back to the form or report.

The text box for the date or time appears on each page of a form (for each item in the table or query on which the form is based) or report.

Inserting the Date and Time in Excel

To insert the system date and time as text in Excel's automatic date and time formats, follow the steps on the next page.

DATE AND TIME

- Press Ctrl+; (semicolon), and then press ↵ to enter the date.
- Press Ctrl+Shift+: (colon), and then press ↵ to enter the time.

To insert the system date and time as a function so it will automatically update each time you activate the spreadsheet:

1. Click on the Function Wizard button on the Standard toolbar or press Shift+F3 to display the Function Wizard dialog box.

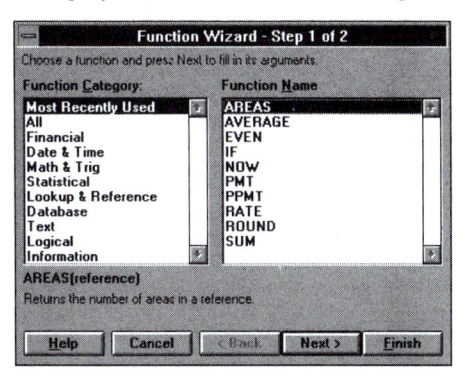

2. Select Date & Time in the Function Category list box to display the names of the Date and Time functions.

3. Select NOW (to enter the system date and time), or TODAY (to enter the system date) in the Function Name list box.

4. Choose Finish.

Inserting the Date and Time in PowerPoint

To insert the date and time on slides, the outline, notes pages, or handouts of a presentation, you must insert the date and time on the Master view. Any item you insert on the Master view appears in the background on each slide or each printed page.

COMMAND AND FEATURE REFERENCE

To insert the date and time in PowerPoint:

1. Select View ➤ Master ➤ Slide Master, Outline Master, Handout Master, or Notes Master to display the Master view.

2. Select Insert ➤ Date or Insert ➤ Time. A text box with // (the date symbol) or :: (the time symbol) appears.

The system date or time appears in the slide show, or the printed version of the slides, outline, handouts, or notes pages.

To enter a text date or time, click on the Text Tool button in the Drawing Tools, and then click in the position on the slide, notes page, handout, or outline where you want the date or time to appear. Type the date or time you want in the text box. The size of the text box changes to accommodate each character you type.

Inserting the Date and Time in Word

To insert the current date and time in Word as either text or a field code:

1. Position the insertion point where you want to insert the date or time.

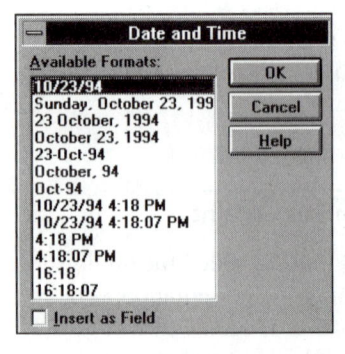

2. Select Insert ➤ Date And Time to display the Date And Time dialog box.

3. Select the date or time format in the Available Formats list box.

4. To enter the date or time as a field code, select the Insert As Field check box.

5. Choose OK to insert the selected date or time.

SEE ALSO: *Control; Control Properties; Field Code; Function; Master View*

Drag and Drop

Use the drag-and-drop feature to move or copy selected text, graphics, or any item a short distance within a worksheet, presentation, or document or to another displayed worksheet or document.

TIP: *To move or copy an item a farther distance, cut or copy the selection to the Clipboard, and then paste it into a different location.*

When you are dragging and dropping an item, the mouse pointer appears with a small box that has a gray dotted border with a dotted gray vertical line.

Moving or Copying with Drag and Drop

Select the item you want to move or copy, and then:

- Drag the selection to a new location to move it.
- Press and hold down the Ctrl key while you drag the selection to copy it.

SEE ALSO: *Cut, Copy, and Paste; Duplicate*

Draw

Use the Drawing tools to create a drawing in a file. You can draw directly on the form or report in Design view, the worksheet, slide, or document. To draw or see drawings, you must be in Slide or Notes Pages view in PowerPoint, and Page Layout or Print Preview view in Word.

COMMAND AND FEATURE REFERENCE

Displaying the Drawing Tools

Display the Drawing toolbar in the application in which you want to create a drawing:

- In Access, the drawing toolbar, called the Toolbox, appears by default when you change to Form Design or Report Design view.

- In Excel and Word, click on the Drawing button on the Standard toolbar to toggle the display of the Drawing toolbar.

- In Power Point, the Drawing toolbar appears by default when you change to Slide or Notes Pages view. To display the Drawing+ toolbar, right-click on any of the displayed toolbars, and then select Drawing+.

Using the Drawing Tools

To draw an object, click on one of the drawing tools discussed below, position the mouse pointer in the location where you want the object, and then drag. When you release the mouse button (except for freeforms), the object is complete.

For many drawn objects, you can make a copy of a selected object by holding down the Ctrl key while you drag the object. To draw an object outward from its center, click on the drawing tool and then press and hold down the Ctrl key while you drag the mouse pointer. Or, you can constrain the shape of the object being drawn by holding down the Shift key as you draw.

If you make a mistake and want to cancel a drawing (except for a freeform), press Esc while you are still holding down the mouse button, or select the object and press Del to delete it after it has been drawn.

TIP: *To use the same drawing tool several times, double-click on it when you select it on the Drawing toolbar.*

DRAW **D**

> **TROUBLESHOOTING**
>
> ## Selecting the Drag-and-Drop Feature
>
> What should you do if the drag-and-drop feature does not work in Excel or Word?
>
> **1.** Select <u>T</u>ools ➤ <u>O</u>ptions, and choose the Edit tab in the Options dialog box.
>
> **2.** Select the Allow Cell <u>D</u>rag And Drop check box in Excel, and the <u>D</u>rag-and-Drop Text Editing check box in Word.
>
> **3.** Choose OK in the Options dialog box.
>
> In Excel, make sure the <u>A</u>lert Before Overwriting Cells check box on the Edit tab is also selected so you don't lose any valuable data when you drop a selection into a cell or range.

Use the Line tool to draw a line.

Select the Rectangle or Filled Rectangle tool to draw a rectangle.

Use the Ellipse or Filled Ellipse tool to draw an oval.

Use the Arc or Filled Arc tool to draw an arc of an ellipse.

Use the Freeform or Filled Freeform tool to draw an open or closed polygon or a freeform. (Freeforms are made up of very small straight lines, although they appear to be curved lines.) Click in the window and move the mouse to draw straight line segments, or drag the mouse pointer to create freeform shapes. Click on the starting point to close

COMMAND AND FEATURE REFERENCE

a freeform object. Double-click or press Esc to end the drawing as an open object, or press Backspace to remove the last line segment drawn.

To draw a freehand object, use the Freehand tool. Freehand objects are the same as freeform objects created with the Freeform tool.

Draw an arrow with the Arrow tool to point to important items in a worksheet or slide.

Use the Text Box tool in Excel and Word, or the Text Tool in PowerPoint, to draw a text box that appears as a rectangle with a paragraph mark or the insertion point in it.

In Access, use the Label tool to draw an unbound label. Or, use the Text Box tool to draw a text box with a bound label.

Use a callout to tie a text object to a graphic. To create a callout in a Word document, click on the Callout tool to insert a text box with no borders, and a line pointing to the callout item.

To change the format of a selected Word callout, click on the Format Callout tool, and then select the appropriate options in the Format Callout dialog box.

Use the Create Button tool in Excel or the Command Button tool in Access to draw a blank button to which a macro can be assigned. In addition, the Access Toolbox contains buttons you can use to draw an option group, toggle button, option button, check box, combo box, list box, graph, subform or subreport, and a bound or unbound object frame.

Some of the Drawing tools allow you to change the position of the object or to format a selected object.

Click on the Fill Color tool, and then click on the color or pattern in the pop-up palette that appears.

DRAW

Click on the Line Color tool to display a pop-up color palette, and then select the color you want for the lines of the selected object.

Click on the Line Style tool in PowerPoint and Word to display a pop-up list of line styles, including arrows, and then select the line style. In PowerPoint, click on the Dashed Lines button to display a pop-up list of dashed lines, and then select the style you want in the list.

In PowerPoint, click on the Arrowheads tool and select an arrowhead style to apply to a selected line.

To add a predrawn shape to a slide in a presentation, click on the AutoShapes button, and then select the shape. Position the mouse pointer on the slide, and then drag to create the shape in the size you want.

Click on the Select button when you want to select an object. To select multiple objects or groups, hold down the Shift key while you click on each object. Or, click on the Select button, and then drag to create a rectangle that surrounds the object or group you want to select.

In Excel, click on the Drop Shadow button to apply a drop shadow to a selected object. In PowerPoint, click on the Shadow On/Off button to toggle the display of a drop shadow on a selected object.

In PowerPoint, click on the Shadow Color tool, and then select a color to apply to the drop shadow of a selected object.

Select an object or group that is behind (under) another object or group and click on the Bring To Front or Bring Forward tool to change the order of the stack.

Select an object or group that is in front (on top) of another object or group, and click on the Send To

COMMAND AND FEATURE REFERENCE

Back or Send Backward tool to change the order of the stack.

In Word, select an object or group that you want to appear in front (on top) of your document text, and click on the Bring In Front Of Text button.

In Word, select an object or group that you want to place behind (under) the text in your document, and click on the Send Behind Text button.

To manipulate multiple objects or groups as a unit, select each object or group and click on the Group button.

To remove objects or groups from a single group, select the group and click on the Ungroup button.

Select the object you want to flip, and then choose the Flip Horizontal or Flip Vertical button to create a mirror image. The text in a text box will not flip, but the text box itself will flip horizontally or vertically.

To rotate an object 90 degrees to the right, select the object and click the Rotate Right button. A text box will rotate, but the text in it will not.

Click on the Free Rotate tool in PowerPoint, and then position the mouse pointer over one of the handles of a selection. Drag the handle to rotate the object.

To rearrange the individual line segments of a selected freeform object, click on the Reshape button in Word, or select Edit ➤ Edit Freeform Object in PowerPoint. Drag any of the handles to reshape the object. To add another vertex to the object, hold down the Ctrl key while you click in the position on a line where the vertex will be. To remove a vertex from the object, hold down the Ctrl key and click on the handle of the vertex.

In Word, click on the Snap To Grid tool to display the Snap To Grid dialog box to change the spacing between gridlines, define where the grid begins, or

102

remove the grid. Choose OK after any options are changed.

In Word, select the drawing objects you want to align, and then click on the Align Drawing Objects button to display the Align dialog box. Choose a horizontal, vertical, and relative alignment option, and then choose OK to realign your selection. An object that was aligned relative to the page does not move if the page size is changed.

To place a selected drawing object in a picture or open a separate window in which to create a picture, click on the Create Picture button in Word.

To place a selected object in a frame or create a frame in a Word document, click on the Insert Frame button.

SEE ALSO: *Font; Frame; Graphic*

Drop Cap

Add dropped capital formatting to a paragraph to make selected text at the beginning of the paragraph appear in a large, bold font in a Word document. The selected text is placed in a frame, and the paragraph text wraps around the frame. You can apply borders and shading to the frame that surrounds the dropped capital.

Use scaleable fonts such as TrueType, ATM, or PostScript fonts for the best results with dropped capitals. You must be in Page Layout view to see how the dropped capital appears in your document.

COMMAND AND FEATURE REFERENCE

Creating Dropped Capitals

You cannot place a dropped cap in the margin of a columnar document. To create a dropped capital:

1. Move the insertion point into the paragraph in which you want the first letter to be a dropped capital, or select the first word of the paragraph.

2. Choose F_ormat ➤ _Drop Cap to display the Drop Cap dialog box.

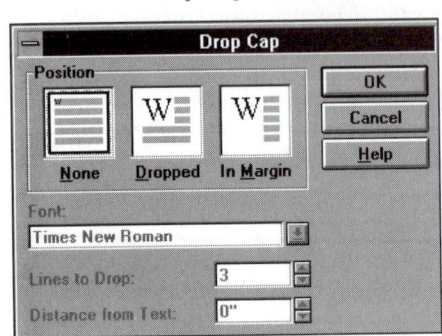

3. In the Position area of the dialog box, select _Dropped to place the selection within the paragraph or In _Margin to place the selection in the margin beside the top of the paragraph.

4. Optionally, select a different font for the selection in the _Font drop-down list.

5. To change the height of the dropped capital letter, change the number in the _Lines To Drop text box.

6. To change the distance between the dropped capital and the paragraph text, change the measurement in the Distance From Te_xt text box.

7. Choose OK in the Drop Cap dialog box.

To remove the dropped capital format from the paragraph that contains the insertion point, select _None in the Position area of the Drop Cap dialog box, and then select OK.

SEE ALSO: *Borders and Shading; Columns; Frame; Graphic*

Duplicate

Both Access and PowerPoint contain a Duplicate feature. Use the feature to copy a selection into an Access form in Design view or on a slide in a presentation. Duplicate bypasses the Windows Clipboard and immediately makes a copy of the selection.

Use Access's Duplicate feature to copy a group of controls, such as a stack of check boxes or option buttons you have placed in a form, below their current positions. When you copy the group with Duplicate, the same spacing and alignment as in the original selection is also copied.

TIP: *To select multiple controls in a form that is displayed in Design view, hold down the Shift key while you click on additional controls.*

In a presentation, you can duplicate a selected object in Slide view or a selected slide in Outline, Slide Sorter, or Notes Pages view. A copy of a selected object is placed immediately in an offset position from the original object. A copy of a selected slide is placed immediately after the original slide.

Duplicating a Selection

To immediately copy an object, slide, control, or multiple controls, bypassing the Windows' Clipboard:

1. Select the object or slide, or the control or multiple controls to duplicate.

2. Choose Edit ➤ Duplicate (or press Ctrl+D in PowerPoint) to copy the selection, and then drag the copy to position it.

COMMAND AND FEATURE REFERENCE

You can also select an object in a presentation slide, and then press the Ctrl key while you drag the object to create a duplicate.

SEE ALSO: *Cut, Copy, and Paste; Drag and Drop*

Envelopes

Use Word's Envelope feature to quickly print an envelope for a document. Word will automatically insert the delivery and return addresses.

You can also mark the delivery and return addresses in your document with bookmarks. Use EnvelopeAddress as the bookmark name for the delivery address and EnvelopeReturn to mark the return address in a document that contains several addresses.

Addressing and Printing an Envelope

To print an envelope with a delivery address entered in the active document:

1. Select the mailing address if the document contains more than one address.

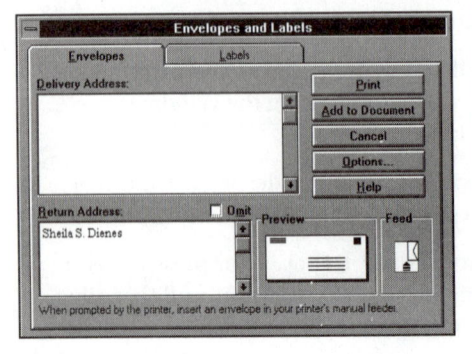

2. Choose Tools ➤ Envelopes And Labels to display the Envelopes And Labels dialog box. If necessary, select the Envelopes tab.

3. If necessary, type a different

ENVELOPES E

return address in the Return Address text box. Or, select the Omit check box to omit printing the return address on an envelope.

4. Select Add To Document to add a section to the beginning of a document that contains the envelope formatting. Or, select Change Document to insert any changes made if you already have an envelope section in a document.

5. Insert the envelope in the printer in the position shown in the Feed area.

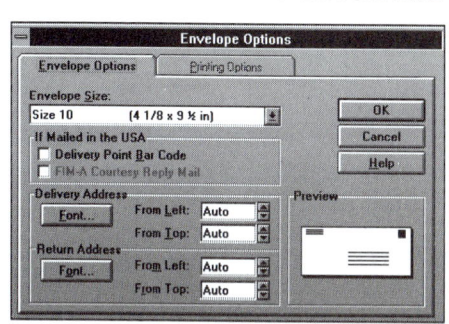

6. If necessary, select Options to display the Envelope Options dialog box. Then change any of the following envelope options on the Envelope Options tab, and choose OK:

- Select the defini-tion of the envelope size you want to use in the Envelope Size drop-down list. Or, select Custom Size to create a new envelope size.

- Select the Delivery Point Bar Code check box to have Word automatically print the bar code of the delivery address's zip code.

- Select the FIM-A Courtesy Reply Mail check box to print a facing identification mark on the front of a courtesy reply envelope.

NOTE: *By default, Word inserts FIM-A codes when the check box is selected. To insert an FIM-C code for bulk mail, insert a BarCode field with the \f "C" switch.*

- Choose Font or Font to change the format of the font in the Delivery Address or Return Address area. Specify the distance

107

COMMAND AND FEATURE REFERENCE

the delivery or return address will be printed from the left and top edges of the envelope.

7. Select Print to print the envelope.

You can also change the style of both the delivery and return addresses directly in a document to which an envelope has been added to change the font and reposition the text on the envelope. Or, move the delivery address (which is inside a frame) directly in the document.

Including Graphics on an Envelope

To print special text or graphics on an envelope each time you create an envelope based on the current template, save the text or graphic as an AutoText entry named EnvelopeExtra1 or EnvelopeExtra2. Word automatically inserts the AutoText entries on each envelope.

To include graphics on an envelope:

1. Create the envelope using the steps and any necessary options described above. Then select Add To Document or Change Document.

2. If necessary, switch to Page Layout view.

3. Type any special text, insert a graphic, or create a drawing.

4. Adjust the position of the special text or graphic on your envelope. If necessary, place text that is not a text object or a graphic you inserted into a frame so it can be positioned on the envelope.

5. Select the text or graphic, and click on the Edit AutoText button on the Standard toolbar or choose Edit ➤ AutoText.

6. Type EnvelopeExtra1 or EnvelopeExtra2 in the Name text box, and select Add.

Delete any text that appears in the Return Address text box in the Envelopes And Labels dialog box, or select the Omit check box to suppress the return address on the envelope when you use the envelope AutoText entries.

Delete the AutoText entry when you no longer want to use it for every envelope based on the template that contains it.

SEE ALSO: *AutoText; Field Code; Font; Frame; Graphic; Labels; Style; Templates*

Exit

Use correct exiting methods so none of your data will be lost when you exit any Microsoft Office or Windows application. If any open files have been changed, the application prompts you to save the changes for each. If a file has not been saved previously, the Save As dialog box for the application appears. Type a name for the file in the File Name text box, and then select OK.

Exiting an Application

There are several ways to exit the active Microsoft Office application:

- Select File ➤ Exit.
- Double-click on its Control menu box.
- Click on the Control menu box or press Alt+Spacebar to reveal the Control menu, and then choose Close.
- Press Alt+F4.

COMMAND AND FEATURE REFERENCE

> **TROUBLESHOOTING**
>
> ### When the Printer Won't Print an Envelope
>
> If your printer cannot print the envelope with the methods described on the Envelopes tab in the Envelopes And Labels dialog box, select Options, and then select the Printing Options tab. Choose the envelope feed that is necessary for your printer, and then choose OK to return to the Envelopes And Labels dialog box.

Exiting Microsoft Office

To exit Microsoft Office and close its toolbar:

- Click on the Microsoft Office button on the Microsoft Office toolbar, and then select Exit.

- Press Ctrl+Esc to display Windows' Task list, highlight Microsoft Office in the list box, and then choose End Task.

SEE ALSO: *File Management; Microsoft Office Manager*

Field

A field is the most basic unit of information in a database. Databases are composed of records, which contain all the information about an item. Records are composed of *fields*, the individual pieces of information in each record. For example, in a database that contains customer names and addresses, each customer's information is contained in one record. The record itself may include fields for the first name, last name, street address, city, state, and zip code.

Defining a Field

Fields are defined in a database. In a table in Access or Excel, the field names appear as labels at the top of each column. In an Access form, the field names appear as labels beside the text or graphics box into which the data for the field is entered.

In Access, there are several types of fields that can be defined, depending on the type of data that will be entered in the field:

- A *text* field contains either alphabetical or numerical characters, or a combination of the two. Text fields can contain up to 255 characters.

- A *memo* field contains up to 64,000 characters consisting of both letters and numbers. Memo fields cannot be sorted or indexed.

- Values to be used in calculations should be placed in a *number* field.

- To insert a date or time value into a record, specify a *date* or *time* field.

- To automatically display numbers as currency, define a *currency* field.

- To have Access automatically increment record numbers in the database, insert a *counter* field. You cannot update the data in a counter field.

- Define a *Yes/No* field (also known as a Boolean field) for a field that can contain only one of two values.

- To insert a graphic or other object into a record, specify an *OLE object* field. OLE object fields cannot be sorted or indexed.

In Excel, the type of data in a field is defined only by the number format you assign to the column of data.

Naming a Field

Use a descriptive name for each field in a database to help you remember what information you need to enter in the field:

- In Access, field names can consist of up to 64 characters, including spaces. However, if you want to use expressions, SQL statements, or macros in the database, do not include spaces in a field name.

- In Excel, field names can consist of up to 255 characters, including spaces.

SEE ALSO: *Database; Field Code; Filter; Mail Merge; Record; Sort; Table*

Field Code

Use field codes when you want Word to automatically enter specific information in a document. For example, use field codes to enter the system date and time, page numbers, the number of pages in a document, and to mark entries for indexes, cross-references, and tables of contents.

Displaying Field Codes in a Document

By default, field codes in Word documents are shaded when the insertion point is placed anywhere in the code. You can change the display to shade all the field codes in your document, or remove the shading attribute. In addition, you can display the field codes instead of their results in your documents.

FIELD CODE F

To display field codes in a document:

1. Select Tools ➤ Options and choose the View tab in the Options dialog box.

2. In the Show area of the tab, select Always to shade all field codes, or Never to remove the shading in the Field Shading drop-down list.

3. To display the codes instead of the results in your documents, select the Field Codes check box.

4. Select OK in the Options dialog box.

Inserting a Field Code

A field code consists of field characters, which look like braces, a field type, and either required or optional instructions.

To insert a field code:

1. Position the insertion point where you want to enter the field code.

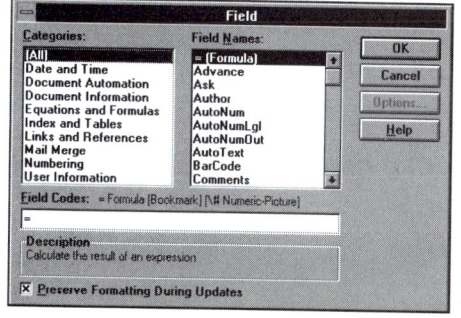

2. Choose Insert ➤ Field to display the Field dialog box.

3. Select the type of field code in the Categories list box.

4. Highlight the field code you want to use in the Field Names list box. The selected name appears in the Field Codes text box.

5. If necessary, type the instructions for the field code after its name in the Field Codes text box. Or, select Options and choose the options for the field code, select Add to Field, and then select OK in the Field Options dialog box.

COMMAND AND FEATURE REFERENCE

6. To keep the formatting you have applied to the field, select the Preserve Formatting During Updates check box (selected by default) to add the Mergeformat switch (*) to the field code instructions.

7. Select OK in the Field dialog box.

You can also insert the field characters by pressing Ctrl+F9, and then typing the field name and instructions within the field characters.

To edit a selected field code, press Shift+F9 to display the actual code, and then use regular editing methods to change any characters necessary.

Toggling between Field Codes and Results

By default, the results of a field code are displayed in your document rather than the actual code. You can toggle the display of a single field between the field code and the results.

To toggle between the field code and the result:

1. Move the insertion point into the field whose display you want to toggle.

2. Right-click on the field and select Toggle Field Codes on the shortcut menu. Or, press Shift+F9 to toggle a selected field code. Press Alt+F9 to toggle all the field codes in a document.

To change the field results into regular text or graphics, press Ctrl+Shift+F9 or Ctrl+6 to unlink the results from the field code.

Updating Fields

Use any of the following methods to update fields in a document:

- Select the field and press F9 (Update).

FILE MANAGEMENT

NOTE: *To select the next field in your document, press F11; to select the previous field, press Shift+F11.*

- Choose Edit ➤ Select All (Ctrl+A) to select the entire document, and then press F9 to update all the fields in the document.

- Right-click on the field, and then select Update Field on the shortcut menu.

- To have Word automatically update the fields when the document is printed, choose Tools ➤ Options and select the Print tab. Select the Update Fields check box in the Printing Options area, and then choose OK.

Press Ctrl+F11 or Ctrl+3 to lock a field so it cannot be updated. Locked fields have the Lock Result (\!) switch added to the field code instructions. Press Ctrl+Shift+F11 or Ctrl+4 to unlock a field.

SEE ALSO: *Field; Link; Object Linking and Embedding*

File Management

Each Microsoft Office application has several commands useful for managing your files.

Backing Up a Message File

In Mail, your messages, message folders, and address book are stored in the file named MSMAIL.MMF. Each time you receive a message or make a change to a folder, the file is automatically updated.

COMMAND AND FEATURE REFERENCE

To create a backup copy of the message file:

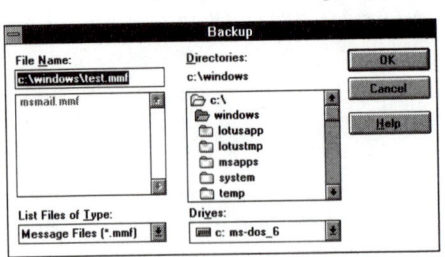

1. Select Mail ➤ Backup to display the Backup dialog box.

2. Enter a new name for the backup file in the File Name text box.

3. Select OK. The file is automatically saved with the .MMF file extension.

If your original message file is corrupted, restore your backup message file the next time you start Mail.

1. Enter the path and name of your backup message file in the File Name text box in the dialog box that appears.

2. Select Yes to confirm that you want to convert the backup file into a message file.

3. Choose OK.

You can read the messages in the backup file without converting them to a message file. However, you cannot send or receive mail without a message file.

Closing an Open File

In Access, Excel, PowerPoint, and Word, you can close a file without exiting the application. Because each open file uses memory in your computer, close any files when you are finished working on them.

To close the active file:

1. In Access, select File ➤ Close Database. In Excel, PowerPoint, and Word, select File ➤ Close.

2. If you have made any changes to the file since you last saved it, a message box appears

FILE MANAGEMENT

asking if you want to save the changes. Choose Yes to save the file, No to close the file without saving the changes, or Cancel to return to the application and continue working on the file.

3. If you choose Yes for a file that you have not saved previously, the Save As dialog box appears. Type a name for the file in the File Name text box, and then choose OK.

Creating a New File

You can have multiple Microsoft Office files open, depending on the amount of memory available in your computer.

To create a new file:

1. Click on the New button on the Standard toolbar, or choose File ➤ New (Ctrl+N). The New Presentation dialog box appears in PowerPoint. In Word, the New dialog box appears when File ➤ New is selected. In Access, choose File ➤ New Database to display the New Database dialog box.

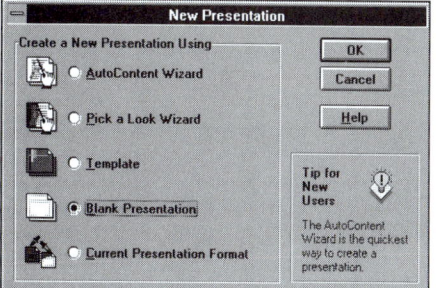

2. Follow the appropriate steps below:

- In Access, type the name for the new database file in the File Name text box, and then choose OK. The .MDB file extension is automatically added to the name, and the Database window for the file appears.

- In PowerPoint, select AutoContent Wizard, Pick A Look Wizard, Template, Blank Presentation, or Current Presentation Format to choose the presentation's format, and then choose OK. If you choose a

COMMAND AND FEATURE REFERENCE

Wizard, answer the questions in each dialog box, and then select Next. Choose Finish in the last Wizard dialog box. If you choose Template, select the name of the template file in the File Name list box in the Presentation Template dialog box, and then choose Apply.

◆ In Word, click on the New button on the Standard toolbar or press Ctrl+N to open a new file based on the NORMAL.DOT template. Or, select File ➤ New to display the New dialog box, choose the name of a template in the Template list box, select Document in the New area, and then choose OK.

When you open a new file in Excel, a new, blank workbook appears.

Inserting a File

You can insert a file in the active Word document at the position of the insertion point:

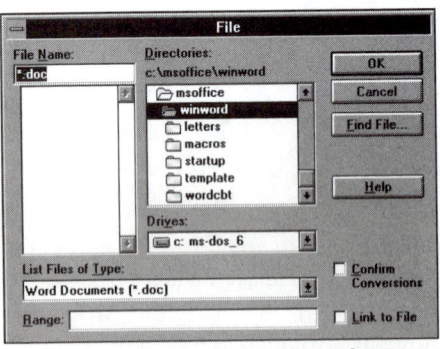

1. Select Insert ➤ File to display the File dialog box.

2. If necessary, select a different drive on which to find the file in the Drives drop-down list, and then select the directory that contains the file in the Directories list box.

3. If necessary, select the type of file to insert in the List Files Of Type drop-down list.

4. Highlight the name of the file to be inserted in the File Name list box.

FILE MANAGEMENT

5. To insert a portion of the selected file, type the name of a bookmark or the range name in the Range text box.

6. To link the inserted file to the active file, select the Link To File check box.

7. To approve the file converter selected by Word to open a file created in another application, select the Confirm Conversions check box.

8. Choose OK to insert the selected file into the document.

Opening a File

Each of the Microsoft Office applications uses a similar procedure to open a file that has been saved on your disk.

To open a file:

1. Click on the Open button on the Standard toolbar, or select File ➤ Open (Ctrl+O) to display the Open dialog box. In Access, select File ➤ Open Database (Ctrl+O) to display the Open Database dialog box.

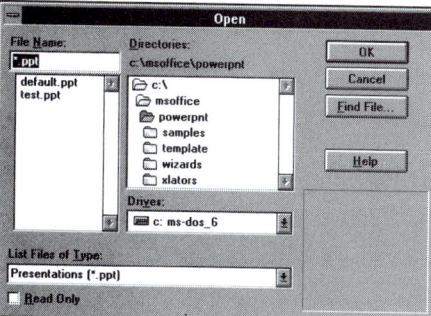

2. If necessary, select a different drive on which to find the file in the Drives drop-down list, and then select the directory that contains the file in the Directories list box.

3. If necessary, select the type of file to open in the List Files Of Type drop-down list.

4. Highlight the name of the file to be opened in the File Name list box.

COMMAND AND FEATURE REFERENCE

5. To open the file so that it can be displayed, but no changes can be saved to it, select the Read Only check box.

6. If necessary, select one of the following options available in the specified application:

- Select Access's Exclusive check box (selected by default) to open the selected database file so no one else can modify the database or objects in it.

- Select Word's Confirm Conversions check box to approve the file converter selected by Word to open a file created in another application.

7. Choose OK in the dialog box.

To change Access's default Exclusive option when shared access is to be allowed to database files, choose View ➤ Options, select Multiuser/ODBC in the Category list box, choose Shared as the Default Open Mode For Databases in the Items list box, and then select OK.

Saving a File

Use a similar procedure to save the active file in Excel, PowerPoint, and Word.

To save the current file for the first time:

1. Click on the Save button on the Standard toolbar, or choose File ➤ Save (Ctrl+S) to display the Save As dialog box.

2. If necessary, select a different drive on which to save the file in the Drives drop-down list, and a different directory in which to store the file in the Directories list box.

FILE MANAGEMENT

3. If necessary, select the type of file to save in the Save File As Type drop-down list.

4. Type the name for the file in the File Name text box.

5. In PowerPoint, if necessary, select the Embed True Type Fonts check box to embed the fonts in the presentation so they can be displayed on a system without those fonts installed.

6. In Excel or Word, if necessary, select Options to display Excel's Save Options dialog box or the Save tab in Word's Options dialog box. Then choose any of the following options and select OK:

- Select the Always Create Backup or Always Create Backup Copy check box to save a backup copy of the current file each time you save it.

- Select the Allow Fast Saves check box (selected by default) to save only the changes made to the current Word document.

- Select the Prompt For Summary Info check box to display the Summary Info dialog box each time you save a new Word file.

- Select the Prompt To Save Normal.dot check box to display a dialog box when you close Word if you have made any changes to the NORMAL.DOT template.

- Select the Save Native Picture Formats Only check box to save only the Windows version of an imported graphic, thereby reducing the size of a Word document.

- Select the Embed TrueType Fonts check box to embed the fonts in a Word document so they can be displayed on a system without those fonts installed.

COMMAND AND FEATURE REFERENCE

- Select the Save **D**ata Only for Forms check box to save the data in a Word form as a single record in a database.

- Select the Automatic **S**ave Every N **M**inutes check box (selected by default) to automatically save the current Word file after the number of minutes specified.

- To prevent others from opening a Word or Excel file, type a password in the **P**rotection Password text box.

- To prevent others from saving changes made to a Word or Excel file, type a password in the **W**rite Reservation Password text box.

- To suggest that others open a Word or Excel file as a read-only file, select the **R**ead-Only Recommended check box.

7. Choose OK in the Save As dialog box.

Each time you click on the Save button or select **F**ile ➤ **S**ave (Ctrl+S) to save an existing file, the Save As dialog box will not appear. To save an existing file to a new file name, select **F**ile ➤ Save **A**s to display the Save As dialog box, type a new name in the File **N**ame text box, and choose OK.

In Access, you can save a new design, layout, or structure of the active database object (table, form, report, query, or module) with **F**ile ➤ **S**ave (Ctrl+S). Use **F**ile ➤ Save **A**s to save the database object to a new name.

In Excel, use **F**ile ➤ Save **W**orkspace to save the sizes and positions of all open workbook files to the RESUME.XLW file. You must open the RESUME.XLW file, which is saved by default in the MSOFFFICE\EXCEL subdirectory, when you want to use the saved workspace.

In Mail, select a message, and then choose File ➤ Save As to display the Save Message dialog box, type a file name in the File Name text box, and choose OK. To save a selected file attachment, select File ➤ Save Attachment, select the file in the Attached Files list box, or type a new name for the file in the File Name text box, and then choose Save. Or, choose Save All to save all the attached files in the directory. Select Close to return to the Mail window.

In Word, choose File ➤ Save All to save all open documents, including templates and macros, and any AutoText entries created during this session of Word.

SEE ALSO: *AutoText; Database; Find File; Form; Graphic; Import/Export Data; Macro; Templates; Workbook*

Filter

To display a subset of data that meets specific criteria in an Excel list, filter the list. When a list of data is filtered, only the rows of data that meet criteria you set are displayed.

TIP: *In Access, use a query to display data in the database that meets specific criteria.*

Data in a filtered list can be edited, printed, and sorted. In addition, you can create a chart using the data in a filtered list and perform calculations on the data.

COMMAND AND FEATURE REFERENCE

Filtering a List with AutoFilter

AutoFilter is the easiest way to specify the criteria to be displayed in an Excel database, also called a *list*.

To use AutoFilter to filter a list:

1. Select one cell in the list, and then choose Data ➤ Filter ➤ AutoFilter. A drop-down list button appears by each of the field names in the top row of the list.

2. Click on the drop-down list button beside the field you want to use as the filtering criteria to display a list of values for the items in that column.

3. Select the value by which the database is to be filtered in the drop-down list. Or, select (Custom) to display the Custom AutoFilter dialog box.

4. Select the comparison operator for the first criterion in the corresponding drop-down list, and then select the value for the first criterion in the field values drop-down list.

5. Select And or Or as the method of comparison.

6. Select the comparison operator for the second criterion in the corresponding drop-down list, and then select the value for the second criterion in the field values drop-down list.

7. Choose OK. Each row that does not meet the criteria is hidden in the list.

The arrow on the drop-down button beside a field that was used to filter the data in the list appears in blue on a color monitor.

FILTER

To remove a filter from the displayed list, click on the drop-down list button beside the appropriate field, and then select (All) in the list, or choose Data ➤ Filter ➤ Show All.

To display AutoFilter drop-down list buttons for only some fields, select the name of the first field, hold down the Shift key and select the name of the last field in a range of adjacent fields, and then choose Data ➤ Filter ➤ AutoFilter..

To turn off the AutoFilter feature, select, Data ➤ Filter ➤ AutoFilter. The check mark beside AutoFilter in the list is removed.

Filtering a List Using Compound Criteria

Perform an Advanced Filter on data using *comparison criteria*, *computed criteria*, or both. In an Advanced Filter, you type the criteria for the filtered list in a *criteria range* in the worksheet. Create the criteria range, which consists of a row of field name labels above at least one blank row, either above or below the list in a worksheet.

> **NOTE:** Use the Copy and Paste buttons on the Standard toolbar to copy the field names to the field name row in the criteria range, because they must exactly match the column labels in the database. You can copy the same column label in the field name row of the criteria range more than once.

To filter the list to display only rows whose values fall within specific limits, use comparison criteria. Specify the limits using any of the following comparison operators: = (equal to); > (greater than); < (less than); >= (greater than or equal to); <= (less than or equal to); and <> (not equal to).

COMMAND AND FEATURE REFERENCE

Follow these rules to specify comparison criteria:

- To display a filtered list that meets all the criteria specified, type the criteria in one row of the criteria range.

- To display list items that meet multiple criteria for items in the same column in the list, display that column label once for each criterion.

- To display a filtered list that meets one set of specified criteria or a different set of criteria, type each set of criteria in a different row in the criteria range.

To filter the list using a formula, use computed criteria. The formula allows you to specify criteria with values that are not in the list. For example, you can filter a sales list so that only names of personnel who have sold more than (a comparison criterion) the average amount (a computed criterion) for July are displayed.

There are several rules to follow concerning a formula entered in a criteria range:

- The formula must produce a TRUE or FALSE result. The rows that contain values producing the TRUE result are displayed in the filtered list.

- The formula must reference a cell in at least one column in the list, and that cell should be relative to the cell in the first row of the column that is being evaluated.

- If you label the formula, use characters other than those used to define the column (field) names in the list.

1. If necessary, insert four rows above the list for the criteria range, and then copy the labels (the field names) to be evaluated in the top row of the criteria range.

2. Enter the comparison or computed criteria in the criteria range.

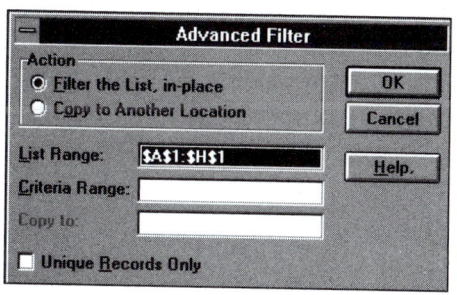

3. Select one cell in the database (list) and choose Data ➤ Filter ➤ Advanced Filter to display the Advanced Filter dialog box. The entire list is selected, and its absolute reference appears in the List Range text box.

4. Click in the Criteria Range text box, and then select the criteria range in the worksheet. Do not include any blank rows in the selection.

5. In the Action area, select Filter The List, In-place to hide any records in the list that do not meet the criteria. Or, select Copy To Another Location, and then specify the range for the filtered list in the Copy To text box.

6. If necessary, select the Unique Records Only check box to exclude any rows that contain duplicate criteria.

TIP: *Select the Unique Records Only check box without specifying a criteria range to hide duplicate records in the list.*

7. Select OK to filter the list.

SEE ALSO: *Cell; Database; Formula; Query; Reference; Sort*

COMMAND AND FEATURE REFERENCE

Find File

Use Microsoft Office's Find File feature to locate a document by its name, key words, author, date, or specific text in the file.

TIP: *You can also use File ➤ Find File in Excel, PowerPoint, and Word to display the Find File dialog box.*

A preview of the file is displayed in the Find File dialog box, or you can select multiple files to open, delete, or print. Save the criteria used to perform a search so it can be used again.

Defining the Search Criteria

To search for a file, enter and save the necessary criteria to perform the search. The criteria specified are automatically used for the next search unless you select or specify different criteria.

To define the search criteria:

1. Click on the Find File button on the Microsoft Office toolbar to display the Find File dialog box.

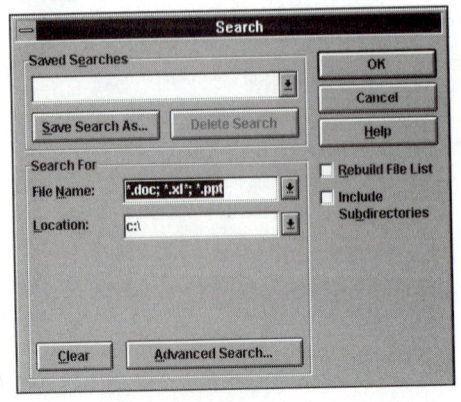

2. Select Search to display the Search dialog box.

3. Select the type of file for which to search, or type the name of the file in the File Name drop-down list in the Search For area of the dialog box. Type a semicolon between

128

FIND FILE

each extension or file name to specify more than one.

4. Select the letter of the drive on which to search in the Location drop-down list. If necessary, type the path in which you want to search.

5. To include subdirectories of the path specified in the Location text box, select the Include Subdirectories check box.

6. Select the Rebuild File List check box to replace the current list of files in the Listed Files list box with a new list that meets the current criteria.

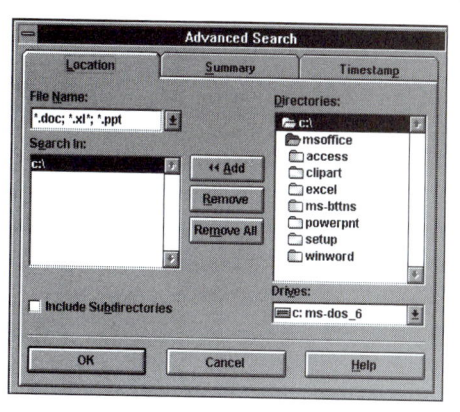

7. To place further restrictions on the search results, select Advanced Search to display the Advanced Search dialog box.

8. Choose options on the Location tab, Summary tab, or Timestamp tab in the Advanced Search dialog box and select OK. On the **Location tab**:

- Select the type of files or type the names of files for which you want to search, separated by a semicolon, in the File Name drop-down list or text box.

- The Search In list box contains the names of directories that will be searched.

- Highlight the directory in which to search in the Directories list box and choose Add to place the selection in the Search In list box.

- Select Remove to clear a highlighted directory name from the Search In list box.

129

COMMAND AND FEATURE REFERENCE

- Select Remove All to clear all the directories from the Search In list box.
- Select the Include Subdirectories check box to search all the subdirectories of the directories in the Search In list box.

On the **Summary tab**:

- Type information in the Title, Author, Keywords, and Subject text boxes that matches that in the Summary Info dialog box. Specify approximate criteria to search for when you use special characters (* for any number of characters, or ? for a single character) to indicate the criteria.

- Highlight one of the options in the Options drop-down list to define how the files in the Listed Files list box in the Find File dialog box will be used in the search. Choose Create New List to replace the current list with only the files that meet the criteria, Add Matches To List to add the names of files that meet the search criteria to the current list, or Search Only In List to list only the files in the current list that match the specified criteria.

- Select the Match Case check box to find only files that contain the exact case of text entered in the Containing Text text box.

- In the Containing Text text box, type text that is in a file you wish to find.

- Select the Use Pattern Matching check box to use advanced search criteria for the text in the Containing Text text box. Select the special character to enter in the Containing Text text box in the Special pop up list.

FIND FILE

On the **Timestamp tab:**

- Enter the range of dates upon which the files for which you are searching were last saved in the Last Saved area of the tab, or created in the Created area. Type the earliest date in the range you want to search in the From text box, and the latest date in the To text box. (Leave the From text box empty to search for all files before the date in the To text box. Leave the To text box empty to search for all files after the date in the From text box.) Type the name of the last person who saved the file or the file's creator in the By text box.

9. To save the specified search criteria, choose Save Search As, type a name in the Search Name text box, and select OK in the Save Search As dialog box.

10. Choose OK in the Search dialog box to begin the search.

To select a saved set of search criteria to use in performing the search, highlight a name in the Saved Searches drop-down list, and then choose OK.

To specify different search criteria, choose Clear to empty all the text boxes and check boxes in the Search dialog box.

Displaying File Information

After you have defined your search criteria and performed a search, the search results are displayed in the Listed Files list box in the Find File dialog box.

To display file information:

1. If necessary, select the file whose information you want to see in the Listed Files list box.

2. Select one of the following options in the View drop-down list.

COMMAND AND FEATURE REFERENCE

- Select Preview (the default) to display part of the selected file without opening it.

- Choose File Info to display information about all the files in the list, such as the name, size, author, and date each file was last saved.

- Select Summary to display the information entered into the highlighted file's Summary Info dialog box, and the file's statistics.

TIP: *You can print a Word document's summary information and statistics using options in the Print dialog box.*

Managing Files in the List

Once a file or multiple files in the Listed Files list box of the Find File dialog box is selected, you can open, copy, delete, or print the selection.

To select a file, click on the name of the file. Hold down the Ctrl key while you click on any additional file names to select them. Or, hold down the Shift key while you click on the last file in a range to select a range of files in the list.

To manage files in a list:

1. Click on the Find File button on the Microsoft Office toolbar to display the Find File dialog box.

2. If necessary, perform a search, and then highlight the file or files to be managed in the Listed Files list box.

3. To open the highlighted file(s), choose Open. Or, select Commands, and then choose one of the following options in the pop-up list:

Print	Opens the Print dialog box. Choose the options to print all the files in the selection, and then select OK.

FIND FILE

- **Delete**   Deletes the selected files from your disk. Choose Yes in the dialog box that appears asking you to confirm the deletion.

- **Copy**   The Copy dialog box appears. Enter the path for a copy of the selected file in the Path text box. Or, select New to create a new directory, enter the path in the Name text box, and then select OK in the Create Directory dialog box. Choose OK in the Copy dialog box.

NOTE: *When you use the Copy command in Find File, make certain that each file in your selection is assigned a unique file name. You can use wildcards to indicate the names of files you copy.*

- **Sorting**   The Options dialog box appears. In the Sort Files By area, select Author, Creation Date, Last Saved By, Last Saved Date, Name, or Size to sort the files in the Listed Files list box alphabetically, chronologically, or from smallest to largest. In the List Files By area, choose File Name to display the name you assigned to the file, or Title to display the title assigned in the Summary Info dialog box. If no title was assigned to a file, the file name is listed between hyphens. Select OK in the Sorting Options dialog box.

4. Choose Close in the Find File dialog box.

SEE ALSO: *File Management; Print; Summary Info*

COMMAND AND FEATURE REFERENCE

Find and Replace

Use the Find feature to search for and select text or other characters, formats, special characters, and other items in Access, Excel, PowerPoint, and Word. Use the Replace feature to both search for the specified items and replace a found item with a specified item.

Finding Items

Follow these steps to search for a specific item. Comparable options in each application's Find dialog box are described below.

1. Select Edit ➤ Find (Ctrl+F) or click on the Find button on the Table Datasheet toolbar in Access to display a Find dialog box similar to Word's.

2. Type the text or characters to find in the Find What text box, or select one of the last four items searched for in the drop-down list in Word.

3. Select one of the following options in the Search drop-down list, or in the Search In and Direction areas.

- Choose Down to search from the position of the insertion point to the end of the selection, database, or file.

- Choose Up to search from the position of the insertion point to the beginning of the selection, database, or file.

- Select All to search the entire file beginning at the insertion point.

FIND AND REPLACE

- Select By Rows to search across each row in a worksheet.
- Choose By Columns to search down each column in a worksheet.
- To search for the item in the active field in the entire database, select Current Field.
- To search for the item in each field in the entire database, choose All Fields.

4. In Access, select Any Part Of Field, Match Whole Field, or Start Of Field in the Where drop-down list. In Excel, select Formulas, Values, or Notes in the Look In drop-down list as the items to search.

5. Choose any of the following options to limit the search results, depending on the active application:

- Select the Match Case check box to find an item with the exact uppercase and lower-case letters as those in the Find What text box.
- Select the Find Whole Words Only check box to find only text that is a whole word.
- Select the Use Pattern Matching check box to use advanced search operators and expressions in Word.
- Select the Sounds Like check box to find homonyms of the text in the Find What text box.
- Select the Search Fields As Formatted check box to find an item based on the format assigned to the field.
- Select the Find Entire Cells Only check box to search for a cell that contains the same characters as those in the Find What text box.

COMMAND AND FEATURE REFERENCE

- Choose No Formatting to remove all specified formatting from the search.

- In Word, choose F_ormat, and then select _Font, _Paragraph, _Language, or _Style to display each command's dialog box. Choose the formatting for which to search in the corresponding dialog box.

- Select Sp_ecial, and then choose a character in the pop up list to enter in the Fi_nd What text box.

6. Select _Find Next or Find Fir_st to start the search. The first instance of the item you are searching for appears highlighted.

NOTE: *In Word, you can edit your document while the Find or Replace dialog box is displayed. Click in the document window or press Alt+F6 to activate the document window. Click in the dialog box to activate it when you are finished.*

7. If necessary, select _Find Next to find the next instance of the document item.

8. To edit the found item, select Close. Or, choose _Replace to display the Replace dialog box.

9. When the beginning or end of the file is reached during the search process, a dialog box appears asking if you want to continue the search. Select _Yes to continue the search back to the location of the insertion point.

10. Choose OK to remove the message box that appears to tell you when the search is complete.

11. When you have finished searching for the document item, select Close or press Esc.

To repeat the last search after the Find dialog box is closed, press Shift+F4 to search without opening the dialog box.

FIND AND REPLACE

> **TROUBLESHOOTING**
>
> ### Searching for Formats
>
> Do you want to search for all characters to which a specific format has been applied in a Word document? You can perform a search for only formatting, without specifying any characters. To find formatting only, remove all the characters from the Find What text box and position the insertion point in the text box. Then choose Format and select the format for which you want to search. To find text without searching for formatting, make sure no formats appear in the area under the Find What text box.

Replacing Items

To replace a found item with specific characters, display the Replace dialog box:

1. Select Edit ➤ Replace (Ctrl+H), or choose Replace in the Find dialog box to display the Replace dialog box.

2. If necessary, type the text to be found in the Find What text box.

3. Type the text with which to replace a found item in the Replace With text box.

> **TIP:** *To delete the item for which you are searching, remove all the characters from the Replace With text box, and then choose Replace.*

4. Choose any of the options in the active application's dialog box to define and limit the search. The options are described in the previous section, "Finding Items."

COMMAND AND FEATURE REFERENCE

5. Select Find Next to start the search and highlight the first instance of the item.

6. Select Replace to replace the highlighted item with the characters in the Replace With text box. Or, choose Find Next to find the next instance of the document item without replacing the currently highlighted item.

7. Repeat step 6 as necessary.

8. When each instance of the searched for item has been found, a dialog box appears asking if you want to continue the search. Select Yes to continue the search back to the location of the insertion point.

9. Choose OK to remove the message box that appears when the search is complete.

10. Choose Close or press Esc to return to the file.

Select Replace All to automatically find all instances of the search item and replace it with the characters in the Replace With text box.

SEE ALSO: *Font; Format; Go To; Message Finder; Paragraph; Style*

Folder

In Mail, create folders in which to store your messages. Your main folders can contain other folders, called subfolders. Folders are either private, so only you can see the data stored, or shared, so all the people in your postoffice can see the messages in the folder.

Creating a Folder

To create a main folder or subfolder:

1. If necessary, display the folder list pane in the mail window, and then select File ➤ New Folder to display the New Folder dialog box.

2. Type a name for the folder in the Name text box.

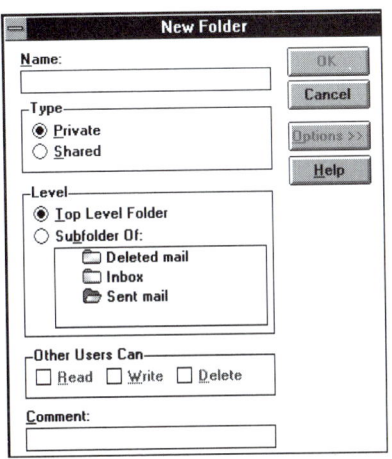

3. If necessary, select Options to enlarge the New Folder dialog box.

4. In the Type area, select either Private or Shared. If you select Shared, select any of the following options available in the Other Users Can area:

- Select the Read check box (selected by default) to allow everyone in your postoffice to read the messages in the folder.

- Select the Write check box (selected by default) to allow everyone in your postoffice to add messages to the folder.

- Select the Delete check box to allow everyone in your postoffice to delete messages from the folder.

5. In the Level area, select Top Level Folder to create a main folder. Or, select Subfolder Of, and then select the name of the folder that will contain your new folder.

COMMAND AND FEATURE REFERENCE

> **NOTE:** When a main folder contains subfolders, it appears in the list of folders with a plus sign to the left of the folder icon. Click on the plus sign to display the names of all the subfolders in the main folder.

6. If necessary, type a description of the folder's contents in the Comment text box.

7. Choose OK in the New Folder dialog box.

Editing a Folder

You can change any aspect of a selected folder's attributes:

1. If necessary, display the folder list pane in the mail window, and then select a folder in the list.

2. Select File ➤ Folder Properties (Alt+Enter) to display the Folder Properties dialog box, similar to the enlarged New Folder dialog box.

3. Change any of the options described in "Creating a New Folder," above.

4. Choose OK.

To delete a main folder or a subfolder, select the name of the folder in the folder list pane in the mail window, and then click on Mail's Delete button or choose File ➤ Delete (Ctrl+D). Choose Yes to confirm the deletion.

To promote a private subfolder, point to it in the folder list pane of the mail window, hold down the left mouse button, and then hold down the Home key while you drag the subfolder to a different level position.

Moving or Copying a Private Folder

A private folder can be moved or copied so that it becomes the subfolder of a folder.

NOTE: *To copy a folder to another location, hold down the Ctrl key while you drag its icon in the mail window's folder list pane to a different location.*

To move or copy a private folder:

1. Select the name of the folder in the folder list pane of the Mail window, and then click on Mail's Move button or choose File ➤ Move (Ctrl+M) to display the Move Folder dialog box. Or, select File ➤ Copy to display the Copy Folder dialog box.

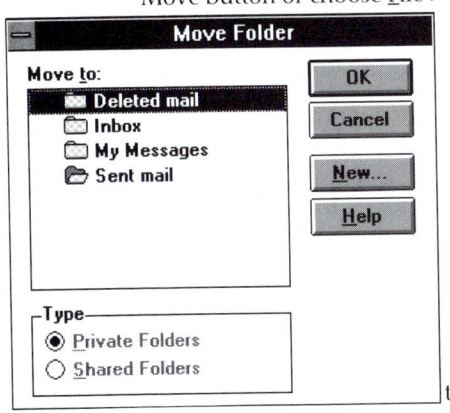

2. Highlight the name of the folder you want to move in the Move To list box, or the name of the folder you want to copy in the Copy To list box, and then drag the highlight to the folder in which you want to place the subfolder.

3. Select OK in the Move Folder or Copy Folder dialog box.

SEE ALSO: *Address Book; Mail*

Font

You can apply a different font and size, or other text attributes such as bold or italic formatting, to selected text in Access, Excel, PowerPoint, and Word.

COMMAND AND FEATURE REFERENCE

Or, you can change the default appearance of the characters you type.

Applying Fonts to Characters

Use drop-down lists and buttons on the Formatting toolbar (displayed by default) to change the font and size, and to apply Bold, Italic, Underline, and special effect formats. Or, display the Font dialog box or tab to format selected text.

To apply fonts to characters:

1. Select the characters to which you want to apply new formatting.

2. Click on the appropriate font buttons on the Formatting toolbar. Or, if necessary, choose Format ➤ Font or Format ➤ Cells (Ctrl+1), and then select the Font tab in Excel and Word. The dialog box containing the font options appears.

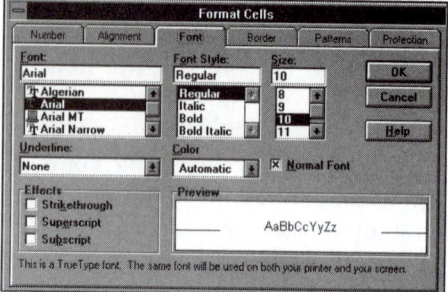

3. Choose any of the following options or their corresponding toolbar buttons:

- Select the name of the font in the Font list box or the Font drop-down list on the Formatting toolbar.

- Select Regular (the default for each font), Bold, Italic, or Bold Italic in the Font Style list. Not all of the style options are available for every font. On the Formatting toolbar, click on the Bold or Italic button to apply the attribute.

- Select a size for the font in the Size list box or in the Font Size drop-down list on the

FONT

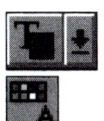

Formatting toolbar. Or, in PowerPoint, click on the Increase Font Size button on the Formatting toolbar to change selected characters to the next largest size in the list, or click on the Decrease Font Size button to change selected characters to the next smallest size in the list.

- Select one of the underline attributes in the Underline drop-down list. Or, select the Underline check box or click on the Underline button on the Formatting toolbar to apply a single underline.

- Click on one of the colors in the Color palette, or in Excel's Font Color palette or PowerPoint's Text Color palette. The text will display in color on a color monitor, and print in color on a color printer.

- In Excel, select the Normal Font check box to set all the attributes of the selected font to the Normal style. Or, toggle the toolbar buttons of any applied attributes to remove them.

4. To apply special effects, select any of the following check boxes or click on the corresponding toolbar button:

- Strikethrough draws a line through text that does not have a revision line through it.

- Superscript raises the text above the baseline.

- Subscript lowers the text below the baseline.

- In PowerPoint, enter a percentage by which superscript or subscript text should be raised or lowered in the Offset text box.

- Hidden hides the text in the document, so it will not appear on screen or in a printed document.

COMMAND AND FEATURE REFERENCE

- Small Caps displays all the text in reduced size capital letters.

- All Caps displays the text in regular size capital letters.

- Select Shadow or click on the Text Shadow button on the Formatting toolbar to apply a shadow effect to text in PowerPoint.

- Select Emboss to apply a raised effect to selected text in PowerPoint.

5. If necessary, choose OK in the dialog box.

Changing the Character Spacing

In Word, you can change the amount of space that appears between characters, the position of the text relative to the baseline, and reduce the spacing between TrueType font characters. *Kerning*, or reducing the distance between two characters to improve the appearance of the text, can only be used with TrueType or ATM fonts, and then only with fonts above a certain size, depending on which font is used.

To change character spacing:

1. Select Format ➤ Font, and then select the Character Spacing Tab in the Font dialog box.

2. Select Normal in the Spacing drop-down list to use the default spacing for the font. Or, select Condensed to decrease the spacing between characters, or Expanded to increase the spacing between characters, and specify the distance in points in the By text box.

3. Choose Normal in the Position drop-down list to place characters on the baseline. Or, choose Raised or Lowered to adjust the text up or down, and then specify the distance in points in the By text box.

4. If necessary, select the <u>K</u>erning For Fonts check box to automatically change the spacing between characters, and then specify the base font size in the P<u>o</u>ints And Above text box.

5. Choose OK.

Changing the Default Font

Follow these steps to set the default font in Excel:

1. Select <u>T</u>ools ➤ <u>O</u>ptions, and then choose the General tab.

2. Select a font name in the St<u>a</u>ndard Font drop-down list.

3. Select a size in the Si<u>z</u>e drop-down list.

4. Choose OK in the Options dialog box.

In Word, the default font and size are determined by the style that is applied to a paragraph. To change the defaults in the current document template to the options set on both the Font and Character Spacing tabs in the Font dialog box, select <u>D</u>efault on the corresponding tab, and then choose <u>Y</u>es to confirm the changes.

NOTE: *In Access, the default font and style are set in each field's control property sheet.*

SEE ALSO: *Format; Format Painter; Style; Templates; Toolbars*

COMMAND AND FEATURE REFERENCE

Footnotes and Endnotes

Use footnotes and endnotes to provide explanations or references to marked items in the text of a Word document. Footnotes appear at the bottom of the page where the marked item appears, and endnotes appear at the end of the chapter, section, or document. Both are separated from document text by a horizontal line. Documents can contain both footnotes and endnotes.

TIP: *Add cross-references to note references to refer several notes to one source.*

Word automatically updates footnote and endnote numbering when a marked item is added to or deleted from a document, and places the text of either in the correct position in the document. Because footnotes and endnotes are so similar, they are called "notes" in this entry.

Adding a Note

By default, footnotes are numbered 1, 2, 3, etc., and endnotes are numbered i, ii, iii, etc.

To add a note:

1. If necessary, select View ➤ Normal or click on the Normal View button on the horizontal scroll bar to change to Normal view.

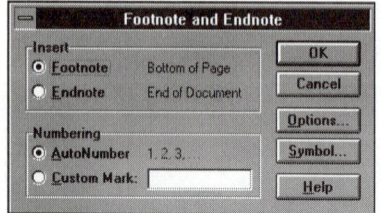

2. Position the insertion point where you want to add a note reference mark and select Insert ➤ Footnote to display the Footnote And Endnote dialog box.

FOOTNOTES AND ENDNOTES

3. Select either Footnote or Endnote in the Insert area of the dialog box to indicate the type of note to add.

4. In the Numbering area, select AutoNumber (selected by default) to automatically update the note numbers in your document. Or, select Custom Mark, choose Symbol to display the Symbol dialog box, select the symbol to use, and then choose OK.

5. To change the format of the notes in your document, select Options to display the Note Options dialog box, select any of the following options on the All Footnotes or All Endnotes tab, and then choose OK.

- In the Place At drop-down list, choose Bottom Of Page to print footnotes just above the bottom margin on the same page as the reference mark, Beneath Text to print footnotes just below the last line of text on the page, End Of Section to print endnotes just after the last line of the section of its reference mark location, or End Of Document to print endnotes after the last line of the document text.

- To change the format of the note numbers, choose Arabic numbers, lowercase or uppercase letters or Roman numerals, or symbols in the Number Format drop-down list.

- Specify the starting number for notes in the Start At text box.

- To define how notes are numbered, choose Continuous to number the notes throughout the document in sequence, or Restart Each Section to start note numbers in each section with the number in the Start At text box. Or, select Restart Each Page, which starts

COMMAND AND FEATURE REFERENCE

footnote numbering on each page with the number in the Start At text box.

- Choose Convert to display the Convert Notes dialog box, choose Convert All Footnotes To Endnotes, Convert All Endnotes To Footnotes, or Swap Footnotes And Endnotes to convert both simultaneously, and then choose OK.

NOTE: *To convert a single footnote or endnote, move the insertion point into the text of the note, right-click on the note, and then select Convert To Footnote or Convert To Endnote.*

6. Choose OK in the Footnote And Endnote dialog box. The note pane appears at the bottom of your screen.

7. Type the note text in the note pane.

8. If necessary, click in the document window to keep the note pane open and continue editing your document. Press Alt+Ctrl+F to add another footnote to the document, or Alt+Ctrl+E to add another endnote to the document at the location of the insertion point, and then type the note text.

9. When you are finished adding or editing notes, choose Close (Alt+Shift+C) in the note pane.

Displaying Notes

Display notes in your document in either the Normal or Page Layout view mode. The note text appears in the note pane in Normal view, and in its correct location in Page Layout view. There are several ways to display the text of notes in your document.

TIP: *You can change the format of the text of individual notes, or change the style of the note text to edit the format*

FOOTNOTES AND ENDNOTES

of all the footnotes or endnotes. To make the note style available to all documents based on the current template, add the style to the template.

To display notes:

- Double-click on the note mark in your document. In Normal view, the note pane opens and the insertion point moves to the note's text in the pane. In Page Layout view, the insertion point moves to the note's text.

- Choose View ➤ Footnotes. In Normal view, the note pane opens to the last viewed note type. To change the view of the note type, select All Footnotes or All Endnotes in the drop-down list at the top of the note pane. In Page Layout view, the View Footnotes dialog box appears. Select View Footnote Area or View Endnote Area, and then choose OK. The insertion point moves to the note text area in the document.

To move to the note mark in the document from the note pane or note area:

- Double-click on the note mark in the note pane or note area of your document to move back to the mark in the document text.

- Or, in Page Layout view, right-click on the note mark and select Go To Endnote or Go To Footnote to move the insertion point to the document window.

Editing Notes

Notes are made up of two parts–the note mark and the note text. To copy, delete, or move a note, select the note reference mark in your document. You can edit the text of a note directly.

Use Word's drag-and-drop feature, or the Cut, Copy, and Paste commands or toolbar buttons to move or copy a note in a document.

COMMAND AND FEATURE REFERENCE

Use one of the following methods to delete notes in your document:

◆ Select the note reference mark in your document, and then press either Backspace or Del.

◆ Choose Edit ➤ Replace (Ctrl+H), and then select Special. Select Footnote Mark or Endnote Mark in the pop-up list, delete the contents of the Replace With text box, and select Replace All to delete all the specified notes in the document.

Editing Note Separators

By default, a short horizontal line, called a *note separator*, separates notes from the document text. If the notes on one page continue on the next, a longer line, called a *continuation separator*, separates the notes from the document text. If necessary, edit these separators so that informational text appears above them.

To edit note separators:

1. If necessary, select View ➤ Normal or click on the Normal View button on the horizontal scrollbar.

2. Select View ➤ Footnotes to display the notes pane.

3. Select All Footnotes or All Endnotes in the drop-down list at the top of the note pane, and then click in the note pane.

4. Select the drop-down list again, and choose Footnote Separator or Endnote Separator, which appear as a two-inch line, or Footnote Continuation Separator or Endnote Continuation Separator, which appear as a line spanning from the left to the right margin.

5. The separator appears in the pane. Type the text you want to appear above the note separator.

Or to delete it, double-click on the Note Separator to select it, and then press Backspace or Del.

6. To return the separator to its default appearance, select Reset (Alt+Shift+R).

7. Select Close (Alt+Shift+C) to close the pane when you are finished.

SEE ALSO: *Cut, Copy, and Paste; Drag and Drop; Find and Replace; Master Document; Style; Templates*

Form

Forms can be created and used for data entry in Access and Excel. In Word, forms are created both for data entry and to be printed.

Creating Forms in Access

Once you have created an Access database, you can create a form in which to enter or edit data in the database. The form must be based on a table or query that is already created for the database.

To create forms in Access:

1. Click on the Form tab in the Database window to display the list of Forms for the database.

2. Select New to display the New Form dialog box.

3. Select the table or query on which to base the form in the Select A Table/Query drop-down list. The data in the table or query will also appear in the form.

COMMAND AND FEATURE REFERENCE

TIP: *Highlight the name of the table in the Tables pane of the Database dialog box, and then click on the New Form button on the Database toolbar to display the New Form dialog box. Or, click on the AutoForm button on the Database toolbar to automatically create a form using the ields in the selected table and display it in Form view.*

4. Select Form Wizards, and then select the name of the Wizard in the Form Wizards dialog box. A brief description of the highlighted Wizard appears below the list box. Choose OK to display the first Wizard dialog box.

TIP: *Select AutoForm to bypass the Form Wizard dialog boxes and create the form automatically. The form appears in Form view, so you can immediately enter data into the fields.*

5. Select the name of a field to place on the form in the Available Fields list box, and then click on the > button to add it to the Field Order On Form list box. Repeat this step until each field you want on the form appears in the correct order in the Field Order On Form list box. Or, to add all the fields, click on the >> button.

6. To change the order of the fields in the Field Order On Form list box, click on the < button to return the selected field to the Available Fields list box. Select the name of the field you want to appear before the returned field in the Field Order On Form list box, select the returned field in the Available Fields list box, and then click on the > button.

7. When the field names appear in the correct order in the Field Order On Form list box, select Next to move to the next Wizard dialog box.

8. Select Standard, Chiseled, Shadowed, Boxed, or Embossed as the style for the form, and then select Next to display the next Wizard dialog box.

9. Enter a title for the form in the text box, and then select Open The Form With Data In It to display the form in Form view so you can add data to it, or Modify The Form's Design to display the form in Design view. Select the check box to display Cue Cards for either view.

10. Select Finish to create the form.

11. Choose File ➤ Save Form (Ctrl+S) to display the Save As dialog box. Type a name for the form in the Form Name text box, and then choose OK to save the new form.

To close the form in either view, double-click on the Control menu box, or click on it and select Close (Ctrl+F4). If you made any changes to the form in Design view, select Yes in the dialog box that appears to confirm that you want to save the changes.

There are four different views you can use with forms:

Click on the Design View button to create or edit the structure of a form.

Click on the Form View button to enter or edit data in the database, or to display records in the database.

Click on the Datasheet View button to display multiple records in the underlying table or query simultaneously. The records are displayed in rows, with each field in a column.

Click on the Print Preview button to display the form the way it will appear when it is printed.

COMMAND AND FEATURE REFERENCE

Creating Forms in Excel

Forms are created automatically when you create a list, or database, in Excel. The form for the list appears in the dialog box that is displayed when you select Data ➤ Form. Use the form to add, edit, or delete records in the list.

The form's field names are the column labels entered in the first row of the list. Each field name has a corresponding text box in which the data for the field is entered or displayed on the form.

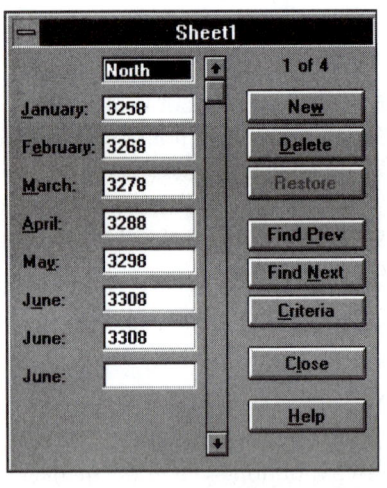

To create forms in Excel:

1. Select one cell in the list, and then choose Data ➤ Form to display the dialog box for the form.

2. The number of the currently displayed record appears at the top right side of the form's dialog box. Use any of the following methods to display a different record in the form:

- On the form's scroll bar, click on the ↓ button to move to the same field in the next record, or on the ↑ button to move to the same field in the previous record.

- Select Find Prev to display the previous record, or Find Next to display the next record in the list.

- To move ten records from the current record, click below the scroll box to move forward, or above the scroll box to move backward.

- Drag the scroll box to the top of the scroll bar to display the first record, or to the bottom of the scroll bar to display a blank form after the last record in the list.

3. Select Ne*w* to display a blank form, and then type the data for each field in the appropriate text box. Press ↵ to enter the record at the end of the list and display another form for a new record.

4. If necessary, display a record to be removed in the form's dialog box, and then select *D*elete. Choose OK to confirm the deletion in the message box that appears.

5. To edit an existing record, display the record, and then change the necessary data in the form and press ↵. To restore the original data in the field, select *R*estore before you press ↵ or display a different record.

6. To display a blank form in the dialog box into which comparison criteria can be entered to filter the list, select *C*riteria, and then enter the criteria in the appropriate field. Select Find *N*ext to display the first, and if necessary, any subsequent records in the form. Select Find *P*rev to display the previous record that meets the criteria.

7. When you are finished adding or editing records in the form, choose C*l*ose to return to your worksheet.

Creating Forms in Word

Word comes with many built-in forms already created, or you can create custom forms in Word by adding form field codes to a document template. Forms can be designed to be filled out online, or to be printed and filled out by hand. Create a new document template for each custom form.

COMMAND AND FEATURE REFERENCE

> **TIP:** *Use tables, frames, borders, and shading to create an attractive, useful online form.*

To create forms in Word:

1. Select File ➤ New to display the New dialog box, select Template in the New area, and choose OK.

2. Type the text of the form.

3. To display the Forms toolbar, right-click on one of the displayed toolbars and select Forms on the shortcut menu, or select Insert ➤ Form Field to display the Form Field dialog box, and choose Show Toolbar.

4. Move the insertion point to the position in the document where you want to insert a form field, and then click on the Text Form Field button, Check Box Form Field button, or the Drop-Down Form Field button on the Forms toolbar to define the type of field.

5. Click on the Form Field Options button on the Forms toolbar, and then select any of the following options for the selected type of form field:

- In the Type drop-down list, highlight Regular Text to require the user to type characters such as text, numbers, symbols, or spaces; Number to require the user to enter a number in the form field; Date to require the user to enter a date; Current Date/Current Time to make Word enter the system date or time; or Calculation to have Word perform a calculation on an expression entered in the form field.

- Specify the length for the text form field in the Maximum Length text box.

- To enter text that will appear by default in

the form field, type the text in the D̲efault Text text box. If Calculation is selected in the Ty̲pe drop-down list, enter the expression in the E̲xpression text box.

- Select Uppercase, Lowercase, First Capital, or Title Case as the format for the characters in the form field in the Text F̲ormat drop-down list. If Calculation is selected in the Ty̲pe drop-down list, the text box is called Number F̲ormat. Select general, decimal, comma, comma with two decimal places, currency, percent, or percent with two decimal places as the number format.

- Select A̲uto to size the check box relative to the font and point size of the surrounding text. Or, choose E̲xactly, and then specify a measurement in points in the text box.

- Select Not Chec̲ked to clear the check box, or C̲hecked to select the check box by default in a check box form field.

- Type the text you want as an item in a drop-down list in the D̲rop-Down Item text box.

- Select A̲dd to add the text in the D̲rop-Down Item text box to the I̲tems In Drop-Down List list box.

- Select R̲emove to remove the item highlighted from the I̲tems In Drop-Down List list box.

- The items that will appear in the drop-down list in the form field appear in the I̲tems In Drop-Down List list box.

- To change the order of a selected item in the I̲tems In Drop-Down List, click on the ↑ or ↓ button in the Move area.

COMMAND AND FEATURE REFERENCE

- Select a macro from the Entry drop-down list to run automatically when the form field is selected, and from the Exit drop-down list to run when the insertion point leaves the form field.

- Type the name of the bookmark that will be associated with the form field and referenced by a macro in the Bookmark text box. To allow the field to be filled-in online, select the Fill-In Enabled, Check Box Enabled, or Drop-Down Enabled check box.

6. If necessary, select Add Help Text, choose any of the following options on the Status Bar tab and the Help Key (F1) tab, and then choose OK:

- Choose None (the default) to have no help available for the form field.

- In the AutoText Entry drop-down list, select an AutoText entry to use as the help text.

- Type the help text for the form field in the Type Your Own text box.

7. Repeat steps 4 through 6 as necessary to complete your form.

8. Click on the Protect Form button on the Forms toolbar if you want to create a form to be filled in online.

9. Click on the Save button on the Standard toolbar, or choose File ➤ Save (Ctrl+S) to display the Save As dialog box. Type a name for the template in the File Name text box, and then choose OK to save the form as a template.

10. Select File ➤ Close (Ctrl+W) to close the template.

FORM F

Editing an Access Form

After an Access form has been created, change to Design view to change the structure of the form:

1. Select the Form tab in the Database window, and then select the name of the form whose design is to be edited.

2. Choose Design. The form's current structure appears in Design view, and the Toolbox is displayed.

NOTE: *To toggle the display of the Toolbox in Design view, click on the Toolbox button on the Form Design toolbar.*

3. If necessary, click on the Field List button on the Form Design toolbar to display the list of fields in the form's underlying table or query. Highlight the name of a field in the list, and then drag it to the position you want on the form to create a bound control.

4. Select one of the following tools in the Toolbox to create new controls:

- Click on the Select Objects button to select controls in the Design window. The tool is selected by default.

- Click on the Label button, and then click in the position in the form to create a text box for an unbound label. Type the label text in the text box, which expands to accommodate the text.

- Click on the Text Box button, and then click in the form to create an unbound text box with an attached label.

- Click on the Option Group button, and then click in the position on the form where you want to place an option group

159

COMMAND AND FEATURE REFERENCE

to display the Option Group Wizard dialog box. Answer the questions in the dialog box, and then choose Next. Choose Finish in the last dialog box to create the option group. (The Control Wizards button is toggled on by default.)

- To create a toggle button, click on the Toggle Button button in the Toolbox, and then click in the position for the button in the form. Click on the Properties button on the Form Design toolbar to display the properties sheet for a selected toggle button, and then select Layout Properties in the drop-down list. Type the text that is to appear on the toggle button in the Caption area.

- To create an option button or check box, click on the corresponding button in the Toolbox, and then click in the position for the object in the form. Both option buttons and check boxes appear with attached labels.

- If necessary, toggle on the Control Wizards button, click on the Combo Box or List Box button, and then click in the position in the form to create a combo box or list box using the Control Wizard.

- Click on the Graph button, and then click in the position for the chart in the form. The Graph Wizard automatically appears.

- Click on the Subform/Subreport button, and then click in the position in the form to create a subform with an attached label.

- Click on the Object Frame or Bound Object Frame button and then click on the form to create the corresponding frame for an object.

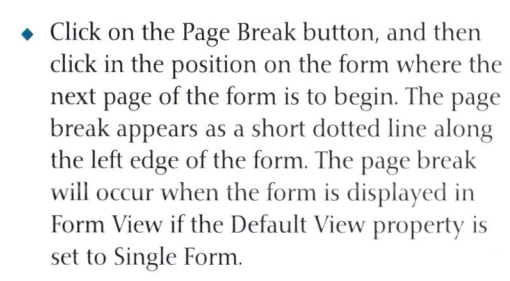

FORM

- Click on the Page Break button, and then click in the position on the form where the next page of the form is to begin. The page break appears as a short dotted line along the left edge of the form. The page break will occur when the form is displayed in Form View if the Default View property is set to Single Form.

- If necessary, toggle on the Control Wizards button, click on the Command Button button, and then click in the form where you want to create a command button to activate an event or macro. Follow the steps in the Command Button Wizard to create the button and link the action to it.

- Click on the Tool Lock button before you select one of the tools in the Toolbox to keep the selected tool active so you can create multiple tools of the same type.

5. Select File ➤ Save (Ctrl+S) to save the changes to the form.

6. Click on the Form View button on the Form Design toolbar to switch to Form view.

Filling In a Word Form

The fields in a Word form will not be activated until you protect the document. To protect a form, click on the Protect Form button on the Forms toolbar, or select Tools ➤ Protect Document, choose Forms in the Protect Document dialog box, and then choose OK.

TIP: *Protect the document while you are creating the template, so the protection is saved with the template. Any documents that are opened on the basis of the template will also be protected.*

COMMAND AND FEATURE REFERENCE

To edit a form field, click on the Protect Form button on the Forms toolbar or select Tools ➤ Unprotect Document to remove the document protection.

Several things happen to a protected Word form:

- Characters can be typed only in form fields or unprotected sections of the document.

- The form fields are activated according to the type of form chosen for each field. Macros assigned to a field as you enter or exit and the help you have assigned to a form field are also activated.

- Results of the fields rather than the field codes are displayed.

- The insertion point can be moved only to form fields and unprotected sections of the document.

- Some document commands are not available at all, and others are available only for the form fields and unprotected sections of the form.

- Users who know the password for the document protection can unprotect the document.

Once document protection is assigned to a form, you can easily move the insertion point from one form field to the next to fill in a form online.

1. Select File ➤ New to display the New dialog box, and then highlight the name of the template that contains the online form.

2. Select Document in the New area, and then choose OK.

3. Use any of the following methods to move from one field to another. Fill in the form as necessary.

- To enter the data and move to the next field in the form, press Tab, ↵, →, or ↓.

- To move to the previous field, press Shift+Tab, ←, or ↑.
- Press F4 or Alt+↓ to select a drop-down list in the selected field.
- Press ↑ or ↓ to select an item in the drop-down list.
- To select a check box in the field or clear a selected check box, press the spacebar or X.
- Press F1 to display Help (if there is any) for the selected field.
- To insert a Tab in the selected field, press Ctrl+Tab.

4. Save the filled-in form as a document file.

To print only the data to fill in a preprinted form, select the Print Data Only For Forms check box on the Print tab in the Options dialog box. To save only the data, select the Save Data Only For Forms check box on the Save tab in the Options dialog box.

SEE ALSO: Borders and Shading; Control; Control Properties; Field Code; Filter; Protection; Query; Record; Templates; Toolbars

Format

The format of the characters displayed on the screen and printed when the file is printed includes the font and size assigned to the characters; any attributes, such as bold, italic, and underline; borders, patterns, and shading; and the alignment of the characters between the margins or in a cell.

COMMAND AND FEATURE REFERENCE

In Access, Excel, and Word, you must define the format for values that are entered in a database, worksheet, table, or field.

NOTE: *In Access, define the number format by selecting it on the control's property sheet.*

Changing the Format of a Number in Excel

The format applied to a cell determines how a number is displayed in the cell. Excel stores and calculates numbers with up to fifteen decimal places.

Numbers are assigned the General number format by default in Excel. In General format, if a number is entered in such a way that Excel assumes it should appear in a certain format, one of the built-in number formats is automatically assigned to it. For example, numbers preceded by a currency symbol are assigned currency format, and numbers followed by a percent sign are assigned percent format.

The Formatting toolbar contains a variety of buttons to use as shortcuts for formatting numbers in the worksheet.

To change the number format of selected cells:

Click on the Currency Style button on the Formatting toolbar to change the format of selected cells to the current currency style. By default, the style displays a dollar sign before the number and two decimal places.

Click on the Percent Style button to change the format to the current percent style. By default, the percent style multiplies the value in the cell by 100 and displays % (percent sign) after it.

Click on the Comma Style button to display numbers in selected cells in the current comma style. By

FORMAT

default, numbers appear with commas between thousands and with two decimal places.

Click on the Increase Decimal button to increase the number of decimal places for selected numbers by one.

Click on the Decrease Decimal button to decrease the number of decimal places for selected numbers by one.

To define a specific format for numbers in selected cells:

1. Select the cells to be formatted.

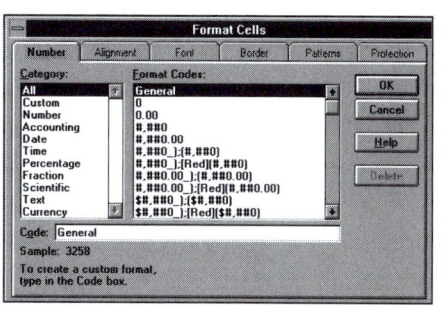

2. Choose Format ➤ Cells (Ctrl+1) to display the Format Cells dialog box, and select the Number tab.

3. Select the type of number format in the Category list box.

4. Select the code for the format in the Format Codes list box, or enter a custom code in the Code text box.

TIP: *Edit one of the built-in codes to create a new number format code. Excel automatically adds a custom code to the appropriate number format category.*

5. Choose OK to change the number format.

To delete one of the custom codes, highlight it in the Format Codes list box, and then choose Delete. Excel's built-in codes cannot be deleted.

SEE ALSO: *Alignment; Borders and Shading; Font; Style*

COMMAND AND FEATURE REFERENCE

Format Painter

Use Format Painter to copy the formats of selected text to other text in Excel, PowerPoint, and Word.

Copying Formats to Characters

To copy the formats applied to existing characters:

1. Select the characters whose formatting you want to copy.

2. Click on the Format Painter button on the Standard toolbar.

3. Select the text to which the format is to be copied. As the text is highlighted, the format is copied to it.

4. Repeat steps 2 and 3 for each set of characters to which you want to copy the format.

To copy the format of selected text to several locations, double-click on the Format Painter button, and then select each occurrence of the text to which the format is to be copied. Click on the Format Painter button again to toggle it off when you are finished.

NOTE: *If you copy a paragraph mark in Word, you can paste the paragraph style and any additional formats applied to the paragraph to other text. If a paragraph mark and some text in the paragraph are selected, the formats applied to the paragraph and the formats applied to the selected text are copied.*

SEE ALSO: *Alignment; Font; Format; Paragraph*

Formula

Use formulas in Access, Excel, and Word to automatically calculate values. In Access, formulas are called expressions.

Entering Expressions in Access

Use expressions to calculate data entered in a form. The expression itself is also entered in the form in a text box control, in which the expression is entered directly, or as a calculated control, in which the expression is the source of the control. Each time the form is used, any expressions in it are automatically recalculated.

Expressions are composed of operators, constant values, field names, control names, and functions, and must begin with = (equal sign). With the form displayed in Design view, either type expressions into the control, or use Expression Builder to select the elements of the expression.

To enter an expression with Expression Builder:

1. Select the text box into which you want to place an expression.

2. Click on the Properties button on the Form Design toolbar to display the properties list for the control. If necessary, select the Data Properties category in the properties sheet.

3. Select the Control Source option area, and then click on the Build button beside the Control Source option area to display the Expression Builder dialog box.

COMMAND AND FEATURE REFERENCE

> **TROUBLESHOOTING**
>
> ## Turning Off Automatic Calculation
>
> By default, formulas are automatically recalculated each time a change is made to one of the dependent values. However, in a very large workbook with many formulas, this can slow down your work. To turn off automatic calculation, select Tools ➤ Options, choose the Calculation tab, select Manual in the Calculation area, and then choose OK.

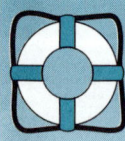

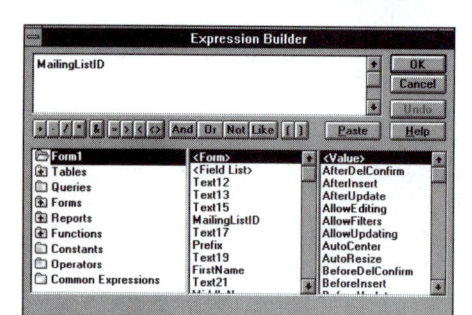

4. Type the expression in the text box. Or, double-click on an element in the left list box to select a reference or element category, select the reference or element in the center or right list box, and then choose Paste.

NOTE: *Select Undo to reverse the last change made in the expression text box.*

5. Choose the operator(s) for the expression in the row of operator buttons below the expression text box.

6. Repeat steps 4 and 5 until the expression is complete, and then choose OK to enter the expression in the control.

Entering Formulas in Excel

One of the basic uses of a worksheet is to perform calculations on values. Use a formula entered in a cell in Excel to automatically calculate operations and display the results in the cell.

A formula must begin with an = (equal sign). You can use numbers (constants), cell references, or range names as the values in formulas. Use the following arithmetic or comparison operators to indicate what operations are to be performed with the values: + (addition); – (subtraction or negation); / (division); * (multiplication); % (percent); ^ (exponentiation); = (equal to); > (greater than); < (less than); >= (greater than or equal to); <= (less than or equal to); <> (not equal to).

By default, formulas are not displayed in a worksheet, but the results of the formulas are. To display a formula entered in a cell, select the cell. The formula appears in the formula bar.

NOTE: *To display formulas in a worksheet instead of their calculated results, select Tools ➤ Options, choose the View tab, select the Formulas check box in the Window Options area, and then choose OK.*

Use parentheses to indicate which set of values is calculated first in a more complex formula. Otherwise, Excel performs calculations in the following order: negation, percent, exponentiation, multiplication and division, addition and subtraction, text joining, and comparison.

To edit a formula, select the cell that contains the formula, and then click in the entry area of the formula bar to position the insertion point, or press F2 (Edit) to place the insertion point at the end of the data in the cell. Use any of the following methods to edit the formula:

- Move the insertion point by either clicking in a different location or by pressing ← and →.

- When the insertion point is positioned where data is to be added, type the new data.

COMMAND AND FEATURE REFERENCE

- To delete the character to the right of the insertion point, press Del.

- To delete the character to the left of the insertion point, press Backspace.

- Drag to highlight any characters to be replaced, and then type the new characters.

- Press ↵ or click on the Enter Box on the formula bar to enter the edited data.

Entering Formulas in Word

Formulas can be entered in calculated form fields in a Word form, in a Formula field code, in a bookmark, or in a table with T_able ➤ F_ormula.

SEE ALSO: *Control Properties; Field Code; Form; Function*

Frame

Frames are used to create a group of Access controls, around charts and chart elements in Excel, to position both text and graphics on each slide in a PowerPoint presentation, or to position text or graphics on a page in a Word document. Frames expand to accommodate their contents, or you can manually change the size and position of a selected frame.

Creating a Frame in a Word Document

By default, document text wraps around a frame. Switch to Page Layout or Print Preview mode to see how the frame and its contents look in the document.

FRAME

TIP: *Insert an empty frame in a document to hold the size and position for an item to be inserted later.*

To create a frame in a Word document:

1. Click on the Drawing button on the Standard toolbar to display the Drawing toolbar, and then click on the Insert Frame button on the Drawing toolbar. Or, choose Insert ➤ Frame.

2. Move the mouse pointer into the document window, where it changes into a crosshair. Position the crosshair where the frame is to be inserted.

3. Drag the crosshair down and to the right. A dotted line appears as you drag.

4. When the frame appears in the correct size, release the mouse button to insert the frame in the document.

TIP: *To add a frame around selected items in a document, click on the Insert Frame button on the Drawing toolbar or choose Insert ➤ Frame. For example, include a caption with the item in a frame so that the caption moves with the item.*

Editing a Frame

To edit a frame, click on it to select it. A selected frame appears with eight small black squares, called *handles*, on its cross-hatched borders. Or, click in the frame to edit its contents. If the insertion point is placed inside the frame, only the cross-hatched border of the frame appears.

To edit a frame with your mouse:

- Point to the frame's border to make the mouse pointer appear as a four-headed arrow, and then drag the frame to a different position.

COMMAND AND FEATURE REFERENCE

> ### TROUBLESHOOTING
>
> ### Formatting Text in a Word Frame
>
> If you want to change the format of text within a frame, you can type and format the text in a frame in the same way you would in a document. Use the indent markers on the Ruler or choose Format ➤ Paragraph to indent a selected paragraph within a frame. Or, right-click in the frame, and then choose one of the commands on the shortcut menu to format the contents of the frame. However, apply any styles to the text before you insert a frame around it so the style does not reposition the frame.

- Click inside the frame, where the mouse pointer appears as an I-beam, and then use the regular editing methods to insert or delete the contents of the frame.

- Position the pointer on one of a selected frame's handles, where it changes into a two-headed sizing pointer, and then drag the handle away from the frame to make it larger, or toward the frame to make it smaller.

In Word, a selected frame can be formatted to exact specifications.

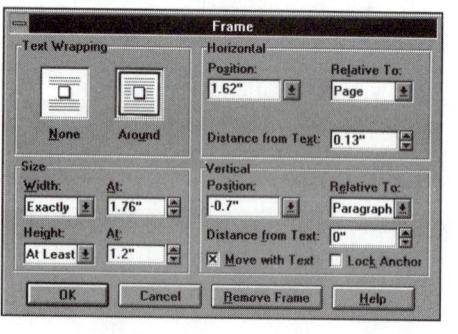

1. Select Format ➤ Frame to display the Frame dialog box.

2. Choose any of the options on the following page, and then choose OK in the Frame dialog box.

172

FRAME

- In the Text Wrapping area, choose None to break document text above the frame and allow the text to continue below the frame, or Around to allow text to flow around the frame. There must be at least one inch between the margin or column boundary and the frame for the text to wrap completely around the frame.

- In the Width drop-down list, select Auto to allow a frame to span from the left margin to the right margin, or select Exactly, and then specify an exact width for the frame in the At text box.

- In the Height drop-down list, choose Auto to allow the frame to be as tall as the height of its tallest contents. Or, choose At Least to specify the minimum height for the frame, or Exactly to specify the exact height for the frame in the At text box.

- In the Horizontal area, specify an exact measurement or select Left, Right, Center, Inside, or Out-side as the position for the frame in the Position drop-down list to define the frame's position on the page. In the Relative To drop-down list, select the frame's position relative to a margin, the edge of the page, or in a column. Specify how much space will separate the frame from surrounding text in the Distance From Text text box.

- In the Vertical area, specify an exact measurement or select Top, Bottom, or Center in the Position drop-down list to specify the frame's position. In the Relative To drop-down list, choose the frame's position relative to a margin, the edge of the page, or a paragraph. Specify how much space will separate the frame from surrounding text

COMMAND AND FEATURE REFERENCE

in the Distance From Text text box. Select the Move With Text check box to move the frame vertically on the page as paragraphs are added or deleted in the document. Select the Lock Anchor check box to anchor the frame to a specific paragraph.

- To remove the selected frame, choose Remove Frame. The frame's contents are moved to the paragraph above the one in which the frame was anchored.

To remove the frame and delete its contents, select the frame and press Backspace or Del.

SEE ALSO: *Captions; Chart; Control Properties; Draw; Graphic; Paragraph*

Function

Access, Excel, and Word come with some built-in formulas, called *functions*. Functions can be used alone or combined with your own formulas.

Entering Functions

A function is composed of two parts–its name entered in either uppercase or lowercase letters, and its *arguments*, the values on which operations are performed. To type a function in a control, worksheet cell, or a Formula field:

1. Type = (equal sign) if the function is the beginning of the formula, and then type the function's name followed by the left parenthesis.

2. Type the function's arguments.

3. Type the right parenthesis to close the formula.

Using AutoSum in Excel

To calculate the sum of the values in cells above or to the left of the active cell, click on the AutoSum button on Excel's Standard toolbar. AutoSum automatically suggests that the cells above or to the left be included in the formula. If the suggested range is incorrect, drag through the range whose values are to be totaled, and then press ↵ to enter the formula into the cell.

Use AutoSum to simultaneously enter more than one sum. Select the row in which the sums of values in corresponding columns are to appear, and then click on the AutoSum button. To total the values in rows, select the column in which the totals are to appear and click on the AutoSum button. Or, use AutoSum to simultaneously total the values in both rows and columns. Select the rows and columns to be totaled, and also the row or column of cells in which the totals are to appear, and then click on the AutoSum button.

In a worksheet that includes subtotaled rows or columns of data, use AutoSum to calculate the grand totals. Select all the data, including the constant values in the worksheet, and select the row or column in which the grand totals are to appear. Then click on the AutoSum button.

Using the Function Wizard

Most of the functions you use will be in Excel. Use Excel's Function Wizard to enter selected functions in a cell or to help you create and simplify your own formulas.

To use the Function Wizard:

1. Select the cell in which to place a formula.

COMMAND AND FEATURE REFERENCE

2. Click on the Function Wizard button on the Standard toolbar to display the Function Wizard–Step 1 of 2 dialog box.

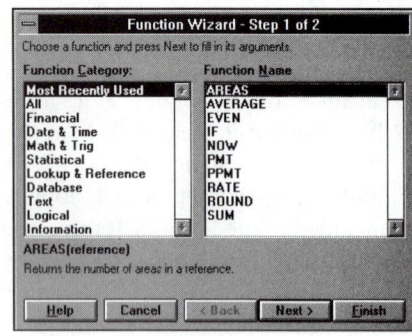

3. Select the type of function in the Function Category list box.

4. If necessary, type a letter to scroll to the first function that begins with that letter in the Function Name text box. Continue to scroll through the list until the name is displayed, and then select the name.

5. Select Next to display the Function Wizard–Step 2 of 2 dialog box.

NOTE: *You can also type = (equal sign) and the name of the function to use in the formula in the active cell, and then press Ctrl+A to display the Function Wizard≈Step 2 of 2 dialog box.*

6. Type each number (or the cell reference of each value) in the text box. Do not type any spaces in the formula.

7. Select Finish when the necessary values have been entered in the Wizard dialog box. The dialog box disappears, and the results are displayed in the selected cell.

To edit a function with the Function Wizard, select a cell that contains a function and then click on the Function Wizard button.

SEE ALSO: *Control Properties; Field Code; Formula; Table*

Goal Seek

Use Excel's Goal Seek feature to save time otherwise spent in performing a trial-and-error analysis by specifying the result a formula is to return. Goal Seek allows Excel to adjust the value in one other cell so the formula returns the needed result.

The cell whose value is to be changed cannot contain a formula. Instead, it must contain a value that is either directly or indirectly dependent on the formula for which a result is sought.

1. Select the cell that contains the formula for which a specific result is required.

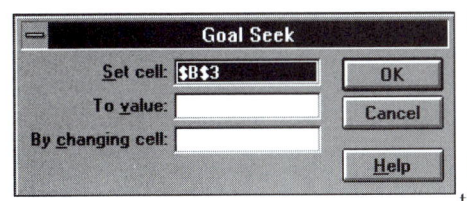

2. Choose Tools ➤ Goal Seek to display the Goal Seek dialog box.

3. The reference to the selected cell (the one that contains the formula for which specific results are required) is entered in the Set Cell text box. Click in the To Value text box, and then type the required results for the formula.

4. Click in the By Changing Cell text box, and then select the cell that contains the value that must be changed to produce the desired results for the formula.

5. Select OK. The Goal Seek Status dialog box appears, describing the progress of the goal seeking.

6. If necessary, select Pause to stop the calculation. Then choose Step to calculate the desired results step-by-step. To resume normal calculation, select Continue.

COMMAND AND FEATURE REFERENCE

7. Choose OK to enter the value necessary to produce the desired results in the cell selected in step 4.

To return the value in the changing cell to its original value, click on the Undo button on the Standard toolbar, or use Edit ➤ Undo (Ctrl+Z) immediately after you approve the change.

SEE ALSO: Auditing; Undo/Redo

Go To

Use Go To to move quickly to another location in the same file in Access, Excel, and Word. In Excel, you can also move to a location in another open workbook file. When Go To is used, the insertion point moves to the location specified.

Going to a Location in an Access Database

To move to a specific record in the active form, table, or query:

1. Press F5, and then type the number of the record.

2. Press ↵ to move to the specified record.

Or, use the following methods to move to specific records:

Click on the First Record button at the bottom of the form or datasheet, or choose Records ➤ Go To ➤ First to move to the first record.

Click on the Last Record button at the bottom of the form or datasheet, or select Records ➤ Go To ➤ Last to move to the last record.

GO TO

Click on the Next Record button at the bottom of the form or datasheet, or select <u>R</u>ecords ➤ <u>G</u>o To ➤ <u>N</u>ext to move to the next record.

Click on the Previous Record button at the bottom of the form or datasheet, or select <u>R</u>ecords ➤ <u>G</u>o To ➤ <u>P</u>revious to move to the previous record.

TIP: *When you want to enter a new record, select Records ➤ <u>G</u>o To ➤ Ne<u>w</u> to display a blank record at the end of the datasheet or form.*

Going to a Location in an Excel Worksheet

To select the cell or range specified:

1. Select <u>E</u>dit ➤ <u>G</u>o To (F5) to display the Go To dialog box.

2. Select the name of a range in the <u>G</u>o To list box, or type the reference of the cell to select in the <u>R</u>eference text box, and then choose OK.

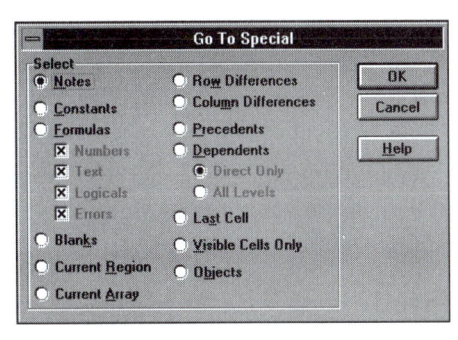

3. Or, select <u>S</u>pecial to display the Go To Special dialog box.

NOTE: *Before choosing Go To Special, select one cell in a worksheet to select every occurrence of the specified item in the worksheet, or a range to select every occurrence of the specified item in the range.*

COMMAND AND FEATURE REFERENCE

4. Select any of the following options, and then choose OK to select each occurrence of the specified item in the selected worksheet or range:

- Select Notes (Ctrl+Shift+?) to select each cell that contains a note.

- To select each cell whose value does not begin with = (equal sign), choose Constants.

- Choose Formulas, and then select any of these check boxes to highlight each cell that contains a formula returning the desired results. Select Numbers to select cells that return a number; select Text to highlight cells that return text; select Logicals to highlight cells that return TRUE or FALSE values; and select Errors to highlight cells that return error values.

- To select every empty cell, choose Blanks.

- To select the range around the active cell bounded by blank cells, choose Current Region (Ctrl+* on keypad).

- Choose Current Array (Ctrl+/) to select each cell in the array that contains the active cell.

- Choose Row Differences (Ctrl+\) to highlight the cells in each row that are different from the cell used for comparison in that row.

- Choose Column Differences (Ctrl+Shift+ |–| (vertical bar)) to highlight the cells in each column that are different from the cell used for comparison in that column.

- To highlight cells that are referred to by the formula in the active cell, choose Precedents. Select Direct Only (Ctrl+[) to highlight only the direct precedents, or All Levels (Ctrl+Shift+{) to select all precedents of the formula.

GO TO

- To highlight cells that contain formulas that refer to the active cell, choose D̲ependents. Select Di̲rect Only (Ctrl+Shift +]) to highlight only direct dependents, or All L̲evels (Ctrl+Shift+}) to highlight all the dependents of the active cell.

- To move to the last non-blank cell in the worksheet, select Las̲t Cell.

- To select only cells that are not hidden, choose V̲isible Cells Only.

- Choose Obj̲ects to select all the graphic objects in the selection.

Going to a Location in a Word Document

To move to the last three positions of the insertion point, press Shift+F 5. Or, follow these steps to move to a specific location in the active document:

1. Choose E̲dit ➤ G̲o To (F 5), or double-click in one of the first two sections of the status bar to display the Go To dialog box.

2. Highlight a document item in the Go To W̲hat list box.

3. To move to the next specified document item, choose Nex̲t. To move to the previous item, choose P̲revious.

TIP: *Type a number in the E̲nter Document Item text box, and then select Go T̲o to move the insertion point to that item. Or, type snpn, where n is the number, in the E̲nter Document Item text box to move to a specific section number and page number.*

4. When you are finished moving to document items, select Close in the Go To dialog box.

SEE ALSO: *Find and Replace*

181

COMMAND AND FEATURE REFERENCE

Graphic

Enhance the appearance of your work by adding graphics to your files. There are several ways to add a graphic to a file, depending on the active Microsoft Office application–paste the graphic from the Clipboard, draw a graphic using the Drawing tools, or insert a graphic file into the active file. You can insert graphics into an Excel worksheet, on a PowerPoint slide, or in a Word document.

Editing a Graphic

Graphics in Excel are inserted within a frame, but graphics in PowerPoint and Word are not. The methods you can use to edit a selected graphic depend on the application in which it is inserted. To select the graphic, click on it. A selected graphic appears with eight handles surrounding it.

NOTE: *To change the application window used to extensively edit an inserted graphic in Word, choose Tools ➤ Options, select the Edit tab, and then choose Microsoft Word, Microsoft Drawing, or Microsoft Graph in the Picture Editor drop-down list.*

The following are some of the changes you can make to your graphics:

- To resize a selected graphic, position the pointer over one of its handles. When the pointer appears as a two-headed arrow, drag a corner handle to resize the graphic but keep its original proportions, or drag one of its middle handles to resize the graphic but lose its original proportions.

- To move a selected graphic, position the mouse pointer over the graphic, and then drag the object to a different location.

GRAPHIC

TIP: *In Word, insert a frame around the selected graphic in order to move it. Otherwise, you can use drag and drop to move the graphic to a different location in the document.*

- To copy a selected graphic, hold down the Ctrl key while you drag the graphic to a new location.

- To edit a selected graphic in an Excel worksheet, choose Format ➤ Object (Ctrl+1) to display the Format Object dialog box. On the Patterns tab, select the border and shadow, and the fill for the frame of the graphic. On the Protection tab, choose whether the object is locked or unlocked. On the Properties tab, select the positioning and printing options for the object.

- To edit a graphic created or inserted with Insert ➤ Object, choose Edit ➤ *Type Of* Object ➤ Edit, or double-click on the graphic to display the application used to create the graphic.

- To insert a border around a selected graphic in PowerPoint, click on the Line On/Off button on the Drawing toolbar. Click on the Shadow On/Off button on the Drawing toolbar to add a drop shadow to the graphic or the border, depending on which is selected.

- To add a border to a selected graphic in a Word file, click on the Borders button on the Formatting toolbar, and then click on the Outside Border button. Or, choose Format ➤ Borders And Shading, select Box or Shadow, and then choose OK.

- To add shading around a graphic in a Word document, click on the Page Layout View button by the horizontal scroll bar to change to Page Layout view, select the graphic, and then select Insert ➤ Frame. Select Format ➤ Frame, and then use the options in the Size area of the Frame dialog box to resize the frame so it is

COMMAND AND FEATURE REFERENCE

larger than the graphic. Select the cross-hatched frame. Then select the shading in the Shading drop-down list on the Borders toolbar, or choose Format ➤ Borders And Shading, select the Shading tab, and select the shading in the Custom Shading list box to apply to the area between the frame and the graphic.

- To crop a selected graphic in a Word document, press the Shift key while dragging a handle to the center of the graphic. The cropping measurements are displayed in the status bar. Or, choose Format ➤ Picture to crop the picture to exact specifications, and then select OK in the Picture dialog box. The following options are available in the Picture dialog box:

    Crop From Specify the measurement to crop from the Left, Right, Top, or Bottom of the graphic.

    Scaling Specify the percentage of the graphic's original dimensions in the Width and Height text boxes.

    Size Specify the graphic's dimensions in the Width and Height text.boxes.

    Reset Returns the graphic to its orignal size and cropping.

    Frame Displays the Frame dialog box in order to format the frame around a graphic.

- To extensively edit a graphic created with Draw or inserted with Insert ➤ Picture in a Word document, double-click on it. The graphic appears in a separate window, and the Drawing toolbar is displayed above the status bar. Use the Drawing tools to add or remove graphics, apply color or line styles to the graphic, or add text to the graphic.

GRAPHIC

> **TROUBLESHOOTING**
>
> ## Saving Graphics in Native Format
>
> If you insert a graphic created on a different platform, such as a graphic created on a Macintosh, Word saves both the original graphic and its interpretation of the graphic in the document. You can save disk space by saving the graphic only in Word's interpretation (its native format) in your document. Select Tools ➤ Options and choose the Save tab. Select the Save Native Picture Formats Only check box in the Save Options area, and then choose OK.

Inserting a Graphic File

Excel, PowerPoint, and Word each come with graphics filters, used to interpret many different graphics file formats. These filters are automatically used when you insert a graphic, even one created in another application, into a worksheet, slide, or document.

Microsoft Office comes with many clip art files that can be used in your files. They are found in the MSOFFICE\CLIPART directory, and are in .WMF (Windows Metafile) format.

TIP: *The easiest way to insert a picture in a file is to use the ClipArt Gallery. See the ClipArt entry for additional information.*

To insert a graphic file in a document:

1. Activate the cell, slide, or position the insertion point in the document where you want a graphic to appear.

2. Choose Insert ➤ Picture to display the Insert Picture dialog box.

COMMAND AND FEATURE REFERENCE

3. Select the name of the file to insert in the File Name list box.

4. To see a sample of the graphic in the Preview area of the dialog box, select the Preview Picture check box.

> **NOTE:** In Word, select the Save Picture in Document check box to save Word's interpretation of the graphic rather than the actual graphic file in your document. Or, select the Link To File check box and clear the Save Picture In Document check box to save the link in the document rather than the graphics file. You can also select the Link To File check box when inserting a picture in PowerPoint.

5. Select OK to insert the picture in the file.

Linking a Graphic File

Because graphic files tend to take up a lot of disk space, save some space by linking a graphic file to the application file rather than inserting it in the file. When a graphic is inserted into a file, the size of the graphic file is added to the size of the application file. In effect, the graphic file is saved twice–once as the graphic file, and once in the application file.

> **NOTE:** The only way to insert a graphic into a control in an Access form is to link the graphic to the control while in Form Design view.

When the link rather than the graphic is stored, a placeholder for the graphic is inserted in the file. A depiction of the graphic or an icon representing the graphic is displayed in the placeholder. The graphic takes longer to display when it is linked because it must be recreated from its source file.

TIP: *To speed up document scrolling, have Word use only placeholders in documents that contain graphics. Choose Tools ➤ Options, and then select the View tab. Select the Picture Placeholders check box in the Show area, and then choose OK in the Options dialog box.*

SEE ALSO: *Chart; ClipArt; Control Properties; Cut, Copy, and Paste; Draw; Frame; Link; Object Linking and Embedding*

Guides

In PowerPoint, display the guides to help align objects on a slide. The guides are horizontal and vertical straight-edges, and are themselves aligned to an underlying, invisible grid. When an object is moved near one of the guides, it snaps to the guide. The guides are only active when they are displayed.

Aligning Objects with the Guides

A PowerPoint object is aligned according to its selection rectangle. Either the corner or center of the object, whichever is closer to a near guide, is aligned along the guide.

To align objects in either Slide View or Notes View:

1. Select View ➤ Guides to toggle on the display of the guides in the center of the slide or notes page.

2. If necessary, drag a guide to a different location on the slide or notes page. As you drag the guide, the measurement from its starting point appears.

3. Drag the object near the guide to align it along the guide. Hold down the Shift key while you drag the object to restrict it to either horizontal or vertical movement.

4. If necessary, select <u>V</u>iew ➤ <u>G</u>uides to toggle off the display of the guides.

Use ↑, ↓, ←, and → to move a selected object only slightly. Hold down the Alt key (to turn off the underlying grid) while moving the object with one of the arrow keys to nudge it into position.

SEE ALSO: *Graphic; Presentation*

Header and Footer

Headers can be displayed and printed in the top margin of each page of a printed document in Access, Excel, and Word, and footers can be displayed and printed in the bottom margin of each page. The method used to add headers and footers to a file depends on the active Microsoft Office application.

Creating a Header or Footer in Access

You can create headers and footers in Access as controls on both forms and reports. To create headers and footers, the form or report must be in Design view. Page, form, and report headers and footers can be created only in pairs.

TIP: *To remove an unwanted page, form, or report header or footer, position the mouse pointer over the section heading in Design view, and then drag the section to change its height to none. Or, change its Visible property to No.*

HEADER AND FOOTER

There are five sections in a form in Design view, four of which are headers and footers. Create the following kinds of headers and footers for a form:

- Use a *form header* to display instructions for using the form or buttons that allow the user to open other forms or to perform another task. A form header appears at the top of the form in Form view, and at the top of the first page when the form is printed.

- Create a *page header* to display the same information, such as the title of the database, at the top of each printed page.

- The *page footer* is used to display the same information, such as the page number or date, at the bottom of each printed page.

- Create a *form footer* to display instructions for using the form, or buttons that allow the user to perform specific tasks at the bottom of the form in Form view, and at the bottom of the last page when the form is printed.

NOTE: *To prevent a form header or form footer from being printed, set its Display When property to Screen Only.*

To create a header and footer for a form:

1. Display the form in Design view.

2. Select Format ➤ Page Header/Footer or Format ➤ Form Header/Footer to create both the header and the footer specified.

A report can contain up to seven different types of sections, six of which are headers and footers. Create the following kinds of headers and footers for a report:

- Use a *report header* to display items, such as a company logo or the title of the report, only once at

COMMAND AND FEATURE REFERENCE

the top of a report. It appears before the first page's page header when the report is printed.

- To display items at the top of every page, create a *page header* in the report.

- Create a *group header* to specify items, such as a name for a group, at the beginning of a group of records in the report.

- Use a *group footer* to specify items, such as a total for the group, at the end of each group.

- Use a *page footer* for items, such as page numbers, that will appear at the bottom of each page in the report.

- A *report footer* appears before a page footer at the end of the printed report. It contains items that pertain to the entire report, such as the report's total.

To create a header and footer for a report:

1. Display the report in Design view.

2. Select Format ➤ Page Header/Footer or Format ➤ Report Header/Footer.

3. To add a group header or group footer, select View ➤ Sorting And Grouping to display the Sorting And Grouping dialog box.

4. Select the field or expression on which to sort in the drop-down list for the first item.

5. In the Group Properties area of the Sorting And Grouping dialog box, select Yes in the Group Header and Group Footer property areas.

To remove a group header or footer, select No as the Group Header or Group Footer property in the Sorting And Grouping dialog box, and then choose OK to confirm the removal.

Creating a Header or Footer in Excel

A header and footer appear by default on each page printed in an Excel file. However, you can customize the header and footer for any portion of a workbook that is printed.

To create a header or footer in Excel:

1. Click on the Print Preview button on the Standard toolbar, and then choose Setup, or select File ➤ Page Setup to display the Page Setup dialog box.

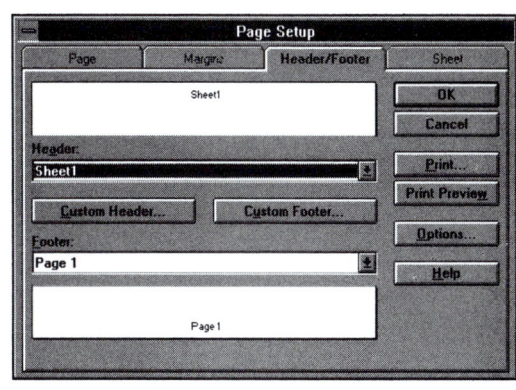

2. Select the Header/Footer tab.

3. Select one of the predefined headers and footers in the Header and Footer drop-down lists.

4. Or, select Custom Header or Custom Footer to display the corresponding dialog box.

5. Type the text for the header or footer in the Left Section, Center Section, and Right Section text boxes.

6. If necessary, do any of the following:

> Click on the Font button to change the font and attributes of selected text.

> Click on the Page Number button to insert the page number in the position of the insertion point.

> Click on the Total Pages button to insert the total number of pages in the position of the insertion point.

COMMAND AND FEATURE REFERENCE

Click on the Date button to insert the current date in the position of the insertion point.

Click on the Time button to insert the system time in the position of the insertion point.

Click on the Filename button to insert the name of the file that contains the worksheet being printed.

Click on the Sheet Name button to insert the name of the worksheet being printed.

7. Choose OK in the Header or Footer dialog box to return to the Page Setup dialog box.

8. Choose OK in the Page Setup dialog box to insert the specified header and footer in the document.

The header and footer appear on the screen only when the area being printed is displayed in Print Preview view.

Creating or Editing a Header or Footer in Word

Use Word's Header And Footer toolbar to easily create, move between, and display the header or footer in a document. You can use a negative indent to print a header or footer in the left margin.

To create or edit a header or footer in Word:

1. Select View ➤ Header And Footer to change to Page Layout view, display the Header And Footer toolbar, and activate the header area of the current page.

2. Type the text for the header of the document within the dashed lines. Use Word's regular formatting techniques to format the text.

3. Click on the Switch Between Header And Footer button on the Header And Footer toolbar to move the insertion point into the footer.

4. Type the text and apply the formatting you want for the footer.

5. If necessary, click on any of the following buttons on the Header And Footer toolbar to insert the corresponding field code in the active header or footer in the position of the insertion point:

> Click on the Date button to insert the current Date.

> Click on the Page Numbers button to insert the page number field code.

> Click on the Time button to insert the current Time.

6. To change any of the page layout options for the document, click on the Page Setup button to display the Page Setup dialog box.

7. To adjust the distance between the header or footer and the text of the document, drag the margin boundary on the vertical ruler up or down.

8. Optionally, click on the Show/Hide Document Text button to hide the dimmed text in your document.

9. Select Close to remove the Header And Footer toolbar and return to the document in the original view.

To edit the text or update a field code in a header or footer, activate the header or footer and display the Header And Footer toolbar.

COMMAND AND FEATURE REFERENCE

- In Page Layout view, double-click on either the header or footer.
- In Normal view mode, select <u>V</u>iew ➤ <u>H</u>eader And Footer.

Creating Different Headers and Footers in Word

You can have a different header and footer for the first page of a document, for odd and even pages in a document, or for document sections.

To create different headers or footers in Word:

1. Display the Header And Footer toolbar.

2. Click on the Page Setup button on the Header And Footer toolbar, and then select the <u>L</u>ayout tab.

3. To make the header and footer on the first page different from those in the rest of the document, select the Different <u>F</u>irst Page check box in the Headers And Footers area.

4. To have different headers and footers appear on odd and even pages in the document, select the Different <u>O</u>dd And Even check box in the Headers And Footers area.

5. Select OK in the Page Setup dialog box.

6. If necessary, create the header and footer for the first page. To omit a header and footer on the first page, leave the areas blank.

7. Or, create the header and footer for the odd pages in the document. Click the Show Previous or Show Next button on the Header and Footer toolbar to move to the odd or even page header or footer, and then create the header and footer you want to appear on odd or even pages.

8. Choose <u>C</u>lose to return to the document.

If headers and footers are inserted in documents that contain more than one section, all the headers and footers will be the same for the entire document because the sections are connected. "Same as Previous" appears in the top right corner of the header or footer area.

To create different headers and footers for a section, click on the Same As Previous button on the Header And Footer toolbar to disconnect the previous section's header and footer. All subsequent sections will then have the same header and footer as the section after the broken connection, unless the connection is broken for those sections as well.

To establish a connection with the header or footer in the previous section of a document, move the insertion point into the section and click on the Same As Previous button on the Header And Footer toolbar, and then choose Yes to confirm that the header and footer in the previous section are to appear in this section.

SEE ALSO: *Control Properties; Field Code; Margins; Master View; Page Setup; Sort; Toolbars*

Help

Each Microsoft Office application contains extensive online help. You can search for keywords, view demonstrations with "Examples and Demos," display Basic commands for the application, or read step-by-step instructions for a specific task.

COMMAND AND FEATURE REFERENCE

Getting Context-Sensitive Help

There are several ways to quickly get help with the current command or dialog box:

- Double-click on the Help button on the Standard toolbar in Excel, PowerPoint, and Word to make the Search dialog box appear, and then begin typing the keyword or topic on which you want help.

- Click on the Help button on the Standard toolbar, and then select a command to display help for that command.

- Click on the Help button on the Standard toolbar, and then click on a toolbar button or any other screen hot spot to display help for that item.

- Press F1 when a menu command is highlighted.

- Select Help in a dialog box to get help related to that dialog box.

- Click on one of the icons or underlined topics in a Help window.

Use the menu commands in the Help window to define a bookmark or add a note to a topic, to copy a Help topic to the Clipboard, or to print a Help topic.

- Select Bookmark ➤ Define to place a bookmark in a Help topic, or select the name of an existing bookmark on the Bookmark drop-down menu.

- Select Edit ➤ Copy to copy the text of a Help topic to the Clipboard. Paste it into a Word document to edit or print the text.

- Select Edit ➤ Annotate to add a note to a Help topic. Click on the paper clip beside an annotated topic title to display the Annotate window with the note.

HELP

- Choose <u>F</u>ile ➤ <u>P</u>rint Topic to print the current Help topic.

Getting "How To" Help

Often, a "How To" window will open on your screen when a Help topic is selected. Use the buttons on the window's button bar to control How To Help. Select Print to print the topic, Index to display the Help Index, On Top to make the How To window stay on top of the active window for reference, or Close to close the How To window.

Using Cue Cards

In Access and PowerPoint, use the Cue Cards to assist with the current task. Cue Cards appear in a separate window, and provide step-by-step instructions on how to perform a specific task. If the Cue Cards do not appear on your screen, choose <u>H</u>elp ➤ C<u>u</u>e Cards to display the Cue Cards, and then click on the button beside the task to display the steps necessary to complete the task. Choose Next at the bottom of the displayed Cue Card to return to the next page in the list of steps.

On the button bar in the Cue Cards window, select <u>M</u>enu to return to the original Cue Cards task list, <u>S</u>earch to display the Search dialog box, or <u>B</u>ack to display each previously displayed screen of Cue Cards in turn.

NOTE: *Select <u>H</u>elp ➤ <u>E</u>xamples And Demos for a demonstration of a selected procedure in Excel and Word. Click on the button beside the procedure you want to see. If necessary, click on the button beside the topic in the list that appears.*

197

COMMAND AND FEATURE REFERENCE

Import/Export Data

You can convert data created in other applications (and stored in a different file format) to the format used in Access, or use data in an Access database in other applications by importing or exporting data. Or, attach a table of data created in another application to an Access database.

Attaching a Table

Attached tables are stored in the file format of the application used to create the file, and appear in the Database window with the corresponding attached table icon. Only the location and other information about the attached file are stored in the Access database. Data in an attached table can be added or edited in Access, but processing takes longer.

NOTE: *If you plan to use Access exclusively when working with a database created in another application, import the database file rather than attaching it. Access works more efficiently with files in its own format.*

The steps necessary to attach a table to an Access database depend on the type of table that is being attached. For example, tables created in some applications may require a password, which was saved in the other application, in order to open and attach the table to an Access file.

In general, follow these steps:

1. Activate the Database window of the file to which a table is to be attached.

IMPORT/EXPORT DATA

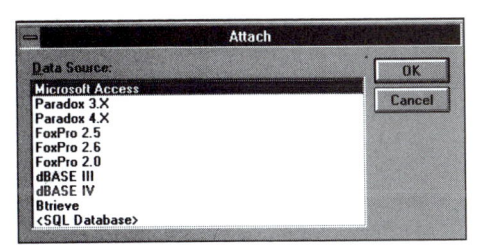

2. Select File ➤ Attach Table to display the Attach dialog box.

3. Select the type of table to attach to the database in the Data Source list box.

4. Choose OK. The Select File dialog box appears.

5. If necessary, select the drive and directory in which the file is stored. Highlight the name of the file to attach in the File Name list box, and then choose Attach.

NOTE: *Select the Exclusive check box in the Select File dialog box to obtain faster performance while working with an attached table.*

6. If the Select Index Files dialog box appears, select the name of the index file that is associated with the file being attached in the File Name list box, and then choose Select.

7. Choose OK in the message box that appears to inform you that the file was successfully attached.

8. Choose Close in the Select File dialog box to return to the Database window.

To delete an attachment to an Access database, select the attachment in the Database window, choose Edit ➤ Delete (Del), and then choose OK to confirm the deletion. Only the attachment is deleted–the source database file remains on your disk.

To speed up performance when using an attached table:

- To insert new records in the table, open the table or a form based on the table, and then choose the <u>R</u>ecords ➤ <u>D</u>ata Entry command to hide all existing records. Select <u>R</u>ecords ➤ <u>S</u>how All Records to redisplay the hidden records.

- Create a form for the attached table, and then change the Default Editing property to Data Entry. Each time the form is opened, a blank form appears so data entry can begin immediately.

- Create a query to display only the data in an attached table that is necessary for a specific purpose.

If an attached file is moved or renamed, or the table in the source file is renamed, Access will not be able to find it. To update the attachment:

1. Select <u>F</u>ile ➤ Add-<u>i</u>ns ➤ A<u>t</u>tachment Manager to display the Attachment Manager dialog box.

2. Select the check box of each attachment to be updated in the list box, and then choose OK.

3. Follow any instructions that appear, and then choose Close in the Attachment Manager dialog box.

Exporting Data

You can export the data saved in an Access database for use in another application. For example, export a mailing list to a Word data source rather than re-entering all the names and addresses in the database.

NOTE: *If Access field names are too long for an application to which the data is being exported, Access adjusts the length of the field names.*

The steps necessary to export data depend on the application and the method selected to receive the exported records. In general, follow the steps on the next page.

IMPORT/EXPORT DATA

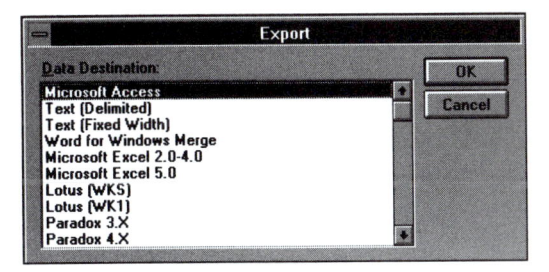

1. With the database file that contains the records to be exported open, select File ➤ Export to display the Export dialog box.

2. Select the application or method for the export in the Data Destination list box, and then choose OK.

3. In the Select Microsoft Access Object dialog box that appears, select the database table or query to be exported in the Objects In *Name* list box, and then choose OK.

4. In the Export To File dialog box that appears, type the name for a new file or select the name of an existing file that is the destination for the data, and then choose OK.

If the name of an existing Excel 5 workbook file is selected, the data is placed on a new sheet in the file.

Importing Data

Data created in other applications can be imported into a table in an Access database. If the data is in a spreadsheet or a text file, Access creates field names based on the field names in the first row of data. Access then tries to assign an appropriate data type to the fields in the new table.

To import data into a table:

1. With the Access database file into which you want to import data open and the Database window active, select File ➤ Import to display the Import dialog box.

COMMAND AND FEATURE REFERENCE

2. Select the name of the application or the type of data that is to be imported in the Data Source list box, and then choose OK to display the Select File dialog box.

3. If necessary, choose a different drive and directory. Then select the name of the file that contains the data to be imported in the File Name list box, and choose Import.

4. Select any of the following options, depending on the type of data being imported, and then choose OK:

- Select the First Row Contains Field Names check box to have Access use the text or column labels in the first row of the file as the names of fields.

- In the Table Options area, select Create New Table to import the data into a new table in the database file. Or, choose Append To Existing Table, and then select the name of the table to which the new records are to be added. The imported records must have a structure in which each field has the same name, is the same data type, and appears in the same order as those in the existing table.

- In the Spreadsheet Range area, select Sheet Name, and then highlight the name of the worksheet that contains the data to be imported. If necessary, type the reference of the range that contains the data in the Range text box. Or, select Named range, and then choose the name of a range in the drop-down list.

- If the data being imported is in a delimited text file, choose Options. Then, if necessary, select the name of a defined import specification in the Specification Name drop-down list in the Import Text Options dialog box.

IMPORT/EXPORT DATA

♦ When importing a fixed-width text file, choose <u>E</u>dit Specs to create or edit an import file specification.

Setting Import/Export Specifications

Define the specifications that are necessary to import text files created in other applications, or edit existing defined specifications. Save the specifications to a unique name so they can be used to import text files in the future.

To set import/export specifications:

1. Open the Access database file into which you want to import text and activate the Database window.

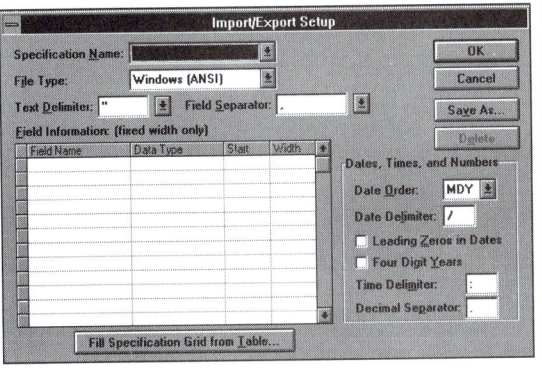

2. Select <u>F</u>ile ➤ Imp/Exp <u>S</u>etup to display the Import/Export Setup dialog box.

3. Select any of the following options to define or edit import specifications, and then choose OK.

♦ If necessary, select the name of an existing import specification that is to be edited in the Specification <u>N</u>ame drop-down list.

♦ Select the type of file that contains the text being imported in the F<u>i</u>le Type drop-down list.

203

COMMAND AND FEATURE REFERENCE

- Select the character that is used as a text delimqiter in the file being imported in the Text Delimiter drop-down list.

- Select the character that is used to indicate where the next field begins in the Field Separator drop-down list.

- For each field in a fixed-width text file, specify the name, data type, the starting number of the column, and the width of the field in the source file in the Field Information (Fixed Width Only) list box. Or, choose Fill Specification Grid From Table, select the name of an existing table in the Access database that contains similar field names and definitions in the Table drop-down list, and then choose OK.

- In the Dates, Times, And Numbers area, select the format for dates being imported in the Date Order drop-down list, and then type the character used between portions of the date in the Date Delimiter text box. Select the Leading Zeros In Dates check box if dates in the file contain leading zeros, and select the Four-Digit Years check box if the dates are expressed with all four digits for the year. Type the character that appears between portions of the time in the Time Delimiter text box. Type the character that is used as a decimal in the source file in the Decimal Separator text box.

- To save the text options selected as a defined import specification, select Save As, type a name for the specification in the Name text box, and then choose OK.

SEE ALSO: *Control Properties; Database; File Management; Mail Merge; Table; Workbook*

Indent

Indentation is the distance between the text and the margins in a Word document. The indentation can be changed for an entire paragraph or for the paragraph's first line. Text can be indented from either the left or the right margin.

Indenting a Paragraph

To indent a single paragraph to the next or previous tab stop, move the insertion point into the paragraph or select the paragraph, and then use one of the following methods:

- Click on the Increase Indent button on the Formatting toolbar or press Ctrl+M to increase the indentation of an entire paragraph to the next tab stop.

- To decrease the indentation of an entire paragraph to the previous tab stop, click on the Decrease Indent button on the Formatting toolbar or press Ctrl+Shift+M.

- To create a hanging indent, press Ctrl+T.

- To decrease a hanging indent, press Ctrl+Shift+T.

Indenting a Paragraph with Exact Measurements

Follow these steps to specify the exact measurements for the current paragraph:

1. Select Format ➤ Paragraph, and then select the Indents And Spacing tab in the Paragraph dialog box.

2. In the Indentation area, specify the distance to indent the paragraph from the Left or Right margin.

COMMAND AND FEATURE REFERENCE

Enter a negative number in the corresponding text box for text to appear in either margin.

3. Select (None), First Line, or Hanging in the Special drop-down list to define the indentation for the first line of the paragraph.

4. Specify the distance the first line will be indented in the By text box.

5. Choose OK in the Paragraph dialog box.

TIP: *Use the indent markers on the Ruler to quickly change the indentation of the paragraph at the position of the insertion point.*

SEE ALSO: *Margins; Paragraph; Ruler; Tabs*

Labels

Create mailing and other types of labels in both Access and Word. In Access, use the Mailing Label Report Wizard to design the labels. In Word, use the options on the Labels tab in the Envelopes And Labels dialog box to create one label or an entire page of the same label, or Mail Merge to create different labels using the records in a database.

Creating Labels in Access

To create mailing labels with Access' Mailing Label Wizard:

1. Select the Report tab in the Database window.

2. Choose New to display the New Report dialog box.

LABELS

3. Highlight the name of the table or query that contains the records to be used to create the text of the labels in the Select A Table/Query drop-down list.

4. Choose Report Wizards to display the Report Wizards dialog box. Select Mailing Label in the list box, and then choose OK.

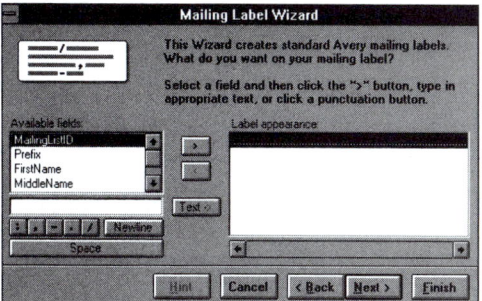

5. The Mailing Label Wizard dialog box appears. Select the field whose data is to appear first on the label in the Available Fields list box, and then click on the > button to insert it in the Label Appearance area.

TIP: *To remove the last field, text, punctuation, or other character inserted in the Label appearance area, click on the < button.*

6. If necessary, type text in the text box below the Available Fields list box, and then click on the Text button to insert the text in the next position in the Label Appearance area.

7. Click on any of the buttons below the Available Fields list box to insert the corresponding character after the field name in the Label Appearance area. For example, click on Space to insert a space character after the last field inserted.

8. Repeat steps 4 through 6 to insert each field in the necessary position in the Label Appearance area, and then select Next.

207

COMMAND AND FEATURE REFERENCE

9. Select the field on which to sort the labels in the Available Fields list box, and then click on the > button to insert it in the Sort Order list box.

10. Repeat step 8 for each field on which to sort the labels, and then choose Next.

11. Select the type and dimensions for the label in the list box. If necessary, choose English or Metric as the Unit Of Measure, and choose Sheet Feed or Continuous as the Label Type. Then select Next.

12. Select the font, size, color, and attributes for the label text, and then select Next.

13. Select whether to display the labels as they will appear when printed, or to change the label design. If necessary, select the Open Cue Cards check box to display the steps for the procedure.

14. Select Finish to display the labels or switch to Design view.

15. If the labels are displayed, click on the Save button on the Form Design toolbar or select File ➤ Save (Ctrl+S) to save the report. If the labels are displayed in Design view, save the report after any changes are made.

Creating a Label in Word

Word allows you to print one label or a page of labels with the same text. Select one of Word's built-in label definitions, which are based on many different Avery label types and sizes, or customize a label definition to use with another brand of labels whose dimensions are not among those in the list.

Set up the printer on which the labels will be printed before you select the type of label. The selected printer driver determines how the labels will be set up and printed.

LABELS

To create a label in Word:

1. Select the text in a document to be printed, and then choose Tools ➤ Envelopes And Labels to display the Envelopes And Labels dialog box.

2. Select the Labels tab. The selected text appears in the Address text box.

NOTE: *If necessary, type the text that is to appear on the label in the Address text box.*

3. Choose any of the following options on the Labels tab:

- Select the Use Return Address check box to display the default return address in the Address text box when you want to print it on a single label or on each label on the page of labels.

NOTE: *If you type a new return address in the Address text box and select Print or New Document, choose Yes to confirm that it is the default return address.*

- Select the Delivery Point Bar Code check box to include the POSTNET bar code on a mailing label.

- In the Print area, select Full Page Of The Same Label to create a table of labels. Or, select Single Label, and then specify the number of the row and column in which to place the label text in the Row and Column text boxes.

- Choose New Document to place a full sheet of labels in a table in a new document, which can then be saved as a file.

COMMAND AND FEATURE REFERENCE

> **TIP:** *Labels are automatically created with the Normal style. To change the format of the text on the label, change the Normal style in the document for which the labels are being created.*

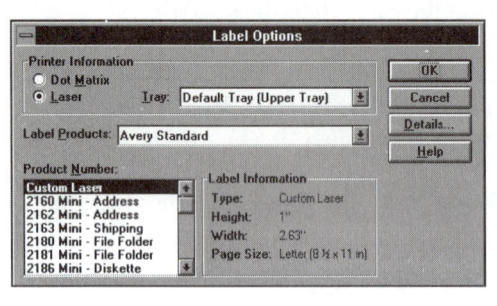

4. Click on the Label area, or select Options to display the Label Options dialog box.

5. Select any of the following label and printer specifications, and choose OK in the dialog box:

- Select Dot Matrix or Laser to define the type of printer in the Printer Information area. If Laser is selected, highlight the method used to feed the labels to the printer in the Tray drop-down list.

- Highlight the kind of label being used in the Label Products drop-down list.

- Select the label to use in the Product Number list box. A description of the label appears in the Label Information area.

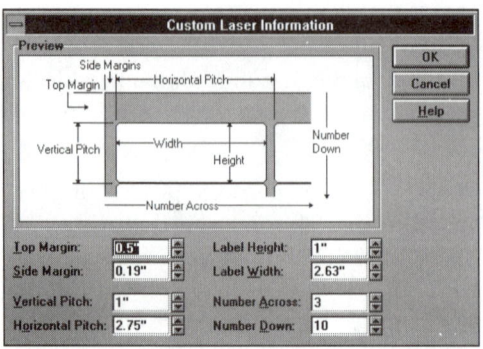

6. If necessary, click on the Label Information area or select Details to display the Custom *Printer* Information dialog box.

LABELS

7. Select any of the following options to customize the selected label, and then choose OK:

- In the Top Margin text box, specify the distance between the top edge of the page and the top edge of the labels in the first row for a page of laser printer labels. The top margin for dot matrix labels should be 0.

- In the Side Margin text box, specify the distance between the left edge of the page and the left edge of the labels in the first column.

- In the Vertical Pitch text box, specify the distance between the top edge of one label and the top edge of the label below.

- In the Horizontal Pitch text box, specify the distance between the left edge of one label and the left edge of the label on its right.

- In the Label Height text box, specify the distance between the top and bottom edges of the label.

- In the Label Width text box, specify the distance between the left and right edges of the label.

- In the Number Across text box, specify the number of labels in a row on the page.

- In the Number Down text box, specify the number of labels in a column on the page.

8. If necessary, choose OK again in the Label Options dialog box.

9. Select Print to print the single label or the page of labels.

SEE ALSO: *Envelopes; File Management; Form; Mail Merge; Print; Report; Style*

COMMAND AND FEATURE REFERENCE

Line Spacing

The line spacing in a paragraph defines the height of each line in the text. The height of a line depends on the font used in the paragraph. For example, if a 12-point font were selected, the height of a single spaced line would be just over 12 points, so some white space, called *leading*, is included above the text and below the baseline of the text above. The height of a 12-point double-spaced line is about 24 points. Set the line spacing to adjust the amount of white space that appears above the text in each line.

The line spacing in a line that contains an oversized character is adjusted to accommodate the character. Adjust the line spacing so that all the lines are evenly spaced in the paragraph.

By default, Word's line spacing is set for single spaced lines. Set the line spacing to a preset definition, or customize the line spacing for a document.

Changing the Line Spacing in a Paragraph

To change the line spacing of the paragraph that contains the insertion point:

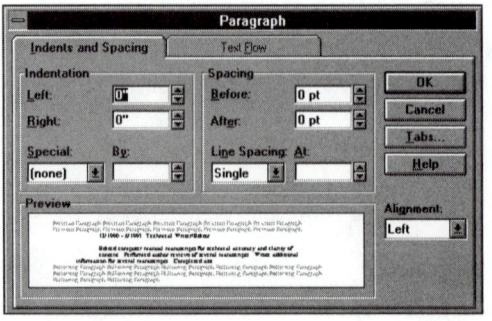

1. Choose Format ➤ Paragraph, and then choose the Indents And Spacing tab.

2. Select one of the following line spacing options in the Li$\underline{n}$e Spacing drop-down list in the Spacing area:

- Choose Single (Ctrl+1) to adjust the line height to the tallest character in the line.

- Select 1.5 Lines (Ctrl+5) to adjust the line height to 1.5 times that of single spacing.

- Select Double (Ctrl+2) to double the line height of single spacing.

- Choose At Least, and then specify the minimum line height in the $\underline{A}$t text box.

- To prevent Word from adjusting the line height, choose Exactly, and then specify the exact line height in the $\underline{A}$t text box.

- Select Multiple to adjust the line spacing to a specific multiple of single spaced text, and then specify the number of lines (3 is the default) in the $\underline{A}$t text box.

3. Choose OK in the Paragraph dialog box.

SEE ALSO: *Drop Cap; Paragraph*

Link

A link between two files occurs when the information regarding the location of the data in a source file is inserted in a client file. The client file stores the location of the source of the data, not the actual data in the source. When data or files are linked, the data in the source document can be changed, and then automatically updated in the destination (client) document.

COMMAND AND FEATURE REFERENCE

Linking Data

The source file must be saved before data in it can be linked to another file.

To link data:

1. In the source file, select the data to be linked, and then click on the Copy button on the Standard toolbar, or select Edit ➤ Copy (Ctrl+C).

2. Activate the client file, and position the insertion point or activate the cell in which the link is to be established.

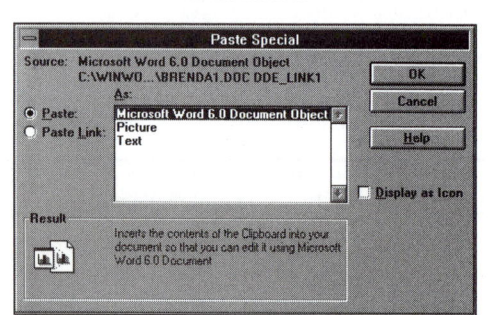

3. Select Edit ➤ Paste Special in the client file to display the Paste Special dialog box for the selected data.

> **NOTE:** *In Excel, if you are linking selected data from a source worksheet into a client worksheet, the Paste Special dialog box that appears does not contain a path, but does contain various options to use for pasting data. To establish a link with the selected data, select the cell or range in the client worksheet, choose All (the default) in the Paste area, and then choose Paste Link.*

4. The path and file name of the selected data appear in the Source area of the dialog box. Select Paste Link to insert the selected data into the client file as a link.

5. Select one of the following options as the paste method in the As list box. An explanation of each option for pasting the link appears in the Result area of the Paste Special dialog box.

> ***Application Name* Object**   The Clipboard contents are linked to the document as a graphic.
>
> **Formatted Text (RTF)**   The Clipboard contents are linked to the document as text data with its current formatting.
>
> **Unformatted Text**   The contents of the Clipboard are linked to the document as unformatted text.
>
> **Picture**   The Clipboard contents, such as those from a .WMF file, are linked to the document as a graphic.
>
> **Bitmap**   The contents of the Clipboard, such as those from a .BMP file, are linked to the document as a bitmap.

6. To make the link appear as an icon in the client file, select the Display As Icon check box.

7. Optionally, select Change Icon, select any of the following options in the Change Icon dialog box, and then choose OK to change the icon displayed in the client file:

- Choose one of the icons in the Icon list box to appear in the client file.

- If necessary, type the text that is to appear below the icon in the client file in the Caption text box.

- Select Browse to search for other files that contain additional icons from which to choose. The name of the file that contains

COMMAND AND FEATURE REFERENCE

the icons displayed in the Icon list box appears in the File Name text box in the dialog box.

8. Choose OK in the Paste Special dialog box.

> **NOTE:** *A link in a Word document is stored as a field code. Changes made to the formatting of the item in the source are not updated if the *MERGEFORMAT switch is in the field.*

Select Paste in the Paste Special dialog box to paste the selection into the client file in one of the formats listed in step 5, above.

Linking a File

To insert a link to all the data in a server file into the client file:

1. Position the insertion point in the client document in which the link is to be inserted, choose Insert ➤ Object, and then select the Create From File tab in the Object dialog box.

> **NOTE:** *In Access, a link can be established between a file and a control in a form or report that is displayed in Design view. Select the control, and then choose Edit ➤ Insert Object to display the Insert Object dialog box.*

2. Select the name of the file to be linked to the client file in the File Name list box.

> **TIP:** *If necessary, choose Find File to display the Find File dialog box, Browse to display the Browse dialog box, or Network to display the Disk Connect dialog box when you must search for the file to link.*

3. Select the Link or Link To File check box to link the data in the source to the client file.

4. To make the link appear as an icon in the client file, select the Display As Icon check box.

5. Optionally, select Change Icon to select a different icon to display in the client file, and then select OK.

6. Select OK in the Object or Insert Object dialog box.

To insert the source file without linking it to the client file, clear the Link or Link To File check box in step 3 above.

Modifying a Link

There are several ways to edit a link–break an established link, reconnect a link to a file that has been moved or renamed, store the link as a picture in the client file document, specify how the link will be updated, update the link yourself, or lock a link in the client file.

To modify a link:

1. Activate the file that contains the link, and then choose Edit ➤ Links to display the Links dialog box.

2. Choose any of the following options, or use the information displayed in the following items, to edit a link:

- The Source File or Links list box displays the names and paths of all the links in the active document. Select the link to be modified, and then perform the necessary edits. Select multiple links in the list box by holding down the Ctrl key as you click on additional links.

- The Item column in the Source File or Links list box displays the name or range of the item that is linked.

- The Type column displays the name of the source application.

COMMAND AND FEATURE REFERENCE

- The Status column displays the method used to update the link. In the Update area, choose <u>A</u>utomatic to update the link whenever the source is changed, or <u>M</u>anual to manually update the link selected in the <u>S</u>ource File or <u>L</u>inks list box.

- Choose <u>U</u>pdate Now to update all the links highlighted in the <u>S</u>ource File or <u>L</u>inks list box.

- To edit the data in the selected link, choose <u>O</u>pen or <u>O</u>pen Source to open the source document. Or, select the linked item in the client file, and then choose <u>E</u>dit ➤ <u>O</u>bject to open the source document of the selected link.

TIP: *Any edits you make to linked data in a Word document will be lost when the links are updated. Highlight the links in the client document so you will not edit them. To highlight the source of the links in a Word source document, display bookmarks in the document.*

- Highlight a link lost when the source was moved or renamed, and then choose Change Source to display the Change Links or Change Source dialog box. Type the path and name of the file to link in the <u>C</u>hange Links To or File Name text box, and then choose OK.

- Select <u>B</u>reak Link to break the link highlighted in the <u>S</u>ource File or <u>L</u>inks list box. The data remains in the file, but it can no longer be updated. A broken link cannot be reconnected.

- Select the <u>L</u>ocked check box to prevent a selected link from being updated.

LINK L

> **TROUBLESHOOTING**
>
> ## Updating Links in Excel and Word
>
> Do you want to display or print the most recent data available, even if the links to the file are manual links?
>
> By default, Excel displays a message box asking if automatic links are to be updated. To update the links without displaying the message box, choose Tools ➤ Options, select the Edit tab, clear the Ask To Update Automatic Links check box, and then choose OK.
>
> You can have Word automatically update manual links to all documents when they are printed. Select Tools ➤ Options, and then choose the Print tab. Select the Update Links check box in the Printing Options area of the dialog box, and then choose OK.

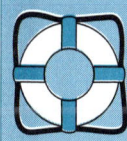

- Select the Save Picture In Document check box (selected by default) to save the link as a picture of the linked data in a Word document rather than the actual information. If the link is a graphic, clear the check box to reduce the size of the client file. However, the link will take longer to display because the picture must be created after the data in the source file is interpreted.

3. Choose OK in the Links dialog box.

SEE ALSO: *Bookmark; Control; Field Code; File Management; Find File; Object Linking and Embedding; Print*

COMMAND AND FEATURE REFERENCE

Macro

Create or record macros to automate tasks that you perform regularly. In Access, macros can be assigned to forms, reports, sections, and controls. Macros can be assigned to menus, shortcut keys, or toolbars for easy access in Excel and Word.

Use Access's Macro Builder to create a macro in a form or report in Design view, or create a macro in the Macro pane of the Database window. Use Excel's Visual Basic toolbar and Word's Macro Record and Macro toolbars to record a macro or to edit a recorded or written macro.

NOTE: *Each Microsoft Office application comes with many useful macros already built into it and assigned to toolbar or button bar buttons.*

Access's macros are stored as database objects in the database file. In Excel, macros can be stored in the workbook in which you intend to use them, or in the Personal Macro Workbook, so they will always be available. Word's macros are stored in the NORMAL.DOT template by default, and can be assigned to a toolbar, menu, or key sequence.

Adding Conditions to Macros in Access

Add *conditions* to the actions in a macro that should only be carried out if certain requirements are met. A condition is a logical expression that returns a value of either true or false. The actions in the macro are carried out differently depending on the results of the condition.

MACRO

To add conditions to macros in Access:

1. Click on the Macro tab in the Database window, highlight the macro to which conditions are to be added, and then choose Design.

2. Click on the Conditions button on the Macro toolbar, or choose View ➤ Conditions to display the Condition column in the Macro window.

3. Click in the Condition column beside the action to which a condition is to be added, and then type the condition. Or, click on the Build button on the Macro toolbar to display the Expression Builder dialog box, and then assemble the condition.

4. Click on the Save button on the Macro toolbar, or choose File ➤ Save (Ctrl+S) to save the macro.

To carry out adjacent actions that meet the same condition in a macro, make sure the actions appear one after the other in the Action column. Enter the condition in the Condition column beside the first action, and enter . . . (ellipsis) in the row below the condition (beside the second and any subsequent actions). When the macro is run, the action beside a condition that is false is ignored, and the next different condition (without an ellipsis) is evaluated.

Creating and Running an Access Macro

Create macros as database objects in Access to make forms, reports, tables, and other database objects work together. For example, create a macro to print a monthly summary report or to open a report while you are working in Form view. Macros can also be used within other macros.

TIP: *While you are designing a form, attach a macro to a button in the form. To run the macro, just click on the button while you are in Form view.*

COMMAND AND FEATURE REFERENCE

The macros you create as database objects are written in Access Basic. You can also type Access Basic instructions in macros.

Access database macros consist of *actions*, the events that the macro is to perform, and *action arguments*, the specific information that is necessary to carry out each action.

To create and run an Access macro:

1. Click on the Macro tab in the Database window to display the Macro pane, and then choose New, or select File ➤ New ➤ Macro to display both the Macro window and the Macro toolbar (below the Form Design toolbar in the Microsoft Access window).

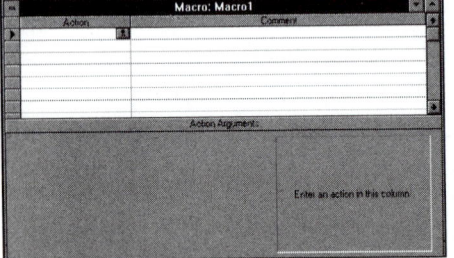

2. Select the first action for the macro in the Action drop-down list. Or, display the Database window beside the Macro window, and drag a table, form, query, report, or macro from the Database window into a row in the Action list in the Macro window. An action is automatically added to open the table, form, query, or report, or to run the macro.

TIP: *To describe the purpose of a macro, leave the first row in the Action column blank, and type the description in the first row in the Comment column. Begin the macro in the second row in the Action/Comment pane of the Macro window.*

3. Click on the first argument for the action in the Action Arguments pane of the Macro window, and then type or select the appropriate option for the argument in its drop-down list. A brief explanation of the current argument appears in the area beside the arguments.

MACRO

> **TROUBLESHOOTING**
>
> ## Renaming Database Objects
>
> Do you want to change the name you assigned to a database object? In Access, tables, queries, forms, reports, macros, and modules are all database objects, and each is saved to a specific name. To rename a database object, highlight the object in the appropriate pane of the Database window, and then choose File ➤ Rename to display the Rename *Database Object* dialog box. Type the new name in the *Object Name* text box, and then choose OK.
>
> A database object name can consist of up to 64 characters, including letters, numbers, and spaces. Do not use . (period), ! (exclamation mark),' (backquote character), [ ] (brackets), leading spaces (spaces before any other characters), or ASCII characters 0 through 32 in the name of any database object.

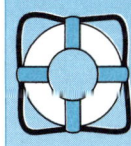

NOTE: *Press F6 to move the insertion point between the Action/Comment pane and the Action Arguments pane in the Macro window.*

4. Repeat step 3 for each argument for the first action.

5. Optionally, type an explanation for the selected action on the corresponding line in the Comment area of the Macro Window.

6. Repeat steps 2 through 5 to enter each step in the macro.

7. Click on the Save button on the Macro toolbar or select File ➤ Save (Ctrl+S) to display the Save As dialog box. Type a name for the macro in the Macro Name text box, and then choose OK to save the macro as a database object.

COMMAND AND FEATURE REFERENCE

8. To run the macro, click on the Run button on the Macro toolbar or choose <u>M</u>acro ➤ <u>R</u>un. To run a macro in the active Database window, highlight the name of the macro, and then choose <u>R</u>un.

The order in which the actions appear in the Macro Window is the order in which the actions are carried out when the macro is run. If the actions do not appear in the correct order, click on the row selector to select the entire row containing the action, point to the center of the row selector, and drag the row to a different position in the list.

To ensure that each action entered in a database macro takes place in the correct order:

1. Click on the Single Step button on the Macro toolbar or choose <u>M</u>acro ➤ <u>S</u>ingle Step, and then click on the Run button or choose <u>M</u>acro ➤ <u>R</u>un. The Macro Single Step dialog box appears with the name of the first action and its arguments.

2. Choose <u>S</u>tep to perform the first action and display the name of the next action, <u>H</u>alt to stop the macro at the current step, or <u>C</u>ontinue to run the rest of the macro normally.

3. If the action cannot be carried out, a message box appears. Select <u>H</u>alt, and then correct the arguments for the action in the Macro window.

To edit a macro, click on the Macro tab in the Database window, highlight the name of the macro in the Macro pane, and then choose <u>D</u>esign. Follow the steps used when creating a macro, above, to add new actions on blank lines in the Macro window. If necessary, move the actions to the correct position in the Action list, and then save the changes you made to the macro.

MACRO M

> ### TROUBLESHOOTING
>
> ### Changing the Display of the Macro Window
>
> Do you want to change Access' default Macro window so that it appears with the Macro Name and Condition columns as well as the Action and Comment columns each time you create a new macro? Choose View ➤ Options, select Macro Design in the Category list box, change the Show Macro Names Column and Show Conditions Column options to Yes in the Items area, and then choose OK.

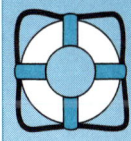

TIP: *To insert a blank row above the row that contains the insertion point in the Action/Comment pane of the Macro window, choose Edit ➤ Insert Row. To delete the row that contains the insertion point, choose Edit ➤ Delete Row. Any characters in the row will also be deleted.*

To delete an action, click on the row selector, and then choose Edit ➤ Delete (Del) or Edit ➤ Delete Row.

Creating a Macro Group in Access

Create a *macro group* to collect a set of related macros in the same Macro window (database macro). Each macro in a group can run independently of the other macros in a group.

A macro group is a named database object. Each macro in the group is also assigned a unique name.

To create a macro group:

1. Create a macro, as described earlier in "Creating and Running an Access Macro."

225

COMMAND AND FEATURE REFERENCE

2. Click on the Macro Names button on the Macro toolbar, or choose View ➤ Macro Names to display the Macro Name column in the Action/Comment pane of the Macro window.

3. Click in the row in the Macro Name column beside the macro's first action, and then type a name for the macro.

4. Repeat steps 1 and 3 as necessary for each macro in the macro group.

5. Click on the Save button on the Macro toolbar, or choose File ➤ Save (Ctrl+S) to save the macro group to a single named database object.

6. To run a macro in a macro group, type the name of the macro group followed by a . (period), and then type the name of the macro (*MacroGroupName.MacroName*) in any location in which you can enter the name of a macro to run.

Creating and Running a Macro in an Access Form or Report

Use Macro Builder to attach a macro to a form, report, or control, and have the macro run automatically when a certain event occurs. For example, attach a macro to a command button in a form, so that when you click on the button, the macro runs.

To create and run a macro in an Access form or report:

1. Display the form or report in Design view.

2. Click on the Properties button on the Form Design or Report Design toolbar, or choose View ➤ Properties to display the properties sheet for the form or report.

3. If necessary, click on the control to which a macro is to be attached to change the display of the properties sheet, and then select Event Properties in the drop-down list.

MACRO M

4. Click on the property in the properties sheet to which a macro is to be attached, and then click on the Build button beside the property's option area to display the Choose Builder dialog box.

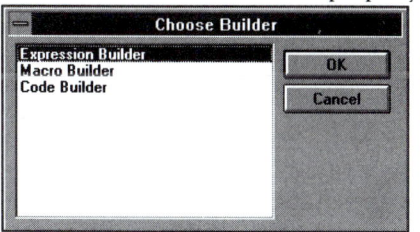

Choose Builder dialog box options:
- Expression Builder
- Macro Builder
- Code Builder

TIP: *To attach an existing macro to the form, report, or control, select the name of the macro in the property's drop-down list.*

5. Highlight Macro Builder, and then choose OK. The Save As dialog box appears.

6. Type a name for the macro in the Macro Name text box, and then choose OK to display the Macro window.

7. Create a macro to be attached to the form, report, or control using the steps outlined above in "Creating and Running an Access Macro," and then click on the Save button on the Macro toolbar to save the new macro.

The macro will automatically run when the event occurs in Form or Report view. Or, you can run the macro independently by selecting it in the Macro pane of the Database window and choosing Run.

Recording and Running an Excel Macro

Create macros to perform tasks that you often repeat in Excel. You can record often-used commands and keystrokes with Excel's Macro Recorder, or write macros in Visual Basic, Excel's macro language.

COMMAND AND FEATURE REFERENCE

> **TIP:** When you are recording a macro in Excel, display the Visual Basic toolbar to make your work easier. The Visual Basic toolbar appears automatically when you edit a macro.

For a macro to run, it must be in a *module*–a special sheet in a workbook for storing macros–in an open workbook file. To insert a module before the active worksheet in a workbook, click on the Insert Module button on the Visual Basic toolbar or select Insert ➤ Macro ➤ Module.

> **NOTE:** By default, the Macro Recorder uses relative references while recording macros. Choose Tools ➤ Record Macro ➤ Use Relative References to toggle on the use of absolute references while recording a macro.

A macro can be stored in the current workbook, so it is available whenever you are working in it; in a new workbook, which you must remember to open before you use the macro; or in Excel's Personal Macro Workbook, which is always open (but hidden), and which Excel controls automatically. If you create or edit a macro in the Personal Macro Workbook, Excel automatically displays a message asking if you want to save any changes you made to the workbook file (PERSONAL.XLS) when you exit Excel.

> **NOTE:** To display the Personal Macro Workbook (after you have created a macro in it), choose Window ➤ Unhide, select PERSONAL.XLS in the Unhide Workbook list box, and then choose OK.

To record and run an Excel macro:

1. Click on the Record Macro button on the Visual Basic toolbar, or choose Tools ➤ Record

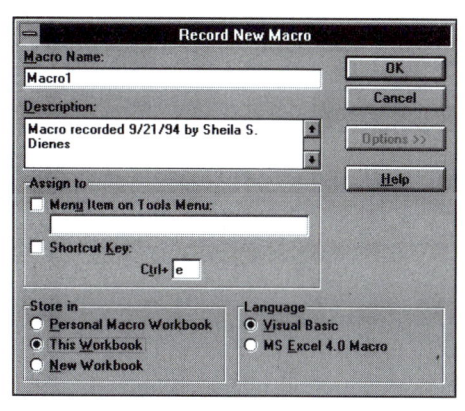

MACRO

Macro ➤ Record New Macro to display the Record New Macro dialog box.

2. Select Options to enlarge the Record New Macro dialog box.

3. Optionally, type a descriptive name for the macro in the Macro Name text box, and a brief description of the macro's function in the Description text box.

4. Optionally, select the Menu Item On Tools Menu check box, and then type a name for the macro to appear on the Tools drop-down menu so it can be selected.

5. To assign a shortcut key to use to run the macro, select the Shortcut Key check box and type a letter in the Ctrl+ text box.

TIP: *Create a toolbar for your macros, and then assign each macro to the toolbar. Click on the corresponding button on your macro toolbar to run the macro.*

6. In the Store In area, select Personal Macro Workbook, This Workbook, or New Workbook as the location in which to store the macro.

7. If necessary, choose Visual Basic (the default) or MS Excel 4.0 Macro in the Language area.

8. Choose OK in the Record New Macro dialog box.

9. Perform the actions and select the commands necessary for the macro, and then click on the Stop Macro button on the Visual Basic toolbar or choose Tools ➤ Record Macro ➤ Stop Recording.

COMMAND AND FEATURE REFERENCE

10. To run the macro, click on the Run Macro button on the Visual Basic toolbar, select Tools ➤ *Macro Name*, press Ctrl+*letter*, or click on the toolbar button to which the macro is assigned.

To edit a macro, you must display it on your screen. If the macro is stored in the Personal Macro Workbook, you must unhide the workbook before you can edit the macro.

- Choose Tools ➤ Macro to display the Macro dialog box, highlight the name of the macro in the Macro Name/Reference list box, and then choose Edit to display the module that contains the macro.

- Position the insertion point where you want to begin recording in a macro module, and choose Tools ➤ Record Macro ➤ Mark Position For Recording. Then choose Tools ➤ Record Macro ➤ Record At Mark to start the Macro Recorder.

- To delete a macro, choose Tools ➤ Macro, highlight the name of the macro in the Macro Name/Reference list box, and then choose Delete.

- Optionally, to display a macro that is assigned to a toolbar button, right-click on the toolbar, and then choose Customize in the shortcut menu to display the Customize dialog box. Then right-click on the toolbar button, choose Assign Macro in the shortcut menu to display the Assign Macro dialog box, select the name of the macro in the Macro Name/Reference list box, and choose Edit.

- To add informational text for the macro on the status bar, choose Tools ➤ Macro, select Options to display the Macro Options dialog box, and then type the text that is to appear on the status bar when you point to the toolbar button or highlight the menu item assigned to the macro.

MACRO

Use any of the following buttons on the Visual Basic toolbar to help you edit a displayed macro:

Click on the Menu Editor button or choose Tools ➤ Menu Editor to display the Menu Editor dialog box when you want to add a macro to a menu, change the current menu commands, create new menus or menu bars, and edit or delete existing menus or menu bars.

Click on the Object Browser button or choose View ➤ Object Browser (F2) to display the Object Browser dialog box when you want to display a list of the objects, procedures, methods, and properties currently loaded in Excel or in the active workbook.

To display the Debug window (and any errors in the active macro) and to place the module in Break mode, click on the Step Macro button or choose View ➤ Debug Window (Ctrl+G).

Click on the Resume Macro button to resume stepping through a macro that is paused to display an error message.

Click on the Stop Macro button to stop recording a macro, or stop a macro that is running.

Click on the Toggle Breakpoint button or choose Run ➤ Toggle Breakpoint (F9) to insert or delete a *breakpoint* in the position of the insertion point. A breakpoint changes the macro to Break mode, and halts the macro's execution. Select Run ➤ Clear All Break-points to remove all the breakpoints in a macro.

Select a *watch expression*, an expression that contains variables that you define using Tools ➤ Add Watch. Then click on the Instant Watch button or choose Tools ➤ Instant Watch (Shift+F9) to display its current value.

COMMAND AND FEATURE REFERENCE

To run the next line of Visual Basic code in a macro and then return to Break mode, click on the Step Into button or choose Run ➤ Step Into (F8).

To run the next line of code and other procedures before returning to Break mode, click on the Step Over button or choose Run ➤ Step Over (Shift+F8).

Recording and Running a Word Macro

Record the commands and keystrokes used to perform a task you often repeat while working in Word. Use the mouse to select menu commands or to scroll while recording a macro, but not to select text or move the insertion point in the document window.

As you record a macro, Word uses the WordBasic programming language to compile the macro. You can also use WordBasic to create more complex macros in Word, including instructions that cannot be recorded.

> **TIP:** *If you record something in a macro accidentally, immediately click on the Undo button on the Standard toolbar or select Edit ➤ Undo Ctrl+Z. The undone action will not play back when the macro is run.*

To record and run a Word macro:

1. Select Tools ➤ Macro, and then choose the Record button in the Macro dialog box, or double-click on REC on the status bar to display the Record Macro dialog box.

2. Type a name for the macro in the Record Macro Name text box, and a description in the Description text box.

3. If necessary, select All Documents (Normal.dot) or the active template in the Make Macro Available To drop-down list as the location to store the macro.

MACRO

4. Optionally, select Toolbars, Menus, or Keyboard as the method to access the macro in the Assign Macro To area, and then perform the steps necessary to assign the macro.

5. Choose OK in the Record Macro dialog box to display the Macro Record toolbar. While you are recording, the mouse pointer appears with a graphic of a cassette tape.

6. Select the commands and type the keystrokes necessary for the macro.

7. Click on the Stop button on the Macro Record toolbar, or double-click on REC on the status bar to stop recording the macro. Or, choose Tools ➤ Macro and select Stop Recording in the Macro dialog box.

8. To run a macro, highlight the name of the macro in the Macro Name list box and choose Run, or click on the toolbar button, press the shortcut keys, or select the menu item to which the macro was assigned.

9. If necessary, select Close in the Macro dialog box to return to your document.

To temporarily stop recording the commands and keystrokes in a macro, click on the Pause button on the Macro Record toolbar. Click on the Pause button again when you are ready to resume recording your macro.

To delete a macro, select Tools ➤ Macro to display the Macro dialog box, highlight the name of the macro in the Macro Name list box, and then choose Delete. Choose Yes to confirm the deletion.

To edit a macro you have recorded (or written using WordBasic), choose Tools ➤ Macro to display the Macro dialog box, highlight the name of the macro in the Macro Name list box, and then choose Edit. The macro appears in a document window below the Macro toolbar.

COMMAND AND FEATURE REFERENCE

Use any of the following buttons to help perform the edits, and then click on the Save button on the Standard toolbar or choose File ➤ Save Template to save the macro to its current name:

NOTE: *To save the text of a macro in a file that is separate from the template file that contains the macro, choose File ➤ Save Copy As, type a name in the File Name text box, and then choose OK in the Save As dialog box.*

Select the macro to be edited in the Active Macro drop-down list. Only the names of currently open (for editing) macros appear in the list.

Click on the Record button to begin recording a new macro.

Position the insertion point where a command is to be inserted in the active macro, click on the Record Next Command button, and then select the command to be inserted in the macro. The command is inserted in the active macro document and simultaneously carried out.

TIP: *To insert new commands or actions in the active macro, display a regular document window (so most of the commands will be available), and then use the buttons on the Macro toolbar to edit the active macro. Use Window ➤ DocumentNumber to switch back and forth between the macro document and the regular document to check on the macro's progress as you edit it.*

Click on the Start button (Alt+Shift+S) to run the active macro.

To run the macro and highlight each step as it is performed, click on the Trace button (Alt+Shift+R).

Click on the Continue button (Alt+Shift+O) to resume running a paused macro. When a macro is paused, the Continue button appears depressed.

MACRO

Click on the Stop button to stop running the active macro or to stop recording a new macro.

Click on the Step button (Alt+Shift+E) to highlight the first instruction in a macro. Click on the Step button again to carry out the highlighted instruction, and then highlight the next macro instruction. With the Step button, each step in subroutines is also highlighted.

Click on the Step Subs button (Alt+Shift+U) to highlight the first instruction in the main subroutine of the active macro. Click on the Step Subs button again to carry out the first instruction and highlight the next instruction in the main subroutine. With the Step Subs button, all instructions in the subroutines of the main subroutine are ignored.

To display the Macro Variables dialog box to change values of the variables in a paused macro, click on the Show Variables button (Alt+Shift+V).

Click on the Add/Remove REM button to add or remove REM at the beginning of a statement in the active macro. Statements that contain REM are ignored when the macro is run.

Click on the Macro button or choose Tools ➤ Macro to display the Macro dialog box.

Click on the Dialog Editor button to start and run the Dialog Editor, or to activate it if it is already running. Use the Dialog Editor to create dialog boxes for your macros.

SEE ALSO: *AutoCorrect; AutoText; Control; Control Properties; Form; Formula; Report; Table; Templates; Toolbars; Window*

COMMAND AND FEATURE REFERENCE

Mail

Use Microsoft Mail to create and send a message, or to send an online Access database table, form, query, or report, Excel workbook, PowerPoint presentation, or Word document to other people for their comments or revisions, or to fill in a form. The people to whom an online file is sent must have the same Microsoft Office application, and Mail or a compatible program.

Creating a Mail Message

To create a Mail message:

1. Click on the Microsoft Mail button on the Microsoft Office Manager toolbar to open Mail.

2. If necessary, type your password in the Password text box, and then choose OK.

3. Click on the Compose button on the button bar, or choose Mail ➤ Compose Note (Ctrl+N) to open the Send Note window.

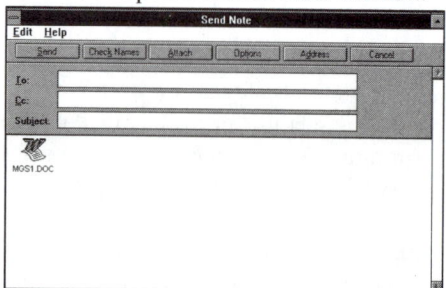

4. Type the name of the person who is to receive the message in the To text box. Or, select Address to display the Address dialog box, highlight the name of the person to whom the file is to be sent in the Directory list box, and then choose To in the Add area.

5. Repeat step 4 for each person to whom the file is to be sent.

6. Highlight the name of the person in the Directory list box to whom to send a copy of the file, and then choose Cc. Repeat this step for each person who is to receive a copy.

TIP: *You can also type the name(s) of people to whom a copy of the file is to be sent in the Cc text box. If you type names in the To or Cc text boxes, select Check Names in the Send Note window to have Mail make sure each name is correctly entered and appears in your Address Book.*

7. Choose OK in the Address dialog box.

8. Type the subject of the message in the Subject text box.

9. Click in the message area, and then type the text of your message.

10. Choose Send to send the message (and a file that is attached to the message).

To attach a file to the message before it is sent, select Attach to display the Attach dialog box, highlight the name of the file in the File Name list box, and then choose Attach. Select Close to return to the Send Note window.

To change the default options for the message, select Options in the Send Note window to display the Options dialog box. Select the Return Receipt check box to receive a message when the message is opened. Select the Save Sent Messages check box (selected by default) to save a copy of the message in your Sent Mail folder. Choose the High, Normal, or Low priority option for the message in the Priority area (for the recipient's information), and then choose OK.

COMMAND AND FEATURE REFERENCE

Receiving a Mail Message

Electronic mail that is sent to you appears by default in your Inbox folder each time you open Mail.

To open a message you have received, double-click on the icon to the left of the message in the list of messages. Or, highlight the description of the message in the list, and then choose File ➤ Open.

Choose any of the following options on the button bar:

To display the contents of the next message in the list, click on the View Next Message button or choose View ➤ Next (Ctrl+>).

To redisplay the contents of the previous message in the list, click on the View Previous Message button or choose View ➤ Previous (Ctrl+<).

To send a reply to only the sender of a message you received, click on the Reply To Sender button or choose Mail ➤ Reply (Ctrl+R), type your reply in the message area of the Send window, and then choose Send.

To send a reply to both the sender and to each name in the To and Cc text boxes, click on the Reply To All button or choose Mail ➤ Reply To All (Ctrl+A). Then type your reply in the message area of the Send window and choose Send.

To send the open or highlighted message to someone else, click on the Forward Message button or choose Mail ➤ Forward (Ctrl+F). Then specify the names to whom the message is to be forwarded in the To text box, type any comments in the message area of the FW: *Subject* window, and choose Send.

To move the open or highlighted message to a different folder, click on the Move Message button or choose File ➤ Move (Ctrl+M) to display the Move Message dialog box. If necessary, select Private

MAIL

Folders or Shared Folders in the Type area to display the name of the folder to which the message is to be moved. Then, highlight the name of the folder in the Move To list box and choose OK.

TIP: *If necessary, select New in the Move Message dialog box to create a new folder of the type specified in the Type area.*

To delete an open or selected message, click on the Delete Message button or choose File ➤ Delete (Ctrl+D).

WARNING: *A deleted message cannot be undeleted! Make certain you do not need a message before you delete it.*

Sending an Online Document

You can choose how the file is sent–to each person simultaneously, or to selected people in a specific order.

With Mail running, follow these steps to send a file to several people:

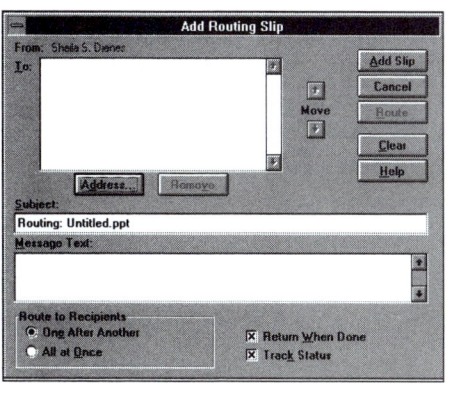

1. Activate the file to be sent online, and then choose File ➤ Add Routing Slip. Your name appears in the From area of the Routing Slip or Add Routing Slip dialog box.

2. To select the people to whom to send the document, choose Address, highlight the name of a person in the Directory list box, and choose Add. Repeat this step for each person who is to receive the file, and then select OK in the Address dialog box.

COMMAND AND FEATURE REFERENCE

> **NOTE:** *To delete a name in the To list box, highlight the name and select Remove.*

3. If necessary, use the ↑ and ↓ Move buttons to arrange the names in the list in the order in which you want the document to be routed to each recipient.

4. If necessary, type the subject of the file or its name in the Subject text box.

5. Type any messages or instructions to the file's recipients in the Message Text text box.

6. In the Route To Recipients area, choose One After Another to send the document to the people in the order in which they are listed in the To list box, or All At Once to simultaneously send a copy of the document to all the people in the To list box.

7. If the file was sent to everyone simultaneously, select the Return When Done check box to have the file returned to you when the last person finishes and selects File ➤ Send.

8. Or, if the file was sent individually to each person in the order in which they are listed in the To list box, select the Track Status check box to receive a message when the file is forwarded to the next person on the list.

> **TIP:** *In Word, select Revisions, Annotations, or Forms in the Protect For drop-down list to protect the document from any changes to its text.*

9. Select Route to send the document to each person listed in the To list box.

- ◆ To return to the active file in order to edit it before sending it, choose Add Slip in the Add Routing Slip dialog box.

- To make changes to the routing slip, choose File ➤ Edit Routing Slip to display a dialog box similar to the Add Routing Slip dialog box.

- To send the active file to the people listed in the To list box or to an individual, select File ➤ Send to display the Send dialog box. Choose Route *File* To *Person* to use the routing slip, and then choose OK to send the file.

- To create a new routing slip, select File ➤ Edit Routing Slip, and then choose Clear.

To send a file as an attachment to a note (without using a routing slip):

TIP: *In Access, you must send a file as an attachment to a note. Open the file, and then highlight the database object you want to send in the appropriate pane of the Database window. Choose File ➤ Send to display the Send dialog box, highlight the format for the file in the Select Format list box, and then choose OK. Access creates a file of the selected database object in the selected format, and then the Send Note window appears with the new file attached.*

1. Activate the file, and then choose File ➤ Send to display the Send Note window. An icon representing the active file appears in the message area of the window.

2. Follow steps 4 through 10 in "Creating a Mail Message," above.

Merging Revisions Made to a Word Document

If a Word document is sent to the names on the list simultaneously, each person's revisions or annotations will be sent back in a separate document. You can merge the revisions or annotations into the original document, where up to eight individuals'

COMMAND AND FEATURE REFERENCE

revisions will appear in different colors. Be sure the document is protected for revisions in the Routing Slip dialog box so the revisions are marked in each document.

NOTE: *A Word document that is sent in sequence to each person in the list collects all the revisions and annotations in the one document. The revised document is returned after the last recipient is finished.*

SEE ALSO: *Address Book; Annotation; Folder; Form; Mail Merge; Message Finder; Postoffice Manager; Revision*

Mail Merge

Use Word's Mail Merge feature to combine a *data source* with a *main document*. The data source is a database file that contains the information that changes for each document. The main document contains the text that stays the same in each document, and the merge field codes, which instruct Word where to insert the data source information in the main document text.

There are three basic steps to performing a Mail Merge–specify the file that is the main document, then specify the data source, and finally, merge the data source with the main document.

Creating a Main Document

To create the document that contains the text and field codes that will be merged with the records in the data source:

1. Open a new or existing document to use as the main document.

MAIL MERGE

2. Select Tools ➤ Mail Merge to display the Mail Merge Helper dialog box.

3. Choose Create in the Main Document area.

4. Select one of the following types of documents to create:

- Highlight Form Letters to create a merge document that is a form letter.

- Select Mailing Labels to create a merge document for various types of Avery labels.

- Highlight Envelopes to set up a merge using envelopes as the type of document.

- Select Catalog to organize lists of data.

- Select Restore To Normal Word Document to change a main document back into a normal Word document by removing the relationship it has with the data source.

5. Select Active Window to use the current document as the main document, or New Main Document to open a new document window for the main document.

Designating a Data Source

To specify the database file that contains the fields that will be inserted in the merge field codes in the main document:

1. Select Get Data in the Data Source area of the Mail Merge Helper dialog box.

2. Choose one of the following options in the drop-down list:

- Select Create Data Source to display the Create Data Source dialog box.

- Choose Open Data Source to display the Open Data Source dialog box, select the file

COMMAND AND FEATURE REFERENCE

that contains the data in the File Name list box, and choose OK. Database files created in other applications, such as Access or Excel, can be used as the data source for a Mail Merge.

- Select Header Options to display the Header Options dialog box, and then choose Create to display the Create Header Source dialog box, or Open to display the Open Header Source dialog box. A *header source document* is a document that contains only the merge fields of a data source. Save a header source file so the merge fields it contains can be used in many different merge documents. If a merge field must be changed, it can be changed in the header source document instead of in each data source document.

3. If Create Data Source or Create Header Source was selected in step 2, you can type a new field name in the Field Name text box and select Add Field Name to add the new field name to the Field Names In Header Row list box.

NOTE: *A field name must begin with a letter and can contain as many as 40 characters made up of letters, numbers, and the underline character, but cannot contain any spaces.*

4. To move or delete a field name, highlight it in the Field Names In Header Row list box, and then select the ↑ or ↓ Move button to change its position, or choose Remove Field Name to remove the name from the list box.

TIP: *To filter the records in an existing database file, select MS Query.*

5. When the data or header source is created, select OK in the dialog box, type a name for the file

MAIL MERGE

in the File Name text box, and then choose OK in the Save Data Source or Save Header Source dialog box.

6. Select Edit Data Source to display the Data Form dialog box so records can be entered. Or, choose Edit, and then select Header *Filename* to enter records in the header source document. Select File ➤ Save As to display the Save As dialog box, type a different name for the changed header source file in the File Name text box, and choose OK.

Editing a Data File

To add records to or delete records from the data source:

1. Choose Edit Data Source after a new data source is created, or click on the Edit Data Source button on the Mail Merge toolbar in the main document window to display the Data Form dialog box.

2. Type the appropriate information in the first text box, press Tab to enter that information in the field, and then move to the next text box.

3. Repeat step 2 until all the data is entered in the first record, and then select Add New to enter the data in the record and display a blank data form for the next record.

4. To display an existing record, type the number of the record in the Data Form in the Record text box and select Find. Or, click on the First Record, Previous Record, Next Record, or Last Record button in the Record area to display the specified record.

NOTE: *Make any changes necessary to the record that is displayed in the Data Form dialog box, and then choose Restore to undo the changes or Add New to save the changes. To remove the record displayed in the Data Form from the data source, select Delete.*

COMMAND AND FEATURE REFERENCE

5. If necessary, select Find to display the Find In Field dialog box, type the text to find in the Find What text box, and select the name of the field in which to search for the text in the In Field drop-down list. Then choose Find First or Find Next to find the next record and display it in the Data Form dialog box. Choose Close to return to the Data Form.

NOTE: *Select View Source to display the entire data source in a table on your screen. Each record is a row in the table, and the Database toolbar appears above the document window.*

6. When all the records for the data source have been added or edited, choose OK in the Data Form Dialog box.

When you close the main document, a dialog box appears asking if the changed data source document should be saved. Choose Yes to save the changes.

Editing the Main Document

After you have specified an open data source, insert the field names in the data source document as merge fields in the main document:

1. If necessary, click on the Mail Merge Helper button on the Mail Merge toolbar to display the Mail Merge Helper dialog box. Then choose Edit in the Main Document area to set up the main document.

2. Position the insertion point where a merge field is to be inserted in the main document, and then click on the Insert Merge Field button on the Mail Merge toolbar and choose the field to insert. Repeat this step for each location in the main document that will contain a merge field.

3. Insert the necessary punctuation or edit the text and other document items in the main document.

MAIL MERGE

4. Click on the Save button on the Standard toolbar to save the main document.

If any changes were made to the Word data source that is attached to the main document, choose Yes in the dialog box that appears to save the data source file.

Inserting Fields in a Word Data Source

You can add, remove, or edit the field names in the data source file:

1. Click on the Edit Data Source button on the Mail Merge toolbar in the main document window to display the Data Form dialog box.

2. Choose View Source to display the data source document window.

3. Click on the Manage Fields button on the Database toolbar to display the Manage Fields dialog box.

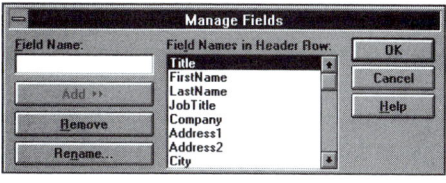

4. Type a new name in the Field Name text box.

5. Select Add to add the new field to the Field Names In Header Row list box.

6. If necessary, highlight a field in the Field Names In Header Row list box, and then select Remove to remove the field name from the data source.

7. Optionally, highlight a field name in the Field Names In Header Row list box, and then select Rename to display the Rename Field dialog box. Type the new name in the New Field Name text box, and then choose OK.

COMMAND AND FEATURE REFERENCE

8. Select OK in the Manage Fields dialog box.

Add the new field information directly in the corresponding cell in the data source table, or click on the Data Form button on the Database toolbar, and then add the new field data into each record.

Merging the Data File and the Main Document

After the main document and the data source files are created, merge the two files to insert the records in the data source into the merge field codes in the main document:

1. If necessary, click on the Mail Merge Main Document button on the Database toolbar or select Window ➤ *Filename* to activate the main document.

2. Click on the View Merged Data button on the Mail Merge toolbar. The fields from the first data record are displayed in the main document merge field locations.

3. If necessary, click on the First Record, Previous Record, Next Record, or Last Record button, or type the number of the record to display in the Go To Record text box on the Mail Merge toolbar and press ↵.

4. If necessary, click on the Mail Merge button on the Mail Merge toolbar to display the Merge dialog box, select any of the following options, and then choose Merge:

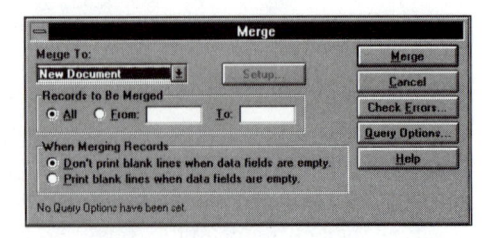

- In the Merge To drop-down list, select New Document to create a new merged

MAIL MERGE

document, Printer to send the merged data directly to the printer, Electronic Mail to send the merged data to mail addresses, or Electronic Fax to send the merged data to fax numbers.

- If you select Electronic Mail or Electronic Fax in the Merge To drop-down list, choose Setup to display the Merge To Setup dialog box. Select the field that contains the address or phone number in the Data Field With Mail/Fax Address drop-down list, and type the text that is to appear as the subject for each document sent in the Mail Message Subject Line text box. Select the Send Document As An Attachment check box to send the document as an attachment to a mail or fax message instead of sending the document text as an unformatted message. Then choose OK to return to the Merge dialog box.

- In the Records To Be Merged area, select All to merge all the records in the data source or that meet the specified filtering criteria with the main document, or type the starting and ending numbers of a range of records to merge in the From and To text boxes.

- Select Don't Print Blank Lines When Data Fields Are Empty or Print Blank Lines When Data Fields Are Empty to define whether blank lines are to be printed when a record in the data source contains empty fields.

- If necessary, select Check Errors to display the Checking And Reporting Errors dialog box. Choose Simulate The Merge And Report Errors In A New Document, Complete The Merge, Pausing To Report

COMMAND AND FEATURE REFERENCE

Each Error As It Occurs, or Complete The Merge Without Pausing–Report Errors In A New Document. Then choose OK to define how errors that occur during the merge are to be reported.

TIP *You can also click on the Check For Errors button on the Mail Merge toolbar to select how to check for errors during the merge.*

- To filter the records in the data source so that only records that meet specific criteria are printed, or to sort the records in the data source, select Query Options. Specify the filtering and sorting criteria, and then choose OK.

5. Or, on the Database toolbar, click on the Merge To Printer button to send all the merged documents directly to the printer, or the Merge To New Document button to send all the merged documents to a single new document.

SEE ALSO: *Database; File Management; Filter; Mail; MS Query; Query; Sort*

Margins

Margins define the distance from the edge of the paper to the beginning of the text or data on a printed page. Some items, such as headers, footers, and objects inserted in a frame, can be printed in the margins. The minimum margins that can be set depend on the size of the paper and the printer being used. Margins can be defined for Access

MARGINS

forms and reports, Excel worksheets, and Word documents.

Setting the Margins for an Access Form or Report

To specify the margins for a printed form or report in Access:

1. Open the database file that contains the form or report.

2. Highlight the form or report whose margins are to be changed in the corresponding pane of the Database window. Then choose Open for a form or Preview for a report.

3. Select File ➤ Print Setup to display the Print Setup dialog box.

4. Specify the measurement for the Left, Right, Top, and Bottom margins in the corresponding text box in the Margins area.

5. Choose OK to set the margins for the active database object.

NOTE: *To set different default margins for all new database objects, select View ➤ Options, select Printing in the Category list box, specify the distance from the edge of the paper in the Left Margin, Right Margin, Top Margin, and Bottom Margin option areas, and then choose OK.*

Setting the Margins for an Excel Worksheet

To quickly set the page margins, adjust column widths, and adjust the distance between the header and footer and the top or bottom edge of the page in an Excel worksheet:

1. Click on the Print Preview button on the Standard toolbar, or choose File ➤ Print Preview to display the active worksheet in the Print Preview window.

251

COMMAND AND FEATURE REFERENCE

2. If necessary, select <u>M</u>argins to toggle on the display of margin and column-width handles.

3. Position the mouse pointer over one of the handles until it appears as a cross with two arrows (the arrows point in the directions in which you can move the handle), and then drag the handle to adjust the margin, column width, or the position of the header or footer on the page.

To set exact margins for a printed page containing the current worksheet:

1. Select <u>F</u>ile ➤ Page Set<u>u</u>p to display the Page Setup dialog box, and choose the Margins tab.

2. Specify the <u>T</u>op, <u>B</u>ottom, <u>L</u>eft, and <u>R</u>ight margins in the corresponding text boxes.

3. Specify the distance from the edge of the page for the header and footer in the He<u>a</u>der and <u>F</u>ooter text boxes.

4. To center the data on the printed page, select the Hori<u>z</u>ontally and <u>V</u>ertically check boxes in the Center On Page area.

5. Choose OK to define the margins for the current worksheet.

Setting the Margins in a Word Document

By default, the top and bottom margins are set at 1 inch, and the left and right margins at 1.25 inches in a Word document based on the NORMAL.DOT template. Margins can be set for each section of a Word document.

TIP: *Use the Ruler to quickly set the margins in the current section of the active document in either Page Layout or Print Preview view.*

To set exact margin measurements, adjust the position of the header or footer, or create a binding

MARGINS M

offset, use options on the Margins tab of the Page Setup dialog box:

1. Position the insertion point in the section of the document whose margins you want to change.

2. Select File ➤ Page Setup, and choose the Margins tab in the Page Setup dialog box.

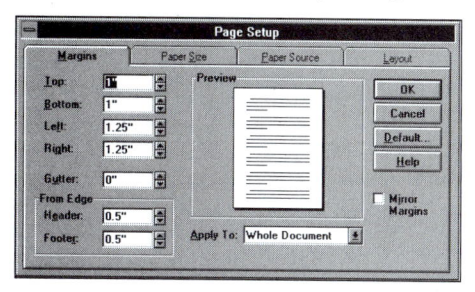

3. Specify the Top, Bottom, Left, and Right margins in the corresponding text boxes.

4. If necessary, choose any of the following options, and then choose OK in the Page Setup dialog box:

- In the Gutter text box, specify the amount of additional space to allow for the binding margin of a document. The gutter is added to the Left or Inside margin.

- In the From Edge area, specify the distance from the edge of the page for the position of the document's header and footer in the Header and Footer text boxes.

TIP: *For a large header or footer, the top and bottom margins settings are automatically adjusted so the entire header or footer is in the margin.*

- Choose Whole Document, Selected Text, This Point Forward, Selected Sections, or This Section as the portion of the document

COMMAND AND FEATURE REFERENCE

   whose margins are to be reset in the <u>A</u>pply To drop-down list.

- Select the M<u>i</u>rror Margins check box to change the widths of the inside and outside margins for facing pages if printing is to appear on both sides of the paper. In the <u>I</u>nside text box, specify the distance from the left edge of the paper to the left edge of the text on the odd-numbered pages, and the distance between the right edge of the paper and the right edge of the text on the even-numbered pages. In the <u>O</u>utside text box, specify the distance from the right edge of the paper to the right edge of the text on the odd-numbered pages, and the distance between the left edge of the paper and the left edge of the text on the even-numbered pages.

- Select <u>D</u>efault to change the default margins in the current template to the settings specified on the <u>M</u>argins tab, and then choose <u>Y</u>es to confirm the change.

SEE ALSO: *Header and Footer; Indent; Page Break; Page Setup; Print Preview; Ruler*

Master Document

Use a *master document*, a file that contains subdocuments, to manage long documents in Word. The subdocument files can be opened and edited, renamed, and relocated. When you save changes to the subdocument, the changes will also be updated in its associated master document.

MASTER DOCUMENT

Master documents can contain up to eighty subdocuments, and can be as large as 32 MB, not counting graphics. Change to Master Document view to create a new master document or to turn an existing document file into a master document. Both the Outline and the Master Document toolbars appear when you are in Master Document view. Switch to Normal view to work with the entire master document.

The template created for a master document will override a different subdocument template except for special subdocument formatting such as columns, margin settings, and special page number settings. Styles or formatting can be applied to the master document or to any of its subdocuments.

Each subdocument is in a separate section of the master document. Each section of a master document can have different headers and footers.

Changing a Document into a Master Document

Each subdocument is assigned its own file name based on the text of the first subdocument heading. However, if a file in the directory is already named what Word would normally choose, the subdocument is assigned a numbered file name based on the text.

To change a document into a master document:

1. Activate the document to be changed into a master document.

2. Select View ➤ Master Document to display the Outline and Master Document toolbars.

3. Use the Outline toolbar to arrange the headings in the document. By default, Word's built-in heading styles are applied to headings in the document.

COMMAND AND FEATURE REFERENCE

4. Select the headings and text to be included in subdocuments, and then click on the Create Subdocument button on the Master Document toolbar. A new subdocument is created each time Word finds the same heading level as the first heading level in the selection.

5. Save the master document. Each subdocument will also be saved as a file.

Or, to convert a subdocument into master document text, position the insertion point in the subdocument, and then click on the Remove Subdocument button on the Master Document toolbar. The converted portion of the master document retains its section formatting.

Creating a New Master Document

If you are creating a document that will be very long, create it as a master document:

1. Click on the New button on the Standard toolbar, press Ctrl+N, or select File ➤ New and choose OK to create a new document.

2. Choose View ➤ Master Document to display the Outline and Master Document toolbars.

3. Type the master document's outline. Make sure the outline headings are in Word's built-in heading styles.

4. Select the text to be included in a subdocument, and then click on the Create Subdocument button on the Master Document toolbar.

5. Click on the Save button on the Standard toolbar to save the master document. Each subdocument will also be saved as a file.

To remove a subdocument from the master document, select the subdocument's icon and press the Backspace or Del key. If you wish, you can also delete the file from your disk.

MASTER DOCUMENT

Editing a Subdocument

You can edit subdocuments using the same techniques as those you use to edit any other documents:

1. Double-click on the subdocument icon in the master document to open the subdocument file.

2. If necessary, close the master document to allow others to access it.

3. Edit the subdocument as you would any other document.

4. Save the subdocument.

Inserting a Subdocument into a Master Document

You can insert an existing Word file as a subdocument in a master document:

1. Open the master document file, and then select View ➤ Master Document to change to Master Document view.

2. Position the insertion point where you wish to insert a new subdocument.

TIP: *When the insertion point is positioned on the lower End Of Section mark in a section, the new subdocument will be inserted in its own section as a separate subdocument. If the insertion point is positioned into an existing subdocument, the new subdocument will be a subdocument of the existing subdocument. Split the subdocument to place the new subdocument in the master document. A master document can contain up to eight layers of subdocuments.*

3. Click on the Insert Subdocument button on the Master Document toolbar to display the Insert Subdocument dialog box.

4. Select the name of the file to insert in the File Name list box, and then choose OK.

COMMAND AND FEATURE REFERENCE

The document is inserted into the master document with its original file name. If the document is based on a different template or is formatted differently than the master document, the settings in the master document will be used in the subdocument when it is opened in the master document. The template and formatting settings in the subdocument file will be used when the subdocument file is opened with File ➤ Open (Ctrl+O) or by clicking on the Open button on the Standard toolbar.

To reposition a subdocument within the master document, click on its icon to select the subdocument, and then drag it to the new location in the master document.

To reposition a heading in a subdocument, select the heading and drag it to a new location in the subdocument or in another subdocument.

Locking a Subdocument

If you share the use of a master document with other people, you can lock the subdocuments you create. A locked subdocument appears with a padlock icon on it, and can be opened only as a read-only file by anyone other than the author of the subdocument. The author's identity is taken from the Summary Info AUTHOR field code. However, anyone can unlock a locked subdocument.

To lock a subdocument:

1. With the master document open and in Master Document view, click on the icon of the subdocument to be locked or unlocked.

2. Click on the Lock Document button on the Master Document toolbar to lock an unlocked subdocument or to unlock a locked subdocument.

If you are locking a subdocument that you have changed since you last saved it, choose Yes to save the changes and lock the subdocument.

MASTER DOCUMENT

Merging and Splitting Subdocuments

Merged subdocuments are saved as a single subdocument of the master document. After subdocuments are merged, their original, individual subdocument files can be deleted.

To merge subdocuments:

1. If necessary, reposition the subdocuments that are to be merged so they are next to each other in the master document.

2. Click on the icon of the first subdocument.

3. Hold down the Shift key while you click on the icon of the next and any subsequent subdocuments that are to be merged.

4. Click on the Merge Subdocument button on the Master Document toolbar.

5. Save the master document.

To split a subdocument, position the insertion point where you want to begin a new subdocument, and then click on the Split Subdocument button on the Master Document toolbar.

Moving or Renaming a Subdocument File

Open a subdocument from within its master document when you want to save the subdocument to a different file name and location without breaking its link to the master document.

To move or rename a subdocument file:

1. With the master document open and displayed in Master Document view, double-click on the icon of the subdocument to be moved or renamed. Leave the master document open.

2. Select File ➤ Save As to display the Save As dialog box.

COMMAND AND FEATURE REFERENCE

3. Type the new name and path for the subdocument in the File <u>N</u>ame text box, and then choose OK in the Save As dialog box.

4. Click on the document's Control menu box, and then choose <u>C</u>lose (Ctrl+W) to close the subdocument.

5. Save the master document.

SEE ALSO: *File Management; Header and Footer; Outline; Page Numbers; Style; Summary Info; Templates; View*

Master View

PowerPoint's Master views allow you to set all the items that will appear on each slide of a presentation, on each page of a handout, on each printed page of an outline, or on each printed page of notes. Use Master views to apply formatting to text; set background colors, borders, and patterns for each slide in a presentation; and add the slide or page number, a company logo, the date, or any item you want to appear on each slide or printed page.

Applying a Slide Master Format

The Slide Master determines the format of each slide in the presentation, and the notes, outline, and handouts prepared for the presentation. Many items, such as place holders for the title and text for each slide in the presentation, are already set up for use on the Slide Master each time you create a presentation. You can add background objects such as a company logo, the page number, or the date to the Slide Master so the objects appear on each slide in the presentation.

MASTER VIEW M

To make changes to the existing Slide Master:

1. Select View ➤ Master ➤ Slide Master to change the current presentation to Slide Master view.

2. On the Slide Master view, change the format of existing items or add new items to the background of each slide in the presentation, and then drag the object to its correct position on the slide.

- To insert text on the Slide Master that will appear on each presentation slide (such as the title of the presentation or the name of your company), click on the Text Tool on the Drawing toolbar, and then drag on the Slide Master view to create a text box. Type the text in the new text box.

- To insert the system date on each slide, choose Insert ➤ Date.

- To insert page numbers, select Insert ➤ Page Number.

- Click on the Insert Clip Art button on the Standard toolbar or choose Insert ➤ Clip Art to choose a graphic from the ClipArt Gallery.

- Select Insert ➤ Picture to select a picture object for each slide in the presentation.

3. To see how the changes appear in your presentation, click on the Slide View button on the horizontal scroll bar or select View ➤ Slides to return to Slide view.

You can also change the appearance of individual slides to provide some diversity in the presentation. Use the commands on the Format drop-down menu to change the format of selected text, the background of the slide, or the slide's color scheme.

For example, to delete background items from the current slide, choose Format ➤ Slide Background,

COMMAND AND FEATURE REFERENCE

clear the Display Objects On This Slide check box, and then choose Apply.

WARNING: *If you apply a template to a presentation, it affects every slide in the presentation, not just the current slide. In addition, any formatting and background objects you added to the Slide Master will be lost.*

To return the current slide to the elements and formatting in the Master Slide:

- Choose Format ➤ Slide Layout, and then choose Reapply to return the current slide's style to the formatting in the Master Slide.

- To return the background, text, and fill colors on the current slide to the colors on the Master Slide, choose Format ➤ Slide Color Scheme, choose Follow Master, and then choose Apply.

- To return the background objects on the Master Slide to the current slide, choose Format ➤ Slide Background, select the Display Objects On This Slide check box, and then choose Apply.

Using the Other Master Views

The formatting and background items on the Slide Master appear on the miniature slides on notes and handouts, and the text formatting appears in an outline based on the presentation. Those elements on the Slide Master appear in Notes Pages View, Outline View, and on printed pages containing notes, handouts, or outlines.

Notes, handouts, and outlines also have their own masters, to which you can add items that appear on each page. Outline Master, Handout Master, and Notes Master all work in the same way as the Slide Master.

For example, change to Handout Master to add a header and footer or a graphic to each page of a handout, and change to Outline Master to insert the company name and page numbers on each printed page of the outline. Or, change to Notes Master to reposition the slide or the notes area and to add page numbers on each notes page.

SEE ALSO: *Clip Art; Date and Time; Font; Header and Footer; Page Numbers; Slide Show*

Message Finder

Use Mail's Message Finder to search for messages you have received. With Message Finder, you must specify the criteria to use to perform the search. Once the messages that meet the criteria are found, use Mail's regular methods to open, read, forward, and reply to them.

To find a message:

1. Select File ➤ Message Finder to open the Message Finder window.

TIP: *You can have multiple Message Finder windows open simultaneously, each containing a different set of search criteria.*

2. Type the information for which to search in the From, Subject, Recipients, or Message Text text boxes. To search for multiple criteria in one of the search categories, type a semicolon between the items.

NOTE: *To search for messages that meet criteria in multiple search categories, type the criteria in more than one search text box.*

COMMAND AND FEATURE REFERENCE

3. If necessary, choose Where To Look, select the name of the folder in the Look In list box, and then choose OK.

4. Select Start to begin the search.

As Message Finder finds each message that meets the specified criteria, it appears in a list below the Message Finder window. When the message you want appears in the list, choose Stop to stop the search.

To close the Message Finder window, double-click on its Control menu box.

SEE ALSO: Find and Replace; Mail

Microsoft Office Manager

Each time you start Windows, the Microsoft Office Manager runs automatically, because Setup placed the Microsoft Office application icon in the Windows StartUp group. By default, Office Manager displays the Microsoft Office toolbar with small buttons near the top-right corner of your screen. When any of the Office applications are active and maximized, the Microsoft Office toolbar appears on its title bar.

Customizing Microsoft Office

The Microsoft Office toolbar contains a button that you can click on to start each of the Microsoft Office applications, as well as the Find File button and the Microsoft Office button. You can add or remove buttons on the toolbar, items on the Microsoft Office drop-down menu, or change the display of the toolbar.

MICROSOFT OFFICE MANAGER

To customize Microsoft Office:

1. Click on the Microsoft Office button on the Microsoft Office toolbar, and then choose Customize to display the Customize dialog box.

2. Select the appropriate tab to make changes to the Microsoft Office Toolbar, Menu, or View.

3. Make any changes necessary, and then choose OK in the Customize dialog box to implement the changes.

The following options can be changed on the Toolbar and Menu tabs:

- Select the check box of an application in the list box, and then choose Edit to display the Edit Program Item dialog box. Type any startup switches in the Parameters text box, and type the path in which to store files created with the application in the Working Directory text box. Choose OK to add the application's button to the Microsoft Office toolbar or its name to the drop-down menu.

TIP: *Choose Browse to select the path and command for the Command Line and Working Directory text boxes.*

- To add an application whose name does not appear in the list box, select Add. Type the name of the application in the Description text box, the path and command necessary to start the application in the Command Line text box, and the path in which to store files created with the application (if necessary) in the Working Directory text box. Select the picture that is to appear on a toolbar button in the Button Image drop-down list. Choose OK to add the application's button to the toolbar or its name in the drop-down menu.

COMMAND AND FEATURE REFERENCE

- In the list box, highlight the name of an application whose toolbar button or position on the drop-down menu is to be changed, and then click on the ↑ or ↓ Move button to change its location.

- In the list box, highlight the name of an application whose toolbar button or name on the drop-down menu is to be removed, and then choose <u>R</u>emove. The applications that Setup placed on the toolbar or drop-down menu cannot be removed.

The following options can be changed on the <u>V</u>iew tab:

- In the Toolbar Button Size area, select <u>S</u>mall Buttons (the default) to make the Microsoft Office toolbar appear on the right side of the title bar of a maximized application window, Regular <u>B</u>uttons to make the toolbar moveable, or <u>L</u>arge Buttons to increase the size of the buttons on a moveable toolbar.

- Select the T<u>o</u>olbar Is Always Visible check box (the default) to keep the toolbar on your screen.

- Select the Sho<u>w</u> ToolTips check box (the default) to display the name of the application when you point to a button on the Microsoft Office toolbar.

- Select the Show T<u>i</u>tle Screen At Startup check box (the default) to display the Microsoft Office Manager dialog box when it automatically starts.

SEE ALSO: *Customize; Toolbars; View*

Module

Use Access Basic to create programming code to make your database objects work together. When you write code in Access Basic, it is written in a unit called a *procedure*, a set of statements that performs an operation or calculates a value. Each statement must appear on a single line in the procedure. The procedures are organized and stored in a *module*.

NOTE: *In Excel, a module is a sheet in a workbook in which Visual Basic macros are stored.*

A database can contain a form or report module, in which you create *event procedures*–actions that are automatically performed in response to a specific event that takes place while you are working in a form or report. Or, you can create a global module, an object in a database that contains procedures that can be run from anywhere in the database, in the Module pane of the Database window.

NOTE: *To create a global module, click on the Module tab in the Database window, and then choose New. Type the code in the Module window that appears, and then click on the Save button on the Module toolbar or choose File ➤ Save (Ctrl+S) to save the module as a named database object.*

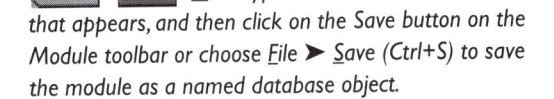

Use modules to create customized functions to calculate values, create messages that appear when an error occurs while running a procedure, create databases and objects, perform system operations, perform an operation on each record, one at a time, in a set of records, and set arguments in the code while it is running to customize its execution.

COMMAND AND FEATURE REFERENCE

Creating an Event Procedure

Modules that are created for forms and reports in a database are built into the form or report for which they are created. (Macros are separate database objects.)

To create an event procedure:

1. Display the form or report in Design view.

2. Use either of the following methods to open the Module window:

- If necessary, click on the object for which an event procedure is to be created, and then click on the Properties button on the Form Design or Report Design toolbar or choose View ➤ Properties to display its property sheet. Click in the option area for the property, click on its Build button, choose Code Builder in the Choose Builder dialog box, and then choose OK.

- Right-click on the form, report, section, or control for which an event procedure is to be written, select Build Event in the shortcut menu to display the Choose Builder dialog box, select Code Builder, and then choose OK.

3. Type the code for the procedure between the Sub and End Sub statements.

NOTE: See Microsoft Access Building Applications for additional information on entering code in a module.

4. Click on the Save button on the Module toolbar or choose File ➤ Save (Ctrl+S) to save the module.

To run the procedure, carry out the event on the form or report.

MS QUERY

SEE ALSO: *Control; Control Properties; Macro; Shortcut Menus*

MS Query

Use Microsoft Query to collect and arrange data from tables in various data sources in Excel and Word. For example, use MS Query to collect data from an Access database, and use it as a data source for a Word Mail Merge. With MS Query, you specify the criteria that define which data is to be retrieved, and how it is to be displayed.

The data that is displayed can be edited, or you can add new data, which will be stored in the same file as the data that was retrieved. You can perform calculations on the displayed data, format and sort the data, and then copy it to a different application for use.

Creating a Query

To collect and arrange data from tables in a different data source:

1. Double-click on the Microsoft Query icon in the Microsoft Office group window.

2. Double-click on the Control menu box on MS Query Cue Cards dialog box to close it.

TIP: *Select the Don't Display This Card On Startup check box in the MS Query Cue Cards window to prevent the display of the Cue Cards window each time MS Query is started.*

COMMAND AND FEATURE REFERENCE

> **TROUBLESHOOTING**
>
> ### Controlling the Table List
>
> Do you want to filter the list of tables that appears in the Table list box? If the list box contains table names rather than file names, you can select which table names are displayed in the list box by selecting tables created by a specific person in the Owner drop-down list, or stored in a specific database in the Database drop-down list in the Add Tables dialog box.

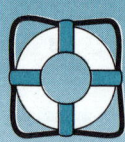

3. Click on the New Query button on the MS Query toolbar, or choose File ➤ New Query to display the Select Data Source dialog box.

4. If the data source you want to use is not listed in the Available Data Sources list box, choose Other to display the ODBC Data Sources dialog box. Type the name of the data source in the Enter Data Source text box or select it in the list box, and then choose OK.

5. Highlight the name of the data source to be queried in the Available Data Sources list box in the Select Data Source dialog box, and then choose Use.

6. If necessary, select the path and name of the file that contains the data source and choose OK. Enter the ID or password for the file, if necessary.

NOTE: *The Available Data Sources list box in the Select Data Source dialog box contains the names of each data source you have previously queried. Choose Remove to remove the highlighted data source from the list box.*

7. The Add Tables dialog box appears. Depending on the options displayed, highlight the name of the file that contains the data in the Table

MS QUERY

Name list box, or highlight the table in the Table list box and choose Add.

8. Choose Close to return to the Query window.

TIP: *More than one table can be used in a query. However, the tables must be joined. See Chapter 6 in the* Microsoft Query User's Guide *for detailed information about joining tables.*

The Query window appears with a Tables pane, which contains the list of fields in the selected table in alphabetical order, and the Data pane, where the data in selected fields appears.

To create a subset of the data in the database, add fields to the Data pane using any of the following methods:

- Double-click on the field name in the Tables pane.

- Drag the field name from the Tables pane to a blank column in the Data pane.

- Type the name of a field that is listed in the Tables pane into the first cell in a blank column in the Data pane and press ↵.

- Click in the first cell in a blank column, and then select the name of the field from the drop-down list.

- Select Records ➤ Add Column, select a field name in the Field drop-down list, and choose Add. Choose Close to remove the Add Column dialog box.

- To add more than one field, select the first field in the list in the Table pane, and then hold down the Ctrl key while you click on additional field names or hold down the Shift key while you click on the last name in a range of names. Then drag the selection to the Data pane.

COMMAND AND FEATURE REFERENCE

- To add all the fields in the order in which they appear in the source, highlight the * (asterisk) at the top of the list of fields in the Tables pane, and drag it to a column in the Data pane.

- To add all the fields in alphabetical order, double-click on the name of the field list in the Tables pane to select the entire list, and then drag the selection to a column in the Data pane.

To remove a field from the Data pane, click on the name of the field (the column heading) to select the column, and then choose Records ➤ Remove Column.

Working with a Query

Once you have created a query, use the buttons on the MS Query toolbar and the commands on the menus to manipulate and format the data. The following methods can be used to work with the displayed data:

Click on the Open Query button or choose File ➤ Open Query to open a previously saved query.

Click on the Save File button or choose File ➤ Save Query to save the displayed query.

Click on the View SQL button or choose View ➤ SQL to display the structured query language statement used to retrieve the current data.

Click on the Show/Hide Tables button or choose View ➤ Tables to toggle on or off the display of the Tables pane.

Click on the Show/Hide Criteria button or choose View ➤ Criteria to toggle the display of the Criteria pane.

Click on the Add Tables button or choose Table ➤ Add Tables to select additional tables for the query in the Add Tables dialog box.

Click on the Criteria Equals button or choose Criteria ➤ Add Criteria to change the criteria that define which records are displayed.

Click on the Cycle Thru Totals button to cycle through the sum, average, count, minimum, and maximum values in the selected column.

Click on the Sort Ascending button or choose Records ➤ Sort ➤ Ascending to sort the records alphabetically or from 0 to 9 by the values in the selected column.

Click on the Sort Descending button or choose Records ➤ Sort ➤ Descending to sort the records from Z to A or from 9 to 0 by the values in the selected column.

Click on the Query Now button or choose Records ➤ Query Now to display the results of a query if Auto Query is not turned on.

Click on the Auto Query button or choose Records ➤ Automatic Query to toggle Auto Query on or off. If Auto Query is on, each time you make a change the results of the query are displayed.

SEE ALSO: *Database; Mail Merge; Query; Table*

New File

SEE: *File Management*

COMMAND AND FEATURE REFERENCE

Note

Use notes to describe complex formulas or provide explanations for items in an Excel worksheet. Text notes can be displayed and printed, if necessary; sound notes can be played later. Notes are attached to a cell in a worksheet.

NOTE: *You must have recording hardware and a sound driver installed before you can create or play back a recorded note.*

Creating a Note

Right-click on one of the displayed toolbars and select Auditing in the shortcut menu, or choose View ➤ Toolbars, select the Auditing check box in the Toolbars list box, and choose OK to display the Auditing toolbar.

To create a note:

1. Select the cell to which a note is to be added.

2. Click on the Attach Note button on the Auditing toolbar, or choose Insert ➤ Note to display the Cell Note dialog box.

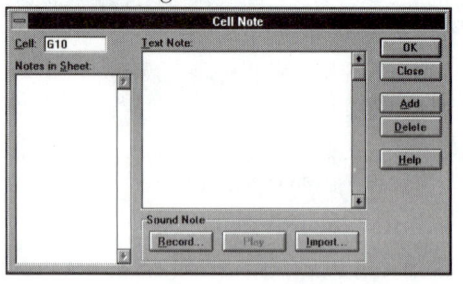

3. Type the text of the note in the Text Note text box, and then choose Add. The cell and the

NOTE

beginning of the note appear in the Notes In Sheet list box.

4. If necessary, enter another cell reference in the Cell text box, select the text in the Text Note text box, and then repeat step 3.

5. To create a sound note in the selected cell, choose Record in the Sound Note area to display the Record dialog box. Choose Record, and then speak into your microphone to create a sound note. When you are finished, choose Stop, and then select OK to save the sound. Choose Add in the Cell Note dialog box to attach it to the cell.

NOTE: *Sound notes appear in the Notes In Sheet list box with the cell reference followed by an * (asterisk).*

6. To attach an existing sound file to the selected cell, choose Import to display the Import Sound dialog box, select the name of the sound file in the File Name list box, and then choose OK. Select Add in the Cell Note dialog box.

TIP: *Highlight a sound note in the Notes In Sheet list box, and then choose Play in the Sound Note area of the Cell Note dialog box to hear the recorded sound.*

7. If necessary, highlight a note in the Notes In Sheet list box, and choose Delete to remove the note from the cell. Or, to remove only the sound portion of a note that contains both sound and text, select the note in the Notes In Sheet list box, choose Erase in the Sound Note area, and then choose OK.

8. Choose Close to return to the worksheet.

Each cell that contains a note appears with a small, red square in its upper-right corner. To remove the note indicators in all workbooks, choose Tools ➤ Options, select the View tab, clear the Note Indicator check box in the Show area, and choose OK.

COMMAND AND FEATURE REFERENCE

To see information about the selected cell, including the text of a text note, click on the Show Info Window button on the Auditing toolbar or choose Tools ➤ Options, select the View tab, select the Info Window check box in the Show area, and then choose OK to display its Info Window.

To print the contents of the Info Window, select Window ➤ Arrange, select Vertical in the Arrange Windows dialog box, and then choose OK. Activate the worksheet window and select the cell whose information is to be printed. Then activate the Info Window and click on the Print button on the Standard toolbar or choose File ➤ Print (Ctrl+P) and select OK.

SEE ALSO: Annotation; Auditing; Find and Replace; Formula; Go To; Page Setup; Print; Reference; Spelling

Object Linking and Embedding

Use Object Linking and Embedding (OLE) to exchange data between the Microsoft Office applications. With OLE, objects, such as graphics, equations, worksheets, documents, and drawings can be linked or embedded in a file. An embedded object becomes part of the file, and can be edited from within the file. A linked object is edited in its source file, and changes made to it are updated when you open the file that contains the link.

NOTE: *Both the application used to create the object (the source) and the one used to create the destination for the object must support dynamic data exchange (DDE) or OLE to link an object, and must support OLE to embed an object.*

OBJECT LINKING AND EMBEDDING

Creating and Embedding a New Object

An object is data of any type that is created in the active application or another application that supports OLE or DDE. Objects can be embedded in each of the Microsoft Office applications.

In Access, you must display the form or report in Design view in order to create and embed an object.

To create and embed a new object:

1. Position the insertion point in the location in the form or report, worksheet, or document, or activate the slide in which the object is to be embedded.

2. In Access, choose Edit ➤ Insert Object to display the Insert Object dialog box, and select Create New. In Excel, PowerPoint, and Word, select Insert ➤ Object, and then choose the Create New tab or Create New to display the Object or Insert Object dialog box.

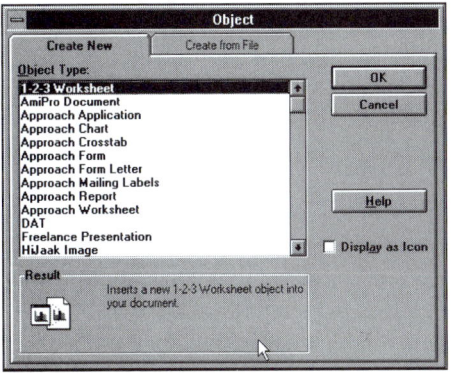

3. Select the kind of object you want to embed in the Object Type list box.

4. To display the object as an icon in your document, select the Display As Icon check box. When the check box is cleared, the object appears as a miniature version of the data selected for the object.

5. Choose OK to open the application used to create the object (the source).

COMMAND AND FEATURE REFERENCE

6. Create the object in the source application.

7. To embed the object and return to the destination file, select File ➤ Exit And Return To *Destination* in the source application, if it has the command, and then choose Yes to confirm that you want to embed the object in the destination file. Or, if necessary, click in the file outside the object.

8. Click on the Save button on the toolbar that is displayed or choose File ➤ Save (Ctrl+S) in the destination file to save both the file and the embedded object.

Editing an Embedded Object

You can open the source and edit an object from within the client application:

1. Double-click on the object in the destination file. Or, select the object, choose Edit ➤ *(Source Application)* Object, and then choose Edit. The source application opens with the object's file already active.

2. Make the necessary changes to the object.

3. Select File ➤ Exit And Return To *Destination* in the source application, if it has the command, and then choose Yes to confirm that you want to embed the object in the destination file. Otherwise, click in the destination file outside the object.

4. Click on the Save button on the toolbar that is displayed or choose File ➤ Save (Ctrl+S) in the destination file to save the changes in both the file and the embedded object.

Embedding an Existing File

In Access, you must display the form or report in Design view in order to embed an object.

OBJECT LINKING AND EMBEDDING

> **TROUBLESHOOTING**
>
> ### How Do I Activate a Different Application?
>
> You can use Windows commands to switch to a different open application. Hold down Alt, and then press Tab to cycle through the open Windows applications. When the destination application and file name appear, release the Alt key. Or, press Ctrl+Esc to display the Windows Task List, highlight the name of the application, and then choose Switch To.

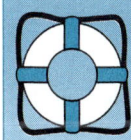

To embed an object in an existing file:

1. Position the insertion point in the location in the form or report, worksheet, document, or on the slide in which the object is to be embedded.

2. In Access, choose Edit ➤ Insert Object to display the Insert Object dialog box, and select Create From File. In Excel, PowerPoint, and Word, select Insert ➤ Object, and then choose the Create From File tab or Create From File to display the Object or Insert Object dialog box.

3. In Access and PowerPoint, type the path and name of the file to be embedded in the File text box. If necessary, select Browse to display the Browse dialog box to search for the file. In Excel and Word, select the name of the file to be embedded in the File Name list box.

4. Select the Display As Icon check box to display the object as an icon in the destination file.

5. Choose OK in the Object or Insert Object dialog box to embed the object in the destination file.

6. Click on the Save button on the toolbar that is displayed or choose File ➤ Save (Ctrl+S) in the destination file to save the destination file.

COMMAND AND FEATURE REFERENCE

Embedding Part of a File

You can embed the selected portion of a file as an object in the client file:

1. Position the insertion point where the object is to be embedded.

2. Open the source application and file, and then select the data to be embedded.

3. In the source application, click on the Copy button on the displayed toolbar, or choose <u>E</u>dit ➤ <u>C</u>opy (Ctrl+C), and then switch back to the destination file.

4. Select the destination application's <u>E</u>dit ➤ Paste <u>S</u>pecial command to display the Paste Special dialog box, and choose <u>P</u>aste.

5. Highlight the item (or the first item that includes "Object" in its name) in the <u>A</u>s list box.

6. To display the object as an icon in the destination file, select the Display As Icon check box.

7. Choose OK.

Modifying the File Format of an Object

You can convert the file format of an object created in an application that is not installed on your system to a format your system supports.

Or, you can change an embedded object into a graphic to reduce the size of the destination file. An embedded object appears by default as a picture of the embedded data, with all the data in the object.

WARNING: *If you change an object into a graphic, the original data is no longer embedded in the object, and the object can be edited as a drawing.*

To modify the file format of an object:

1. Select the object whose file format is to be changed.

2. In Excel, PowerPoint, and Word, choose Edit ➤ (Source Application) Object ➤ Convert to display the Convert dialog box.

NOTE: *In Access, choose Edit ➤ Type Of Object ➤ Change To Picture, and then choose Yes to permanently change the object into a picture.*

3. Select the kind of file format for the object in the Object Type list box. To change the object into a graphic, select a format that includes "Picture."

4. Choose Convert To to permanently convert the file format, or Activate As to temporarily convert the file format.

5. Choose OK in the Convert dialog box.

SEE ALSO: *Chart; Control; Draw; Field Code; Link*

Open

SEE: *File Management*

COMMAND AND FEATURE REFERENCE

Outline

Switch to Outline view in Excel, PowerPoint, and Word to display important data or text in the current worksheet, presentation, or document, or create a new outline. When you create an outline in Excel, the outline symbols appear. When you are in Outline view, the Outline toolbar appears to the left of the active window in PowerPoint, and just above the active window in Word, replacing the Ruler.

Using Outline View in Excel

Create an outline in Excel to display worksheet data in a summary report. In an Excel outline, as much data as necessary can be hidden or displayed.

In a worksheet outline, ranges of rows or columns are grouped, with each group containing the detail and summary data. An Excel outline can have up to eight levels of vertical and horizontal groups.

TIP: *Only one outline can be created for a worksheet. To create a second outline of the data, copy the worksheet to a different location in the workbook.*

To create an outline:

- When worksheet data is arranged with detail data directly above or to the left of summary data and formulas, select the data to be grouped, and then choose Data ➤ Group And Outline ➤ Auto Outline to create an automatic outline.

- Select Data ➤ Group And Outline ➤ Group to create an outline using detail data that is selected in either rows or columns.

OUTLINE

- Select a cell in a list, and then choose Data ➤ Subtotals to automatically subtotal and outline the list items.

The selected data appears with outline symbols above and/or to the left of the data.

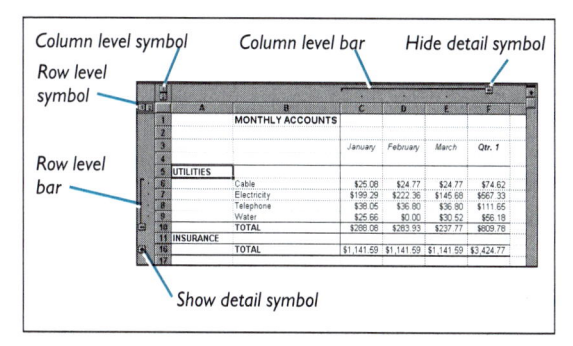

Column level symbol *Column level bar* *Hide detail symbol*
Row level symbol
Row level bar

	A	B	C	D	E	F
1		MONTHLY ACCOUNTS				
2						
3			January	February	March	Qtr. 1
4						
5	UTILITIES					
6		Cable	$25.08	$24.77	$24.77	$74.62
7		Electricity	$199.29	$222.36	$145.68	$567.33
8		Telephone	$38.05	$36.80	$36.80	$111.65
9		Water	$25.66	$0.00	$30.52	$56.18
10		TOTAL	$288.08	$283.93	$237.77	$809.78
11	INSURANCE					
16		TOTAL	$1,141.59	$1,141.59	$1,141.59	$3,424.77
17						

Show detail symbol

- Click on one of the *row or column level symbols* to display a specific level of data.

- Click on the *row or column level bar* to hide the corresponding detail rows or columns.

- Click on the *hide detail symbol* to hide the rows or columns indicated by its level bar.

- To display hidden detail rows or columns, click on the *show detail symbol*.

To have Excel apply automatic styles to each level of data that is to be outlined, choose the Automatic Styles option before the outline is created. To choose the option, select the data to be outlined, choose Data ➤ Group And Outline ➤ Settings to display the Outline dialog box, select the Automatic Styles check box, and then choose OK. To change the formatting for a level, change the style for that level.

To remove an outline or part of an outline, select the range that contains the outline, and then select Data ➤ Group And Outline ➤ Clear Outline.

COMMAND AND FEATURE REFERENCE

Or, to hide the outline symbols in a worksheet, select the range that contains the outline, choose Tools ➤ Options, choose the View tab, clear the Outline Symbols check box, and then choose OK.

Using Outline View in PowerPoint and Word

The text in an outline appears in *levels*, or different amounts of indentation in PowerPoint and Word. A title or heading appears at the first level (no indentation) and subsequent data appears at the next level (one indent). Up to five levels of indentation in PowerPoint and up to nine indentation levels in Word are possible.

> **TIP:** Click on the Report It button on PowerPoint's Standard toolbar to open or activate Word and display the text of your presentation outline in it. Switch to Word's Outline view to edit the presentation text. When you are finished, select Tools ➤ Macro, highlight PresentIt in the Macro Name list box, and then choose Run to return to PowerPoint and display the changes made to the text of the presentation.

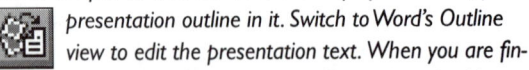

Switch to PowerPoint's Outline view to create or display only the text of a presentation. The title and text on each slide in a presentation appear beside the number of the slide and the slide icon. If a slide contains a graphic, small pictures appear on the slide icon.

Switch to Word's Outline view to display only document text to which one of Word's heading or paragraph styles was applied. Or, create an outline for your documents, and then fill in the paragraph text later.

To change to Outline view in PowerPoint and Word, click on the Outline View button on the horizontal scroll bar of the presentation or document window or choose View ➤ Outline.

OUTLINE

Use any of the following buttons on PowerPoint's and Word's Outlining toolbar to work with text in an outline:

TIP: *When a collapsed title or heading is moved, promoted, or demoted, all the subtext is moved with the heading. Select all the text to be moved, promoted, or demoted in an expanded title or heading.*

Click on the Promote button (Alt+Shift+←) to increase (move to the left) the level of the current heading, title, or text.

Click on the Demote button (Alt+Shift+→) to decrease (move to the right) the level of the current heading, title, or text.

TIP: *In Word, the plus icon next to a heading indicates that the heading has subtext, and the minus icon indicates that it does not have subtext. A small square icon indicates text in a paragraph (subtext). Click between the icon and the heading to select only the heading.*

You can also drag the slide or plus or minus icon beside an item to the left to promote it and any paragraph text, or to the right to demote it. To promote or demote only paragraph text, drag the paragraph icon (the small black or gray square) to the left or to the right. As you drag, a vertical line appears on the screen. Release the mouse button when the line is in the location in which you want the outline item.

In Word, click on the Demote To Body Text button (Ctrl+Shift+N) to change a heading into paragraph text.

Click on the Move Up button (Alt+Shift+↑) to move the selected item up one line. The moved item remains in the same outline level.

COMMAND AND FEATURE REFERENCE

Click on the Move Down button (Alt+Shift+↓) to move the selected item down one line. The moved item remains in the same outline level.

You can also drag the slide or plus icon up or down to move the heading and body text. Drag Word's minus icon or the paragraph icon up or down to move only the heading or the paragraph text. As you drag, a horizontal line appears on your screen. Release the mouse button when the line is in the location in which you want the outline item.

To expand the text on a single selected slide in PowerPoint or one level of heading text in Word, move the insertion point into a title or heading and click on the Expand button (Alt+Shift++). Or, double-click on the Expand button or the plus icon to expand all Word's heading text.

To expand the text on all slides in a PowerPoint presentation, click on the Show All button (Alt+Shift+A).

To collapse the text on a single selected slide in PowerPoint or one level of heading text in Word, move the insertion point into the title or heading and click on the Collapse button (Alt+Shift+ –). Or, double-click on the Collapse button or the minus icon to collapse all Word's heading text.

To collapse the text on all slides in a PowerPoint presentation, click on the Show Titles button (Alt+Shift+1).

To expand all the heading and paragraph text in Word, click on the All button (Alt+Shift+A). To expand the outline to only a specified level, click on the button that displays the corresponding level number.

In Word, click on the Show First Line Only button (Alt+Shift+L) to toggle the display between collapsing the current paragraph into its first line

OUTLINE

and expanding the first line of text into the whole paragraph.

Click on the Show Formatting button (/ on the numeric keypad) to toggle the display of character formatting in the outline.

When you print the outline in PowerPoint, it is printed just as it appears on your screen, including the slide numbers and icons, and the text formatting. Use View ➤ Master ➤ Outline Master to add a header and footer to each printed page.

In Word, only the headings and body text that appear on your screen are printed. Use View ➤ Header And Footer to add a header and footer to each printed page.

Numbering Word's Outline Headings

To automatically number the headings to which one of Word's built-in styles have been applied in an outline:

1. In Outline view, select Format ➤ Heading Numbering to display the Heading Numbering dialog box.

2. Select the numbering style to be used in the outline.

3. If necessary, select Modify to display the Modify Heading Numbering dialog box, customize the heading numbers, and then choose OK.

4. Choose OK in the Heading Numbering dialog box.

To remove heading numbers from a section of the outline, position the insertion point in the section, select Format ➤ Heading Numbering, choose Remove.

SEE ALSO: *Database; Header and Footer; Master Document; Master View; Presentation; Print; Slide Show; Style; View; Workbook*

COMMAND AND FEATURE REFERENCE

Page Break

Access automatically breaks form and report pages according to the options selected in the Print Setup dialog box. Excel inserts automatic page breaks on the basis of the paper size, margins, and scaling options in the Page Setup dialog box. Word automatically inserts a soft page break when a page is full and starts a new page in the document. If the document is edited, the soft page breaks are automatically adjusted.

To manually start a new page, add a manual or *hard* page break. A hard page break is not automatically adjusted when the file is edited. However, you can adjust the location of a hard page break by deleting it and inserting one in a different location.

Inserting Hard Page Breaks

To insert a page break control in a section of an Access form or report displayed in Design view, click on the Page Break button in the Toolbox, and then click in the position on the form or report at which a new page is to start.

In Excel, manual page breaks are inserted above and/or to the left of the selection.

- To insert both a horizontal and a vertical page break, select the cell at which a new page is to begin, and choose Insert ➤ Page Break.

- To insert a horizontal page break, select the row at which a new page is to begin and choose Insert ➤ Page Break.

- To insert a vertical page break, select the column at which a new page is to begin and choose Insert ➤ Page Break.

PAGE NUMBERS

- To remove a selected manual page break, select a cell just below a horizontal page break or to the right of a vertical page break. Then select Insert ➤ Remove Page Break.

- To remove all the manual page breaks in a worksheet, click on the Select All button at the left of the column headings to select the entire worksheet, and then select Insert ➤ Remove Page Break.

To insert a hard page break in a Word document, position the insertion point where you want to start a new page, and then press Ctrl+↵. Or, select Insert ➤ Break to display the Break dialog box, choose Page Break (the default) in the Insert area, and then choose OK.

To delete a hard page break in a Word document, click on the Normal View button on the horizontal scroll bar, or select View ➤ Normal. Select the hard page break (a horizontal line with "Page Break" on it), and then press Del.

SEE ALSO: *Columns; Control; Page Setup*

Page Numbers

You can add automatic page numbers to the printed pages in an Access form or report, an Excel worksheet, a PowerPoint presentation, or a Word document.

NOTE: *In PowerPoint, page numbers can be placed on notes pages, slides, outlines, and handouts. See "Master View" for information on numbering pages in PowerPoint.*

COMMAND AND FEATURE REFERENCE

Numbering Pages in Access

To number the pages in an Access form or report, insert a text box control in the position in which the page numbers are to appear, and then enter the Page property in the text box:

1. If necessary, click on the Database Window button on the Database toolbar to activate the Database window.

2. Highlight the name of the form or report on the Form or Report pane in the Database window, and then select Design.

3. Click on the Text Box button in the Toolbox, and then click in the location on the form or report in which you want to place the text box.

4. Click on the Properties button on the Form Design or Report Design toolbar to display the property sheet dialog box for the new text box.

5. If necessary, select Data Properties in the drop-down list.

6. Click in the Control Source property area, and then type **=Page** to number the pages of the form or report.

NOTE: *To enter the page number in relation to the total number of pages in a report, type* **="Page "&Page&" of "&Pages** *to format the page numbers as "Page N of TotalN."*

7. Double-click on the property sheet dialog box's Control menu box to close it.

8. Click on the Save button on the Form Design toolbar, or select File ➤ Save (Ctrl+S) to save the changed design of the form or report.

PAGE NUMBERS

The text box for the page number appears on each page of a form (for each item in the table or query on which the form is based) or report.

Numbering Pages in Excel

By default, page numbers appear in the footer on each printed page in Excel.

To change the starting page number when printing the current worksheet, choose File ➤ Page Setup, select the Page tab in the Page Setup dialog box, type the number that is to appear on the first page in the First Page Number text box, and then choose OK.

Numbering Pages in Word

To insert page numbers in a Word document in a frame within the header or footer, select Insert ➤ Page Numbers. You can drag the page number to any position in the document, but the header or footer will expand as you drag, depending on the new location.

NOTE: *Another way to number the pages in a document is to select View ➤ Header And Footer to display the Header And Footer toolbar, position the insertion point where the page numbers are to appear, and then click on the Page Numbers button.*

To insert page numbers:

1. Position the insertion point in the section of the document where page numbering is to be added.

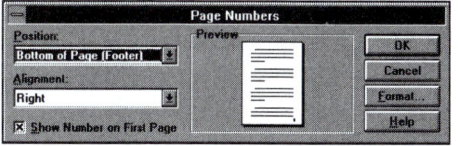

2. Select Insert ➤ Page Numbers to display the Page Numbers dialog box.

COMMAND AND FEATURE REFERENCE

3. Choose any of the following options to insert page numbers:

- Select Top Of Page (Header) or Bottom Of Page (Footer) in the Position drop-down list as the location for the number on each page.

- Select Left, Center, Right, Inside, or Outside in the Alignment drop-down list as the position between the left and right margins for the number on each page.

- Select the Show Number On First Page check box to display the page number on the first page of the document or section.

4. Select OK in the Page Numbers dialog box.

To change the format of page numbers:

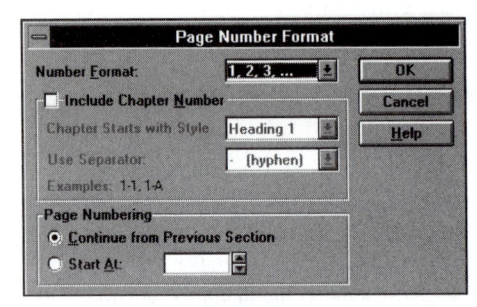

1. Select Insert ➤ Page Numbers, and then choose Format to display the Page Number Format dialog box.

2. If necessary, select the format for the numbers in the Number Format drop-down list.

> **TIP:** *You can also apply character formatting to a selected page number in a header or footer. Apply a style to the page number if you want page numbers in all your documents based on the template to have the same format.*

3. To insert the chapter number just before the page number, select the Include Chapter Number check box. If necessary, highlight a style for the chapter number in the Chapter Starts With Style drop-down list, and choose the character to be used as the separator between the chapter and the page numbers in the Use Separator drop-down list.

4. Select <u>C</u>ontinue From Previous Section to maintain consecutive numbers in adjacent document sections, or enter the number on which the section's page numbering is to begin in the Start <u>A</u>t text box.

5. Choose OK in the Page Number Format dialog box.

6. Choose OK again in the Page Numbers dialog box.

TIP: *Number the pages of a document before you divide it into sections. The headers and footers in each section are connected unless you break the connection with the Same As Previous button on the Header And Footer toolbar.*

To delete all the page numbers in a document or the section in which the insertion point is placed (if the connection between sections is broken), display the Header And Footer toolbar, select the page number, and then press Backspace or Del.

SEE ALSO: *Form; Header and Footer; Master View; Report*

Page Setup

The page setup defines the way each page in an Access form or report, an Excel worksheet, and a Word document appears when it is printed, including the margins, page layout, paper size, and the printer's paper source. The available paper size and source options depend on the printer that is set up to be used in all Windows applications.

COMMAND AND FEATURE REFERENCE

In PowerPoint, the command is called Slide Setup. It allows you to define the dimensions and numbering of the slides, and the orientation for slides, notes, handouts, and outlines.

Setting Up the Page

To define the appearance of the printed page or slide:

1. Activate the file whose page setup you want to change. In Word, you can also position the insertion point in the document section whose page setup you want to change.

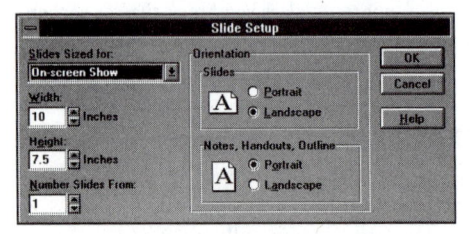

2. Select File ➤ Print Setup in Access, File ➤ Slide Setup in PowerPoint, or File ➤ Page Setup in Excel and Word to display the corresponding dialog box.

3. If necessary, specify the arrangement of each page as Portrait (the pages are taller than they are wide) or Landscape (the pages are wider than they are tall). In PowerPoint, select the orientation in the Slides and/or Notes, Handout, Outline area for the view to be printed.

4. Select a predefined paper size in the Paper Size or Slides Sized For drop-down list. In PowerPoint and Word, you can also select Custom or Custom Size and enter a measurement to define the width and height of the paper in the Width and Height text boxes.

5. Select any of the following options to further define the page setup:

NOTE: *In Access, choose More to display additional options in the Print Setup dialog box. In Excel's Page Setup dialog box, choose the options on the Page or Sheet tabs. In*

PAGE SETUP

Word's Page Setup dialog box, choose the options on the Paper Size, Paper Source, and Layout tabs.

Data Only	In Access, select the check box to print only the data in a preprinted form.
Items Across	Specify the number of columns to be printed in an Access form or report.
Row Spacing/ Column Spacing	Specify the amount of space between rows or columns on each page of an Access form or report.
Item Size	Select the Same As Detail check box to print the whole form or report. To print only a portion of the form or report, specify the size in the Width and Height text boxes.
Item Layout	To print forms or reports with more than one column specified in the Items Across text box, select Horizontal to print across the page or Vertical to print down one column, and then continue at the top of the next column.
Scaling	Select Adjust To, and then reduce or enlarge the Excel worksheet on the printed page to as little as 10 percent or as much as 400 percent of its normal size. Or, select Fit To to reduce the current worksheet so it will fit on the specified (or fewer) number of wide or tall pages.
Print Quality	Select the printer resolution to be used for the active Excel

COMMAND AND FEATURE REFERENCE

	worksheet. The greater the number of dots per inch, the higher the quality of the printed page.
First Page Number	Select Auto (the default) to begin numbering the pages of an Excel print job at 1, or at the next consecutive page number in the print job. Or, type the number that you want to appear on the first page.
Number Slides From	Specify the starting number to appear on the first slide in the presentation.
Print Area	Enter the range that is to be printed each time you print the active Excel worksheet.
Print Titles	In the Rows To Repeat At Top and the Columns To Repeat At Left text boxes, enter the range for the rows and columns that contain data that is to be printed on each page in the active Excel worksheet.
Gridlines	Select the check box to print the active worksheet's gridlines on each page.
Notes	Select the check box to print any notes in the active Excel worksheet on separate pages.
Draft Quality	Select the check box to speed up printing an Excel worksheet by printing few graphics and no gridlines.
Black and White	In Excel, select the check box to print colored objects in black and white on a color printer, foreground objects that are not

PAGE SETUP

completely white in black, and background objects that are not completely black in white.

Row and Column Headings — Select the check box to print the row and column headings in an Excel worksheet. You must select this option to include cell references when you print notes.

Page Order — Choose Down, Then Across to print and number the printed pages beginning at the top of the worksheet, continuing down, and then moving to the right. Or choose Across, Then Down to print and number the printed pages beginning at the top of the worksheet, continuing to the right, and then moving down.

Paper Source — For the first page of a Word document, choose which printer tray to use or select Manual Feed to define the location of the paper in the First Page list box. Choose options in the Other Pages list box to define the location of the paper for each page except the first in a Word document. In Access, select the location for all printed pages of the form or report in the Source drop-down list.

Section Start — In Word, highlight in the drop-down list the document location at which a new section is to begin and the previous section is to end. Select Continuous to begin a new section without inserting a page break; New Column to start the new section at the top of the next

COMMAND AND FEATURE REFERENCE

> ### TROUBLESHOOTING
>
> ## Working with Sections in a Word Document
>
> Do you want to include text in a document that has a different page layout than the rest of the document? You can insert a section break in a document to include a section with text that is formatted differently from the previous sections in the document. For example, in a newsletter, the first page may contain a one-column section (for the title, publisher, etc.) and a three-column section (for the news). The formatting for a section is stored in its section break. To copy text in a section, include the section break in the selection if you want to copy the format of the section and insert a section break in the new location.

column; New Page to insert a page break and begin the new section at the top of the next page; Even Page to begin the new section on the next even-numbered page; or Odd Page to begin the new section on the next odd-numbered page.

Vertical Alignment To define the vertical alignment of the text on each page, select one of the following options from the drop-down list: Top to align the top line of text along the top margin, Center to center the text between the top and bottom margins, or Justified to increase the space between paragraphs so the top line of text is aligned along the top margin and the bottom line of text is aligned along the bottom margin.

PARAGRAPH

S<u>u</u>ppress Endnotes	Select the check box to print the endnotes that are placed at the end of the current section directly before the endnotes at the end of the next section.
<u>A</u>pply To	In the drop-down list, select the portion of a Word document to which the changes in the Page Setup dialog box will apply.
<u>D</u>efault	Select the button to change Word's Paper <u>S</u>ize, <u>P</u>aper Source, or <u>L</u>ayout settings so the changes made apply to all new documents.

4. Choose OK in the Page Setup dialog box.

SEE ALSO: *Alignment; Footnotes and Endnotes; Form; Header and Footer; Indent; Margins; Note; Print; Report*

Paragraph

A paragraph consists of all the text and graphics that appear before a ¶ (paragraph mark) in Word. Formatting applied to the entire paragraph is stored in its paragraph mark. The format of the active paragraph is automatically applied to the next paragraph created when you press ↵.

NOTE: *To display paragraph marks and other nonprinting characters on your screen, toggle on the Show/Hide ¶ button on the Standard toolbar.*

299

COMMAND AND FEATURE REFERENCE

- To begin a new paragraph, position the insertion point at the end of a paragraph, and then press ↵. A paragraph mark is inserted, the current paragraph ends, and the insertion point moves to the beginning of the next paragraph.

- To manually begin a new line of text in a document without starting a new paragraph, press Shift+↵.

- To apply a different format to an existing paragraph, position the insertion point in the paragraph, or select the entire paragraph, including the paragraph mark. Then apply the desired format.

NOTE: *You can easily apply the same format to all paragraphs in a document by applying a paragraph style. By default, all paragraphs appear in Normal style in Word.*

Setting Paragraph Spacing

To specify the amount of space that appears between paragraphs:

1. Position the insertion point in the paragraph or select the entire paragraph.

2. Select Format ➤ Paragraph to display the Paragraph dialog box, and choose the Indents And Spacing tab.

3. In the Spacing area, enter a measurement in the Before and After text boxes to indicate the amount of spacing that is to appear before or after the current paragraph.

4. Choose OK in the Paragraph dialog box.

SEE ALSO: *Alignment; Borders and Shading; Bullets and Numbering; Indent; Line Spacing; Style; Tabs*

PARAGRAPH P

Password

In Access, a blank password is automatically created for each user account to verify the identity of the user. In Excel and Word, passwords are used to assign various levels of protection to files to keep data secure.

Passwords are case sensitive. In Access, passwords can contain up to 14 characters. In Excel and Word, they can contain as many as 15 characters made up of numbers, letters, symbols, and spaces.

Assigning a Password to an Access User Account

Although Access automatically assigns a blank password to each user account, each user should change the blank password to a real password so Access can verify the user's identity. The password is used when a user logs on to Access.

WARNING: *Change your password frequently to ensure the security of the data in the database.*

To assign a password to an Access user acount:

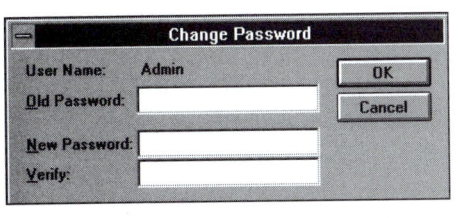

1. Select Security ➤ Change Password to display the Change Password dialog box with the name of the current user at the top.

2. To change an existing password, type the current password in the Old Password text box. Leave the text box blank if you are changing the blank password assigned by Access.

301

COMMAND AND FEATURE REFERENCE

> **TROUBLESHOOTING**
>
> ### What If a User Forgets His/Her Password?
>
> When an Access user's password is lost or forgotten, a person who belongs to the Admins group can clear the existing password. Choose Security ➤ Users, select the name of the user account whose password has been lost in the Name drop-down list, choose Clear Password, and then select Close. The user can then create a new password for his/her account.

3. Type the new password in the New Password text box. For security, Access displays asterisks instead of the characters in the text box.

4. Type the new password in the Verify text box, where asterisks are again displayed.

5. Choose OK to change the password.

The next time you start Access, the Logon dialog box appears. Type the name that is assigned to your user account in the Name text box, type your current password in the Password text box, and then choose OK to run Access.

WARNING: Be sure to store your password in a safe place, because you cannot recover it if you forget it. If you forget your password, a user with Administer permissions in your workgroup must clear your current password.

Assigning a Password to an Excel or Word File

To protect a file from being opened by others, assign a protection password to the file. Only a person who knows the password can open the document. You must save a file with a protection password before the protection goes into effect.

PASSWORD

Or, assign a write reservation password to a file so others can open it as a read-only file. Any changes made to a read-only file cannot be saved.

WARNING: *Keep a list of passwords you assign to your files. You must enter the protection password that is assigned to a file before the file can be opened, and you must enter the write reservation password before the file can be opened without read-only status.*

To assign a password to an Excel or Word file:

1. Activate the file to which a password is to be assigned, select File ➤ Save As (F12), and select Options. The Save Options or Options dialog box appears with the Save tab selected.

NOTE: *In Word, you can also choose Tools ➤ Options and select the Save tab to display the file protection options.*

Assign the password, and then choose OK in the Options dialog box. If you assigned a protection password, click on the Save button on the Standard toolbar to save the file so the password protection can go into effect.

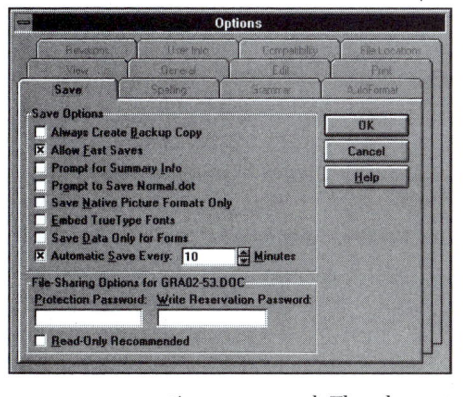

2. In the File Sharing or File-Sharing Options For *Filename* area, type a password in the Protection Password text box to create a protection password, or in the Write Reservation Password text box to create a write reservation password. The characters you type appear as asterisks.

3. Select OK to display the Confirm Password dialog box.

303

COMMAND AND FEATURE REFERENCE

4. Type the password again in the Reenter Protection/Write Reservation Password text box, and then select OK in the Confirm Password dialog box.

5. Select OK again in the Save As dialog box.

NOTE: *Instead of assigning a write reservation password, you can recommend that a document be opened as read-only so no changes can be saved to it. If you select the Read-Only Recommended check box in the Options dialog box, a dialog box asking whether to open the file as read-only will appear each time the file is opened.*

To change a protection or write reservation password:

1. Open the file. If the file has a write reservation password, do not open it with read-only status.

2. Select File ➤ Save As (F12) and select Options.

3. Highlight the asterisks that appear in the Password Protection or Write Reservation text box, and type a new password.

4. Type the password again in the Reenter Protection/Write Reservation Password text box.

5. Select OK in the Confirm Password dialog box, and again in the Save As dialog box.

NOTE: *To remove a protection or write reservation password, highlight the asterisks in the corresponding text box and press Del, and then save the file. If a file protected with a write reservation password is opened as read-only, the original file cannot be saved. Instead, select File ➤ Save As (F12) to save the file to a new name.*

SEE ALSO: *Annotation; File Management; Permissions; Protection; Revision*

Permissions

To secure the data or objects in an Access database, a workgroup administrator assigns *permissions* to individual user accounts or to groups of users in his/her workgroup. Permissions allow or prohibit access to the database or to objects in the database.

Changing Ownership

The *owner*, who is usually the creator of a database or a database object, automatically has Administer permissions for the database or object. The owner can be a user account, or ownership can be assigned to a group.

TIP: *To change the ownership of a database, create a new database, and then import the contents of the old database into the new one.*

To change ownership:

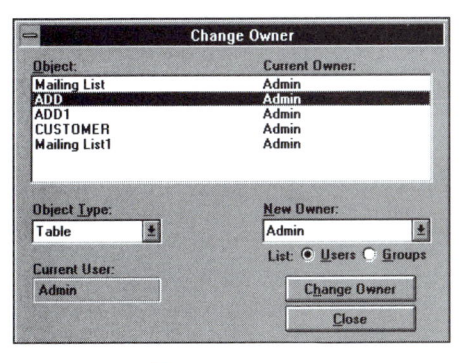

1. Open the database that contains an object whose ownership is to be changed, and then select Security ➤ Change Owner to display the Change Owner dialog box.

2. If necessary, select a different type of database object in the Object Type drop-down list to change the list of objects in the Object list box.

COMMAND AND FEATURE REFERENCE

3. Select the database object in the Object list box.

4. If necessary, select Users or Groups in the List area to display the list of users or the list of groups in the New Owner drop-down list.

5. Select the name of the user or group that is to be the new owner of the selected object in the New Owner drop-down list.

6. Choose Change Owner to change the ownership of the object.

7. Repeat steps 2 through 5 as necessary, and then select Close.

Creating a Group or User Account

The easiest way to secure a database is to create groups with different permissions to access certain portions of the database file, and then add user accounts to the groups. A user account may be included in more than one group, thereby increasing the amount of access allowed to the user. User accounts must be stored in the workgroup that the user will use.

NOTE: *There must always be at least one user account in the Admins group.*

By default, Access creates the Admins, Users, and Guests groups, and the Admin and Guest user accounts. None of these groups or user accounts can be deleted. All user accounts are added to the Users group by default and, with the exception of the Guest account, cannot be removed. To remove a user account other than the Guest account from the Users group, you must delete it.

When you create a new group or user account, the name you assign can contain up to 20 characters and can consist of letters, numbers, spaces, and

PERMISSIONS

some symbols. However, the name cannot contain any leading spaces, any of the ASCII characters from 0 to 31, or any of the following symbols: " (quotation mark); / (slash); \ (backslash); [ ] (brackets); : (colon); ; (semicolon); , (comma); ? (question mark); * (asterisk); | (vertical bar); < (less than); > (greater than); + (plus); = (equal to).

To create a group account:

1. With the database file for which permissions are to be assigned open, select Security ➤ Groups to display the Groups dialog box.

2. Type the name for the new group in the Name text box, and then select New to display the New User/Group dialog box.

3. In the Personal ID text box, type a PID (personal identifier).

NOTE: *The PID that is assigned to each user account and group name can contain up to 20 characters. Access uses a combination of the name and the PID to identify the account.*

4. Select OK in the New User/Group dialog box, and then select Close in the Groups dialog box.

NOTE: *To delete a group, select the name of the group in the Name drop-down list, choose Delete and then choose OK to confirm the deletion. Choose Close in the Groups dialog box.*

COMMAND AND FEATURE REFERENCE

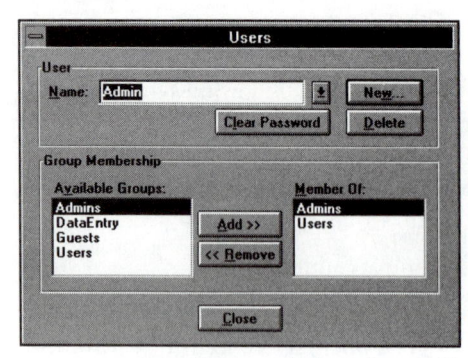

5. To create a user account and add it to a group, select Security ➤ Users to display the Users dialog box.

6. In the User area, type the name for a new user account in the Name text box, and then choose New to display the New User/Group dialog box.

NOTE: *To delete a user account, select the name of the account in the Name drop-down list, choose Delete, and then choose OK to confirm the deletion.*

7. Type a PID in the Personal ID text box, and then choose OK to return to the Users dialog box.

8. In the Group Membership area, select the name of a group in the Available Groups list box to which the user account is to be added, and then select Add to place the name of the group in the Member Of list box.

9. Repeat step 8 for each group to which the user account is to be added.

NOTE: *If a user account is added as a member of a group by mistake, highlight the name of the group in the Member Of list box, and then choose Remove.*

10. Choose Close to return to the database.

Only user account names can be used to log on to Access. They are not case-sensitive during the log-on procedure.

PERMISSIONS

> **WARNING:** *If a deleted group or user account name is being re-created, or if the name is being created in a different workgroup, both the name and the PID must be exactly the same as the original name and PID, including the case of each letter. The workgroup administrator should keep a list of each name and PID that is assigned so an account can be recovered, if necessary.*

Granting Permissions

To assign permissions for access to a specific database object, the user must be logged on to Access as a user in the Admins group of the workgroup that created the database object, the owner of the database object, or a user in a group that is assigned Administer permissions for the object. To assign permissions for a database, the user must be logged on as a user in the Admins group, or as the owner of the database.

> **WARNING:** *The permissions assigned to an individual user account are combined with the permissions assigned to any groups to which the user belongs, even though only the permissions assigned to the selected user appear in the Permissions dialog box. For example, if a user is allowed Read Design permission and is a member of a group that has Modify Design permission, the user also has Modify Design permission.*

Before a database can be secure, remove all the permissions from the Admin user and Users group, which contains all the users in the workgroup. Then assign the necessary permissions to each user.

To assign permissions:

1. With the database for which permissions are to be assigned open, choose Security ➤ Permissions to display the Permissions dialog box.

COMMAND AND FEATURE REFERENCE

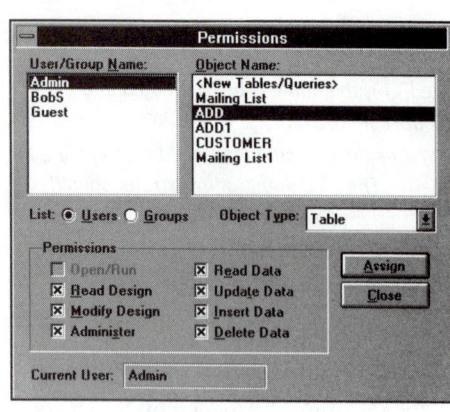

2. If necessary, select Users or Groups to display the names you want in the User/Group Name list box.

3. Select a name in the User/Group Name list box to which permissions are to be assigned.

4. If necessary, select the kind of database objects to be displayed in the Object Name list box in the Object Type drop-down list.

5. Select the database object for which the permissions are to be assigned in the Object Name list box.

> **TIP:** *To assign permissions to the selected group or user that will be used for all new objects of the selected type created in the active database, highlight <New Object Type> in the Object Name list box.*

6. In the Permissions area, select any of the following check boxes to grant the corresponding permission for the selected object to the selected user or group. Clear the check boxes of permissions that are to be removed.

> **NOTE:** *A permission that is not available to the selected user or group appears grayed or ghosted in the dialog box.*

Open/Run Allows the user or group to open a database or a report or form in the database, or to run a macro in the database.

Open Exclusive Allows the user to open a database and prevent other users from making changes to data or database objects.

PERMISSIONS

TIP: *To prevent other users from opening the database, select the Exclusive check box in the Open Database dialog box. To prevent others from making any changes to the data, select the Read Only check box in the Open Database dialog box.*

Read Design Allows users or groups to display tables, queries, forms, reports, macros, and modules in Design view when selected.

Modify Design Allows users or groups to display database objects in Design view, and modify and delete tables, queries, forms, reports, macros, and modules in the selected database.

Administer Allows the user full access to all objects and data in the selected database. A user with Administer permission has the ability to grant or remove permissions.

Read Data Allows the user to read the data in tables and queries.

Update Data Allows the user or group to display and edit the existing data in tables and queries, but not to add or delete any data.

Insert Data Allows the user or group to display existing data in tables and queries, but not to change or delete it. However, the user or group can add new data to the table or query.

Delete Data Allows the user or group to display and delete existing data in tables and queries. However, the user or group cannot change the existing data or add new data to the table or query.

7. Choose Assign to assign the permissions.

8. Choose Close to return to the database.

COMMAND AND FEATURE REFERENCE

When a database object is edited and saved to the same name, the permissions that are assigned in the object stay with the object. However, all the permissions are lost if the database object is saved to a different name, imported, exported, or cut and pasted into a different object.

SEE ALSO: Password; Print Security; Workgroup

Pivot Table

Create a pivot table in Excel to summarize data in a *list* or database, and display the summary so it can be analyzed. A pivot table allows you to rotate the row and column headings in order to display different views of the data, and can be updated when the data in the source changes.

The summary of the data is created using calculations you define with Excel's summary functions.

Creating a Pivot Table

Use data in an Excel list, a worksheet range with labeled columns, a collection of ranges with labeled rows and columns, an existing pivot table, or data from a different database application as the source data in a pivot table. Then specify the data to use in the source as the *fields* (data categories, often the column or row labels) and *items* (data subcategories, often the data that appears in a field) that are to appear in the pivot table.

Multiple pivot tables can be placed on an worksheet, or you can create them on separate worksheets in the workbook. Use the PivotTable Wizard

PIVOT TABLE

to select the source data and design the layout of the pivot table.

To create a pivot table:

1. Select <u>D</u>ata ➤ <u>P</u>ivotTable to display the first PivotTable Wizard dialog box.

2. Select <u>M</u>icrosoft Excel List Or Database, <u>E</u>xternal Data Source, Multiple <u>C</u>onsolidation Ranges, or Another PivotTable as the data source for the new pivot table, and then choose Next.

TIP: *To place the data in an external data source on the active worksheet, select <u>D</u>ata ➤ Get E<u>x</u>ternal Data to open Microsoft Query. Select the fields that contain the necessary data, and then choose <u>F</u>ile ➤ <u>R</u>eturn Data To Microsoft Excel to place the table with the selected data in an Excel worksheet.*

3. In the PivotTable Wizard–Step 2 of 4 dialog box, enter the location of the data source selected in the first PivotTable Wizard dialog box. For example, type or select a range in the <u>R</u>ange text box if you selected <u>M</u>icrosoft Excel List Or Database, or select <u>G</u>et Data to open Microsoft Query if you selected <u>E</u>xternal Data Source.

4. Choose Next to define the layout of the pivot table. Drag the fields (the column labels in an Excel list) from the source data into the <u>R</u>ow and <u>C</u>olumn areas in the dialog box to create the row labels and column labels in the pivot table.

TIP: *Add as many fields to the pivot table as you like. The more fields that are added, the more detail appears in the pivot table.*

5. Drag the fields that are to be summarized from the source data into the <u>D</u>ata area of the dialog box.

COMMAND AND FEATURE REFERENCE

> **TROUBLESHOOTING**
>
> ### Inserting a Pivot Table in an Unopened Workbook
>
> The workbook that contains the worksheet in which you insert a pivot table does not have to be open. If you want to create a pivot table in a worksheet that is in a closed workbook file, type the path, name of the workbook, name of the worksheet, and the cell reference for the top-left cell in the pivot table. If the pivot table is to be placed on a new worksheet in the workbook, leave the PivotTable Starting Cell text box empty.

6. To display data for only one type of item at a time in the pivot table, drag its field into the Page area of the dialog box. This creates a drop-down list above the pivot table, from which you can select the type of data to display.

7. Choose Next to display the PivotTable–Step 4 of 4 dialog box. Select the first cell for the pivot table or type the cell reference in the PivotTable Starting Cell text box.

8. If necessary, type a name for the pivot table in the PivotTable Name text box.

9. Select any of the following options (all are selected by default) to create the pivot table:

- To create totals for the data in columns, select the Grand Totals For Columns check box.

- To create totals for the data in rows, select the Grand Totals For Rows check box.

- To save a duplicate set of the source data for the pivot table, select Save Data With Table Layout. If you clear this check box,

PIVOT TABLE

hidden source data is lost when the file containing the pivot table is closed, and other data in other pivot tables that use the new pivot table as a source is lost.

TIP: *If the Save Data With Table Layout check box is cleared, click on the Refresh Data button on the Query And Pivot toolbar to restore the lost data.*

- To apply an autoformat to the pivot table, select the AutoFormat Table check box.

10. Choose Finish to create the pivot table and display the Query And Pivot toolbar.

By default, Excel uses the Sum function to calculate and summarize the data if the data field contains numeric data, and the Count function to total the number of the items if the data field contains text.

Customizing a Pivot Table

Once a pivot table has been created, it can be customized and formatted. Use the buttons on the Query And Pivot toolbar and the pivot table's shortcut menu to customize the active pivot table.

To change the layout of the displayed pivot table, drag a field button to a different row, column, or page orientation, or drag an item to a different position in the same field.

Select any cell in the pivot table, and then click on the Pivot Table Wizard button or select Data ➤ PivotTable to display the PivotTable Wizard–Step 3 of 4 dialog box. To delete a field or item, just drag it off the Page, Column, Row, or Data area of the dialog box. To change a field's or item's position, drag it to the new location in the appropriate area of the dialog box. When you have made the necessary changes, select Finish.

COMMAND AND FEATURE REFERENCE

To delete a row, column, or page field from the pivot table displayed on a worksheet, drag its button out of the pivot table and into the worksheet.

To delete a data field from the pivot table, right-click on the data field, and then select Delete in the shortcut menu.

To return a deleted data field or add a new data field to the pivot table, right-click on the table and select Add Field in the shortcut menu. Then select the name of the field to be added in the list.

To update changes made to the source data in the pivot table, click on the Refresh Data button on the Query And Pivot toolbar, or right-click on the pivot table and select Refresh Data.

To change the format of selected cells in the pivot table, select the cells, and then right-click on the selection. Choose Format Cells to display the Format Cells dialog box, and then change the necessary format for the selected cells.

To change the way the data in the pivot table is calculated:

1. Select a cell that contains a value in the data area in the pivot table and click on the Pivot Table Field button or choose Data ➤ PivotTable Field to display the PivotTable Field dialog box.

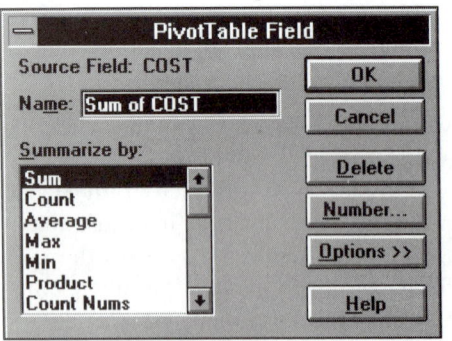

2. If necessary, type a different data field name in the Name text box.

TIP: To delete the selected data field, choose Delete in the PivotTable Field dialog box.

PIVOT TABLE

3. In the §ummarize By list box, select one of the following functions to calculate the summary for the values in the data field specified in the Name text box:

Sum	(The default) Calculates the total of all the values in the data.
Count	Returns the total number of records in the data.
Average	Calculates the average of the values in the data.
Max	Returns the largest value in the data.
Min	Returns the smallest value in the data.
Product	Calculates the product of the values in the data.
Count Nums	Returns the number of records that contain values in the data.
StdDev	Calculates the standard deviation in a sample of the data.
StdDevp	Calculates the standard deviation in all the data.
Var	Estimates the variance, using a sample of the data.
Varp	Estimates the variance, using all the data.

4. To change the format of the values displayed in the data area of the pivot table, select №umber to display the number options in the Format Cells dialog box, select the format, and then choose OK.

5. To change the type of calculation for a data field by creating a summary that compares the values in cells in the data area, select a cell in the data area of that field, and then select Options.

COMMAND AND FEATURE REFERENCE

6. Select one of the following types of custom calculation for the selected data field:

Difference From	Calculates the data in the data area as the difference between the field specified in the Base Field list box and the item specified in the Base Item list box.
% Of	Calculates the data in the data area as a percentage of the field specified in the Base Field list box and the item specified in the Base Item list box.
% Difference From	Calculates the data as the difference between the specified Base Field and Base Item, and displays the result as a percentage of the data.
Running Total In	Calculates a running total for successive items in the specified field.
% Of Row	Calculates the data in a row as a percentage of the total value in the row.
% Of as Column	Calculates the data in a column a percentage of the total value in the column.
% Of Total	Calculates the data in the data area as a percentage of the total of all data in the pivot table.
Index	Calculates the data using the formula: ((cell value)*(Grand Total))/((Grand Row Total)*(Grand Column Total)).
Normal	Removes the custom calculation from the field.

7. If necessary specify the field specified in the Base Field list box or the item specified in the Base Item list box for the calculation.

8. Choose OK in the PivotTable Field dialog box.

Customizing the Way the Table Is Displayed

Create a group in a data field for data that should be summarized in a category not contained in the data source. Group items so you can display a summary of the group, group numbers into a range, or group dates and times into larger units of time.

Select the items to be grouped in a field in the pivot table, and then click on the Group button on the Query And Pivot toolbar. Or, right-click on the selection, choose Group And Outline, and select Group to create a field for the group and an item containing the group in the field in the pivot table.

TIP: *To group items in a page field, drag the page field button to a row or column and then group the items. Then drag the group field back to the position for the page field.*

Select a group that contains items to be ungrouped in a field in the pivot table, and then click on the Ungroup button on the Query And Pivot toolbar. Or, right-click on the selection, choose Group And Outline, and select Ungroup to remove each item from the group.

In a pivot table that has multiple row or column fields, or that contains grouped items, display summary data for items that are hidden.

To hide an item and display its summary data, double-click on the item in an outer row or column field in the table. Or, select a cell that contains an item in the outer row or column field, and click on the Hide Detail button on the Query And Pivot toolbar.

COMMAND AND FEATURE REFERENCE

To hide details and display summary data for all items in a field, select the field button and click on the Hide Detail button on the Query And Pivot toolbar, or right-click on the field button, select Group And Outline in the shortcut menu, and then select Hide Detail.

To redisplay an item and hide its summary data, double-click on the item in an outer row or column field in the table. Or, select the cell that contains the summary item in the outer row or column field, and click on the Show Detail button on the Query And Pivot toolbar.

To redisplay details and hide summary data for all items in a field, select the field button, and then click on the Show Detail button on the Query And Pivot toolbar. Or, right-click on the field button, select Group And Outline in the shortcut menu, and choose Show Detail.

To create a pivot table for each item in the page field on a separate worksheet in the active workbook, click on the Show Pages button on the Query And Pivot toolbar. Or, right-click on the table, select Show Pages, highlight the name of the field in the Show All Pages Of list box, and choose OK in the Show Pages dialog box.

The items in a field that is added to a pivot table are automatically sorted in ascending order according to their labels. To sort the items in a field in descending order, select an item in the field or the item's field button, and then click on the Sort Descending button on the Standard toolbar. To return the items to ascending sort order, select an item in the field or the field button, and then click on the Sort Ascending button on the Standard toolbar.

To sort items by their values, select the field name that contains the items to be sorted, and then choose Data ➤ Sort to display the Sort dialog box. Select a cell in the data area for the item by which

POSTOFFICE MANAGER

to sort (Values is automatically selected in the Sort area), and then choose OK.

SEE ALSO: *AutoFormat; Crosstab Query; Filter; Format; MS Query; Shortcut Menus*

Postoffice Manager

A workgroup post office (WGPO) is a directory that contains the information for the mail accounts in a workgroup. To send or receive mail, each person must be a member of the same workgroup, must have a copy of Mail installed on his/her computer, and must have a Mail account set up in the WGPO. The WGPO is set up and managed by one person (usually the workgroup administrator) in a directory on one computer. The WGPO can contain many different workgroups.

NOTE: *To send or receive mail from people in other workgroups, the Microsoft Mail PostOffice Upgrade for Windows for Workgroups must be installed.*

Managing the WGPO

Postoffice Manager is available in Microsoft Mail only on the computer of the person who set up the WGPO.

NOTE: *The WGPO is set up by default when you install Windows for Workgroups on a network.*

To administer the WGPO:

1. If necessary, click on the Microsoft Mail button on the Microsoft Office Manger toolbar to open Mail, type your password, and choose OK.

321

COMMAND AND FEATURE REFERENCE

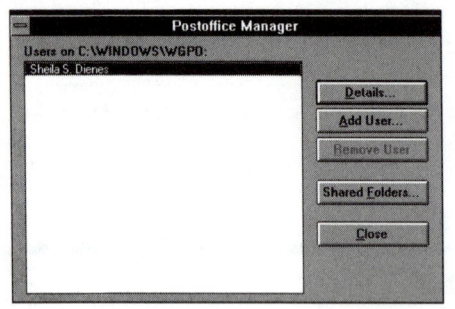

2. Select <u>M</u>ail ➤ <u>P</u>ostoffice Manager to display the Postoffice Manager dialog box.

3. Select any of the following options to manage the WGPO:

<u>D</u>etails To change any of the details for a post office account, select the name of a user in the Users On *Path* list box, and then choose <u>D</u>etails. A dialog box appears that contains the person's <u>N</u>ame, <u>M</u>ailbox (address), <u>P</u>assword (only asterisks appear), Phone #<u>1</u>, Phone #<u>2</u>, <u>O</u>ffice, <u>D</u>epartment, and No<u>t</u>es about the user or the postoffice account. Change any necessary item, and then choose OK to modify the details for the account.

<u>A</u>dd User To add a new user to the WGPO, select <u>A</u>dd User, and then enter the <u>N</u>ame, <u>M</u>ailbox (address), <u>P</u>assword, Phone #<u>1</u>, Phone #<u>2</u>, <u>O</u>ffice, <u>D</u>epartment, and No<u>t</u>es about the user or the postoffice account in the corresponding text box, and choose OK.

<u>R</u>emove User Select the name of a user to be removed from the WGPO in the Users On *Path* list box, and then select <u>R</u>emove User. Choose <u>Y</u>es to confirm that the person's name is to be removed from the WGPO.

Shared To display the number of shared
Folders folders, number of messages in the shared folders, the amount of space the messages are using on the hard disk that contains the WGPO, and the amount of space that can be recovered by compressing the messages, select Shared Folders. Choose Close to return to the Postoffice Manager.

4. Choose Close to exit the Postoffice Manager.

SEE ALSO: *Folder; Mail*

Presentation

With PowerPoint, you can easily create professional-looking presentations that include text, graphics, and color. The presentation can be placed on slides, displayed from a computer, or printed on transparencies, and can include notes for the speaker and handouts for the audience.

PowerPoint comes with more than 100 templates that define the backgrounds, colors, and master views that will appear on each slide. Or, you can create a custom look for the background and master slide view.

Creating a Presentation

The easiest way to create a presentation is to use the AutoContent Wizard or the Pick A Look Wizard. Both are available in the PowerPoint dialog box that appears when you start PowerPoint, and in the

COMMAND AND FEATURE REFERENCE

New Presentation dialog box that appears when you click on the New button on the Standard toolbar or choose File ➤ New (Ctrl+N) to start a new presentation while PowerPoint is running.

Each page of a presentation is called a *slide*. A slide contains the text that is to be presented, along with the background colors and graphics applied to the entire presentation with the template selected. Each slide can be edited separately. The slides are assigned an order within the presentation.

To create a presentation:

1. Click on the Microsoft PowerPoint button on the Microsoft Office Manager toolbar to start PowerPoint.

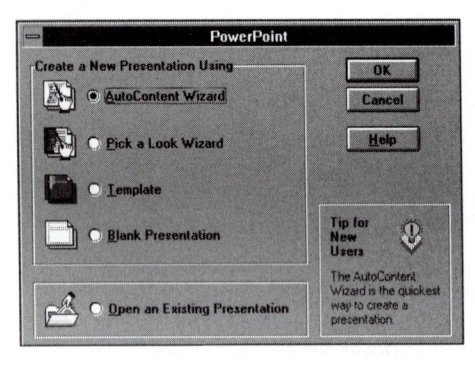

2. Read the Tip Of The Day, and then choose OK to close the dialog box and display the PowerPoint dialog box.

3. Choose any of the following options, and then choose OK in the PowerPoint dialog box:

> **TIP:** *The options selected can be changed any time the presentation is active.*

- Select AutoContent Wizard to create a presentation in which the template is selected for you. Type the text that is to appear on the first slide in the presentation, and select an option describing the goal of the presentation. The presentation is created and displayed in Outline view so you can make any necessary changes to the text.

PRESENTATION

- Select **P**ick A Look Wizard to create a presentation in which you choose the type of output, a design for the background, the views in which the presentation can be printed, and the Slide, Notes, Handout, and Outline master views for the presentation. The Wizard creates the presentation and displays it in Slide view.

- Select **T**emplate to display the Presentation Template dialog box. PowerPoint's Template subdirectory has subdirectories that contain template files to use for creating black and white overheads, color overheads, and slide shows. If necessary, select the subdirectory that contains the template that is to be applied in the **D**irectories list box. Then select the name of the template file in the File **N**ame list box, and choose **A**pply to display the New Slide dialog box. Select the layout for the first slide in the presentation in the Choose An **A**utoLayout list box, and then choose OK.

- Select **B**lank Presentation to display the New Slide dialog box. Choose the layout for the first slide in the Choose An **A**utoLayout list box, and then select OK. The new presentation is created with a blank background.

- Choose **O**pen An Existing Presentation to display the Open dialog box. Select the name of the presentation file to be opened in the File **N**ame list box, and then choose OK. The presentation file contains all the text and graphics assigned to the slides, as well as the notes, handouts, slide show, and outline created for the presentation.

COMMAND AND FEATURE REFERENCE

> **NOTE:** *If a new presentation is started while PowerPoint is running, the Current Presentation Format option appears in the New Presentation dialog box. Select the option to create a new presentation using the same template and displayed in the same view as the active presentation.*

Editing a Presentation

Change the view in which the presentation is displayed to make your work easier.

Click on the Slide View button on the horizontal scroll bar or select View ➤ Slides to display each slide, one at a time, in the presentation. In Slide view, you can change the layout applied to the slide and add graphics to it. Slide view displays each slide exactly as it will appear when printed on transparencies or slides, or displayed in a slide show.

> **TIP:** *Click on the Next Slide button on the vertical scroll bar to display the next slide in Slide view. Click on the Previous Slide button to display the previous slide. Drag the scroll box on the vertical scroll bar to move to a specific slide number while in Slide view.*

Click on the Outline View button on the horizontal scroll bar or choose View ➤ Outline to display the text of the presentation in an outline for an overall view of the ideas presented. If existing slides contain graphics, the slide icon that appears in Outline view beside the text on each slide contains a graphic.

To change to Slide Sorter view and display the Slide Sorter toolbar, click on the Slide Sorter View button on the horizontal scroll bar or choose View ➤ Slide Sorter. All the slides in the presentation appear miniaturized on the screen, and, with a mouse, can easily be moved around in the presentation, copied, or deleted.

PRESENTATION

Click on the Notes Pages View button on the status bar, or choose View ➤ Notes Pages to display a miniaturized version of the current slide above a text box. Type speaker notes for the slide in the text box. While in Notes Pages view, you can enter notes for each slide in the presentation.

To preview the way each slide in the presentation will appear in a slide show, click on the Slide Show button. Or, select View ➤ Slide Show to display the Slide Show dialog box to set the options before running the slide show.

Layout... To change the layout of the current slide, click on the Layout button on the status bar or choose Format ➤ Slide Layout to display the Slide Layout dialog box. Select the layout to which the slide is to be changed in the Change The Layout Of The Slide To list box, and then choose Apply.

New Slide... To insert a new slide in the presentation, click on the New Slide button on the status bar or choose Insert ➤ New Slide (Ctrl+M) to display the New Slide dialog box. The layout of the current slide will be selected. Choose the layout for the new slide in the Choose An AutoLayout list box, and then choose OK.

Template... To change the template that is applied to the current presentation, click on the Template button on the status bar or choose Format ➤ Presentation Template to display the Presentation Template dialog box. If necessary, select the subdirectory that contains the templates for black and white overheads, color overheads, or slide shows. Then highlight the name of the template file in the File Name list box and choose Apply.

SEE ALSO: *Master View; Outline; Print; Slide Show*

COMMAND AND FEATURE REFERENCE

Print

The printer that is currently set up for all Windows applications is the one that will be used to print the active Access database object or Excel, PowerPoint, or Word file. When it is printed, the object or file will appear as it is displayed in the Print Preview window in each of the Microsoft Office applications.

TIP: *Always save a file before you print it. That way, in case of any kind of system error, a copy of the file remains on your hard disk.*

Printing a File

To print the current file or a selection in the file using the current settings in the Print dialog box, click on the Print button on the Standard toolbar.

To change the settings in the Print dialog box and then print the file:

1. If necessary, select the portion of the file to be printed.

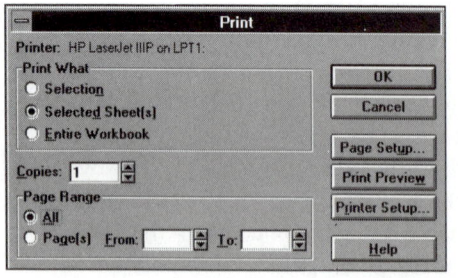

2. Select File ➤ Print (Ctrl+P) to display the Print dialog box, with the name of the printer that is currently set up at the top.

3. Enter the number of copies to be printed in the Copies text box.

4. If multiple copies are specified in Access, PowerPoint, and Word, select the Collate Copies check box to print one entire copy of the file, object, or selection, and then print the next entire copy.

5. Choose any of the following options depending on the active Microsoft Office application:

Print Range In Access, select what portion of the current database object is to be printed. Choose All to print the entire object, Selection to print only selected data, or Pages, and then specify the range of pages in the From and To text boxes.

Print What In Excel, choose Selection, Selected Sheet(s), or Entire Workbook as the portion of the current file to be printed. In PowerPoint, select Slides (with or without builds, if available), Notes Pages, Handouts with 2, 3, or 6 slides per page, or Outline View. In Word, choose Document, Summary Info, or Annotations as the portion of the file to print in the Print What drop-down list. Or, select Styles to print a description of the styles used in the file, AutoText Entries to print the entries in the current and global templates, or Key Assignments to print the customized macro key assignments and descriptions for the current template.

Page Range Indicate which pages of the current file are to be printed. In Excel, select All to print all the pages of the selection indicated in the Print What area, or Page(s) to print the range of pages specified in the From and To text boxes. In Word, Select All to print the whole document, Current Page to print only the page that

COMMAND AND FEATURE REFERENCE

	contains the insertion point, Selection to print a selection in the document, or Pages to print the pages specified. (Type 0 to print an envelope attached to the beginning of a document.)
Slide Range	In PowerPoint, choose All to print the entire file in the view selected in the Print What drop-down list, Current Slide to print only the active slide, Selection to print only the current selection, or Slides to print the specified slides or range of slides.
Print	In Word, select the order in which to print the specified pages in the drop-down list. Choose All Pages In Range to print the range of pages specified in the Pages text box. Or, when printing on both sides of the paper, select Odd Pages, and then choose File ➤ Print (Ctrl+P) again and select Even Pages.
Print to File	To print the active file, object, or selection to a .PRN file so it can be printed on a different printer or a different system in Access, PowerPoint, and Word, select the check box, and then choose OK to display the Print To File dialog box. Type a name for the file in the Output File Name text box, and then choose OK.
Print Hidden Slides	Select the check box to print slides that are hidden in the presentation.
Black & White	Select the check box to print slides with all solid fills in white, all

PRINT

patterned fills in black and white, and to add a narrow black frame to all objects that do not have borders or contain text.

Scale to Fit Paper Select the check box to size each slide in the presentation so it will fit on the paper selected when the printer is set up.

Pure Black & White Select the check box to change all colored fills to white, all text and borders to black, to add borders to any filled object that does not already have a border, and print all pictures in grayscale.

Print Quality In Access, select a high, medium, or low print quality in the drop-down list to define the quality of the data on the page. The higher the quality, the more dots per inch printed, but the slower the data is printed.

4. Select OK in the Print dialog box to print the file, object, or selection.

Setting Up the Printer

Before you print for the first time, or if you change to a different printer, you must set up the printer to use when printing all your Windows applications' files.

TIP: *The fonts that are applied to text in the file may not be available on a different printer. Be sure to check the appearance of the file before you print it.*

To set up the printer:

1. Select File ➤ Print (Ctrl+P) to display the Print dialog box, and then choose Setup, Printer Setup, or Printer to display the Print Setup or Printer Setup dialog box.

COMMAND AND FEATURE REFERENCE

2. In Access, select the name of a printer driver in the Specific Printer drop-down list in the Printer area. In Excel, PowerPoint, and Word, select the name of a printer driver that is available on your system in the Printer(s) list box.

NOTE: *Generally, the default options that are set for the selected printer driver do not need to be changed. However, if you do want to change any of the options for the selected printer driver, choose Setup or Options in the Print Setup or Printer Setup dialog box.*

3. Select Set As Default Printer to make the selected printer the one used to print files in all your Windows applications.

4. Choose OK or Close in the Print Setup or Printer Setup dialog box.

5. Choose Cancel or Close in the Print dialog box.

Setting Word's Default Print Options

To customize some of Word's default printing options for all printed documents:

1. Select File ➤ Print (Ctrl+P) and choose Options, or select Tools ➤ Options and choose the Print tab in the Options dialog box.

2. Select any of the following options:

- Select the Draft Output check box to print documents with little or no formatting, depending on the selected printer.

- Select the Reverse Print Order check box to print the specified pages of the active document, beginning with the last page. Clear the check box to print an envelope or to print the pages first to last.

- Select the Update Fields check box to

PRINT

update all field codes in your documents before printing them.

- Select the Update Links check box to update the links in all documents before printing.

- Select the Background Printing check box (selected by default) to allow you to continue working in Word while documents are being printed. Clear the check box to speed up printing.

- Select the Summary Info check box to print summary information on a page after the regular document text.

- Select the Field Codes check box to print the field codes instead of their results in all documents.

- Select the Annotations check box to print annotations on a page after the regular document text.

- Select the Hidden Text check box to print hidden text, whether or not it is displayed in your documents.

- Select the Drawing Objects check box (selected by default) to print objects created with Draw.

- In the Options For Current Document Only area, select the Print Data Only For Forms check box to print only the data entered in a form field.

- Select the printer tray to be used for printing all Windows applications' files in the Default Tray drop-down list. (See the "Page Setup" entry for information on how to change the tray for a single document section.)

3. Choose OK in the Options dialog box.

COMMAND AND FEATURE REFERENCE

SEE ALSO: *Margins; Page Setup; Print Preview*

Print Preview

Use Print Preview to display an Access database object, or an Excel or Word file exactly as it will appear when printed. The portion of the file that appears in the Print Preview window depends on the location of the insertion point in the active file and which part of the file is specified as the portion to be printed in the Print dialog box.

Changing to Print Preview

To switch to Print Preview in Access, Excel, and Word, click on the Print Preview button on the Database or Standard toolbar. Or, select File ➤ Print Preview.

The Print Preview window appears, along with the Print Preview toolbar or button bar. Use the buttons on the toolbar or button bar to change the appearance of the page or otherwise manipulate the appearance of the file in the Print Preview window.

When you display a database object in Access's Print Preview window:

Click on the Close Window button to close the Print Preview window and return the selected display of the database object.

Click on the Print button to display the Print dialog box. Then change any settings necessary and choose OK to print the database object.

PRINT PREVIEW

To change any of the defined print settings before the database object is printed, click on the Print Setup button to display the Print Setup dialog box.

Click on the Zoom button to reduce the size of the displayed page. Click on it again to return it to its enlarged size.

To create an .RTF file with the contents of the database object, and then open Word and display the .RTF file, click on the Publish It With MS Word button.

To save the database object as an Excel .XLS file, open Excel, and display the new file as a worksheet, click on the Analyze It With MS Excel button.

Click on the Mail It button to copy the contents of the database object to a mail message in a file format you select.

Click on the Database Window button to activate the Database window.

When you change to Print Preview in Excel, the number of the displayed page and the total number of pages appear on the status bar. In Excel's Print Preview window:

Next — Select Next to display the next page that will be printed.

Previous — Choose Previous to display the page before the currently displayed page.

Zoom — To enlarge the display of the current page, click anywhere in the page or select Zoom. To return the display of the current page to its original, reduced appearance, click in the page or select Zoom again.

COMMAND AND FEATURE REFERENCE

Print... Choose Print to return to the default view of the worksheet and display the Print dialog box. Change the settings as necessary, and then choose OK to print the file.

Setup... Select Setup to display the Page Setup dialog box. Change the necessary settings, and then select OK.

Margins Select Margins to toggle on the display of the handles for margins, the position of the header and footer, and the width of each column. Drag the corresponding handle to a new position to change any of the items. As you drag, the measurement appears in the status bar.

Close Select Close to return to the worksheet window.

When you switch to Print Preview in Word, the document is repaginated and the updated page numbers are displayed. In Word's Print Preview window:

To print the file with the current settings in the Print dialog box, click on the Print button. To change the settings in the Print dialog box, select File ➤ Print (Ctrl+P).

To magnify a document, click on the Magnifier button to toggle on magnification (toggled on by default when you first open the Print Preview window), and then move the pointer into the document and click to enlarge the size of the document displayed. Click in the document again to reduce the document to its original size.

PRINT PREVIEW

To display only one page of the document at a time, click on the One Page button.

TIP: *Click on the Next Page or Previous Page buttons on the vertical scroll bar or drag the scroll box to scroll through the document. Or, press PgUp or PgDn to scroll through the displayed document.*

To display two or more pages of the document, click on the Multiple Pages button, and then drag through the number and arrangement of the pages to be displayed.

To change the size of the displayed page, select a magnification in the drop-down list or type a percentage in the Zoom Control text box.

Click on the View Ruler button to display both the horizontal and vertical rulers. To hide the rulers, click on the button again.

If only a small amount of text appears on the last page of the document, click on the Shrink To Fit button to reduce the size of the font so the document can be printed on one less page.

To hide everything on the screen except the document and the Print Preview toolbar, click on the Full Screen button. Click on the button again or press Esc to display all the screen elements.

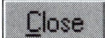

Select Close to return to the document window.

COMMAND AND FEATURE REFERENCE

> **TROUBLESHOOTING**
>
> ### Does Your Document Require Edits?
>
> If you noticed a misspelled word or incorrect punctuation while your document was enlarged in the Print Preview window, you can edit the document without returning to Normal or Page Layout view. If necessary, enlarge the document in the Print Preview window, click on the Magnifier button to toggle it off, and then use Word's regular editing techniques. When you are finished, select File ➤ Save (Ctrl+S) to save the changes to the document.

SEE ALSO: *Margins; Page Setup; Print; Ruler; View*

Print Report

In Excel, reports that contain data on worksheets, *views* (defined settings used to display and print selected data), and *scenarios* (defined sets of input values used in a worksheet model), can be saved in a workbook, and then printed when necessary. To create reports, you must have installed the Report Manager Add-in.

Creating a Report

Reports must contain at least one section. A section in a report contains at least one worksheet, and can contain any views or scenarios that are defined in the worksheet.

PRINT REPORT P

To create a report:

1. Select File ➤ Print Report to display the Print Report dialog box.

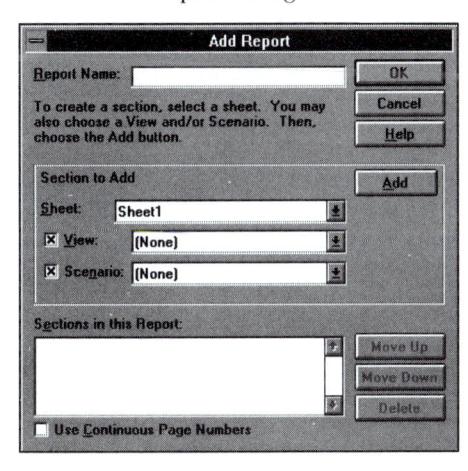

2. Select Add to display the Add Report dialog box.

3. Type a name for the report in the Report Name text box.

4. Select the name of a sheet to include in the first section of the report in the Sheet drop-down list.

5. To add a view or a scenario to the first section of the report, select the name of the view in the View drop-down list, and the name of the scenario in the Scenario drop-down list.

6. Choose Add in the Section To Add area of the dialog box to add the section to the report.

7. Repeat steps 4 through 6 for each section of the report.

8. To change the order of the sections that are in the report, select the section in the Sections In This Report list box, and then choose Move Up to move the selected section before the section above it in the list box, or Move Down to move the selected section after the section below it in the list box.

NOTE: *Select Delete to remove the section highlighted in the Sections In This Report list box from the defined report.*

COMMAND AND FEATURE REFERENCE

> **TROUBLESHOOTING**
>
> ## Installing an Add-In
>
> If the Print Report command does not appear on Excel's File menu, you must install Excel's Report Manager add-in. Select Tools ➤ Add-Ins to display the Add-Ins dialog box, select the Report Manager check box in the Add-Ins Available list box, and then choose OK.
>
> If Report Manager does not appear in the list box, double-click on the Office Setup icon in the Microsoft Office group window, or click on the Microsoft Office button on the Office Manager toolbar, and then select Office Setup And Uninstall to run Setup.

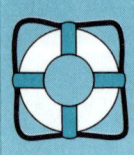

9. Select the Use Continuous Page Numbers check box to number the pages in the report consecutively.

10. Choose OK to create the report.

11. If necessary, choose Close in the Print Report dialog box to return to the worksheet.

To edit the sections in a defined report, display the Print Report dialog box, select the name of the report in the Reports list box, and choose Edit. Make any changes to the report as in steps 3 through 9 above, and then select OK to save the report.

To print a defined report, display the Print Report dialog box, select the name of the report in the Reports list box, and then choose Print to display the Print dialog box. Enter the number of copies to print in the Copies text box, and then choose OK to print the report.

PROTECTION

> **SEE ALSO:** *Page Setup; Print; Print Preview; Scenario; View Manager*

Print Security

If you are a member of the Admins group in Access's current workgroup, you can create and, if necessary, print a security information report. The report contains the names of each group to which each user account belongs, and lists the user accounts that are assigned to each group in the workgroup.

1. Select Security ➤ Print Security to display the Print Security dialog box.

2. In the List area, choose Both Users And Groups, Only Users, or Only Groups to define the contents of the report.

3. Choose OK to create the report.

The report appears in the Print Preview window.

> **SEE ALSO:** *Password; Permissions; Print Preview; Workgroup*

Protection

You can protect the data in a worksheet or the text of a document from being changed by others after a workbook or document file is opened. Protect a

COMMAND AND FEATURE REFERENCE

worksheet, parts of a worksheet, or objects in a worksheet, or protect the layout of the windows and the structure of a workbook. (Assign a password to the worksheet or workbook protections to prevent others from removing the protections.) Assign a write reservation password to a document to protect it.

WARNING: *Keep a list of passwords you use to protect your files. Protection cannot be removed unless you know the password.*

Protecting Data in Excel

In Excel, you can protect a worksheet or parts of a worksheet from any changes. By default, all the cells and objects in a worksheet are *locked* (prevented from being changed) when the worksheet is protected. However, you can unlock selected cells or objects before the worksheet is protected so data can be entered or changed in the unlocked cells, or the objects can be edited in a protected worksheet.

To protect a worksheet:

1. If necessary, select the cells that are to be unlocked so data can be entered in them when the worksheet is protected, and then choose Format ➤ Cells (Ctrl+1).

2. Select the Protection tab in the Format Cells dialog box, clear the Locked check box, and then choose OK.

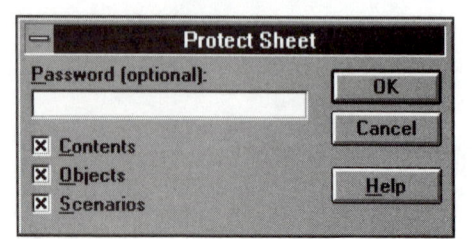

3. Select Tools ➤ Protection ➤ Protect Sheet to display the Protect Sheet dialog box.

PROTECTION

> **TROUBLESHOOTING**
>
> ## Hiding Formulas in a Protected Worksheet
>
> Do you want to hide the formulas that are stored in a worksheet that will be protected? If you want to display the results of the formulas instead of the actual formulas in the formula bar in a protected worksheet, select the cells that contain the formulas to be hidden, choose Format ➤ Cells (Ctrl+1), choose the Protection tab, select the Hidden check box on the Protection tab in the Format Cells dialog box, and then choose OK. Then select Tools ➤ Protection ➤ Protect Sheet to protect the worksheet. Hidden cells can be either locked or unlocked in a protected worksheet.

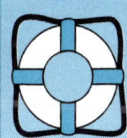

4. Optionally, type a password in the Password (Optional) text box.

5. Select any of the following check boxes to define the worksheet protection. All are selected by default.

- Select the Contents check box to prevent data in all locked cells and items in charts from being changed.

- Select the Objects check box to prevent all graphic objects in the worksheet from being moved, edited, resized, or deleted.

- Select the Scenarios check box to retain the current definitions of scenarios in the worksheet.

6. Choose OK. If a password was entered in step 4, the Confirm Password dialog box appears. Type the password again in the Reenter Protection Password text box, and then choose OK.

COMMAND AND FEATURE REFERENCE

To remove protection from the worksheet, select Tools ➤ Protection ➤ Unprotect Sheet. If a protection password was assigned, the Unprotect Sheet dialog box appears. Type the password in the Password text box, and then choose OK.

A workbook can also be protected. Protect the structure of a workbook so new sheets cannot be inserted in the workbook, and existing sheets cannot be moved, renamed, hidden or unhidden, or deleted. Assign protection to the open windows of the active workbook so they cannot be moved, resized, hidden or unhidden, or closed.

When the structure of a workbook is protected, any activity that requires a new sheet, such as creating a macro or adding a chart sheet, cannot take place in the workbook. When the windows of a workbook are protected, the Minimize and Maximize buttons and the Control menu box are removed from each window's title bar.

To assign protection to the structure or the windows of the active workbook:

1. Select Tools ➤ Protection ➤ Protect Workbook to display the Protect Work-book dialog box.

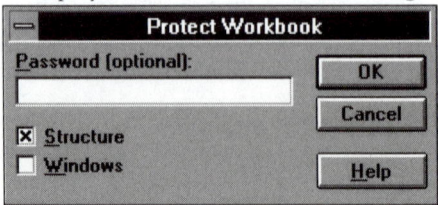

2. Optionally, type a password in the Password (Optional) text box.

3. Select the Structure check box (selected by default) to protect the workbook's structure. Select the Windows check box to protect the workbook's windows.

TROUBLESHOOTING

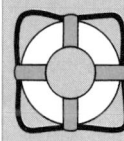

Hiding Data in a Workbook

Do you want to provide a different type of protection to the data in a workbook? You can hide data in rows or columns, hide the whole worksheet, and even hide entire workbooks without assigning protection. Data that is hidden cannot be seen or changed.

To hide a row or column in a worksheet, select a cell in the row or column, and then choose Format ➤ Row ➤ Hide (Ctrl+9) or Format ➤ Column ➤ Hide (Ctrl+0). To redisplay the row or column, select cells above and below the hidden row, or to the left and right of the hidden column, and then choose Format ➤ Row ➤ Unhide (Ctrl+Shift+9) or Format ➤ Column ➤ Unhide (Ctrl+Shift+0).

To hide the active worksheet, select Format ➤ Sheet ➤ Hide. To redisplay the hidden worksheet, select Format ➤ Sheet ➤ Unhide to display the Unhide dialog box, highlight the name of the sheet in the Unhide Sheet list box, and then choose OK. Only one worksheet can be unhidden at a time.

To hide the active workbook, select Window ➤ Hide. To redisplay the hidden workbook, select Window ➤ Unhide when at least one open window is displayed or File ➤ Unhide when all open windows are hidden, to display the Unhide dialog box. Select the workbook to be redisplayed in the Unhide Workbook list box, and then choose OK.

If changes are made to a workbook before it is hidden, a dialog box appears when you close Excel asking if you want to save the changes. Choose Yes to save your changes. The next time the file is opened, it will still be hidden.

COMMAND AND FEATURE REFERENCE

4. Choose OK. If a password was entered in step 2, the Confirm Password dialog box appears. Type the password again in the Reenter Protection Password text box, and then choose OK.

To remove protection from the workbook, select Tools ➤ Protection ➤ Unprotect Workbook. If a protection password was assigned, the Unprotect Workbook dialog box appears. Type the password in the Password text box, and then choose OK.

Protecting the Text of a Word Document

If you don't want others to revise your document, protect the text of a document or a section of the document with a password. Only a person who knows the password can change the text of a protected document. However, others can add annotations or revision marks to a protected document, or fill in fields in a protected form.

To protect the text of a Word document:

1. Choose Tools ➤ Protect Document to display the Protect Document dialog box.

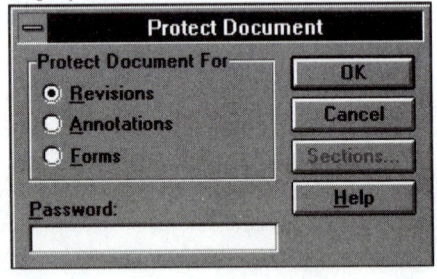

2. Select one of the following options:

- Select Revisions to mark any changes made as revisions while the document is protected. Revisions cannot be accepted or rejected and reviewers cannot turn off revision marking.

PROTECTION P

- Select **A**nnotations to allow reviewers to insert annotations, but not change any of the document contents.

- Select **F**orms to allow users to fill in the form fields, but not change any of the form's text. Then, if necessary, select **S**ections to display the Section Protection dialog box. Select the check box beside each section in the **P**rotected Sections list box (all are selected by default) that is to be protected from changes, and then choose OK.

3. Type the password in the **P**assword text box. An asterisk appears for each character you type.

4. Choose OK to display the Confirm Password dialog box.

5. Type the password again in the Reenter Protection **P**assword text box, and then choose OK.

To turn off the text protection of a document, choose **T**ools ➤ Un**p**rotect Document to display the Unprotect Document dialog box. Type the protection password in the **P**assword text box, and then choose OK.

SEE ALSO: *Annotation; Form; Password; Revision; Scenario*

COMMAND AND FEATURE REFERENCE

Query

Use a query to display a subset of the data in an Access database. With queries, you can select the fields that contain the data to be displayed, specify the criteria that define which records to include, and then display the data in an order you specify. Queries can use the data in more than one table in the database, and can contain data that is the result of calculations. In addition, existing queries can serve as the basis for forms and reports you create.

There are several types of queries you can create in Access:

- Design a *select* query to answer questions about the data in a database.

- Create a *crosstab* query to summarize and filter data, and then display it in a worksheet table.

- Create an *action* query to modify multiple records simultaneously in a database or to create a new table.

- To combine matching data in two or more tables, create a *union* query.

- Create a *pass-through* query to send commands to an SQL database.

- To create or modify tables in a database with SQL statements, create a *data-definition* query.

Creating a Query

Use the Query Wizards to create crosstab queries, queries that find duplicate records, queries that find records in one table that are not matched to records in a related table, and queries that create an archive of specific records in a table.

QUERY

Design a select query to have Access display the results in a *dynaset*, a dynamic view of the data in one or more tables that answers the questions in the query.

A dynaset looks like a table, and data in a dynaset can be entered or otherwise manipulated as in a table. Data that is entered or changed in a dynaset is also entered or changed in the underlying database. In addition, when records are added to or modified in a table on which a query is based, the dynaset is automatically updated when the query is next opened.

To design a select query:

1. Open the database file that contains the tables for which a query is to be created.

2. Select the table in the Table pane of the Database window, and then click on the New Query button on the Database toolbar. Or, select the Query tab in the Database window, and then choose New to display the New Query dialog box.

3. Select New Query. If you used the New Query button on the Database toolbar, the Select Query window appears with the list of fields in the selected table already in the top pane. If you used the Query tab in the Database window, the Add Table dialog box appears.

TIP: *As soon as the Select Query window appears, the Query Design toolbar is displayed. If the Add Table dialog box does not appear automatically, you can click on the Add Table button on the Query Design toolbar to display it.*

4. If necessary, select Tables, Queries, or Both in the View area to display the list of tables and queries from which to create the new query in the Table/Query list box.

COMMAND AND FEATURE REFERENCE

5. Select the name of the table or query whose field list is to be used to create the query in the Table/Query list box, and then choose Add to add the field list to the top pane of the Select Query window.

6. Repeat step 5 for each table or query that contains fields to be used to create the new query.

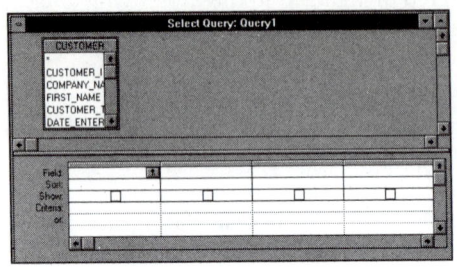

7. Choose Close in the Add Table dialog box to activate the Select Query window.

8. Drag a field from the field list box in the top pane to the first cell in the Field row in the bottom pane (the *query by example*, or QBE grid).

> **TIP:** *To select more than one field at a time to drag to the QBE grid, hold down the Ctrl key while you click on additional fields in the field list box. To select a block of adjacent fields, click on the first field, and then hold down the Shift key while you click on the last field in the block. To place all the fields in the QBE grid in a drop-down list, drag the * (asterisk) at the top of the field list box. Double-click on the field list's title bar to select all the field names, and then drag the selected names to the QBE grid to place each field in a different column in the Field row.*

9. Repeat step 8 for each field that is to be included in the query.

10. Select the cell in the Sort row of the field by which the query results are to be sorted, and then click on the drop-down list button and select Ascending or Descending.

QUERY

> **NOTE:** *If more than one field is to be sorted, Access sorts the left-most field in the query first. Memo and OLE object fields cannot be sorted.*

11. Clear the check box in the Show row for each field that contains data that is not to be displayed in the resulting query.

12. To specify which records are to appear in the query, enter an *expression*–the criteria defining the data to be displayed–in the cell for the field in the Criteria row.

> **TIP:** *If necessary, click on the Build button on the Query Design toolbar to display the Expression Builder dialog box, and then create the expression to define the criteria.*

13. Click on the Save button on the Query Design toolbar, or choose File ➤ Save (Ctrl+S) to display the Save As dialog box.

14. Type a descriptive name for the query in the Query Name text box, and then choose OK.

15. Click on the Datasheet View button on the Query Design toolbar, or choose View ➤ Datasheet to display the results of the query.

To change the design of the active query, click on the Design View button on the Query Design toolbar or choose View ➤ Query Design.

SEE ALSO: *Control; Control Properties; Crosstab Query; Database; Field; Filter; Record*

COMMAND AND FEATURE REFERENCE

Range

A range is a group of adjacent cells in an Excel worksheet, referenced by the top-left cell (the first) and the bottom-right cell (the last) in the group separated by a colon. For example, the range that includes C4, C5, C6, D4, D5, D6, E4, E5, and E6 is called C4:E6.

Naming Cells or Ranges

Assign meaningful names to cells or ranges in a worksheet or workbook. The names can be used in formulas and dialog boxes, or anywhere cell or range references are used. Range names can contain up to 255 characters, but cannot contain any spaces.

> **NOTE:** *You can also assign names to individual sheets in a workbook, and, of course, a name to the workbook file.*

If a defined name is a book-level name, it can be used on any sheet in the workbook, but duplicate names are not allowed. For example, a book-level name defined as "January" can be used on Sheet 1 in a workbook, but if you define a "January" range on Sheet 2, the name is applied to the reference on Sheet 2. Specify a sheet-level name for names that will be used for different ranges on multiple sheets in the same workbook.

To name a cell or range:

1. Select the cell or range to be named.

2. Choose Insert ➤ Name ➤ Define to display the Define Name dialog box.

3. Type a meaningful name for the selection in the Names In Workbook text box to define a book-level

RANGE

name. Or, type the name of the sheet, an ! (exclamation point), and then the name for the selection in the text box to define a sheet-level name.

4. The Refers To text box displays the name of the worksheet and the absolute reference of the cell or range you selected. If necessary, type a new reference in the text box.

5. Select Add to add the name to the Names In Workbook list box.

6. Repeat steps 3 through 5 for each name that is to be defined.

7. Choose OK to define the name.

Or, have Excel create names for cells or ranges on the basis of the labels assigned to columns and rows. When Excel creates names for you, an _ (underline) is automatically inserted to replace a space in a name.

1. Select the cells that contain both the row or column labels and the cells to be named.

2. Choose Insert ➤ Name ➤ Create to display the Create Names dialog box.

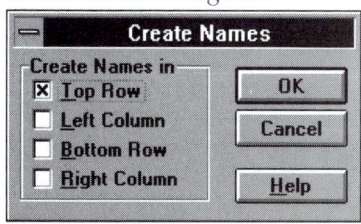

3. In the Create Names In area, select the Top Row, Left Column, Bottom Row, or Right Column check boxes, which define the cells that contain the labels to be used to create the range names.

4. Choose OK.

All names that are defined or created in a workbook appear in the Define Name dialog box.

COMMAND AND FEATURE REFERENCE

> **NOTE:** *To delete a name from the workbook, display the Define Names dialog box, select the name in the Names In Workbook list box, choose Delete, and then select OK.*

To select a named range, click on the Name box drop-down list button (to the left of the formula bar), and then select the name. The named cells are selected on the worksheet.

To insert a name in a formula, type an operator, and then select the name from the Name box drop-down list. Or, choose Insert ➤ Name ➤ Paste to display the Paste Name dialog box. Select the name to be inserted in the formula in the Paste Name list box, and then choose OK.

> **TIP:** *To paste a two-column list containing all the names and their cell references in the worksheet beginning with the active cell, select Insert ➤ Name ➤ Paste, and then choose Paste List.*

To replace all occurrences of a reference with the name for the reference:

1. Select the range that contains references that are to be replaced with a name.

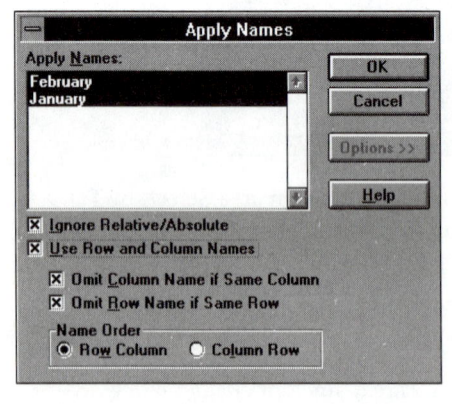

2. Choose Insert ➤ Name ➤ Apply to display the Apply Names dialog box, and then choose Options.

RANGE

3. Select the name to be applied in the Apply Names list box. To select multiple names, hold down the Ctrl key while you click on the names.

4. Select the Ignore Relative/Absolute check box (selected by default) to replace the references with names without regard to the types of references in the references or in the names.

5. Select the Use Row And Column Names check box (selected by default) to replace the references in the selection with the names of row and column ranges that contain the cells if names cannot be found for the cells.

6. If the Use Row And Column Names check box is selected, select any of the following options:

> **Omit Column Name if Same Column** Select the check box to replace a referenced cell that is both in the same column as the formula and in a named row range with the row range name.
>
> **Omit Row Name if Same Row** Select the check box to replace a referenced cell that is both in the same row as the formula and in a named column range with the column range name.
>
> **Name Order** Select Row Column or Column Row to define the order in which range names are listed for references that are replaced by both row and column names.

7. Choose OK to apply the names.

SEE ALSO: *Cell; Formula; Reference; Workbook*

COMMAND AND FEATURE REFERENCE

Record

An Access database consists of *records* that contain all the information about a specific item in one row in a table. Records are composed of *fields*, which define each individual piece of information in a record in a separate column in a table. For example, in a database that contains customer names and addresses, each customer's information is contained in one record. The record itself may include fields for the first name, last name, street address, city, state, and zip code.

Adding Records to a Database

In Access, records can be added to the database in a datasheet (a table or query) or in a form created for the database. Each datasheet and form contains a blank record at the end, which is used to add records to the database. As soon as data is entered in the blank record, a new blank record is added.

Adding Records in a Datasheet

To add records to the database in a datasheet:

1. Select the table in the Tables pane of the Database window, and then choose Open.

2. Choose Records ➤ Data Entry to hide all existing records, and move the insertion point in the first cell displayed.

3. Type the data for the first field.

4. Press Tab to move to the next field, and then type the data.

5. Repeat step 4 until the data for each field is in the record, and then press ↵ to enter the record in the database.

RECORD

Adding Records in a Form

To add records to the database in a form:

1. Select the form in the Forms pane of the Database window, and then choose Open.

2. Choose Records ➤ Data Entry to hide all existing records, and position the insertion point in the first field text box in the new record.

> **TIP:** *To move to the last, blank record in the form without hiding all existing records, click on the New button on the Form View toolbar or choose Records ➤ Go To ➤ New.*

3. Type the data in the first field text box, and then press Tab to move to the next field text box.

4. Repeat step 3 for each field in the form, and then press ↵ to enter the record.

Editing Records

To edit existing records:

1. If necessary, select Records ➤ Show All Records to display all the records in the database.

2. Click on the First Record, Last Record, Next Record, or Previous Record button on the datasheet's or form's status bar, or choose Records ➤ Go To ➤ First, Last, Next, or Previous to display the record to be edited.

3. Press Tab or click on the field name (in a form) to select the existing data to be edited in the cell or field text box, and then type the new data. Or, click in the cell or field text box to position the insertion point, and then type the data to be inserted.

4. Click on the Next Record button or choose Records ➤ Go To ➤ Next to enter the changes to the record and move to the next record.

COMMAND AND FEATURE REFERENCE

> **TROUBLESHOOTING**
>
> ## Finding Records That Contain Specific Characters
>
> If you want to display a record that contains specific data, click in the field text box or the cell that contains the data for which you want to search, and then click on the Find button on the Form View toolbar or choose Edit ➤ Find (Ctrl+F). Type the characters for which to search in the Find What text box. Choose Find Next until the record is displayed, and then choose Close.

SEE ALSO: *Database; Field; Find and Replace; Form*

Reference

Each cell, range, and worksheet in an Excel workbook has a specific name, called a *reference*, that is defined by its location. For example, the reference to the cell in column C and row 4 on Sheet 5 is *Sheet5!C4*. Use references to indicate the values in the cells in formulas.

> **NOTE:** *To enter a reference in a formula with a mouse, type an operator, click on the cell or drag through the range to include in the formula, and then click on the Enter box on the formula bar or press ↵.*

Defining Reference Types in Formulas

Relative references tell Excel where to find a value in a worksheet in relatin on to the current value. Use a

REFERENCE

relative reference to find another cell beginning with the cell that contains the formula. Relative references are the default, and are designated C4 or G9.

An *absolute* reference defines the exact location of a cell. To make a reference absolute, add a $ (dollar sign) in front of the column letter and row number of a cell reference in a formula. For example, C4 is the absolute reference of the value in cell C4.

You can combine relative and absolute references in a formula to form *mixed* references. Type the $ before either the row or column, whichever is to be absolute. For example, to always use the value in column C, but to use rows relative to 4, the mixed reference appears as $C4. To use columns relative to G but always the value in row 9, the reference appears as G$9.

Using Reference Operators

There are three operators to define how references are used in a formula:

- Use : (colon), the range operator, to indicate one reference to all the cells in the range. A range appears as A3:B6.

- Use , (comma), the union operator, to indicate a reference combined from multiple references. A union appears as A3:F3,E1:E8.

- Use (space), the intersection operator, to indicate a common reference within multiple references. An intersection appears as A3:F3 E1:E8.

You can also enter references to a cell or range on a different sheet of your workbook in a formula. Enter the name of the worksheet followed by an exclamation point, and then the cell or range. For example, *Sheet3!B4:D8* refers to range B4:D8 in Sheet 3 of the active workbook. In a worksheet reference, the sheet is always absolute.

COMMAND AND FEATURE REFERENCE

> **TROUBLESHOOTING**
>
> ### Using R1C1 Reference Style
>
> You can change the default A1 reference style, which contains numbered rows and lettered columns, to R1C1 reference style, which contains both numbered rows, preceded by "R," and numbered columns, preceded by "C." For example, the cell in row 4 and column 6 is referenced as R4C6. To change to R1C1 reference style, select Tools ➤ Options, select the General tab, choose R1C1 in the Reference Style area, and choose OK.
>
> By default, all references in R1C1 reference style are absolute. To change any of the references to relative, insert [] (brackets) around the number of the row or column in a formula. For example, R[4]C[6] is the relative reference to the cell that is 4 rows down and 6 columns to the right. R[-4]C6 is a mixed reference to the cell 4 rows up in the sixth column.

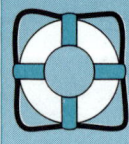

TIP: *It is easier to select the cells or ranges to reference in a different worksheet with your mouse, and let Excel enter the correct syntax.*

References that extend across multiple sheets are called *3D references*. Three-dimensional references use a range of sheets and references to the same cells or ranges in each sheet. For example, to refer to the range A6:D10 in Sheets 3, 4, and 5 of a workbook, the syntax is *Sheet3:Sheet5!A6:D10*.

To enter a 3D reference:

1. Select the cell in which to place the formula and begin typing the formula.

2. Hold down the Shift key and click on the tab of the last worksheet in the range.

3. Select the cell or range to reference, and then click on the Enter box or press ↵.

Moving and Copying References and Formulas

Moving and copying a formula or the data in a formula can affect how the formula is calculated, and therefore the results of the formula.

When a cell is moved:

- The values and references in a cell that is moved do not change.

- References to the moved cell are changed to indicate the new location of the cell in all formulas that refer to the cell.

- Formulas that previously referenced the cell that now contains the contents of the moved cell result in the #REF error message.

- When cells, rows, or columns are inserted or deleted, all affected relative and absolute references are adjusted.

When a cell is copied:

- Relative references and the relative portion of mixed references are adjusted to reflect the new position of the data.

- Absolute references and the absolute portion of mixed references stay the same as in the original formula.

When a sheet in a 3D reference is moved:

- If a new sheet is inserted between the *endpoint sheets* (the first and last sheets in the range), a formula that refers to the 3D reference does not change, but the results of the formula are calculated including the values in the new sheet.

- If a sheet between the endpoint sheets is deleted, a formula that refers to the 3D reference does

COMMAND AND FEATURE REFERENCE

not change, but the results of the formula are calculated without including the values in the moved or deleted sheet.

SEE ALSO: *Cell; Cut, Copy, and Paste; Drag and Drop; Formula; Range*

Relationship

You can establish a *relationship*, a connection between fields that two tables or queries have in common, in an Access database. A defined relationship is helpful when more than one table or query is used to create queries, forms, and reports.

Creating and Defining a Relationship

The tables and queries you create in a database are not automatically related. To create a relationship:

1. Open the database file that contains the tables or queries for which you want to create a relationship.

2. Click on the Relationships button on the Database toolbar, or choose Edit ➤ Relationships to display the Relationships toolbar and window, and the Add Table dialog box.

3. In the View area, select Tables, Queries, or Both to define the list items that appear in the Table/Query list box.

4. Select the first table or query that is to be related in the Table/Query list box, and then choose Add.

RELATIONSHIP

5. Repeat step 4 for each table or query that is to be included in the relationship, and then choose Close to activate the Relationships window.

NOTE: *To redisplay the Add Table dialog box, click on the Add Table button on the Relationships toolbar or choose Relationships ➤ Add Table.*

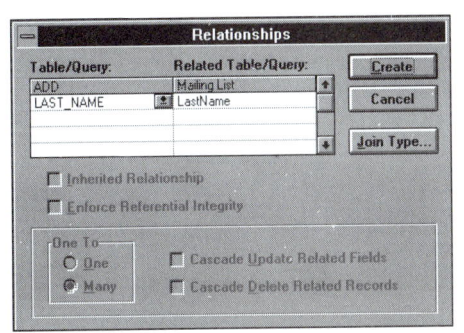

6. Drag the field to be related (in the primary table) from its field list box to a matching field in another field list box (the related table). The Relationships dialog box appears.

7. If necessary, edit the field names in the Table/Query and the Related Table/Query lists.

8. Select any of the following relationship options:

- Select the Inherited Relationship check box to create a relationship between attached tables in the database where the tables are stored.

- Select the Enforce Referential Integrity check box to make certain that the referential integrity rules (the rules that preserve the relationship when records are added or deleted) for the relationship are followed.

NOTE: *The Enforce Referential Integrity check box is available only if the field in the primary table is a primary key or has a unique index, if the fields being related have the same data type, and if both tables are stored in the same Access database.*

363

COMMAND AND FEATURE REFERENCE

- In the One To area, select <u>O</u>ne to establish a one-to-one relationship, or select <u>M</u>any to establish a one-to-many relationship.

NOTE: *In a one-to-one relationship, the value in the primary table's primary key either corresponds only to the value in the matching field or to only one record in the related table, and the value in the related table's primary key is either null or corresponds to only one record in the primary table. In a one-to-many relationship, the value of the primary table's primary key in each record corresponds to the value in the matching field to many records (or to no records) in the related table, and the value in each record in the related table's primary key is either null or corresponds to only one record in the primary table.*

- If the <u>E</u>nforce Referential Integrity check box is selected, select the Cascade <u>U</u>pdate Related Fields check box to make Access change the corresponding values in related tables when the data in the field in the primary table is changed.

- If the <u>E</u>nforce Referential Integrity check box is selected, select the Cascade <u>D</u>elete Related Records check box to make Access delete related records in related tables when the records in the primary table are deleted.

9. Select Join Type to display the Join Properties dialog box, and then choose one of the following options to define how the tables will be joined, and select OK.

- Option <u>1</u>, the default, creates an *equi-join* (also called an *inner join*), in which the records that contain equal values in two tables are added to the dynaset.

- Option <u>2</u> creates a *left outer join*, in which all the records on the left side of the LEFT

RELATIONSHIP

JOIN statement in a query are added to the dynaset, regardless of whether corresponding fields in the table on the right contain matching values. The records that contain matching values from the right table are combined in the dynaset with the records from the left table.

- Option 3 creates a *right outer join*, in which all the records on the right side of the RIGHT JOIN statement in a query are added to the dynaset, regardless of whether corresponding fields in the table on the left contain matching values. The records that contain matching values from the left table are combined in the dynaset with the records from the right table.

10. Choose Create in the Relationships dialog box.

11. Click on the Save button on the Relationships toolbar, or choose File ➤ Save Layout to save the layout of the relationship.

To edit a relationship, you must first display it in the Relationships window.

To display all the relationships in a database, click on the Show All Relationships button on the Relationships toolbar, or choose Relationships ➤ Show All.

To display the relationships for a selected table, click on the Show Direct Relationships button on the Relationships toolbar or choose Relationships ➤ Show Direct.

To edit a displayed relationship, double-click on the relationship line, or click on the line and choose Relationships ➤ Edit Relationship to redisplay the Relationships dialog box, and then change the necessary options.

COMMAND AND FEATURE REFERENCE

To delete a relationship, choose Edit ➤ Delete (Del). To delete a table from a relationship, select the table in the Relationships window, and then choose Edit ➤ Delete (Del).

SEE ALSO: *Database; Field; Table*

Rename

SEE: *Macro*

Repeat

Commands you select and formatting changes you make are stored in Excel and Word until you perform any action except selecting a different cell or moving the insertion point. You can repeat the last command or action that was performed in the active cell or at the position of the insertion point.

TIP: *In Word, you can even repeat the last characters you typed after the insertion point is repositioned.*

Repeating the Last Command or Action

To repeat the previous command or action:

1. Perform the action, select the command, or type new characters.

2. Select the cell or position the insertion point where you want to repeat the action.

REPORT

3. In Excel, click on the Repeat button on the Standard toolbar. Or, in both Excel and Word, select Edit ➤ Repeat *Edit* (F4).

SEE ALSO: *Undo/Redo*

Report

Create a report to present the data in an Access database in a printed document. The source of the data in a report is the underlying table or query on which the report was based. Use controls to establish a connection between the report and the data source. Other items in the report, such as the headers and footers, are part of the report's design.

Creating a Report

Use the Report Wizards to create one of several kinds of predesigned reports:

- Use the AutoReport Wizard to create a single-column, preformatted report that contains all the fields in the table or query on which the report is based.

- To create a single-column report with specific fields, use the Single-Column Wizard.

- To create a report that arranges data into groups and totals the values in each group, use the Groups/Totals Report Wizard.

- To create a report for Avery mailing labels, select the Mailing Label Wizard.

- Use the Summary Wizard to create a report with summary totals for groups.

COMMAND AND FEATURE REFERENCE

- Use the Tabular Wizard to create a report in a table design, with each record displayed in a row, and each field displayed in a column.

- To link the data in a database object to a Word document, use the MS Word Mail Merge Wizard.

Or, create a blank report, in which you specify the design of the report, the format, and the source of the data. To create a blank report:

1. Open the database that contains the records on which the report is to be based.

2. Click on the New Report button on the Database toolbar, or select the Report tab in the Database window and choose New. The New Report dialog box appears.

3. Select a table or query to use as the data source in the Select A Table/Query drop-down list.

4. Choose Blank Report to open a blank report in Design view.

5. Place the necessary controls in the positions desired in the various sections of the blank report.

TIP: *Use the horizontal and vertical rulers and the grid that appears in Design view to help position the controls on the report.*

6. Click on the Save button on the Form Design toolbar, or choose File ➤ Save (Ctrl+S) to display the Save As dialog box. Then type a name for the report in the Report Name text box and choose OK.

To see how the report appears, click on the Print Preview button on the Form Design toolbar or choose File ➤ Print Preview.

If you want to make any changes to the report, click on the Close Window button on the Print Preview toolbar or choose File ➤ Print Preview to return to Design view.

SEE ALSO: *Control; Control Properties; Form; Print; Print Preview; Section*

Revision

Mark revisions in a Word document when you want to track changes made to it by others. The changes made appear by default both on screen and in the printed document in the form of underline and strikethrough characters. If more than one person revises a document for which you are marking revisions, each person's revision marks appear in different colors, and each person's initials and the date and time of the revision are labeled.

Comparing Versions of a Document

You can compare two documents that have different file names or that are in different directories, and add revision marks to indicate where the edited version is different from the original file.

To compare versions of a document:

1. Activate the edited document, and then double-click on the MRK area on the status bar or choose Tools ➤ Revisions to display the Revisions dialog box.

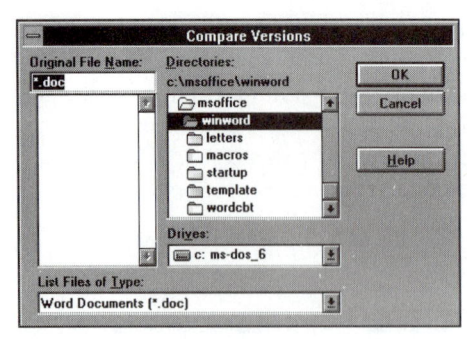

COMMAND AND FEATURE REFERENCE

2. Choose Compare Versions to display the Compare Versions dialog box.

3. Select the name of the original document in the Original File Name list box, and then choose OK. The changes made in the edited version appear as revision marks.

Accept or reject revisions in compared documents the same way you do in a revised document.

Marking and Reviewing Revisions in a Document

Once revision marking is turned on in a document, you can display or hide revision marks and change the format of the marks. Word keeps track of revisions even if they are not displayed in the document.

To track revision marks:

1. Activate the document whose revisions are to be tracked, and then double-click on the MRK area on the status bar or select Tools ➤ Revisions to display the Revisions dialog box.

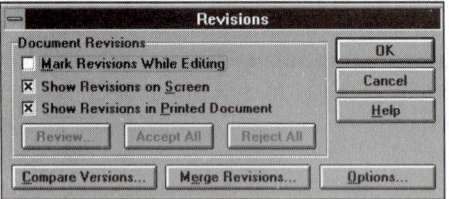

2. Select the Mark Revisions While Editing check box.

3. To display revision marks on your screen, select the Show Revisions On Screen check box (selected by default).

4. To print the revision marks, select the Show Revisions In Printed Document check box (selected by default).

REVISION

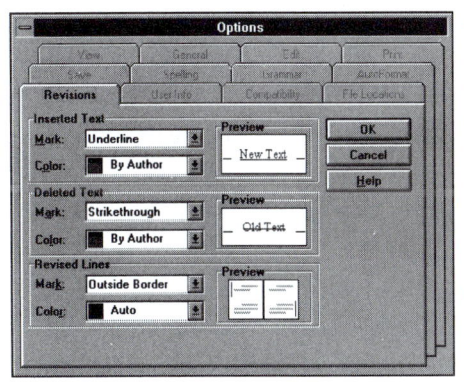

5. To change the format of the revision marks, choose Options to display the Revisions tab of the Options dialog box.

6. Select any of the following options and choose OK:

Mark   Select the mark from the corresponding drop-down list for inserted and deleted text, and for the position of the lines indicating that a paragraph has been revised.

Color   Select the color from the corresponding drop-down list for inserted text, deleted text, and revision lines.

7. Choose OK in the Revisions dialog box.

> **NOTE:** *To turn off revision marking in the document, double-click on the MRK area on the status bar, clear the Mark Revisions While Editing check box, and then choose OK in the Revisions dialog box.*

To see the proposed revisions, review each revision and either accept or reject its inclusion in the document.

1. Activate the revised document, and then double-click on the MRK area on the status bar or select Tools ➤ Revisions.

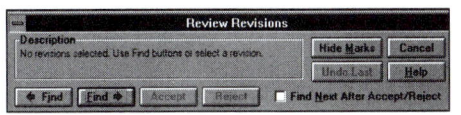

2. Select Review to display the Review Revisions dialog box.

COMMAND AND FEATURE REFERENCE

3. Choose Find → to move to the next revision, or ← Find to move to the previous revision.

4. To have Word automatically move to the next revision, select the Find Next After Accept/Reject check box.

5. To include the proposed revision in your document, select Accept. To remove the revision, choose Reject.

6. To change the acceptance or rejection of the last revision, choose Undo Last.

7. When you are finished reviewing the revisions, select Cancel or Close.

To accept or reject all the revisions without first reviewing them, select either Accept All or Reject All in the Revisions dialog box, and then choose Yes to confirm the acceptance or rejection.

Merging Revisions

When others have added annotations or revisions to a document, you can insert their marked comments and revisions in the original document. The comments and revisions are assigned one of eight colors by Word. If you have more than eight reviewers, the same colors are used over again.

To merge revisions:

1. Activate the revised document.

2. Double-click on the MRK area on the status bar, or select Tools ➤ Revisions.

3. Select Merge Revisions to display the Merge Revisions dialog box.

4. Select the name of the original document in the Original File Name list box, and then choose OK.

TROUBLESHOOTING

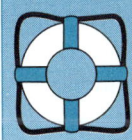

Merging Revisions into the Original Document

Did you send a Word document to members of your workgroup for revisions? If you sent a document with Mail and selected All At Once in the Routing Slip dialog box to send it to all reviewers simultaneously, you can merge each reviewer's revisions into the original document. Double-click on the document's icon when the mail is returned, select OK to confirm that you want to merge the revisions, and then select OK again to merge the revisions into the original document. Repeat this process for each reviewer's document.

SEE ALSO: *Annotation; Mail; Print; Protection*

Ruler

In Word, the horizontal Ruler is displayed by default under the toolbars in Normal view. In Page Layout view and Print Preview, both the horizontal and vertical Rulers are displayed.

NOTE: *In Access, both horizontal and vertical rulers appear when you switch to Design view. Use the rulers to help position the controls when designing a database object.*

COMMAND AND FEATURE REFERENCE

Using the Ruler

Use the horizontal ruler to adjust the indentation of a paragraph, to set the left and right margins, to add or remove tab stops in a paragraph, and to adjust the widths of columns.

To display or hide the horizontal ruler, select View ➤ Ruler.

The vertical Ruler allows you to set top and bottom margins in your document.

To change the margins, indentation, or tab stops in a document, click on the Page Layout View button or choose View ➤ Page Layout to change to Page Layout view. You then have the following options:

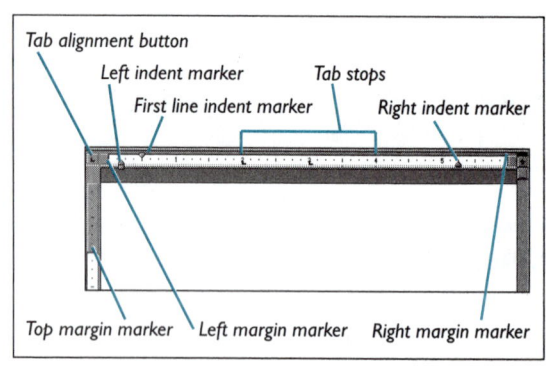

Tab alignment button
Left indent marker
First line indent marker
Tab stops
Right indent marker
Top margin marker
Left margin marker
Right margin marker

- To set the first line indentation of the paragraph that contains the insertion point, drag the *first line indent marker*.

- To adjust the indentation of all lines except the first in the current paragraph, drag the *left indent marker*.

- To adjust the right indentation of all lines in the current paragraph, drag the *right indent marker*.

- To adjust the left or right document margins, drag the *margin marker* on the horizontal ruler.

SCENARIO R

- To adjust the top or bottom document margins, drag the margin marker on the vertical ruler.

- To add tab stops to the current paragraph, click on the *tab alignment button* until the type of tab you want to set appears on the button. Then click in the position for the tab on the horizontal ruler:

L	Left–aligned tab stop
⊥	Centered tab stop
⌐	Right–aligned tab stop
⊥.	Decimal tab stop

- To remove an existing tab stop from the current paragraph, drag the *tab stop marker* off the ruler.

- To adjust the widths of columns, drag the column margin markers.

SEE ALSO: *Columns; Indent; Margins; Paragraph; Tabs; View*

Scenario

In Excel, create a *scenario*, a group of values that is saved with a specific name and inserted into *changing cells* in a worksheet to produce a model of the data. A set of changing cells defines variables, which, when inserted in the worksheet, produce different results in the worksheet model. Each scenario can contain up to 32 changing cells.

COMMAND AND FEATURE REFERENCE

Creating a Scenario

Use Scenario Manager to define variables to be used as input values in the changing cells of a scenario. Changing cells are usually the cells that contain values used in a key formula in the worksheet, rather than an actual formula.

To create a scenario:

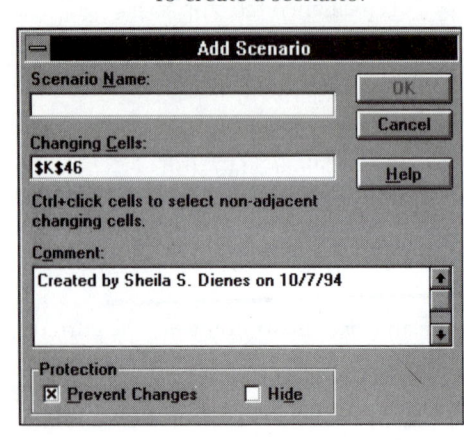

1. Select Tools ➤ Scenarios to display the Scenario Manager dialog box, and then choose Add.

2. Type a name for the scenario in the Scenario Name text box.

3. Specify the scenario's changing cells in the Changing Cells text box.

4. If necessary, type a description of the scenario in the Comment text box.

NOTE: *The Scenario Manager automatically displays the name of the creator and editor, and the date of any change to the selected scenario in the Comments text box. Use this information to track changes made by others in your workgroup.*

5. In the Protection area, select the Prevent Changes check box to prevent any changes to the scenario, and the Hide check box to suppress the display of the name of the scenario in the Scenarios list box in the Scenario Manager dialog box. The protection options are in effect only when the worksheet or workbook is protected.

SCENARIO

6. Choose OK to display the Scenario Values dialog box.

7. Type the input values for each changing cell in the corresponding text box.

8. Choose $\underline{A}$dd to return to the Add Scenario dialog box, and then repeat steps 2 through 7 to create another scenario for the changing cells. Or, choose OK to return to the Scenario Manager dialog box.

9. Choose any of the following options in the Scenario Manager dialog box:

- Choose $\underline{D}$elete to delete the scenario selected in the S$\underline{c}$enarios list box.

- To edit the scenario selected in the Scenarios list box, choose $\underline{E}$dit, and then make the necessary changes in the Edit Scenario dialog box.

- Select $\underline{M}$erge to display the Merge Scenarios dialog box. If necessary, select the name of a currently open workbook in the $\underline{B}$ook drop-down list, select the name of a worksheet that contains the scenarios you want to appear in the Scenarios drop-down list on the Workgroup toolbar or in the Scenarios list in the Scenario Manager dialog box, and then choose OK to merge the scenario names in the two worksheets.

- Choose S$\underline{u}$mmary to have Excel create a report, and then choose Scenario $\underline{S}$ummary or Scenario $\underline{P}$ivotTable as the type of report. Specify the *result cells*, the cells on the worksheet that are recalculated each time a new set of input values are entered in the chang-ing cells, in the $\underline{R}$esult Cells text box. Then choose OK to create a summary report showing the results of all the

COMMAND AND FEATURE REFERENCE

scenarios in the Scenarios list on a separate sheet in the current workbook.

10. Select the name of the scenario to use in the worksheet model in the S̲cenarios list box, and then choose S̲how.

11. Select Close to return to the worksheet.

To display the variables and results of one of the defined scenarios in your worksheet model, display the Workgroup toolbar, and then select the name of the scenario in the Scenarios drop-down list.

SEE ALSO: *Goal Seek; Pivot Table; Protection; Range; Solver*

Section

In Access, a section is a design element used when creating a form or report. In Word, a section is a portion of a document that can be formatted differently from the rest of the document.

Adding Sections to an Access Form or Report

By default, each new Access form and report contains a Detail section, into which the controls for the form's or report's fields are placed.

You can add any of the following pairs of sections to the form's design:

- The *form header* appears at the top of the form when it is displayed onscreen for data entry, and at the top of the first page of the printed form.

- The *form footer* is displayed at the bottom of the form on your screen, and at the bottom of the last page of the printed form.

- The *page header* appears at the top of each page of the printed form.

- The *page footer* appears at the bottom of each page of the printed form.

In addition to the Detail section, any of the following sections can appear in a report:

- The *report header* appears at the top of the printed report.

- The *report footer* appears at the bottom of the printed report.

- The *page header* appears at the top of each page in the printed report.

- The *page footer* appears at the bottom of each page in the printed report.

- The *group header* appears at the beginning of a group of records.

- The *group footer* appears at the end of a group of records.

Page headers and footers, form headers and footers, and report headers and footers must be added as a pair. To insert headers and footers in a form or report:

1. Open the form or report in Design view.

2. Select F_o_rmat ➤ _P_age Header/Footer to add a page header and footer.

3. Select F_o_rmat ➤ Form _H_eader/Footer to add a form header and footer, or F_o_rmat ➤ Report _H_eader/Footer to add a report header and footer.

COMMAND AND FEATURE REFERENCE

> **NOTE:** To add a group header or footer to a report, select View ➤ Sorting And Grouping, select the field in the Field/Expression column for which a group header or footer is to be added, and then select Yes in the Group Header or Group Footer drop-down list in the Group Properties area of the Sorting And Grouping dialog box.

4. Add the necessary controls to the header or footer section.

To hide an unnecessary page, form, or report header or footer, click on the section header, and then click on the Properties button on the Form Design toolbar or select View ➤ Properties to display its property sheet. Then set its Height property to 0, or its Visible property to No.

To change the size of a section, position the mouse pointer over the lower edge of the section until it appears as a vertical arrow intersected by a horizontal line, and then drag the edge up or down. Use the vertical ruler to help determine the size you want.

Adding Sections to a Word Document

Apply the formatting to be used in all sections of the document, and then add a section break to divide a document into sections and insert a section mark. Each section contains the formatting that is applied to the entire document, and the format of each section can be modified as necessary. The formatting applied to the section is saved in its section mark.

> **NOTE:** A section break is automatically inserted when columns; tables of contents, figures, and authorities; or an index are placed in a document.

In Page Layout view, click on the Show/Hide ¶ button on the Standard toolbar to toggle the display of nonprinting characters. When nonprinting characters are displayed in Page Layout view and in Normal view, the section mark appears as a double-dotted line with "End of Section" on it.

To add sections:

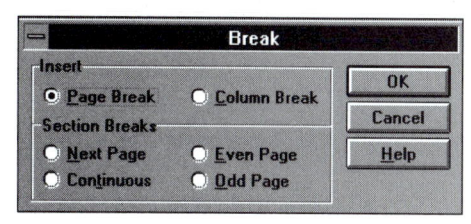

1. Position the insertion point where a section break is to be inserted, and choose Insert ➤ Break to display the Break dialog box.

2. Select one of the following options in the Section Breaks area:

- Select Next Page to insert a section break and begin the new section on the next page.

- To insert a section break and continue on the same page, such as when you want to insert columnar text on a page with regular text, select Continuous.

- Select Even Page to insert a section break and begin the next section on an even-numbered page. The next odd-numbered page is blank if the section break is inserted on an even-numbered page.

- Select Odd Page to insert a section break and begin the next section on an odd-numbered page. The next even-numbered page is blank if the section break is inserted on an odd-numbered page.

3. Choose OK in the Break dialog box.

To delete a section break, select the section mark, and press Del. Both the section break and

COMMAND AND FEATURE REFERENCE

formatting for the text above the section break are deleted, and the text takes on the formatting of the following section.

SEE ALSO: *Columns; Control; Control Properties; Header and Footer; Margins; Page Numbers; Page Setup; Sort*

Sequence

Use Excel's AutoFill feature to quickly enter a series of values in a worksheet range. With AutoFill, you can enter sequential data or copy existing data into a selected range.

Entering a Sequence with AutoFill

Each selected cell or range contains a *fill handle*, a small, black square that appears at the lower-right corner of the selection. To enter an incremental series into a range, drag the fill handle down or to the right. To create a series that decreases in value, drag the fill handle up or to the left.

TIP: *To display the AutoFill shortcut menu, position the mouse pointer over the selection's fill handle, and then hold down the right mouse button as you drag to select the range into which data or a format is to be entered. When you release the right mouse button, the AutoFill shortcut menu appears. Select the appropriate command to fill the selected range with a copy of the data, a sequence, the selection's format, or to create a trend.*

To use AutoFill:

- Select a cell that contains a value you wish to copy to cells in an adjacent range, and then

SEQUENCE

> **TROUBLESHOOTING**
>
> ### Creating and Using Custom Lists
>
> If you often use the same text values in your worksheet, you can create a custom list for Excel to use with AutoFill. Select Tools ➤ Options, and select the Custom Lists tab. Type the list items in the List Entries text box and then choose Add to create the custom list. Or, select Import, select the cells that contain the items in your worksheet, and then select Import again to create a list. Select OK to return to your worksheet.
>
> To have Excel enter the custom list, enter the first list item in a cell, and then select the cell and drag its fill handle through the range of cells to be filled with the list items.

position the mouse pointer over the cell's fill handle until it changes into a + (plus sign). Then drag the fill handle until each cell in the range is highlighted. Release the mouse button to fill the selected cells with the value.

- To create a sequence of values in a range, enter the beginning values in the sequence in at least two cells, and then select the cells and drag the selection's fill handle until the range is highlighted. Release the mouse button to enter the sequence in the range.

- To quickly copy the value (often a formula) in a selected cell at the beginning of a range beside a nonempty range to each cell in the empty range, double-click on the fill handle of the selected cell.

- To create a sequence of values incremented by 1, select the cell that contains the first value, and

COMMAND AND FEATURE REFERENCE

then hold down the Ctrl key while you drag through each cell in the range to be filled.

- To prevent a series from being created using values that would automatically be incremented, select the cells that contain the values, and then hold down the Ctrl key and drag through the range to be filled.

Entering a Trend

Use AutoFill to enter a simple linear trend, in which the fill values are incremented by the example shown in the starting values (entered in the first two cells). You can also have Excel create a longer series incremented by specific values, or a linear or growth trend.

To enter a trend:

1. Select the range to be filled with a series of values.

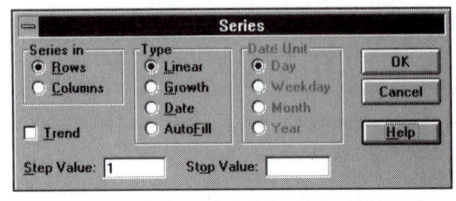

2. Choose Edit ➤ Fill ➤ Series to display the Series dialog box. The selected range is automatically defined as Rows or Columns in the Series In area.

3. Choose one of the following types of series to be created in the range in the Type area:

- Select Linear to create a series by adding the value in the Step Value text box to each cell in the selected range in turn.

- Select Growth to create a series by multiplying the value in the Step Value text box by the value in each cell in the selected range in turn.

- To create a range of dates, select <u>D</u>ate, and then follow step 4.

- To enter values based on existing data in the range into the blank cells in the range, select Auto<u>F</u>ill.

4. If <u>D</u>ate is selected as the type of series, choose D<u>a</u>y, <u>W</u>eekday, <u>M</u>onth, or <u>Y</u>ear in the Date Unit area to define how the series will increase.

5. Enter the amount by which the values in the series are to increase (a positive number) or decrease (a negative number) in the <u>S</u>tep Value text box.

6. If necessary, enter the ending value for the series in the St<u>o</u>p Value text box. The series ends in the selection when the St<u>o</u>p Value is reached.

7. To create a linear or growth trend, make sure <u>L</u>inear or <u>G</u>rowth is selected in the Type area, and then select the <u>T</u>rend check box. When the Trend check box is selected, the step value for the series is calculated on the basis of the starting values in the selected range. A linear trend calculates a best-fit line, and a growth trend calculates values on an exponential curve.

8. Choose OK in the Series dialog box.

SEE ALSO: *Cut, Copy, and Paste; Shortcut Menus; Sort*

Shortcut Menus

Access, Excel, PowerPoint, and Word each contain *shortcut menus*—menus that contain commands specific to the current action or the selected item. Display the shortcut menu to quickly access the

COMMAND AND FEATURE REFERENCE

commands. Shortcut menus are available for many different tasks, including editing charts, pictures, drawings, tables, paragraphs, and embedded objects, and displaying different toolbars.

To display the shortcut menu for an item or a selection, point to the item or position the mouse pointer on the item and click the right mouse button. Then, select the command you want to use in the shortcut menu.

SEE ALSO: *Toolbars*

Slide Show

In PowerPoint, a slide is the most basic part of a presentation. The slides that are created can be transferred to actual slides, printed in color or black and white on transparencies, or presented on a computer in the form of a slide show.

Creating a Slide Show

After a presentation has been created, create a slide show to electronically display each slide in the presentation on the full screen of a computer.

To create a slide show:

1. Open the presentation file for which a slide show is to be created.

2. To display the presentation as a slide show with PowerPoint's default settings, click on the Slide Show button on the horizontal scroll bar. Click the left mouse button or press ↵ to display the next slide in the presentation.

SLIDE SHOW

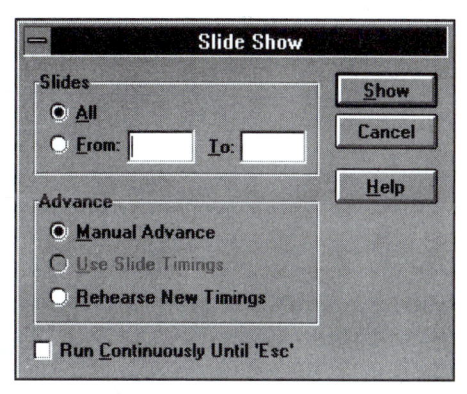

3. Or, to specify the settings for the slide show, select View ➤ Slide Show to display the Slide Show dialog box.

4. Change any of the following options in the Slide Show dialog box:

- Select All in the Slides area to display each slide in the presentation. Or, select From, and then specify the range of slides to display in the From and To text boxes.

- In the Advance area, select Manual Advance to display the next slide in the show by clicking the mouse button or pressing ↵. Or, select Use Slide Timings to automatically display each slide according to the timing set for it.

- Select the Run Continuously Until 'Esc' check box to continue running the slide show until you press the Esc key.

5. Select Show to run the slide show with the settings specified, beginning with the selected slide.

TIP: *Use your mouse to point to an important item on a slide during the slide show. Press B to display a blank screen during the slide show.*

To add a note or drawing to a slide during the slide show:

1. Move the mouse, and then click on the freehand annotation icon at the lower-left corner of the slide to toggle annotation on.

COMMAND AND FEATURE REFERENCE

2. Move the mouse until it appears as a pencil in the position in which you want to add an annotation.

3. Hold down the mouse button and drag to write or draw on the slide.

TIP: *To erase the note or drawing while the slide is still displayed, press E.*

4. Click on the freehand annotation icon again to toggle annotation off.

Hiding a Slide

To prevent a slide in the presentation from appearing during the slide show, hide the slide:

1. Select the slide to be hidden.

TIP: *Display the slide to be hidden in Slide view to select it, or display the presentation in Slide Sorter or Outline views, and then hold down the Shift key while you click on the slide in Slide Sorter view or the slide icon in Outline view to select multiple slides.*

2. Click on the Hide Slide button on the Slide Sorter toolbar, or choose Tools ➤ Hide Slide.

A hidden slide appears in Slide Sorter view with a gray box that contains a diagonal line through it around the number of the slide.

To display a hidden slide during the slide show, move the mouse, and then click on the hidden slide icon that appears at the lower-left side of the slide preceding the hidden slide or press H.

Inserting Special Effects

Add special effects to a slide show to make the presentation more interesting. Create a *transition effect* to

SLIDE SHOW

define the way each new slide replaces the previous slide during the slide show. Create a *build effect* to display one slide as a series of slides with a point on the slide revealed or highlighted in the series.

To add a transition effect to a slide:

1. If necessary, click on the Slide Sorter View button on the horizontal scroll bar to display the presentation in Slide Sorter view.

2. Select the slide for which you want to create a transition effect.

3. Click on the Transition button on the Slide Sorter toolbar or choose Tools ➤ Transition to display the Transition dialog box.

4. Select an effect in the Effect drop-down list. A sample of how it will appear is displayed in the lower-right corner of the dialog box.

5. If necessary, select Slow, Medium, or Fast (the default) in the Speed area to change the speed of the selected effect.

6. Choose OK.

In Slide Sorter view, the transition icon appears below the slide to the left of the timing set for the slide. Click on the transition icon to see the transition special effect.

Select a different transition effect for the selected slide in the Transition Effects drop-down list on the Slide Sorter toolbar.

389

COMMAND AND FEATURE REFERENCE

To add a build effect to a slide:

1. If necessary, click on the Slide Sorter View button on the horizontal scroll bar to display the presentation in Slide Sorter view.

2. Select the slide for which you want to create a build effect.

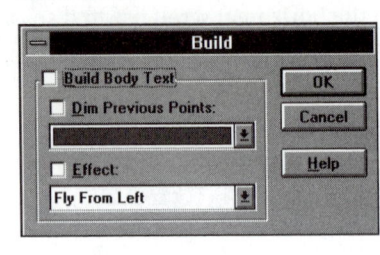

3. Click on the Build button on the Slide Sorter toolbar, or choose Tools ➤ Build to display the Build dialog box.

4. Select the Build Body Text check box to define the selected slide as a build slide.

5. Select the Dim Previous Points check box to dim the preceding points as the subsequent text is built on the slide. Then select a color in which to display the dimmed points in the drop-down list.

6. Select the Effect check box, and then select the effect for animating each point that appears in the drop-down list.

7. Choose OK. The build icon appears below the slide to the left of the timing set for the slide.

To see how the build effect appears, click on the slide's build icon, and then click on the Slide Show button on the horizontal scroll bar to run the slide show. Press Esc after the slide is run to return to Slide Sorter view.

If necessary, select a different build effect for the points on the selected slide in the Build Effects drop-down list on the Slide Sorter toolbar.

SLIDE SHOW

Setting a Timing for Each Slide

If the slides in the slide show are to be displayed automatically, you must set the amount of time each slide is to appear on screen.

To manually set the slide timings:

1. Click on the Slide Sorter View button on the horizontal scroll bar to display the presentation in Slide Sorter view.

2. Select the slide for which a timing is to be set.

3. Choose Tools ➤ Transition to display the Transition dialog box.

4. In the Advance area, select Only On Mouse Click to manually advance the selected slide during the slide show. Or, select Automatically After Seconds, and then specify the amount of time during which the slide is to be displayed in the text box.

5. Choose OK.

To set the slide timings while rehearsing the slide show:

1. Activate the presentation, and then select View ➤ Slide Show to display the Slide Show dialog box.

2. If necessary, specify the range of slides for which timings are to be set in the From and To text boxes in the Slides area.

3. Select Rehearse New Timings in the Advance area, and then select Show to display the first slide with a timing button in the lower-left corner.

TIP: *Display the presentation in Slide Sorter view, and then click on the Rehearse Timings button on the Slide Sorter toolbar to set the timings while rehearsing the slide show.*

COMMAND AND FEATURE REFERENCE

`0:00:11` **4.** When the amount of time the slide is to be displayed during the presentation appears on the timing button, click on it to set the time and display the next slide.

5. Repeat step 4 for each slide that appears.

6. When the timing is set for each slide, select Yes in the dialog box that appears asking if you want to save the timings. The presentation appears in Slide Sorter view with the timing set for each slide on the left below the miniature slide.

NOTE: *Select Use Slide Timings in the Advance area of the Slide Show dialog box, and then select Show to run the slide show with the timings.*

SEE ALSO: *Presentation; Viewer*

Solver

Use Excel's Solver add-in to answer what-if questions involving several variables. Solver can adjust the values in changing cells to find the optimum value defined for a specific cell. Or, use Solver to find the optimum value for a specific cell when limits are placed on at least one value involved in the calculation.

Solving a Problem

To use Solver, define the problem and how it is to be solved:

- Specify the *target cell*, or the objective, that contains the formula that will provide the result.

SOLVER

- Specify the *changing cells*, or the decision variables, which are cells that contain the variable values Solver adjusts to produce the desired value in the target cell. Up to 200 changing cells can be specified for a target cell.

- Specify the *constraints*, or limits imposed to create the target value. A constraint is usually applied to a cell that contains a formula. One upper-limit and one lower-limit constraint can be assigned to each changing cell, and up to 100 constraints can be assigned to other cells in the worksheet model.

Solver changes the values in the changing cells to find a solution within the constraints to the formula in the target cell.

1. Activate the worksheet for which Solver is to be used.

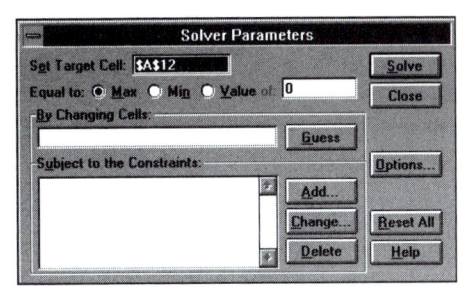

2. Select Tools ➤ Solver to display the Solver Parameters dialog box.

3. Select the target cell in the worksheet. The reference to the selected cell appears in the Set Target Cell text box.

NOTE: *If no target cell is specified, Solver solves the problem by altering the values in the changing cells until all constraints are met. If the target cell does not contain a formula, it must be a changing cell.*

4. In the Equal To area, select Max or Min to allow Solver to maximize or minimize the value in the target cell. Or, select Value Of, and then specify the exact value Solver is to produce in the target cell.

COMMAND AND FEATURE REFERENCE

5. Type the references or names of cells that contain variables that may be changed for the formula in the target cell in the By Changing Cells text box. Or, select Guess to have Solver suggest the changing cells on the basis of the specified target cell.

TIP: *Enter adjacent changing cells as a reference to a range. Separate the references to nonadjacent changing cells with commas.*

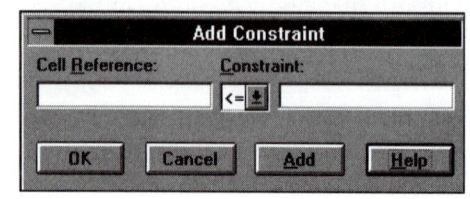

6. Select Add in the Subject To The Constraints area to display the Add Constraint dialog box.

7. Type the reference to the cell for which a constraint is to be applied, often the target cell or one of the changing cells, in the Cell Reference text box.

8. Select the operator for the constraint in the Constraint drop-down list, and then type the value, formula, or cell to specify the value for the constraint in the text box.

NOTE: *If "int" (integer) is selected in the Constraint drop-down list, the value being constrained is limited to whole numbers. Only changing cells can be constrained to integers.*

9. If necessary, select Add, and then repeat steps 7 and 8 to create additional constraints.

10. Choose OK in the Add Constraint dialog box.

NOTE: *Choose Change to edit the constraint highlighted in the Subject To The Constraints list box, or Delete to remove the highlighted constraint.*

11. Choose Solve in the Solver Parameters dialog box to solve the problem, display the results in.

SOLVER

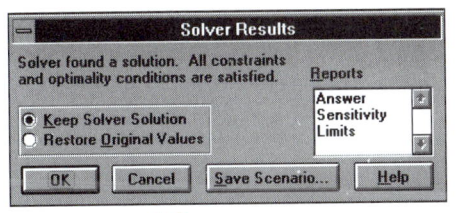

the worksheet, and display the Solver Results dialog box.

12. Select any of the following options in the Solver Results dialog box:

- To replace the original values with Solver's solutions to the problem, select Keep Solver Solution. Or, select Restore Original Values to return the original values to the worksheet.

WARNING: *Solver replaces the values in the changing cells with adjusted values that will produce the desired result in the target cell. If a changing cell contains a formula, the formula will be replaced with a value.*

- To create a report summarizing how Solver achieved the results of the problem on a separate worksheet in the workbook, select Answer to display the original values of the target cell and the changing cells, Sensitivity to show how sensitive the solution is to changes in the target cell formula or the constraints, or Limits to report on the value in the target cell and the upper and lower limits that can be allowed for values in the changing cells, in the Reports list box.

- To save the problem as a scenario, select Save Scenario to display the Save Scenario dialog box. Type a name for the scenario in the Scenario Name text box, and then choose OK.

13. Choose OK in the Solver Results dialog box to return to your worksheet.

COMMAND AND FEATURE REFERENCE

The settings selected for Solver in a worksheet are saved by Solver in the workbook. To return all the selected settings to Solver's defaults before defining another problem, select Reset All in the Solver Parameters dialog box.

Specifying Solver's Options

Set options to manage Solver's solution processes and to save a model or load a saved model.

TIP: *Place different problems on separate sheets in a workbook so Solver can automatically save each set of settings. To save Solver settings for multiple problems on the same sheet in a workbook, create a model or a scenario.*

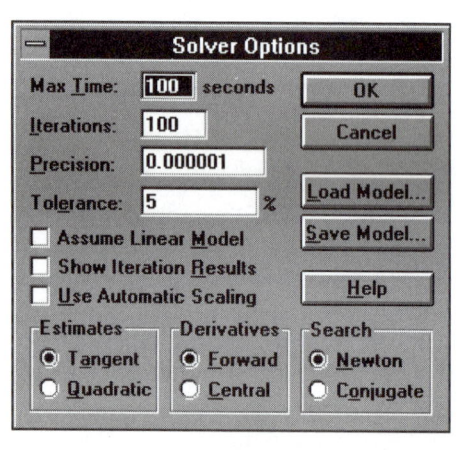

To specify Solver's options:

1. Select Tools ➤ Solver to display the Solver Parameters dialog box, and then choose Options to display the Solver Options dialog box.

2. Select any of the following options:

Max Time Seconds	Specify the maximum amount of time allowed for solving the problem up to 32,767 seconds (9 hours and 10 minutes) in the text box.
Iterations	Specify the maximum number of interim calculations (up to 32,767) allowed when solving the problem in the text box.

SOLVER

Precision	Specify a number in the text box between 0 and 1 to control the precision of the results of the problem. The lower the number, the higher the precision.
Tolerance	Specify the percentage of error allowed for the results when an integer constraint is defined in the problem. The higher the tolerance, the faster the problem is solved.
Assume Linear Model	Select the check box to speed up solving the problem when all the relationships are linear in the worksheet model.
Show Iteration Results	Select the check box to display the results found after each iteration in the problem solving process.
Use Automatic Scaling	Select the check box to use automatic scaling when the values in the target cell and the changing cells are greatly different.
Estimates	Select Tangent to use linear extrapolation from a tangent vector to find the earliest estimates of the basic variables in each one-dimensional search, or Quadratic to use quadratic extrapolation for a nonlinear search.
Derivatives	Select Forward as the type of differencing for estimates of partial derivatives in linear

COMMAND AND FEATURE REFERENCE

	problem solving, or <u>C</u>entral as the type for nonlinear problems.
Search	Choose <u>N</u>ewton as the search algorithm used to determine the direction of the search at each iteration to require fewer iterations, or C<u>o</u>njugate to require more iterations for a large problem.
<u>L</u>oad Model	To select a previously saved model solution, select <u>L</u>oad Model, and then type the reference of the saved model in the Select Model Area text box and choose OK. Choose OK again to confirm that the values representing the solution to the problem are to be entered in their respective cells.
<u>S</u>ave Model	To save the current model solution, select <u>S</u>ave Model, and then type the worksheet reference into which the model is to be placed in the Select Model Area text box and choose OK.

3. Choose OK in the Solver Options dialog box.

4. In the Solver Parameters dialog box, choose <u>S</u>olve to solve the problem with the newly specified options, or Close to return to the worksheet.

SEE ALSO: *Goal Seek; Scenario*

Sort

To change the order of selected data, perform a *sort* on it, or rearrange it numerically, alphabetically, or chronologically. Data in Access, Excel, and Word can be sorted automatically with options you specify.

NOTE: *Slides in a PowerPoint presentation can be sorted manually.*

When you sort data, you arrange it in ascending order (lowest to highest or A–Z) or descending order (highest to lowest or Z–A).

Sorting Data in Access

In Access, sorting the records in a table, form, or query changes the order in which the records are displayed. Sorting the records in a report changes the arrangement of the data in the report. The records can be sorted by the data in one field in either ascending or descending order, or by the data in multiple fields in both ascending and descending order.

To display the records in an open table or form by sorting the records by the data in one field, position the insertion point in the field, and then click on the Sort Ascending or Sort Descending button on the Table Datasheet or Form View toolbar, or select Records ➤ Quick Sort ➤ Ascending or Descending.

NOTE: *To sort the records displayed in a query by the data in one or more fields, display the query in Query Design view, and then specify the order in which to sort the data in the Sort row for the field or fields. The data in the left-most field is sorted first, and then sorted by the data in subsequent fields from left to right in the QBE grid.*

COMMAND AND FEATURE REFERENCE

To sort the records in a form or table by the data in multiple fields:

1. Open the form in Form view or the table in Datasheet view.

2. Click on the Edit Filter/Sort button on the Form View or Table Datasheet toolbar, or select Records ➤ Edit Filter/Sort to display the Filter Sort toolbar and the Filter window for the selected form or table.

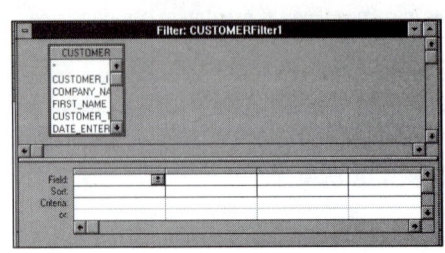

3. Drag the first field on which to sort the records into the Field row in the grid in the bottom pane of the Filter window.

4. In the Sort row for the field, select Ascending or Descending as the sort order in the drop-down list.

5. Repeat steps 3 and 4 for each field that contains the data on which to sort the records.

6. Click on the Apply Filter/Sort button on the Filter/Sort toolbar, or choose Records ➤ Apply Filter/Sort to display the records in the form or table in the specified order.

Although the records are displayed in the form or table in the order specified, they are stored in the form or table in the order in which they were entered.

TIP: *To save the display of the records in a table in the specified order, create a query with the necessary sort order.*

To undo the sort and redisplay the records in the form or table in the order in which they were entered, click on the Show All Records button on the Form View or Table Datasheet toolbar, or choose Records ➤ Show All Records.

SORT

To sort the records that will appear in a report:

1. Open the report in Design view.

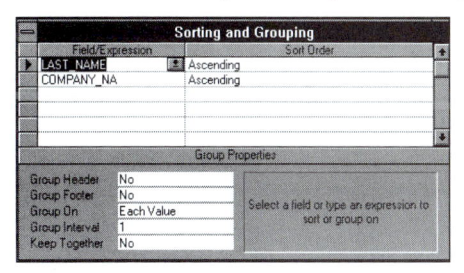

2. Select <u>V</u>iew ➤ Sorting And Grouping to display the Sorting And Grouping window.

3. Select the name of the first field on which the data is to be sorted in the first cell in the Field/Expression column.

4. Select Ascending or Descending in the first cell in the Sort Order column to specify the sort order for the first field.

5. Repeat steps 3 and 4 for each field on which the data in the report is to be sorted. Up to 10 fields can be used to define the sort order.

6. Double-click on the Sorting And Grouping window's Control menu box to close it and return to the report in Design view.

7. Click on the Save button on the Report Design toolbar or choose <u>F</u>ile ➤ <u>S</u>ave (Ctrl+S) to save the changes to the report.

The data in a field that was used to sort records in a report can also be placed in a *group*, a collection of related data. Each group can contain summary information about its data in a header or footer. The summary information can be the result of a calculation, such as the total number of items in the group.

To group data in a report:

1. Open the report in Design view.

COMMAND AND FEATURE REFERENCE

2. Select <u>V</u>iew ➤ <u>S</u>orting And Grouping to display the Sorting And Grouping window.

3. Position the insertion point in the field to be grouped in the Field/Expression column in the Sorting And Grouping window, and then set any of the following properties for the group in the Group Properties pane:

- Select Yes in the Group Header drop-down list to add text or graphics at the top of the selected field's group.

- Select Yes in the Group Footer drop-down list to add text or graphics at the bottom of the selected field's group.

- Select the appropriate Text, Date/Time, or Numeric option to specify how the data is to be grouped in the Group On drop-down list. The options that appear depend on the type of data in the field.

- Type the number in the Group Interval text box to specify the interval that is necessary for the property selected in the Group On drop-down list. For example, when Order Date is the option selected in the Group On drop-down list, type 2 in the Group Interval property text box to report on the data in biweekly groups.

- Select No (the default) in the Keep Together drop-down list to print the group without restricting the header, details, and footer to appear on the same page; Whole Group to print the group's header, details, and footer on the same page; or With First Detail to print the group's header on a page if the first detail will also fit on the page.

4. If necessary, add controls to the group's header and footer.

5. Click on the Save button on the Report Design toolbar, or choose File ➤ Save (Ctrl+S) to save the changes to the report.

Sorting Data in Excel and Word

Sort selected data in an Excel list to organize it in alphabetical, numerical, or chronological order. All the data in each row is rearranged in the list according to the *sort order*–the order specified for data in selected columns of the list.

TIP: *To quickly sort the items in each row of an Excel list by the data in a column, select a cell in the column, and then click on the Sort Ascending button or the Sort Descending button on the Standard toolbar.*

In Excel, data is sorted first by numbers and dates, then by text values, with numbers formatted as text sorted before the text. The logical values TRUE and FALSE are sorted next, then error values in the order in which they occur in the list, and finally empty cells.

TIP: *In Excel, format a number within a group of numbers that contains text as text so that the items in the group will be sorted together. For example, if the group consists of 30, 30a, and 30b, format 30 as text.*

In Word, you can sort up to three types of information in paragraphs, lists separated by commas or spaces, or table rows. Tables are sorted only by the characters in the first table cell. Numbered lists are automatically renumbered after a sort.

TIP: *Sort the data in a mail merge data source before you perform the merge so the results of the printed merge appear in the desired order.*

COMMAND AND FEATURE REFERENCE

In Word, items that start with punctuation marks or other symbols are sorted first, followed by items that start with numbers, then items that start with letters. Uppercase letters precede lowercase letters in the sorted list. Subsequent characters decide the sort order of items that begin with the same character, and subsequent fields decide the sort order if list items contain the same data in a field.

To sort data:

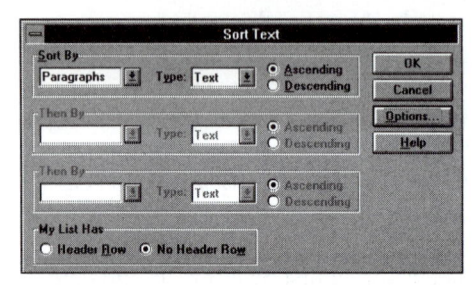

1. Select a cell in an Excel list, and then choose Data ➤ Sort to display the Sort dialog box. Or select the items to be sorted in a Word document, and then choose Table ➤ Sort Text to display the Sort Text dialog box.

2. Choose any of the following options to perform the sort:

Sort By In the Sort By drop-down list, select the column label in Excel, or in Word, choose the field name, column, or Paragraphs as the first type of data on which to sort the selection, and then choose Text, Number, or Date as the kind of data to sort in the Type drop-down list. Choose Ascending or Descending as the sort order.

Then By Select the second, and if necessary, third column label or type of data on which to sort text in the corresponding drop-down list. In Word, choose the type of data to sort in the corresponding Type drop-down list. Select Ascending or Descending

SORT

> **TROUBLESHOOTING**
>
> ### Selecting a Column of Text
>
> What should you do if you want to sort a list of items by a character other than the first character in each item? You can select a column of characters in a Word document. For example, suppose you want to sort the items in a manually entered bulleted or numbered list in a Word document. Hold down the Alt key while you drag to select the first character in each item, and then choose T<u>a</u>ble ➤ Sor<u>t</u> Text and specify the sorting options.

as the sort order for the second and third items being sorted.

My List Has Select Header <u>R</u>ow to disregard the first row of selected data while sorting an Excel list or a Word table, or all rows in a Word table that are defined as heading rows. Or, select No Header Ro<u>w</u> to sort all rows of data in the selection.

3. If necessary, select <u>O</u>ptions to display the Sort Options dialog box, select any of the following options, and then choose OK:

- Select a *custom sort order*, a nonalphabetic or nonnumeric sort order, for the data in the column specified in the Sort By drop-down list in Excel's Sort dialog box in the <u>F</u>irst Key Sort Order drop-down list.

- Select the <u>C</u>ase Sensitive check box to sort words that begin with an uppercase letter before words that begin with the same lowercase letter in an Excel list, or when Text is the type of data specified in the T<u>y</u>pe drop-down list in Word.

COMMAND AND FEATURE REFERENCE

- In Excel, select Sort Top To Bottom (the default for a list) to sort the list or the rows by the data in a single column, or Sort Left To Right (the default for a pivot table) to sort the data or the columns by the data in a single row.

- To sort text outside a table in Word, choose Tabs or Commas as the separator character, or choose Other and type the separator character in the text box.

- In Word, select the Sort Column Only check box to sort a column of table data or text in a newspaper-style column.

4. Choose OK in the Sort or Sort Text dialog box.

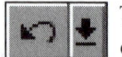

To return the list to its original arrangement, click on the Undo button on the Standard toolbar before you perform any other command or action.

SEE ALSO: *Mail Merge; Query; Section; Sequence; Table; Undo/Redo*

Spelling

Use Microsoft Office's Spelling tool to catch typographical errors or misspelled words in your Excel worksheets, PowerPoint presentations, or Word documents. You can create *custom dictionaries* to add special terminology that is not in the main dictionary to prevent it from being questioned, and *exclude dictionaries* to question the spelling of words in the main dictionary.

SPELLING

Checking Spelling

When you check the spelling in a document, each word that is not in the main or custom dictionaries, or is in the exclude dictionary, is highlighted in your document.

To check spelling:

1. Select the cell or position the insertion point where you want to begin checking the spelling, and then click on the Spelling button on the Standard toolbar, or select Tools ➤ Spelling (F7) to display the Spelling dialog box.

TIP: *To check the spelling of a single word, highlight it, and then click on the Spelling button on the Standard toolbar or select Tools ➤ Spelling (F7). If the word is spelled correctly, select No to return to your file.*

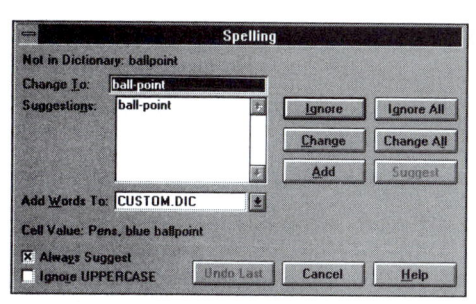

2. If necessary in Word, select Options to display the Spelling tab of the Options dialog box, select any of the following options to use when checking the spelling in a document, and then choose OK:

- Select the Always Suggest check box to have Word display suggestions for the correct spelling of misspelled words in the Suggestions list box.

- Select From Main Dictionary Only to display suggestions from the main dictionary, but not from any custom dictionaries.

COMMAND AND FEATURE REFERENCE

- In the Ignore area, select Reset Ignore All to remove all the words from the current session list for which Ignore All was selected; select the Words In UPPERCASE check box to have Word disregard words that contain only uppercase letters during the Spelling check; and select the Words With Numbers check box to have Word disregard words that contain numbers during the Spelling check.

3. Choose any of the following options for the word that currently appears in the Not In Dictionary area or text box:

- The proposed spelling for the current word appears in the Change To text box. If necessary, edit the spelling or highlight a different spelling in the Suggestions list box.

- Select the correct spelling for the current word in the list of suggested spellings that appears in the Suggestions list box.

- Select the name of the custom dictionary file to which you want to add the current word in the Add Words To drop-down list.

- Choose Ignore to disregard the spelling of the current word.

- Choose Ignore All to disregard the spelling of each occurrence of the current word in the file.

- Select Change to change the spelling of the current word to the spelling that appears in the Change To text box.

- Select Change All to change the spelling of each occurrence of the current word to the spelling that appears in the Change To text box.

SPELLING

- Choose <u>A</u>dd to insert the current word in the selected custom dictionary.

- Choose <u>S</u>uggest to display a list of suggested words for the current word if the Always Suggest check box is cleared.

NOTE: *In PowerPoint, the A<u>l</u>ways Suggest check box appears in the Spelling area in the Options dialog box.*

- In Word and Excel, select <u>U</u>ndo Last to restore the last change made by Spelling.

- In Excel, select the Alwa<u>y</u>s Suggest check box to have Spelling automatically suggest a list of spellings for the current word in the Suggestions list box.

- In Excel, select the Igno<u>r</u>e UPPERCASE check box to prevent Spelling from checking the spelling of words that contain only uppercase letters.

- Choose Cancel or Close to remove the Spelling dialog box and return to the file before Spelling is finished checking the file.

4. When Spelling is finished checking the spelling in the file, choose OK to remove the message box.

Creating a Dictionary of Excluded Words

Any words that are in Microsoft Office's main dictionary are not questioned during a Spelling check. To question the spelling of a correctly spelled word because you prefer a different spelling, create an *exclude dictionary* to be used with the main dictionary.

The exclude dictionary has the same file name as the main dictionary, but it has the .EXC extension. For example, if you are using the US English dictionary, the main dictionary file name is

COMMAND AND FEATURE REFERENCE

MSSP2_EN.LEX. The exclude dictionary associated with it will be named MSSP2_EN.EXC. Use Word to create the exclude dictionary.

To create an exclude dictionary:

1. Click on the New button on the Standard toolbar or press Ctrl+N to open a new document.

2. Type a word you want to exclude and press ↵ to start a new paragraph. Repeat this process for each word in the exclude dictionary.

3. Click on the Save button on the Standard toolbar or choose File ➤ Save (Ctrl+S) to display the Save As dialog box.

4. Choose C:\WINDOWS\MSAPPS\PROOF as the location in which to store the exclude dictionary file.

5. Choose Text Only in the Save File As Type drop-down list.

6. Type a name for the exclude dictionary in the File Name text box. For example, type **MSSP2_EN.EXC**.

7. Choose OK in the Save As dialog box.

8. Press Ctrl+W to close the file, and then select Yes to confirm that the file is to be saved.

9. To save the exclude dictionary, choose Text Only in the dialog box that appears.

Creating a Custom Dictionary

If you often use terminology that is questioned during a Spelling check, create a custom dictionary that contains words that are not in the main dictionary. Words in a custom dictionary will be questioned only when they are misspelled.

Microsoft Office comes with a custom dictionary, and you can create additional custom dictionaries

SPELLING

to use when checking the spelling in a file. The custom dictionaries are Word documents that can be edited using the same techniques as you use for regular documents.

To create a custom dictionary:

1. Select Tools ➤ Spelling (F7), and then choose Options.

2. Use any of the following options in the Custom Dictionaries area of the Spelling tab to create, edit, or remove a custom dictionary:

- Select New to create a new custom dictionary. Type a name for the new dictionary in the File Name text box, and then select OK in the Create Custom Dictionary dialog box. The file is placed by default in the C:\WINDOWS\MSAPPS\PROOF directory.

- Highlight a dictionary in the Custom Dictionaries list box, and then select Edit and choose Yes to open the custom dictionary as a Word document. Choose OK in the Options dialog box to remove it, and then edit the dictionary as necessary. Click on the Save button on the Standard toolbar to save the dictionary as a text-only file, and then press Ctrl+W to close the dictionary file.

- Select Add to add a custom dictionary file stored in a different path to the C:\WINDOWS\ MSAPPS\PROOF directory (and the Custom Dictionaries list box).

- In the Custom Dictionaries list box, highlight the name of a custom dictionary you do not want to use during a Spelling check, and then select Remove to remove it from the list. Choose Yes to confirm that you want to remove the dictionary.

COMMAND AND FEATURE REFERENCE

- Select the name of another language in the Language drop-down list to apply that language's formatting to the selected custom dictionary. Choose (None) to use the dictionary to check text formatted in any language.

3. In the Custom Dictionaries list box, select the check box of any custom dictionary to be used during a Spelling check.

4. Choose OK in the Options dialog box.

SEE ALSO: AutoCorrect; Thesaurus

Style

To present data in Excel worksheets and Word documents with consistent formatting, apply *styles*, defined groups of formatting commands, to the data or text. When a style is applied, each format in the style is simultaneously applied to the selection. Some built-in styles come with Excel and Word.

In Excel, all styles are cell styles. However, a defined style can be applied to an entire worksheet. Cell styles can include any of the formatting that can be applied to a cell using the options on the tabs in the Format Cells dialog box.

There are two types of styles in Word–paragraph styles and character styles. Paragraph styles control all the formatting in a paragraph, including the font and size, line spacing, alignment, tab stops, and the borders and shading. The format applied to a paragraph is stored in its paragraph mark. Character styles are created using the options in the Font dialog box.

Applying a Style in an Excel Worksheet

To apply an existing style in Excel:

1. Select the cells to which you want to apply a defined style.

TIP: *When the Style Box is added to one of the displayed toolbars, you can select the name of one of the defined styles in the workbook to apply to selected cells.*

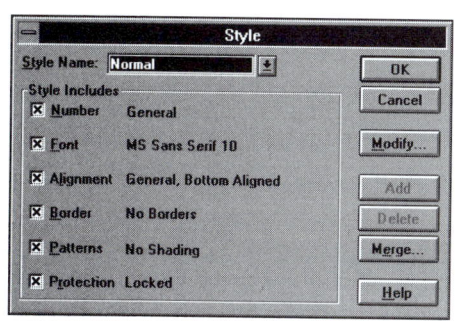

2. Choose Format ➤ Style to display the Style dialog box.

3. Select the name of the style to apply in the Style Name drop-down list.

4. Choose OK.

TIP: *To quickly apply currency, percent, or comma style to selected cells, click on the Currency Style, Percent Style, or Comma Style button on the Formatting toolbar.*

Applying a Style in a Word Document

When you create a new document, select a template that contains the styles to use in the document, and then apply styles to all the document text. If a style is modified, the formatting of all the text to which the style is applied in the document will be changed.

COMMAND AND FEATURE REFERENCE

NOTE: *Click on the Help button on Word's Standard toolbar, and then click on the text to display a message box with information about the formatting and styles applied to the text. Click on the Help button again to remove the message.*

There are several ways to apply a style to text in a Word document. Position the insertion point in the paragraph or select the text.

NOTE: *Paragraph styles appear in bold letters (character styles do not) in the Style drop-down list on the Formatting toolbar and in the Styles list box in the Styles dialog box.*

Use one of the following methods to choose a style:

- Select the name of the style in the Style drop-down list on the Formatting toolbar.

    OR

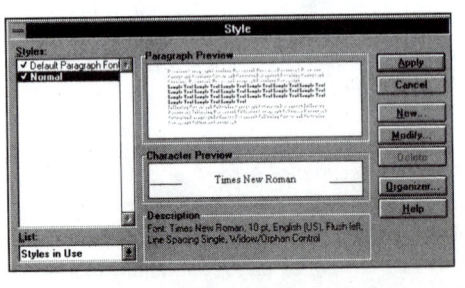

- Select Format ➤ Style to display the Style dialog box, select the name of the style in the Styles list box and then choose Apply.

- Press the shortcut keys assigned to the style. The following is a list of the shortcut keys assigned to some of Word's built-in styles:

Normal	Ctrl+Shift+N
Heading 1	Alt+Ctrl+1
Heading 2	Alt+Ctrl+2
Heading 3	Alt+Ctrl+3

STYLE

List Bullet	Ctrl+Shift+L
Select a Style	Ctrl+Shift+S
Apply the same style	Ctrl+Y
Remove a character style	Ctrl+Spacebar

Copying Styles in Excel

You can copy styles from one open workbook file to another:

1. Activate the workbook to which the styles are to be copied.

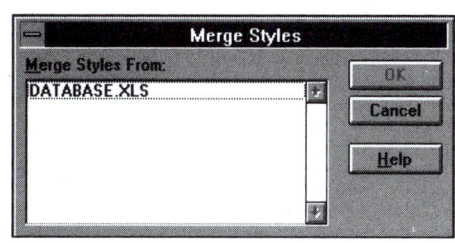

2. Select Format ➤ Style, and then choose Merge to display the Merge Styles dialog box.

3. Select the name of the workbook that contains the styles to be copied in the Merge Styles From list box.

4. Choose OK in the Merge Styles dialog box.

NOTE: *If there are any styles in the active workbook with the same names as the styles being copied, Excel displays a message asking if you want to replace the current styles with the copied styles. Choose Yes to replace all the styles, or No to keep the current styles in the active file. Choose Cancel to cancel the copy procedure.*

5. Choose OK in the Style dialog box to return to the workbook.

Copying Styles in Word

You can copy styles from a document or template to a different document or template to save time and make sure the styles are exactly the same in both.

COMMAND AND FEATURE REFERENCE

1. Choose F̲ormat ➤ S̲tyle, and select O̲rganizer to display the Organizer dialog box.

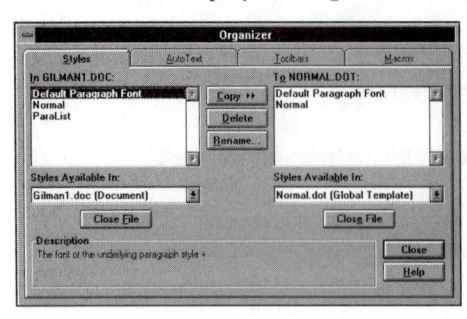

2. If necessary, select the S̲tyles tab.

3. Highlight the name of the style in the I̲n *File Name* list box. Press Ctrl as you select to highlight multiple names in the list box.

4. Select C̲opy to copy the selected style to the T̲o NORMAL.DOT list box.

5. Choose any of the following options to manage the styles:

- Select the name of the file or the template that contains the styles to be copied in the Styles A̲vailable In drop-down list. Then select the name of the file or template to which the styles are to be copied in the Styles Availab̲le In drop-down list.

- Select Close F̲ile to close the document or template file that contains the styles in the I̲n *File Name* list box. Select Close̲ File to close the current file or template that contains the styles in the T̲o *File Name* list box. Each button changes to Open File so you can open a different document or template file.

- Select the corresponding Open File button to display the Open dialog box, and then open a new document or template file. The names of the styles in the file or template appear in the I̲n *File Name* or T̲o *File Name* list boxes.

STYLE

- Choose <u>D</u>elete to remove the highlighted style from the document or template. Select <u>Y</u>es to confirm the deletion.

- Highlight a style to be renamed or to which an alias is to be added, and then select <u>R</u>ename to display the Rename dialog box. Type a different name in the New <u>N</u>ame text box, or type a comma and an alias, and then choose OK.

NOTE: *Rename a style to change the name of a style you created, or to give a built-in style, which cannot be renamed, an alias. Select F<u>o</u>rmat ➤ <u>S</u>tyle, highlight the current name of the style in the <u>S</u>tyles list box, and choose <u>M</u>odify. Type a new name for the style in the <u>N</u>ame text box, or type a comma after the name and then type the style's alias and select OK.*

6. Choose Close in the Organizer dialog box.

Creating or Modifying a Style in Excel

In Excel, styles are stored in the workbook in which they were created. To create or modify a style in Excel:

1. Activate the workbook in which styles are to be created or modified, and then select the cells for which a style is to be defined.

2. Select F<u>o</u>rmat ➤ <u>S</u>tyle to display the Style dialog box.

3. To create a new style, type a new name in the <u>S</u>tyle Name text box, and then choose <u>A</u>dd.

4. Choose <u>M</u>odify to display the Format Cells dialog box.

TIP: *If you modify the formatting in a style, the formatting is automatically applied to all the cells in the workbook to which the style is applied.*

COMMAND AND FEATURE REFERENCE

5. Select any of the formatting that is to be assigned to the style, and then choose OK in the Format Cells dialog box.

6. The formatting selected on each tab in the Format Cells dialog box appears in the Style Includes area of the Style dialog box. If necessary, clear the check boxes of any of the tabs whose formats will not be in the style.

7. Select OK to define the style and apply its formatting to the selected cells.

To delete a style other than one of Excel's built-in styles, select Format ➤ Style to display the Style dialog box, select the name of the style in the Style Name drop-down list, and then choose Delete.

Creating or Modifying a Style in Word

You can create your own styles to use in documents based on the template in which the style is stored.

WARNING: *Although you can redefine Word's Normal style, all new documents are based by default on the NORMAL.DOT template, and many existing styles in other templates are based on the Normal style. Instead, modify the Normal style and save it to a different name. Then apply the new style as necessary.*

To create or modify a style using formatting applied to existing text:

1. Position the insertion point in the paragraph, or select the text whose formatting is to be saved as a style, and then format the text.

2. Click in the Style text box on the Formatting toolbar to highlight the name of the current style.

3. Press ↵ to modify the style, or type a name for a new style, and then press ↵.

STYLE

To create an entirely new style or modify an existing style:

1. Choose Format ➤ Style to display the Style dialog box.

2. To modify an existing style, highlight the name of the style in the Styles list box.

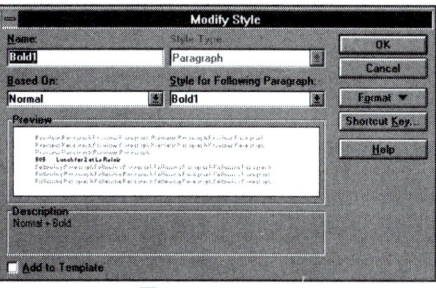

3. Select New or Modify to display the New Style or Modify Style dialog box.

4. If necessary, type a name for the style in the Name text box.

5. If you are creating a new style, select Paragraph or Character in the Style Type drop-down list.

6. Select a style that is similar to the style being created or modified in the Based On drop-down list.

7. Select the style to be automatically applied to a new paragraph begun after the style is applied in the Style For Following Paragraph drop-down list.

8. Optionally, select Shortcut Key and assign a key sequence to the new style.

9. Choose Format, and then select the formatting to be assigned to the style.

10. Select the Add To Template check box to make the style available for any document based on the same template.

11. Choose OK in the New Style or Modify Style dialog box, and then choose Apply in the Style dialog box.

COMMAND AND FEATURE REFERENCE

To remove a style from the current document, select Format ➤ Style to display the Style dialog box, select the name of the style in the Styles list box, and then choose Delete. If the selected style was a paragraph style, the formatting for any paragraph to which the style was applied is changed to Normal style. If the style was a character style, the style is removed from any characters to which it was applied.

> **TIP:** *To display the names of the paragraph styles applied in the current Word document on the left side of the window, display the document in Normal or Outline view, select Tools ➤ Options, and choose the View tab. Adjust the measurement in the Style Area Width text box until it is greater than 0, and then choose OK. If necessary, drag the vertical line along the left edge of the document until the style names appear.*

> **SEE ALSO:** AutoFormat; Help; Print; Style Gallery; Templates; Toolbars; View

Style Gallery

Use Word's Style Gallery to add styles to the document from a different template than the one on which the existing document is based.

> **NOTE:** *To attach a new template (change the document's template) to an existing document, use File ➤ Templates.*

STYLE GALLERY

Copying Styles from a Template

Use the Style Gallery to copy the styles in the selected template to the active document. The template's style takes precedence over the same style in the document. Any style in the template that is not already in the document is added to the document, and styles that are not in the template stay the same in the document.

To copy styles from a template:

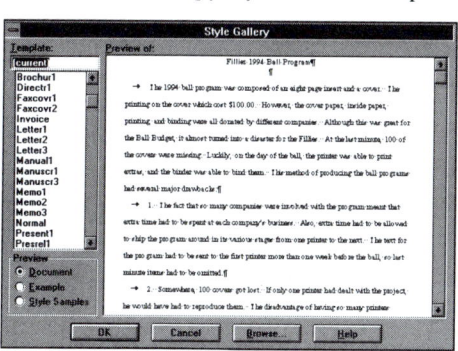

1. With the document whose template you want to change active, select Format ➤ Style Gallery to display the Style Gallery dialog box.

2. Select the name of the template that contains the styles to be added to the document in the Template list box.

3. Select any of the following options:

Preview Select Document to see how the active document appears when styles in the selected template are applied, Example to preview a sample document based on the selected template, or Style Samples to preview a list of the styles in the highlighted template and samples of text formatted with the styles.

Browse When it is necessary to select a template located in a different directory, select Browse to display

COMMAND AND FEATURE REFERENCE

the Select Template Directory dialog box, and then change the directory and choose OK.

4. Choose OK in the Style Gallery dialog box.

To return to the document's original template, click on the Undo button on the Standard toolbar or select Edit ➤ Undo.

SEE ALSO: *AutoFormat; Style; Templates*

Summary Info

In Excel, PowerPoint, and Word, enter summary information in a file so you can use the information to search for the file or display the file's statistics.

NOTE: *Information entered in the Title, Subject, Author, and Keywords text boxes can be used to perform a search. The information in the Comments text box is for your use only.*

Entering Summary Information

To enter summary information for the active file:

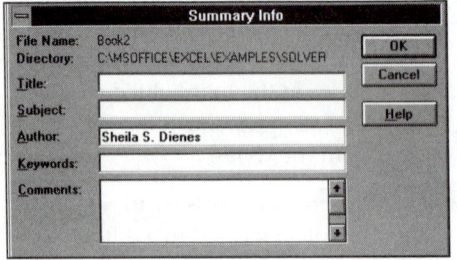

1. Select File ➤ Summary Info to display the Summary Info dialog box.

2. Type a descriptive name for the file in the Title text box.

SUMMARY INFO

3. Type a description of the contents of the file in the Subject text box.

4. The name that appears in the Author text box is the name entered when you set up Microsoft Office. It appears in the User Name text box on the General tab in Excel's Options dialog box, or in Word's User Info dialog box. If necessary, edit the name of the author.

5. Type any words to be used when searching for the file in the Keywords text box. Separate keywords with spaces or commas.

6. Type remarks about the file in the Comments text box.

7. Choose OK in the Summary Info dialog box.

The summary information is saved when you save the file.

NOTE: *Each time a Word document is saved, the statistics for the file are updated. Choose Statistics in the Summary Info dialog box to display the statistics and other information about the active file.*

To display the Summary Info dialog box each time you save a new file:

1. Select Tools ➤ Options, and then choose Excel's General tab or Word's Save tab.

2. Select the Prompt For Summary Info check box.

3. Choose OK in the Options dialog box.

SEE ALSO: *File Management; Print*

COMMAND AND FEATURE REFERENCE

Table

Use tables instead of tabs in Word documents that contain columns of data, for text that is positioned in side-by-side paragraphs, or to place graphics beside text. Tables are made up of rows and columns of data entered into cells. The cells' contents are individual paragraphs, and can be formatted using the same procedures you would use for paragraphs.

NOTE: *An Access table datasheet and Excel worksheet are also tables composed of rows and columns.*

Creating a Table

By default, table gridlines are displayed when you insert a table in your document. Select Table ➤ Gridlines to toggle the display of table gridlines.

Gridlines are not printed when you print the document. To print gridlines in a table, you must add borders to the table.

To create a table:

1. Position the insertion point where you want to place a table.

2. Click on the Insert Table button on the Standard toolbar, and then drag to create a table with the corresponding number of rows and columns.

3. Or, choose Table ➤ Insert Table to display the Insert Table dialog box.

TABLE T

> **NOTE:** *To create a table using existing document text, add paragraph marks, tabs, or commas in the text as separators, and then select the text to change into table text. Choose Table ➤ Convert Text To Table to display the Convert Text To Table dialog box, which is similar to the Insert Table dialog box. The separated text will be placed in individual cells in the table.*

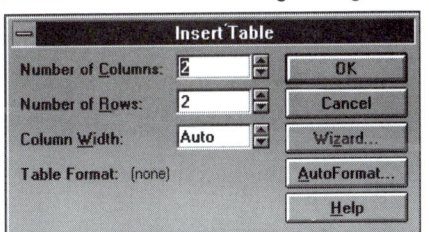

4. Choose any of the following options to create a table to your specifications:

- Specify the number of columns in the table in the Number Of Columns text box.

- Specify the number of rows in the table in the Number Of Rows text box.

- Specify the width of each column, or select Auto to evenly adjust the columns between the left and right margins.

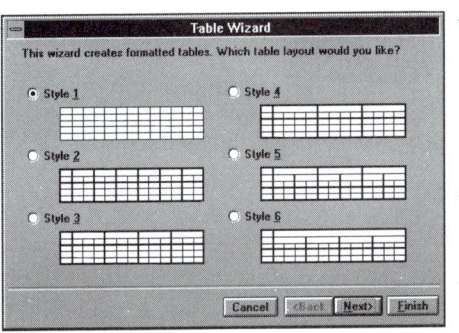

- Select Wizard to create tables in various formats using Word's Table Wizard.

- Select AutoFormat to display the Table AutoFormat dialog box. Select the format for the new table, and then choose OK. The name of the format applied to the table appears in the Table Format area.

425

COMMAND AND FEATURE REFERENCE

5. Choose OK.

TIP: *To insert a tab character in a cell, press Ctrl+Tab.*

To display the end-of-cell mark, which indicates the end of each cell's contents, and the end-of-row mark, which indicates the end of each row, click on the Show/Hide ¶ button on the Standard toolbar to toggle on the display of nonprinting characters.

TIP: *Use Insert ➤ Caption to add captions to tables so the captions will automatically be updated if you insert or delete table in the document.*

Creating Table Headings

Table headings are the data that you want as the "title" of the table. The headings consist of data that is entered in the first row of the table (the *header row*) unless a manual page break is inserted in the table.

Merge two or more cells to place a table heading in one cell that spans several columns in the first row of a table. When cells are merged, their contents are converted to paragraphs within a single cell.

Or, you can split a selected cell (usually a merged cell) to divide its contents according to the number of paragraph marks in the cell. If there is only one paragraph mark, the text is placed in the left cell and empty cells are added to its right.

To create table headings:

1. Select at least two cells to merge or one cell to split.

2. Choose Table ➤ Merge Cells or Table ➤ Split Cells.

The data in the heading row in a table is not automatically repeated across manual page breaks.

TABLE

However, you can have Word repeat the heading row in tables that contain manual page breaks, and automatically update heading text that is edited.

1. Select the row or rows, starting with the first table row, that contain the text to be used as headings.

2. Choose Table ➤ Headings.

To remove the heading text that was updated across manual page breaks, select Table ➤ Headings again.

Editing the Table

The table's appearance can be changed to fit your data.

To delete cells, rows, or columns:

1. Select the cells to be deleted, or a cell in each row or column to be deleted, and then select Table ➤ Delete Cells to display the Delete Cells dialog box.

> **TIP:** *Select an entire row or column, and then choose Table ➤ Delete Rows or Table ➤ Delete Columns to delete the selection.*

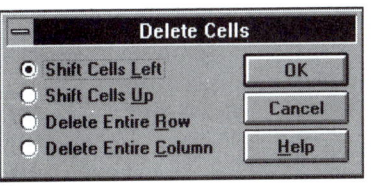

2. Choose one of the following options:

- Select Shift Cells Left to move the remaining cells in the row to the left after the deletion.

- Select Shift Cells Up to move the remaining cells in the column up after the deletion.

- Select Delete Entire Row to delete the row that contains the selected cell.

- Select Delete Entire Column to delete the column that contains the selected cell.

427

COMMAND AND FEATURE REFERENCE

3. Choose OK.

To insert cells, rows, or columns in the table:

1. Select the number of cells, rows, or columns in the position in which they are to be inserted in the table.

2. Click on the Insert Cells, Insert Rows, or Insert Columns button on the Standard toolbar, or choose Table ➤ Insert Cells, Rows, or Columns. If you selected cells, the Insert Cells dialog box appears.

NOTE: *If you selected rows, the rows are moved down to make room for the inserted rows. If you selected columns, the columns are moved to the right so the new columns can be inserted.*

3. Choose one of the following options:

- Select Shift Cells Right to insert cells in the position of the selection and move the originally selected cells to the right.

- Select Shift Cells Down to insert cells in the position of the selection and move the originally selected cells down.

- Select Insert Entire Row to insert a row(s) and move the original selection down.

- Select Insert Entire Column to insert a column(s) and move the original selection to the right.

4. Choose OK.

You can also use either of the following methods to add a row or column:

- With the insertion point in the last cell, press Tab to add another row at the end of a table.

OR

- To add a column on the right edge of the table, select the end-of-row marks and then click on the Insert Columns button on the Standard toolbar.

To change the width of a column, position the mouse pointer on the column's boundary (the gridline), and then drag it to the left to decrease the width or to the right to increase the width. As you drag, the mouse pointer appears as two vertical lines with horizontal arrows attached.

To change the column width with the mouse:

- Drag the column boundary. When you drag, the widths of columns to the right are changed in proportion, so the overall width of the table is not changed.

- Hold down the Shift key while you drag to change the widths of both the column and the column to its right without changing the widths of any other column or of the table.

- Hold down the Ctrl key while you drag the column boundary to change its size, and simultaneously change all columns to the right to the same width without changing the width of the table.

- Drag the table column marker on the Ruler to size all columns to the right proportionally.

- Press Ctrl+Shift as you drag to change the widths of the column and the table, without changing the widths of any other columns.

- Double-click on the right gridline of a column to automatically resize its width with AutoFit.

COMMAND AND FEATURE REFERENCE

To change the width of a column or a cell to exact specifications:

1. Select the cells or columns whose widths are to be changed.

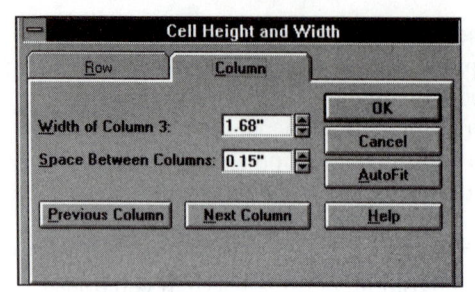

2. Choose Table ➤ Cell Height And Width, and then choose the Column tab.

3. Select any of the following options:

- Specify the width of the selected cell or column in the Width Of Column *Number* text box.

- Specify the amount of blank space between the column boundaries and the cell contents in the Space Between Columns text box.

- Choose Previous Column to select the previous column in the table.

- Choose Next Column to select the next column in the table.

- Select AutoFit to automatically adjust the widths of all the columns in the table that contains the insertion point to their minimum widths.

4. Choose OK.

To quickly change the height of a row, display the table in Page Layout view, and then drag the row marker at the lower edge of the row on the vertical ruler. The size of the table changes proportionally.

TABLE

To specify the exact row height and set other row formatting options:

1. Select the row to be changed.

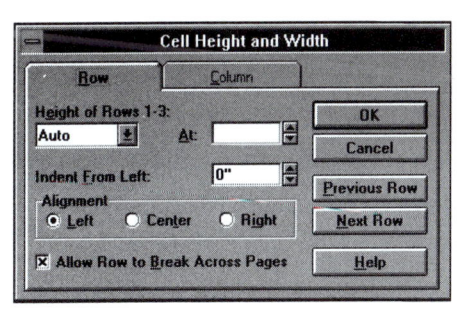

2. Choose Table ➤ Cell Height And Width, and then choose the Row tab.

3. Change any of the following options:

- In the Height Of Row *Number* drop-down list, select Auto to allow Word to adjust the height automatically; or select At Least, and then specify a minimum row height, or Exactly, and then specify an exact row height.

- Specify the measurement for the height of the selected rows in the At text box if you chose At Least or Exactly in the Height Of Row *Number* drop-down list.

- Specify the distance from the left margin to the left edge of the row in the Indent From Left text box.

- In the Alignment area, choose Left to align the row along the left margin, Center to align the row between the left and right margins, or Right to align the row along the right margin.

- Select the Allow Row To Break Across Pages check box (selected by default) to let a table split across a page break at the selected row.

- Choose Previous Row to select the previous table row.

COMMAND AND FEATURE REFERENCE

> ### TROUBLESHOOTING
>
> ## Selecting Cells, Rows, Columns, or Data
>
> Do you find that the commands you want to use are not available on the Tables drop-down menu? If so, make certain that the correct table item is selected.
>
> There are several ways to select items in a table:
>
> - Drag over text in a cell to select the text.
>
> - Click in the *cell selection bar* (the left margin of the cell) to select the cell.
>
> - Click in the *row selection bar* (the left page margin beside the row) or position the insertion point in a cell in the row and choose Table ➤ Select Row to select the entire row.
>
> - Position the mouse pointer on the column's top gridline until it appears as a heavy, black downward-pointing arrow and then click, or position the insertion point in a cell in the column and choose Table ➤ Select Column to select the column.
>
> - Hold down the Shift key while you click on another cell, row, or column to extend the selection.
>
> - Choose Table ➤ Select Table to select the entire table that contains the insertion point.
>
> - Press Tab to select the contents of the next cell, or Shift+Tab to select the contents of the previous cell.
>
> - To extend a selection, hold down the Shift key while pressing ↑, ↓, ←, or →.

TABLE

- Choose <u>N</u>ext Row to select the next table row.

4. Choose OK.

Modifying the Table Format

Use Table AutoFormat to apply predefined styles to a new or existing table, and to size the table automatically:

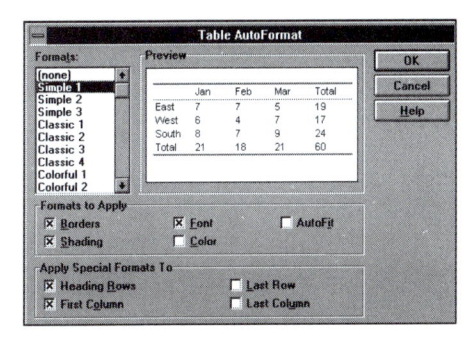

1. Position the insertion point in the table, and then choose T<u>a</u>ble ➤ Table Auto<u>F</u>ormat to display the Table AutoFormat dialog box.

2. Highlight the predefined border and shading format for the table in the Forma<u>t</u>s list box.

3. Choose any of the following options to define the format for the table:

- In the Formats To Apply area, select the check box to apply the borders, shading, font, or color specified in the format. To automatically adjust the size of the table to fit its contents, select the AutoF<u>i</u>t check box.

- In the Apply Special Formats To area, select the corresponding check box to apply special formats to heading rows, the first column, last row, and last column, depending on the selected format.

4. Choose OK in the Table AutoFormat dialog box.

COMMAND AND FEATURE REFERENCE

To change the data in a table to regular document text:

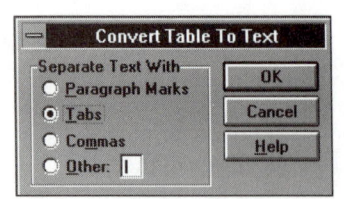

1. Select the table rows that contain the data to be changed into paragraphs, and then choose Table ➤ Convert Table To Text to display the Convert Table To Text dialog box.

2. Select Paragraph Marks, Tabs, or Commas as the character to separate the text in each cell, or choose Other and type a character in the text box.

3. Choose OK.

To place text or a graphic between table rows, position the insertion point in a cell in the row at which the table is to be divided, and then choose Table ➤ Split Table. A paragraph mark is inserted where the table is split. Delete the paragraph mark to reunite the table.

Numbering Table Cells

To automatically number selected cells in a table:

1. Select the cells you want to number.

2. Click on the Numbering button on the Formatting toolbar to display the Table Numbering dialog box.

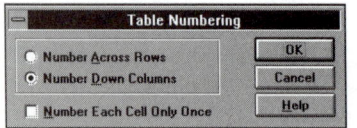

3. Choose any of the following options:

- Select Number Across Rows to number selected cells from left to right across the rows, row by row.

- Select Number Down Columns to number selected cells from top to bottom, column by column.

TABS

- To number each cell rather than each paragraph within a cell, select the Number Each Cell Only Once check box.

4. Choose OK.

SEE ALSO: *Borders and Shading; Bullets and Numbering; Captions; Columns; Paragraph; Ruler; Sort; Tabs; View*

Tabs

By default, Word's tab stops are set at each 0.5 inch between the left and right margins. To insert a tab character and move to the next tab stop, press Tab.

TIP: *Click on the Show/Hide ¶ button on the Standard toolbar to toggle the display of tab characters and other nonprinting characters on your screen.*

Setting Tab Stops

The changes you make to the tab stop settings apply only to selected paragraphs.

To set tab stops using the Ruler:

1. Position the insertion point in the paragraph or select the paragraph(s) whose tab stops you want to change.

2. Click on the Tab Alignment button at the left end of the Ruler to select the type of tab stop to place on the Ruler. As you click, the button cycles through left-aligned, (the default) center aligned, right-aligned, and decimal tab stops.

COMMAND AND FEATURE REFERENCE

3. Click in the position on the Ruler at which you want to place the tab stop.

> **TIP:** *To delete a tab stop you have set, drag it off the Ruler. To move a tab stop you have set, drag it to a different position on the Ruler.*

To precisely define tab stops in the paragraph at the position of the insertion point:

1. Select the paragraph(s) whose tab stops you want to change.

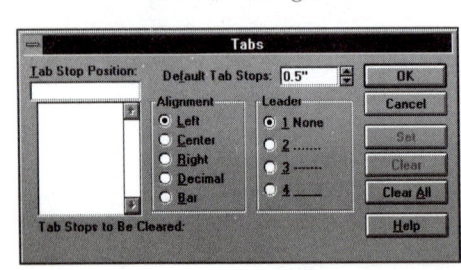

2. Select Format ➤ Tabs to display the Tabs dialog box.

3. Choose any of the following options:

- Type a new tab stop in the Tab Stop Position text box, or select an existing tab stop from the list box.

- Specify the measurement in the Default Tab Stops text box to reset the default tab stops for the entire document.

- In the Alignment area, select Left to align the text to the right, Center to align the text at the center, Right to align the text to the left, Decimal to align along a decimal, or Bar to place a vertical bar at the selected tab stop.

- In the Leader area, select the character to be used as a tab leader for the selected tab stop.

- Choose Set to set the selected tab stop.

- Choose Clear to remove the selected tab stop.

TEMPLATES

- Choose Clear <u>A</u>ll to remove all tab stops except the defaults.

4. Repeat step 3 for each tab stop you want to set in the selected paragraph.

5. Choose OK.

SEE ALSO: *Indent; Margins; Paragraph; Ruler*

Templates

You can use a template file to save the styles, formatting, and text that you use in Word documents that are similar to each other. You can also place AutoText entries and macros used for similar documents in the template. To create a document using the styles, formatting, text, AutoText entries, and macros that are saved in the template file, open a new document based on the template.

NOTE: *PowerPoint presentations are also based on templates that define the background, colors, and text format used for a presentation.*

Creating a Document Based on a Template

Word's template files are stored in the C:\MSOFFICE\WINWORD\TEMPLATE directory. By default, all new documents are created with the NORMAL.DOT template.

COMMAND AND FEATURE REFERENCE

To create a document based on a different template:

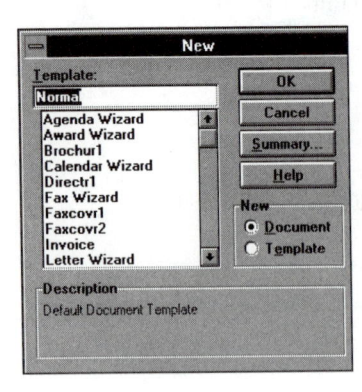

1. Select File ➤ New to display the New dialog box.

2. In the Template list box, highlight the name of the template on which you want to base the new document.

3. If necessary, select Document (selected by default) in the New area.

4. Choose OK.

Creating a New Template

To create a new template:

1. Select File ➤ New to display the New dialog box.

2. Choose Template in the New area, and then select OK.

3. Type any text, create any macros or AutoText entries, define the page setup, customize the toolbars or menus, and create any styles necessary for your document.

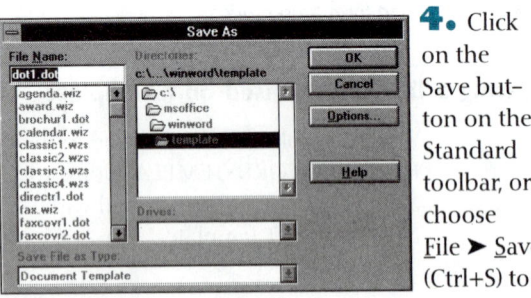

4. Click on the Save button on the Standard toolbar, or choose File ➤ Save (Ctrl+S) to display the Save As dialog box.

5. Type a name for the template in the File Name text box.

TEMPLATES

> **NOTE:** *Word automatically selects the default template directory in which to store the file, and adds the .DOT extension to the name you enter in the File Name text box.*

6. Choose OK in the Save As dialog box.

To edit a template, open the file that contains the template, and then make the necessary changes as you would in a regular document file:

1. Click on the Open button on the Standard toolbar, or choose File ➤ Open (Ctrl+O) to display the Open dialog box.

2. Select Document Templates (*.dot) in the List Files Of Type drop-down list.

3. If necessary, change the directory to C:MSOFFICE\WINWORD\TEMPLATE.

4. Highlight the template file to be edited in the File Name list box.

5. Choose OK in the Open dialog box.

6. Make the necessary changes to the template.

7. Click on the Save button on the Standard toolbar to save the template to the same file name.

Managing Templates

You can attach a different template to an existing document, copy template items to other templates, or customize template items:

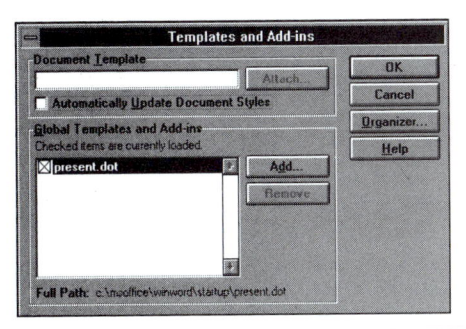

1. Choose File ➤ Templates to display the Templates And Add-ins dialog box.

2. Choose any of the options on the following page.

- Type the name of the template to attach to the current document in the Document Template text box, or select Attach to display the Attach Template dialog box, highlight the name of the template in the File Name list box, and then choose OK.

- Select the Automatically Update Document Styles check box to replace the styles in the current document with those of the same name in the attached template.

- In the Global Templates And Add-ins list box, select the check box of any template that you want to be available whenever you start Word for Windows.

- To add another template to the Global Templates And Add-ins list box, choose Add to display the Add Template dialog box, select the name of a template file in the File Name list box, and then choose OK.

- To remove a template from the Global Templates And Add-ins list box, highlight the name of the template, and then choose Remove.

- Choose Organizer to display the Organizer dialog box when you want to copy styles, macros, AutoText, and toolbars to other documents or templates.

3. Select OK.

SEE ALSO: *AutoText; Macro; Master View; Presentation; Style; Style Gallery*

TEMPLATES T

Thesaurus

Use Word's built-in Thesaurus to find synonyms or antonyms for a selected word or phrase.

Using the Thesaurus

To use Thesaurus to look up the synonyms of a word:

1. If necessary, select a word or phrase to look up.

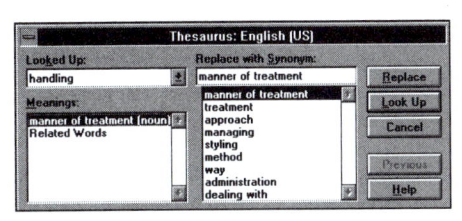

2. Choose Tools ➤ Thesaurus (Shift+F7) to display the Thesaurus dialog box.

TIP: *The selected word is displayed in the Looked Up text box. Once the Thesaurus dialog box appears, you can also type the word you want to look up in the Replace With Synonym text box, or select a word in the Meanings list box.*

3. Choose any of the following options:

- To change the current word in the Looked Up text box, select a word in the Replace With Synonym list box and choose Look Up. The meanings of the word in the Looked Up text box are displayed in the Meanings list box. Synonyms of the word highlighted in the Meanings list box are displayed in the Replace With Synonym list box.

441

- Select <u>R</u>eplace to replace the word selected in your document with the word in the Replace With <u>S</u>ynonym text box and close the Thesaurus dialog box.

- Select <u>L</u>ook Up to look up the word highlighted in the Replace With <u>S</u>ynonym text box.

- Choose <u>P</u>revious to display the last word looked up in the Loo<u>k</u>ed Up text box, and its meanings in the <u>M</u>eanings list box.

- Choose Cancel to return to your document without replacing the selected word.

SEE ALSO: *Spelling*

Toolbars

In Access, Excel, PowerPoint, and Word, toolbar buttons provide easy access to often-used commands, macros, AutoText entries, fonts, and styles. If necessary, you can create buttons for the items you want to place on the toolbar.

TIP: *To display the button's ToolTip (the name of a toolbar button), point to it with your mouse. Glance at the status bar to see a brief description of the button's purpose.*

You can change the position of a displayed toolbar. Drag it onto the work area of your screen to make it a floating toolbar, which can be resized. Or, drag a displayed toolbar to place it vertically along the left or right edge of the window.

TOOLBARS

Creating or Editing Toolbars

You can edit any of the built-in toolbars or create entirely new toolbars to use:

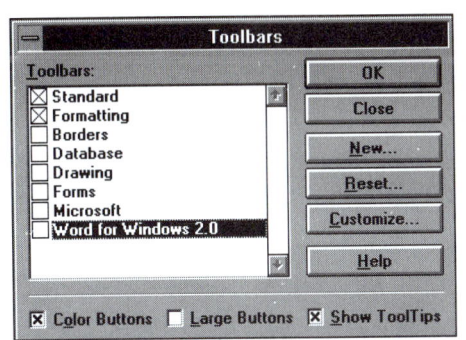

1. Right-click on one of the displayed toolbars, and then select Toolbars in the shortcut menu, or choose View ➤ Toolbars to display the Toolbars dialog box.

2. Choose any of the following options:

- In the Toolbars list box, select the check box of any toolbar you want to display.

- To create a new toolbar, select New to display the New Toolbar dialog box, and then type a name for the toolbar in the Toolbar Name text box. Select the template in which to store the toolbar in the Make Toolbar Available To list box, and then choose OK to display the Customize dialog box.

- Highlight a built-in toolbar that has been changed in the Toolbars list box, and then choose Reset and select OK to return it to its original defaults.

- Highlight a custom toolbar in the Toolbars list box, choose Delete, and then choose Yes to confirm that the toolbar is to be deleted.

- Select the Color Buttons check box (selected by default) to display the toolbar buttons with colors.

- To increase the size of the displayed toolbar buttons, select the Large Buttons check box.

- Select the Show ToolTips check box (selected by default) to display the name and a short description of a button's function when the mouse points to it.

3. Select OK.

Customizing a Toolbar

The Customize dialog box must be displayed before you can add buttons to or remove buttons from a displayed toolbar.

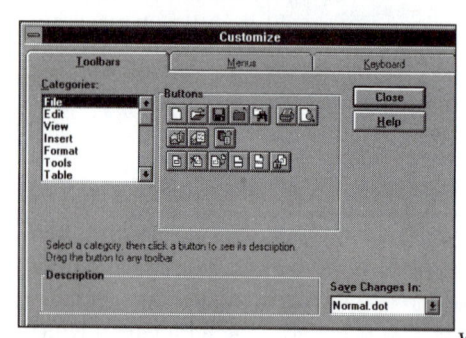

1. Display the toolbar to be customized, and then select View ➤ Toolbars ➤ Customize. In Word, choose the Toolbars tab.

2. In Word, select the template in which you want to save the changes in the Save Changes In drop-down list.

3. Perform any of the following actions:

- To add a button, select an item in the Categories list box. If the item has built-in buttons, they are displayed in the Buttons area. Click on a button to see a description of its function. Drag the button from the Buttons area to its new location on a displayed toolbar.

- To delete a button from a displayed toolbar, drag the button off the toolbar.

- To move a toolbar button on a displayed toolbar, drag the button to a different location or toolbar.

TOOLBARS

- To copy a button, press Ctrl while dragging the button to a different location or toolbar.

- To customize a button, right-click on the button on one of the displayed toolbars to display the shortcut menu. In Access and Excel, select the command that corresponds to the action you want to perform on the button. In Word, select Choose Button Image to display the Custom Button dialog box. Then, click on the image for the button in the button area, type the text that is to appear on a Text Button in the Text Button Name text box, or select Edit to create a new graphic on the button. Choose Assign to place the text or graphic on the selected button.

4. Select Close to return to your document.

SEE ALSO: *Shortcut Menus; Templates*

Undo/Redo

Use Undo to reverse the last change you made in Excel, PowerPoint, and Word. In addition, use Undo to track your last few editing changes in Word.

Using Undo and Redo

Use any of the following methods to reverse your last change:

To reverse your last action, click on the Undo button on the Standard toolbar or choose Edit ➤ Undo (Ctrl+Z).

COMMAND AND FEATURE REFERENCE

To reverse your last several actions in Word, select the Undo drop-down list on the Standard toolbar, and then select the action you want to undo.

To reverse the last action undone in Word, click on the Redo button on the Standard toolbar or select Edit ➤ Redo (F4). To reverse the last several cancellations, click on the Redo drop-down list on the Standard toolbar, and then select the action you want to reverse.

SEE ALSO: *Repeat*

View

In Access, Excel, PowerPoint, and Word, change the way your data appears on screen, and the way you work with the data, by changing the view. Each view is designed for a specific task.

Changing the View in Access

Each time you open a database file in Access, the Database window appears, allowing you to create or select the database object on which to work. Each database object can contain a different view of the records in the database.

With the Database window active, use any of the following methods to change to the corresponding view:

To select a table that contains the records on which to work, create a

VIEW

new table, or edit an existing table, click on the Table tab, or choose View ➤ Tables.

To select a defined query, create a new query, or edit the definition of an existing query, click on the Query tab or choose View ➤ Queries.

Click on the Form tab or choose View ➤ Forms to select an existing form to open or design, or to create a new form for the database.

Click on the Report tab or choose View ➤ Reports to select an existing report to preview or design, or to create a new report for the database.

Click on the Macro tab or choose View ➤ Macros to select an existing macro to run or design, or to create a new macro for the database.

Click on the Module tab or choose View ➤ Modules to select an existing Module to run or design, or to create a new module for the database.

To display the active database object in Design view so you can edit its format or structure, click on the Design view button on the toolbar that appears for the object.

Changing the View in Excel and Word

In Word, click on the Normal View button on the horizontal scrollbar or choose View ➤ Normal to work more quickly as you create, edit, and format your documents. In Normal view, the formatting applied to text appears on screen, but the page layout does not.

COMMAND AND FEATURE REFERENCE

> **TIP:** *To work even faster while in Normal view, limit the number of font sizes and the alignments and spacing available. Select Tools ➤ Options, choose the View tab in the Options dialog box, select the Draft Font check box in the Show area, and then choose OK.*

Click on the Page Layout View button on the horizontal scroll bar or choose View ➤ Page Layout to display a document just as it will appear when printed. Use Page Layout view to make any necessary formatting changes to the document's appearance or to edit the document.

To control how much of the document is displayed, click on the Outline View button on the horizontal scroll bar or choose View ➤ Outline. In Outline view, you can easily change the arrangement of text in the document or the structure of the document.

Click on the Master Document View button on the Outlining toolbar or choose View ➤ Master Document to control the arrangement of subdocuments in a long document.

Click on the Print Preview button on the Standard toolbar or select File ➤ Print Preview to display the worksheet or document at a smaller magnification to see its overall appearance when printed. In Excel, you can change the width of columns, the page margins, and the position of the header and footer while you are in Print Preview.

To display more of the worksheet or document on screen, choose View ➤ Full Screen. All toolbars, menus, scroll bars, Rulers, and the formula bar and status bar are removed. Click on the Full Screen button that appears in its own toolbar while you are in Full Screen view or press Esc to redisplay the screen items.

Changing the View in PowerPoint

Click on the Slide View button on the horizontal scroll bar or choose <u>V</u>iew ➤ <u>S</u>lides to display only the active slide in a presentation. You can edit the appearance of the slide, and add graphics and text to it.

TIP: *To display a different slide while in Slide view, drag the scroll box on the vertical scroll bar until the number of the slide appears, and then release the mouse button.*

Click on the Outline View button on the horizontal scroll bar or choose <u>V</u>iew ➤ <u>O</u>utline to display only the text on each slide in the presentation in an outline. Use Outline view to create and edit the text that will appear on each slide in the presentation.

To display miniaturized versions of each slide in the presentation, click on the Slide Sorter View button on the horizontal scroll bar or choose <u>V</u>iew ➤ Sli<u>d</u>e Sorter to change to Slide Sorter view. You can easily change the order in which the slides appear in the presentation, and set the timings and transitions for each slide to control its appearance on screen during a slide show.

To display the active slide in the presentation with room to add notes for the slide below it, click on the Notes Pages View button on the horizontal scroll bar or choose <u>V</u>iew ➤ <u>N</u>otes Pages to change to Notes Pages view. Use Notes Pages view to create speaker notes for the presentation.

Click on the Slide Show button to run an electronic slide show using the slides in the active presentation. Or, choose <u>V</u>iew ➤ Slide Sho<u>w</u> to display the Slide Show dialog box to set up the options before running the slide show.

COMMAND AND FEATURE REFERENCE

> **SEE ALSO:** *Form; Macro; Master Document; Master View; Module; Outline; Presentation; Print Preview; Query; Report; Table; Zoom*

Viewer

Use PowerPoint's Viewer application to run a PowerPoint slide show, or to allow someone who does not have PowerPoint to run a PowerPoint slide show.

> **NOTE:** *The computer used to run Viewer must be running Windows 3.1 or a later version of Windows.*

Copying PowerPoint Viewer

To allow others who do not have PowerPoint to run a PowerPoint slide show, copy the Viewer application to another disk. PowerPoint Viewer can be shared without purchasing an additional license. However, Viewer does not support all of PowerPoint's presentation features.

To send a PowerPoint slide show to others:

1. Copy all the files on the Viewer disk that comes with Microsoft Office to a 1.44 MB or 1.2 MB disk.

> **WARNING:** *Do not send your original Viewer disk. You may need it to create another copy of PowerPoint Viewer, or to reinstall it on your own computer.*

2. Copy the presentation file onto another disk.

VIEW MANAGER

3. Instruct the presentation's recipient to run VSETUP.EXE on the Viewer disk to set up the Viewer application on his/her computer, and then copy the presentation file to a different subdirectory.

> **NOTE:** *The presentation file must be run from a hard drive so that Viewer can keep up with the transitions defined for each slide.*

Running a Slide Show with Viewer

Once Viewer is installed, follow these steps to run a PowerPoint slide show:

1. Double-click on the Microsoft Office icon in Windows Program Manager or select Window ➤ Microsoft Office in Program Manager to display the Microsoft Office group window.

2. Double-click on the PowerPoint Viewer icon in the Microsoft Office group window to display the Microsoft PowerPoint Viewer dialog box.

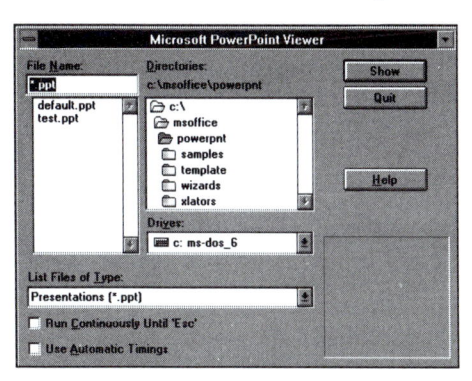

3. Select the name of the presentation to run as a slide show in the File Name list box.

> **NOTE:** *If necessary, select the directory that contains the file of the presentation you want to show in the Directories list box.*

COMMAND AND FEATURE REFERENCE

4. Select the Run Continuously Until 'Esc' check box to continue running the slide show until you press the Esc key.

5. Select the Use Automatic Timings check box to run the slide show with the timings that were set for it.

6. Choose Show.

SEE ALSO: *Slide Show*

View Manager

Use View Manager, an add-in that comes with Excel, to create and save different views of the data in the same worksheet. The defined views can be displayed and printed.

Creating a View

Defined views include the size and position of the window, any frozen panes or titles that are applied, the zoom percentage, the active cell, and the defined print area.

To create different views of your data:

1. Make any necessary changes to the format or appearance of the data in the worksheet.

2. If necessary, select File ➤ Print (Ctrl+P), and then set the print area for the new view.

NOTE: *The area of the view that is to be printed is always saved with the view. By default, the entire worksheet is saved as the print area in the defined view. You can choose whether to save the other print options.*

WINDOW W

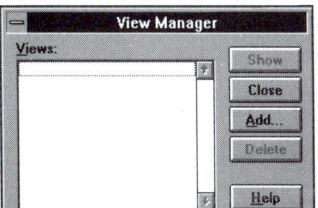

3. Select View ➤ View Manager to display the View Manager dialog box.

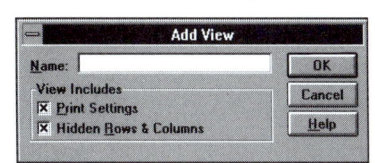

4. Select Add to display the Add View dialog box.

5. Type a descriptive name for the view in the Name text box.

TIP: *All the defined views in the workbook appear in the Views list box in the View Manager dialog box. Include the name of the worksheet in the name of a view, so you can easily determine the contents of the view.*

6. Select the Print Settings check box (selected by default) in the View Includes area to include the current settings in the Print dialog box in the new view.

7. Select the Hidden Rows & Columns check box to include any rows or columns of hidden data as part of the defined view.

8. Select OK to store the defined view of the data.

To delete a stored view, select View ➤ View Manager, highlight the name of the view in the Views list box, choose Delete, and then choose OK to confirm the deletion. Select Close to return to the worksheet.

To display a stored view, select View ➤ View Manager, highlight the name of the view in the Views list box, and then choose Show.

453

COMMAND AND FEATURE REFERENCE

SEE ALSO: *Print Report; Scenario; Workbook*

Window

Use the commands on the Window menu to manage the windows of multiple open database objects in Access, the windows of multiple open files in Excel, PowerPoint, and Word, or the open windows in Mail.

Managing Open Windows

You can use any of the following methods to control the open windows of the active application:

- To display a different part of the current worksheet or document, choose Window ➤ New Window. Any changes made to the data in one window of a file will also appear in other open windows of the same file.

- To display all the open windows of the active application on your screen, choose Window ➤ Arrange or Arrange All.

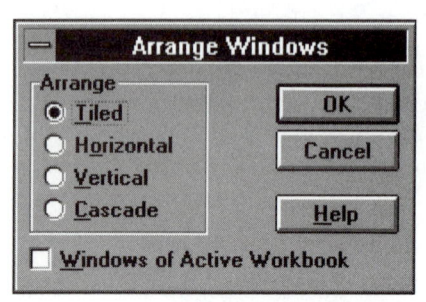

In Excel, choose Window ➤ Arrange to display the Arrange Windows dialog box.

Select Tiled, Horizontal, Vertical, or Cascade in the Arrange area as the way to organize the open windows on your screen. If necessary, select the Windows Of Active Workbook check box to arrange only the open

WINDOW

windows of the active workbook. Choose OK in the Arrange Windows dialog box to arrange the specified open windows.

- In Access, select Window ➤ Tile to arrange the open windows of the database objects so they are equally sized on your screen.

- In Access and PowerPoint, select Window ➤ Cascade to arrange all the open windows (of the database objects in Access) so they are overlapping.

- To activate a different open window in the same application, select Window ➤ *Number*.

- Select Window ➤ Arrange Icons to organize the icons as minimized database objects at the lower-left corner of the Access window.

- In Access, select Window ➤ Hide to hide the active window. To redisplay a hidden window in Access, select Window ➤ Unhide to display the Unhide Window dialog box. Select the name of the window in the Window list box, and then choose OK.

- To divide the active window into two horizontal panes that scroll independently in Excel and Word, double-click on the split box–the small, black rectangle above the vertical scroll bar.

- In Excel, double-click on the split box that appears to the right of the horizontal scroll bar to split the window into two vertical panes.

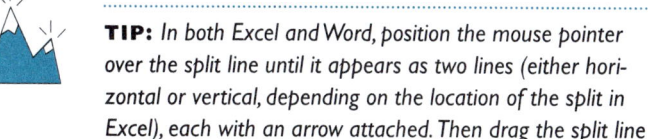

TIP: *In both Excel and Word, position the mouse pointer over the split line until it appears as two lines (either horizontal or vertical, depending on the location of the split in Excel), each with an arrow attached. Then drag the split line until it appears in the desired position.*

COMMAND AND FEATURE REFERENCE

- Or, in Excel, choose Window ➤ Split to simultaneously create four panes in the window.

- In Word, choose Window ➤ Split, move the mouse to position the horizontal gray line where you want to split the screen, and then click the mouse button.

- To remove a split in either Excel or Word, double-click on its split box, or choose Window ➤ Remove Split.

NOTE: *To move between the panes of a split window, click in the pane that contains the data to be edited, or press F6 to move back and forth between or cycle through the panes.*

- In Excel, select Window ➤ Freeze Panes to prevent the row that contains the active cell, all rows above it, and all columns to the left of it from scrolling off the screen as you scroll through the worksheet.

- In PowerPoint, select Window ➤ Fit To Page to resize the active window so that it fits closely around a slide or notes page that was reduced in scale.

SEE ALSO: *Database; Protection; Workbook*

Wizards

SEE: *Form; Report; Style; Table; Templates*

Workbook

The *workbook* is the basic type of file in Excel. A workbook contains 16 worksheets by default, although it may contain up to 255 worksheets if your computer has enough memory.

Managing Worksheets

Each sheet in a new workbook is named with a number on the worksheet tabs that appear just above Excel's status bar.

To change the name of the active worksheet:

1. Double-click on the worksheet's tab, right-click on the worksheet tabs, and then select Rename in the shortcut menu, or choose Format ➤ Sheet ➤ Rename to display the Rename Sheet dialog box.

2. Type the name for the sheet in the Name text box.

3. Choose OK.

To move or copy a sheet in the same workbook:

- Drag its worksheet tab to a different location in the workbook. When the black triangle above the tabs points to the location at which you want to place the sheet, release the mouse button.

- Hold down the Ctrl key while you drag the worksheet's tab to a different location to create a copy of the worksheet. When the black triangle

COMMAND AND FEATURE REFERENCE

points to the location at which you want to place a copy of the sheet, release the mouse button. The copied sheet retains its original name, along with a number in parentheses to indicate that it is a copy.

To move or copy a sheet to a different workbook:

1. Select the worksheet that is to be moved or copied, and then choose Edit ➤ Move Or Copy Sheet to display the Move Or Copy dialog box.

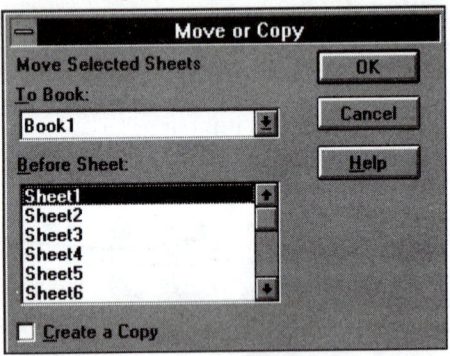

2. In the To Book drop-down list, select the name of the workbook into which the worksheet is to be moved, or into which a copy is to be placed.

3. Select the name of the sheet that will appear to the right of the moved or copied worksheet in the Before Sheet list box.

4. Select the Create A Copy check box to copy the selected worksheet.

NOTE: *If the Create A Copy check box is cleared, the selected worksheet is moved to the workbook.*

5. Choose OK.

To add a worksheet, select the sheet that you want to be positioned after the new worksheet, and then:

- Select Insert ➤ Worksheet.

WORKSHEET

OR

- Right-click on the worksheet tabs and choose Insert to display the Insert dialog box. Select the type of sheet to be inserted in the New list box, and then choose OK to insert it before the selected sheet.

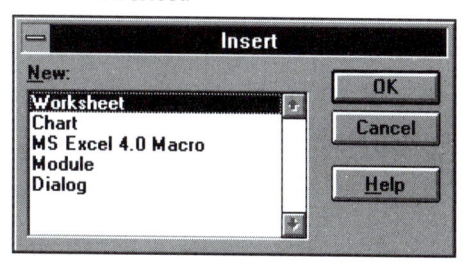

```
┌─────────────────────────────────────┐
│             Insert                  │
├─────────────────────────────────────┤
│ New:                    ┌────────┐  │
│ Worksheet               │   OK   │  │
│ Chart                   └────────┘  │
│ MS Excel 4.0 Macro      ┌────────┐  │
│ Module                  │ Cancel │  │
│ Dialog                  └────────┘  │
│                         ┌────────┐  │
│                         │  Help  │  │
│                         └────────┘  │
└─────────────────────────────────────┘
```

- To delete the selected sheet, right-click on the worksheet tabs and select Delete, or choose Edit ➤ Delete Sheet. Then choose OK to confirm the deletion.

WARNING: *A deleted sheet is permanently deleted, along with all the data it contains.*

Selecting Worksheets in the Active Workbook

The worksheet that is displayed in the Excel window and contains the active cell is the active sheet. However, multiple sheets can be selected simultaneously.

Use any of the following methods to select a worksheet or multiple worksheets in the active workbook:

- To select a different worksheet, click on its tab.

- To select a range of worksheets, click on the tab of the first sheet, and then hold down the Shift key while you click on the last sheet in the range of sheets.

COMMAND AND FEATURE REFERENCE

- To select multiple nonadjacent worksheets, click on the tab of the first sheet, and then hold down the Ctrl key while you click on the tabs of the other sheets.

- Right-click on the worksheet tabs, and then choose Select All Sheets to select every sheet in the active workbook.

SEE ALSO: *Protection; Worksheet*

Worksheet

In Excel, each workbook file is composed of worksheets. *Worksheets* are large tables, with 256 lettered columns and 16,384 numbered rows. The *column heading*, the area that displays the column letter, appears at the top of the column with a gray background. Similarly, the *row heading*, the gray area that displays the row number, appears to the left of the row. The column and row headings appear on screen by default.

TIP: *To select an entire column or row, click on its column or row heading.*

Changing the Column Width and Row Height

To change the width of a column, position the mouse pointer over the left border of the column heading until it appears as a vertical line intersected by a double-headed arrow, and then drag the border to the right to increase its width or to the left to decrease its width.

WORKSHEET

Or, follow these steps to set the exact column width:

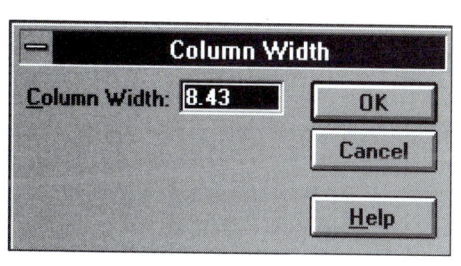

1. Select a cell in the column whose width is to be changed, and then choose Format ➤ Column ➤ Width to display the Column Width dialog box.

2. Type a number from 1 to 255 to specify the width of the column in the Column Width text box.

3. Choose OK.

TIP: *To change the width of a column to the minimum width necessary for selected cells in the column, double-click on the right border of the column heading or choose Format ➤ Column ➤ AutoFit Selection. To return the width of a selected column to the standard width, select Format ➤ Column ➤ Standard Width, and then choose OK in the Standard Width dialog box.*

To change the height of a row, select a cell in the row, and then position the mouse pointer over the lower border of the row heading until it appears as a horizontal bar with a vertical two-headed arrow intersecting it. Then drag the border down to increase the height of the row or up to decrease the height of the row.

Or, follow these steps to set the exact row height:

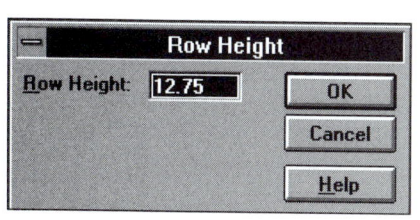

1. Select a cell in the row, and then select Format ➤ Row ➤ Height to display the Row Height dialog box.

461

2. Type a number from 1 to 409 in the Row Height text box to specify the exact height of the row.

3. Choose OK.

> **TIP:** *Double-click on the bottom edge of the row heading or select Format ➤ Row ➤ AutoFit to return the height of the row that contains the active cell to the standard height. The standard height varies according to the size of the font being used.*

Hiding a Column or Row

If your worksheet contains some data you do not want others to see, or data that you do not want to appear in a defined view, hide the column or row of data. The entire column or row, including its heading, is hidden.

To hide a column or row:

◆ Select a cell in the column or row, and then choose Format ➤ Column ➤ Hide or Format ➤ Row ➤ Hide.

◆ Drag the border of the column heading to the left until it is on top of the border for the previous column. Or drag the border of the row heading up until it is on top of the border for the cell above it.

The border of the column before or the row above a hidden column or row appears as a heavy, black border.

To unhide a hidden column or row:

◆ Select a cell in each of the columns adjoining a hidden column, or in each of the rows adjoining a hidden row, and then choose Format ➤ Column ➤ Unhide or Format ➤ Row ➤ Unhide.

- Position the mouse pointer just to the right of the border indicating a hidden column or just below the border indicating a hidden row until it appears as a set of parallel lines with a two-headed arrow attached, and then drag the border to the right to unhide the column or down to unhide the row.

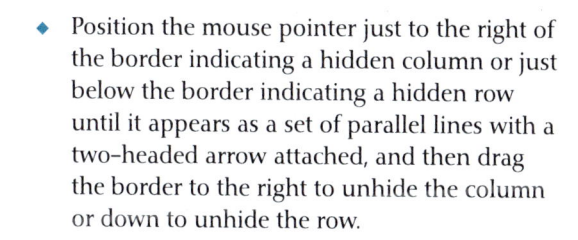

SEE ALSO: *Cell; Range; Table; View Manager; Workbook*

Workgroup

Each user of Access is a member of a workgroup that is defined using the identification information that was entered during Setup. To secure your databases, the workgroup administrator must make the workgroup unique. Otherwise, the workgroup, along with all the permissions assigned to it, can be copied and used by others.

Creating a Unique Workgroup

Specify a workgroup identification number (WID) to create a secure, unique workgroup:

1. Double-click on the MS Access Workgroup Administrator icon in the Microsoft Office group window to display the Workgroup Administrator dialog box.

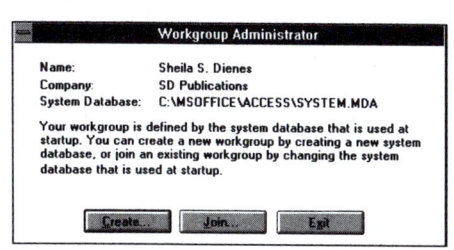

```
                    Workgroup Administrator

    Name:            Sheila S. Dienes
    Company:         SD Publications
    System Database: C:\MSOFFICE\ACCESS\SYSTEM.MDA

    Your workgroup is defined by the system database that is used at
    startup. You can create a new workgroup by creating a new system
    database, or join an existing workgroup by changing the system
    database that is used at startup.

            [ Create... ]   [ Join... ]   [ Exit ]
```

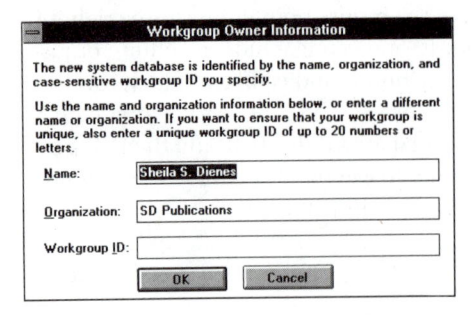

COMMAND AND FEATURE REFERENCE

2. Choose Create to display the Workgroup Owner Information dialog box.

3. Type a WID, consisting of up to 20 numbers, letters, or a combination of the two, in the Workgroup ID text box.

WARNING: *The workgroup administrator should keep a copy of the exact information that appears in the Workgroup System Database dialog box, including the case of the letters in the WID, in a secure place. If the system database must be recreated for any reason, this information must be reentered exactly as it appears, or the database cannot be recovered.*

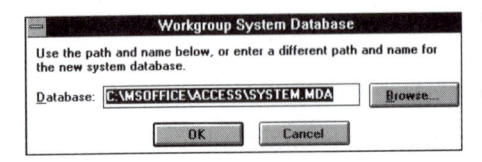

4. Choose OK to display the Workgroup System Database dialog box.

5. If necessary, specify a different path and file name for the system database in the Database text box, and then choose OK.

Joining a Different Workgroup

To join a workgroup other than the one that was set up when you installed Access:

1. Double-click on the MS Access Workgroup Administrator icon in the Microsoft Office group window to display the Workgroup Administrator dialog box.

2. Select Join to display the Workgroup System Database dialog box.

3. Enter the path and file name of the database system you want to join in the Database text box.

4. Choose OK.

The next time you start Access, the user and group accounts, passwords, and other options for the joined system are in effect.

SEE ALSO: Permissions; Print Security

Zoom

You can adjust the magnification of the data displayed on screen in Excel, PowerPoint, and Word. Enlarge the magnification to make the data easier to read, or reduce it to display the overall effect of an entire slide or page.

Adjusting the Magnification

The percentage of magnification is the amount the data is reduced or enlarged on your screen in relation to its normal size. The magnification appears only on your screen, not on a page printed while the magnification is in effect.

To enlarge or reduce the magnification of the data displayed on your screen, select a different magnification in the Zoom Control drop-down list, or type a different percentage of magnification in the Zoom Control text box.

COMMAND AND FEATURE REFERENCE

Or, follow these steps:

1. Choose View ➤ Zoom to display the Zoom dialog box.

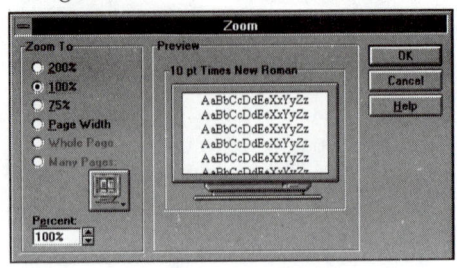

2. Select one of the predefined options in the Magnification or Zoom To area, or specify the percentage of the size of the data displayed in the Custom or Percent text box.

3. Choose OK in the Zoom dialog box.

SEE ALSO: *View*

Index

Note to the Reader:
Boldfaced page numbers indicate principal discussions of topics or definitions of terms. *Italicized* numbers indicate illustrations.

Numbers and Symbols

3D references, in Excel, 360–361
: (colon), as range operator in Excel, 359
, (comma), as union operator in Excel, 359
$ (dollar sign), for absolute references in Excel, 359
# (number sign), for error values in Excel, 24
(space), as intersection operator in Excel, 359

A

absolute references in Excel, **358–359**
Access
  attaching tables from other applications, **198–200**
  cells, 56
  charts, **58–61**
    changing chart type, 61
    creating, 58–60
    editing, 60–61
  clip art, **62–64**
  controls, **67–79**. *See also* forms; reports
    changing default properties of, 78
    changing properties of, **76–78**
    control properties, 76
    creating bound controls, 69
    creating calculated controls, **69–70**
    creating unbound controls, **70–71**
    duplicating, **105–106**
    editing control labels, **71–72**
    Form Wizard and, 68
    on forms, **159–161**
    moving, 72–73
    selecting, 73–74
    sizing, 74–75
    types of, **68**
  Cue Cards, 3–4, 197
  cutting, copying, and pasting, **84–85**
  Database window, 4–5, *4*
  databases, **86–93**. *See also* fields; permissions; records; relationships
    adding records, 179, 356–357
    attaching tables from other applications, **198–200**
    closing, 116–117
    creating, 4, **86–87**, 117
    creating relationships, **362–366**
    entering data, 89
    inserting in Word documents, **89–93**
    linking with Word documents, 368
    navigating with Go To command (F5), **178–179**
    opening, 4, 119–120
    renaming database objects, 223
    saving, 122
    shared access options, 120
    sorting records, **399–400**
    updating databases inserted in Word, 92
  datasheets, adding records in, 356
  Design view, 447
  Drawing tools. *See also specific Drawing tools entries*
    Command Button tool, 100
    displaying, **98**
    Label tool, 100
    Text Box tool, 100
  Duplicate feature, **105–106**
  event procedures, **267–269**
  exiting, **109**
  exporting data, **200–201**, 203–204
  expressions (formulas)
    overview of, **167–168**
    in queries, 351
  fields, **110–112**. *See also* databases; records
    defining types of, 111–112
    naming, 112
    records and, 356
  Form view, 447
  forms. *See also* controls
    adding records in, 357
    attaching macros to, 220, 221, 226–227
    creating, **151–153**
    editing, **159–161**
    expressions (formulas) in, **167–168**
    functions in, 174–175
    headers and footers, 188–190, 378–380
    inserting date and time, **93–94**
    margins, **250–251**

INDEX

page breaks, **288**
page numbering, **290–291**
Print Setup options, **293–299**
sorting records, **399–400**
formulas, **167–168**
 disabling automatic formula recalculation, 168
functions, **174–175**
global modules, 267
Go To command (F5), **178–179**
graphics in, **62–64**, 186
groups. *See also* user accounts; workgroups
 creating, 306–307
 deleting, 307, 309
 naming, 306–307
 printing security reports, 341
headers and footers, **188–190**
 for forms, 188–190
 for reports, 188, 190
importing data, **198–200, 201–204**
 into Access, **201–203**
 attaching tables from other applications, 198–200
 import/export specifications, 203–204
Macro view, 447
macros, **220–227**, 447
 adding conditions, 220–221
 attaching to forms and reports, 220, 221, 226–227
 changing Macro window display, 225
 creating, 221–223
 creating macro groups, 225–226
 editing, 224–225
 overview of, 220
 renaming, 223
 running, 224
mailing labels, **206–208**
managing windows, **454–456**
Module view, 447
modules, **267–269**
number formats, 164
opening screens, **3–5**, *3*, *4*
overview of, **3**
passwords. *See also* permissions
 clearing forgotten passwords, 302
 creating for user accounts, **301–302**
permissions, **305–312**. *See also* passwords
 assigning, 309–312

changing database ownership, 305–306
 creating groups, 306–307
 creating user accounts, 308–309
 deleting groups, 307, 309
 deleting user accounts, 308
 naming groups and user accounts, 306–307
Print dialog box, **328–331**
Print Preview window, **334–335**
procedures, **267–269**
queries, **82–84, 348–351**
 action queries, 348
 crosstab queries, **82–84**, 348
 data-definition queries, 348
 dynasets and, 349
 pass-through queries, 348
 select queries, 349–351
 sorting records, **399**
 types of, **348–349**
 union queries, 348
Query view, 447
records, **356–358**. *See also* databases; fields
 adding to databases, 179, 356–357
 adding in datasheets, 356
 adding in forms, 357
 editing, 357
 fields and, 356
 finding data in, 358
 sorting, **399–403**
 sorting in forms and tables, 399–400
 sorting in queries, 399
 sorting in reports, 401–403
relationships, **362–366**
 between attached tables, 363
 deleting, 366
 displaying, 365
 editing, 365
 enforcing referential integrity, 363, 364
 equi-joins (inner joins) and, 364
 left outer joins and, 364–365
 one-to-one relationships, 364
 right outer joins and, 365
renaming database objects, **223**
Report view, 447
reports. *See also* controls
 attaching macros to, 220, 221, 226–227
 creating, **367–369**
 grouping data, **401–403**

INDEX

headers and footers, 188, 190, **378–380**
inserting date and time, **93–94**
margins, **250–251**
page breaks, **288**
page numbering, **290–291**
Print Setup options, **293–299**
security reports, 341
sorting records, **401–403**
types of, **367–368**
rulers, 373
shortcut menus, **385–386**
sorting records, **399–403**
 in forms and database tables, 399–400
 in queries, 399
 in reports, 401–403
switching between Microsoft Office applications, 1–2
Table view, 446–447
toolbars, 5
troubleshooting
 changing Macro window display in Access, 225
 forgotten passwords, 302
 renaming database objects, 223
 searching for data in records, 358
user accounts. *See also* workgroups
 creating, 308–309
 passwords, **301–302**
 printing security reports, 341
views, **446–447**
Wizards
 Form Wizard, 68
 Mailing Label Wizard, 206–208
 Report Wizards, 367–369
workgroups, **463–465**. *See also* user accounts
 creating unique workgroups, 463–464
 joining a different workgroup, 464–465

access privileges. *See* passwords; permissions
action queries, in Access, 348
active cell, in Excel, 6
Add User option, Mail Postoffice Manager, 322
adding. *See also* entering; inserting
 AutoCorrect entries in Word, 26
 borders to graphics, 183
 buttons to toolbars, 444
 captions to graphics in Word, 52–53
 cells, columns, or rows to tables in Word, 428–429
 conditions to macros in Access, 220–221
 Excel worksheets to workbooks, 458–459
 footnotes and endnotes, 146–148
 frames to graphics, 183
 graphics to envelopes, 108–109
 names to Mail address book, 15–16
 section breaks in Word, 381
 shading to graphics, 183–184
add-ins in Excel
 Report Manager, 340
 Solver, **392–398**
  creating reports, 395
  saving problems as scenarios, 395–396
  Solver Options dialog box, 396–398
  solving problems, 392–395
 View Manager, **452–454**
address book, **15–17**. *See also* Mail
 adding names, 15–16
 creating personal groups, 16–17
 deleting names from groups, 17
addressing envelopes, 106–108
Advanced Search dialog box, **129–131**. *See also* Find File dialog box
 Location tab, 129–130
 Summary tab, 130
 Timestamp tab, 131
Align Drawing Objects button, in Word, 103
aligning
 objects with guides in PowerPoint, **187–188**
 text in Excel, PowerPoint, and Word, **17–19**
 text for printing in Word, 298
all caps option, 57, 144
Alt key
 + F4 (Exit), 109
 + Spacebar (Control menu), 109
annotations, **19–22**. *See also* Word for Windows
 deleting, 21
 displaying, 20
 inserting, 20–21
 overview of, 19
 pen annotations, 20
 protection and, 347
 viewing or listening to, 21–22

INDEX

voice annotations, 21
answering Mail messages, 238
Apply To option, Word Page Setup dialog box, 299
applying
  fonts, 142–144
  styles
    to Excel worksheets, 413
    to Word documents, 413–415
Arc tool, 99
Arrow tool, 100
Arrowheads tool, in PowerPoint, 101
assigning
  passwords, **301–304**. *See also* locking; protection
    to Access user accounts, 301–302
    to Excel and Word files, 302–304
  permissions in Access, 309–312
Assume Linear Model option, Excel Solver dialog box, 397
attaching
  files to Mail messages, 237, 241
  macros to forms and reports in Access, 220, 221, 226–227
  tables from other applications in Access, 198–200
  templates to Word documents, 420, 440
Auditing toolbar, in Excel, 22–25
AutoCaption feature, in Word, 53–55
AutoContent Wizard, in PowerPoint, 323–324
AutoFill feature, **382–385**. *See also* Excel
  displaying AutoFill shortcut menu, 382
  entering linear trends, 384–385
  entering sequences, 382–384
  entering text values, 383
AutoFilter feature, in Excel, 124–125
AutoFormat feature, **28–32**
  in Excel, 28–29
  Table AutoFormat feature in Word, 433
  in Word, 29–32
AutoLayout feature, in PowerPoint, 32–33
automatic formula recalculation, 168
AutoShapes button, in PowerPoint, 101
AutoSum function, in Excel, 175
AutoText entries, **35–38**. *See also* Word for Windows
  copying between templates, 38, 440
  creating, 35–36
  deleting, 36
  editing, 36
  inserting, 37
  renaming, 37–38
axes, for charts, 59

B

backing up message files in Mail, 115–116
balancing columns of text in Word, 67
bar codes, on envelopes, 107
Black and White option, Excel Page Setup dialog box, 296–297
bold font style, 142
bookmarks, **38–41**. *See also* Word for Windows
  copying or moving, 41
  creating, 39–40
  deleting, 39, 40
  displaying, 40
  editing, 40–41
  navigating, 39
  overview of, 38–39
Boolean fields in databases, **111**
borders, **42–48**
  adding to graphics, 183
  defined, **42**
  in Excel, 42–43, 101
  in PowerPoint, 44–47
  in Word, 47–48
bound controls, **68**. *See also* Access; controls
  changing control properties, 76
  creating, 69
breaks
  column breaks in Word, 67
  page breaks in Access, Excel, and Word, 288–289
  section breaks in Word, **380–382**
    adding, 381
    deleting, 381–382
    displaying, 380–381
    formatting and, 298, 380, 381–382
    overview of, 380–381
    page numbers and, 293
    printing sections, 297–298
Bring in Front of Text button, in Word, 102
Bring to Front tool, 101
build effects, in PowerPoint slide shows, 390

470

INDEX

bullets, **49–52**
  in PowerPoint, 49
  in Word, 49–52
buttons, customizing toolbar buttons, **444–445**

C

calculated controls, **68**. *See also* Access; controls
  changing control properties, 76
  creating, 69–70
calculated criteria, for filtering Excel databases, 125–127
Callout tool, in Word, 100
capitalization
  changing case in PowerPoint and Word, 57
  in passwords, 301
  and sorting in Word, 404
captions, **52–55**. *See also* graphics; Word for Windows
  adding to graphics, 52–53
  AutoCaption feature, 53–55
  changing numbering format, 55
  deleting, 53
  editing, 53
  formatting, 55
  updating caption numbers, 54
case
  changing in PowerPoint and Word, 57
  in passwords, 301
  and sorting in Word, 404
cells, **56**. *See also* Excel; tables in Word
  in Access, PowerPoint, and Word, 56
  active cell, 6
  aligning data in, **17–19**
  centering data across, 18
  changing cells
    in scenarios, **375–376**
    in Solver problems, 393, 394, 395
  changing number formats, 164–165
  copying, 361
  deleting tracer arrows, 23
  entering and editing data in, 56
  moving, 361
  notes, **274–276**
  ranges, **352–355**
    deleting range names, 354
    inserting range names in formulas, 354
    naming cells and ranges, 352–353
    replacing references with reference names, 354–355
    selecting named ranges, 354
  references, **358–362**
    3D references, **360–361**
    dollar sign ($) in, 359
    entering in formulas, 358, **359–361**
    moving and copying, **361–362**
    R1C1 reference style, 360
    reference operators (colon, comma, and space), 359
    relative versus absolute references, **358–359**
    replacing references with reference names, **354–355**
  selecting, **56**
  target cells in Solver problems, 392–393
  tracing cell dependents, **23**
  tracing cell precedents, **25**
centering text or data, in Excel cells, 17
Change Password dialog box, in Access, 301–302
changing. *See also* editing
  attributes of Mail folders, 140
  AutoCorrect entries in Word, 26
  caption number format in Word, 55
  case in PowerPoint and Word, 57
  character spacing (kerning), 144–145
  chart type, 61
  column widths
    in Excel worksheets, 460–461
    in Word tables, 429–430
  control properties in Access, 76–78
  cross-references in Word, 81
  database ownership in Access, 305–306
  default control properties in Access, 78
  default font, 145
  file format of embedded objects, 280–281
  layout of columns of text in Word, 67
  Macro window display in Access, 225
  number formats in Excel, 164–165
  passwords in Excel and Word, 304
  revision mark format in Word, 371
  row height
    in Excel worksheets, 461–462
    in Word tables, 430–433
  slide layouts in PowerPoint, 327

INDEX

styles
  in Excel, 417–418
  in Word, 418–419
  table format in Word, 433–434
  templates in PowerPoint, 327
changing cells. *See also* cells
  in Excel scenarios, 375–376
  in Excel Solver problems, 393, 394, 395
chapter numbers in page numbers in Word, 292–293
character spacing (kerning), in Word, 144–145
character styles, in Word, 412–413
charts, **58–61**
  changing chart type, 61
  creating, 58–60
  editing, 60–61
checking spelling, **407–409**
choosing. *See* selecting
clearing. *See also* deleting
  forgotten passwords in Access, 302
clip art, **62–64**. *See also* graphics
Clipboard, cutting, copying, and pasting, **84–85**
closing, databases and files, 116–117
colon (:), as range operator in Excel, 359
colors, **42–48**. *See also* shading
  coloring fonts, 143
  in Excel, 42–43
  in PowerPoint, 44–47
  in Word, 47–48
Column Spacing option, Access Print Setup dialog box, 295
columns
  in Excel
    centering data across, 18
    changing column widths, 460–461
    hiding, 462
    overview of, 7
    printing options, 296, 297
    unhiding, 462–463
  in Word tables
    adding, 428–429
    changing column widths, 429–430
    deleting, 427–428
    inserting, 428
    selecting, 432
columns of text, **65–67**. *See also* text; Word for Windows
  changing layout, 67
  column breaks, 67
  creating, 65–66
  graphics in, 66
  selecting for sorting, 405
comma (,), as union operator in Excel, 359
comma number format style in Excel, 164–165
Command Button tool, in Access, 100
comparing versions of a document, **369–370**
comparison operators, in Excel filters, 125–126
constraints, in Excel Solver problems, 393, 394
Control menu box, 109
controls, **67–79**. *See also* Access; forms; reports
  control properties, **76–79**
    changing, 76–78
    changing default properties, 78
  creating, **69–71**
    bound controls, 69
    calculated controls, 69–70
    unbound controls, 70–71
  duplicating, **105–106**
  editing control labels, 71–72
  Form Wizard and, 68
  on forms, **159–161**
  moving, 72–73
  selecting, 73–74
  sizing, 74–75
  types of, **68**
converting
  footnotes and endnotes, 148
  Word documents to master documents, 255–256
  Word tables to documents, 434
copying
  AutoText entries between Word templates, 38, 440
  bookmarks in Word, 41
  buttons on toolbars, 445
  cells in Excel, 361
  with drag and drop, 97
  Duplicate feature in Access and PowerPoint, 105–106
  formatting with Format Painter, 166
  graphics, 183
  Mail folders, 141
  PowerPoint Viewer application, 450–451
  private Mail folders, 140–141
  references and formulas in Excel, 361–362
  styles
    in Excel, 415

472

INDEX

in Word, 415–417, 421–422
worksheets in Excel, 457–458
copying and pasting, **84–85**
counter fields, in databases, **111**
Create Button tool, in Excel, 100
Create Picture button, in Word, 103
creating
  AutoText entries in Word, 35–36
  bookmarks in Word, 39–40
  charts, 58–60
  columns of text in Word, 65–66
  controls in Access, **69–71**
    bound controls, 69
    calculated controls, 69–70
    unbound controls, 70–71
  cross-references in Word, 79–81
  crosstab queries in Access, 82–84
  custom spelling dictionaries, 410–412
  database files, 4
  databases, **86–89**
    in Access, 4, 86–87, 117
    in Excel, 88–89
  documents in Word, 118
    from templates, 437–438
  drop caps in Word, 103–104
  embedded objects, 277–278
  event procedures in Access, 267–269
  exclude spelling dictionaries, 409–410
  fields in databases, 111–112
  files, 117–118
  forms, **151–158**
    in Access, 151–153
    in Excel, 154–155
    in Word, 155–158
  frames in Word, 103, 170–171
  groups in Access, 306–307
  headers and footers, **188–195**
    in Access, 188–190
    in Excel, 191–192
    in Word, 192–195
  macros
    in Access, 221–223
    creating macro groups in Access, 225–226
    in Excel, 227–229
    in Word, 232–233
  Mail folders and subfolders, 139–140
  Mail Merge main documents, 242–243
  Mail messages, 236–237
  mailing labels, **206–211**
    in Access, 206–208
    in Word, 208–211
  master documents, 256
  new line of text without creating a paragraph in Word, 300
  notes in Excel, 274–276
  outlines, **282–287**
    in Excel, 282–284
    in PowerPoint and Word, 282, 284–287
  paragraphs in Word, 300
  passwords for Excel and Word files, 302–304
  personal groups in Mail address book, 16–17
  pivot tables in Excel, 312–315
  presentations in PowerPoint, 117–118, 323–326
  queries in Microsoft Query, 269–272
  reports in Excel, 338–341
  scenarios in Excel, 375–378
  slide shows in PowerPoint, 386–387
  slides with PowerPoint AutoLayout feature, 32–33
  speaker notes in PowerPoint, 327
  styles, **417–419**
    in Excel, 417–418
    in Word, 418–419
  table headings in Word, 426–427
  tables in Word, 424–426
  templates in Word, 438–439
  toolbars, 443–444
  user accounts in Access, 308–309
  workgroups in Access, 463–464
cropping graphics, in Word, 184
cross-references, **79–82**. *See also* master documents; Word, **79**
  changing or deleting, 81
  creating, 79–81
  footnotes, endnotes and, 146
  section or chapter cross-references in headers and footers, 79
crosstab queries in Access, **82–84**, 348. *See also* queries
Cue Cards, 3–4, 197. *See also* Help
currency fields in databases, **111**
currency number format style in Excel, 164
custom spelling dictionaries, 410–412
customizing
  Microsoft Office, **264–266**
  pivot table display in Excel, 319–321
  pivot tables in Excel, 315–319
  toolbar buttons, 445
cutting and pasting, **84–85**. *See also* moving

473

INDEX

D

data entry, in databases, 89
data markers, for charts, 59
Data Only option, Access Print Setup dialog box, 295
data series
　for charts, 59
　entering in Excel, 382–384
databases, **86–93**. *See also* files; tables in Word
　in Access, **86–93**. *See also* fields; permissions; records; relationships
　　attaching tables from other applications, **198–200**
　　closing, 116–117
　　creating, 4, **86–87**, 117
　　creating relationships, **362–366**
　　entering data, 89
　　entering new records, 179
　　inserting in Word documents, **89–93**
　　navigating with Go To command (F5), **178–179**
　　opening, 4, 119–120
　　renaming database objects, 223
　　saving, 122
　　shared access options, 120
　　sorting records, **399–400**
　　updating databases inserted in Word documents, 92
　in Excel (lists), **86–93**. *See also* fields; filtering
　　creating, **88–89**
　　entering data, 89
　　filtering with AutoFilter feature, **124–125**
　　filtering with comparison or calculated criteria, **125–127**
　　inserting in Word documents, **89–93**
　　sorting, **403–406**
　　updating databases inserted in Word documents, 92
　filtering Excel databases, **123–127**
　　with AutoFilter feature, 124–125
　　with comparison or calculated criteria, 125–127
　　overview of, 123
　linking with Word documents, 368
　relationships in Access, **362–366**
　　between attached tables, 363
　　deleting, 366

　　displaying, 365
　　editing, 365
　　enforcing referential integrity, 363, 364
　　equi-joins (inner joins) and, 364
　　left outer joins and, 364–365
　　one-to-one relationships, 364
　　right outer joins and, 365
data-definition queries, in Access, 348
date fields in databases, **111**
dates, inserting, **93–96**
　in Access, 93–94
　in Excel, 94–95
　in PowerPoint, 95–96
　in Word documents, 96
DDE (Dynamic Data Exchange), 276. *See also* Object Linking and Embedding (OLE)
decimal number format styles in Excel, 165
Default option, Word Page Setup dialog box, 299
defining. *See also* creating
　fields in databases, 111–112
deleting
　annotations in Word, 21
　AutoCorrect entries in Word, 26
　AutoText entries in Word, 36
　bookmarks in Word, 39, 40
　borders and shading
　　in PowerPoint, 46
　　in Word, 48
　buttons from toolbars, 444
　captions in Word, 53
　cells, rows, or columns in Word tables, 427–428
　cross-references in Word, 81
　footnotes and endnotes, 150
　forgotten passwords in Access, 302
　frames in Word, 174
　groups in Access, 307, 309
　Mail folders, 140
　Mail messages, 239
　manual page breaks in Access, Excel, and Word, 288–289
　names from Mail address book groups, 17
　page numbers in Word, 293
　passwords in Excel and Word, 304
　protection in Excel workbooks, 346
　protection in Excel worksheets, 344
　range names in Excel, 354
　relationships in Access, 366

INDEX

with Replace dialog box, 137
scenarios in Excel, 377
section breaks in Word, 381–382
styles in Word, 420
tab stops in Word, 436
tracer arrows in Excel, 23
user accounts in Access, 308
worksheets in Excel, 459
dependent cells, in Excel, **23**
Derivatives option, Excel Solver dialog box, 397–398
Design view, in Access, 447
Details option, Mail Postoffice Manager, 322
direct cell dependents, **23**
direct cell precedents, **25**
disabling
AutoCorrect feature in Word, 27
automatic formula recalculation, 168
revision marking in Word, 371
displaying. *See also* hiding
annotations in Word, 20, 21–22
Auditing toolbar in Excel, 23
AutoFill shortcut menu in Excel, 382
bookmarks in Word, 40
Cue Cards, 3–4
Drawing tools, 98
field codes in Word documents, 112–113
file information in Find File dialog box, 131–132
footnotes and endnotes, 148–149
nonprinting characters in Word, 299, 380–381, 435
relationships in Access, 365
revision marks in Word, 370
section marks in Word, 380–381
shortcut menus, 382, 385–386
styles in Word, 414, 420
tab characters in Word, 435
Tip of the Day dialog box, 11
documents. *See also* Word for Windows
attaching templates to, 420, 440
comparing versions of, **369–370**
converting
to master documents, **255–256**
tables to, **434**
creating, 118
from templates, **437–438**
displaying field codes in, 112–113
editing
in Print Preview window, **538**
while finding or replacing data, **136**

inserting
databases in, **89–93**
field codes in, **113–114**
files in, **118–119**
into master documents, **257–258**
linking with Access databases, 368
margins, **252–254**, 374–375
master documents, **254–260**. *See also* cross-references
converting documents to, 255–256
creating, 256
editing subdocuments, 257
inserting subdocuments into, 257–258
locking subdocuments, 258
merging and splitting subdocuments, 259
moving or renaming subdocument files, 259–260
overview of, 254–255
merging revisions to, **241–242**
navigating, 13, 39
navigating with Go To command (F5), **181**
opening
documents in other file formats, 120
as read-only, 304
password-protecting, 301, **302–304**
revisions, **241–242**, **369–373**
changing format of revision marks, 371
comparing versions of a document, **369–370**
disabling revision marking, 371
displaying revision marks, 370
merging, 241–242, **372–373**
printing revision marks, 370
protection and, 346
reviewing, accepting, or rejecting, **371–372**
saving, 121–122, 123
summary information, **422–423**
dollar sign ($), for absolute references in Excel, 359
Draft Quality option, Excel Page Setup dialog box, 296
drag-and-drop feature, **97**
Drawing tools, **97–103**. *See also* graphics
in Access
Command Button tool, 100
Label tool, 100
Text Box tool, 100

INDEX

Arc or Filled Arc tools, 99
Arrow tool, 100
Bring to Front tool, 101
displaying, **98**
Ellipse or Filled Ellipse tools, 99
in Excel
   Create Button tool, 100
   Drop Shadow button, 101
   Text Box tool, 100
Fill Color tool, 100
Flip Horizontal or Flip Vertical tools, 102
Freeform or Filled Freeform tools, 99–100
Freehand tool, 100
Group tool, 102
Line Color tool, 101
Line tool, 99
in PowerPoint
   Arrowheads tool, 101
   AutoShapes tool, 101
   Edit Freeform Object command, 102
   Free Rotate tool, 102
   Line Style tool, 101
   Shadow Color tool, 101
   Shadow On/Off tool, 101
   Text tool, 100
Rectangle or Filled Rectangle tools, 99
Rotate tools, 102
Select tool, 101
Send to Back tool, 101–102
Ungroup tool, 102
in Word
   Align Drawing Objects tool, 103
   Bring in Front of Text button, 102
   Callout tool, 100
   Create Picture tool, 103
   Format Callout tool, 100
   Insert Frame tool, 103, 171
   Reshape tool, 102
   Send Behind Text button, 102
   Snap to Grid tool, 102–103
   Text Box tool, 100
drop caps, in Word, **103–104**
Drop Shadow button, in Excel, 101
Duplicate feature in Access and PowerPoint, **105–106**
Dynamic Data Exchange (DDE), 276. *See also* Object Linking and Embedding (OLE)
dynasets, in Access, 349

E

Edit Freeform Object command, in PowerPoint, 102
Edit menu, in Word, Bookmark command, 39
editing. *See also* changing
   AutoCorrect entries in Word, 26
   AutoText entries in Word, 36
   bookmarks in Word, 40–41
   captions in Word, 53
   charts, 60–61
   control labels in Access, 71–72
   embedded objects, 278
   footnotes and endnotes, 149
   forms in Access, 159–161
   formulas in Excel, 169–170
   graphics, **182–184**
      adding borders, 183
      adding frames, 183
      adding shading, 183–184
      copying, 183
      cropping in Word, 184
      moving, 182
      resizing, 182
   links, 217–219
   macros
      in Access, 224–225
      in Excel, 230–232
      in Word, 233–235
   Mail Merge data files, 245–246
   Mail Merge main documents, 246–247
   note separators, 150–151
   records in Access, 357
   relationships in Access, 365
   scenarios in Excel, 377
   slide layouts in PowerPoint, 33–34
   subdocuments in Word, 257
   tables in Word, 427–433
   toolbars, 443–444
   Word documents
      in Print Preview window, 338
      while finding or replacing data, 136
Ellipse tool, 99
e-mail. *See also* Mail
   sending Mail Merge documents via, 249
embedding, **277–281**. *See also* Object Linking and Embedding (OLE)
   in Access, 277, 281
   changing file format of embedded

INDEX

objects, 280–281
creating and embedding new objects, 277–278
editing embedded objects, 278
embedding existing files, 278–279
embedding part of a file, 280
embossed font style, 144
endnotes. *See* footnotes and endnotes
endpoint sheets, in Excel, 361
enforcing referential integrity in Access, 363, 364
entering. *See also* adding; inserting
  data in databases, 89
  references in Excel formulas, 358, 359–361
  sequences (series) in Excel, 382–384
  summary information for files, 422–423
  text values in Excel, 383
  trends in Excel, 384–385
envelopes, **106–109**. *See also* Word for Windows
  adding graphics to, 108–109
  addressing and printing, 106–108, 110
  postal bar codes, 107
  troubleshooting, **110**
equi-joins (inner joins), in Access, **364**
erasing. *See* deleting
error values, in Excel, **24**
errors, tracing in Excel worksheets, 24
Estimates option, Excel Solver dialog box, 397
event procedures, in Access, **267–269**
.EXC file extension, in Word, 409–410
Excel
  add-ins
    Report Manager, **340**
    Solver, **392–398**
    View Manager, **452–454**
  aligning data in cells, **17–19**
  AutoFill feature, **382–385**
    displaying AutoFill shortcut menu, 382
    entering linear trends, 384–385
    entering sequences, 382–384
    entering text values, 383
  AutoFilter feature, **124–125**
  AutoFormat feature, **28–29**
  borders and shading, **42–43**, 101
  cells, **56**. *See also* ranges; references
    active cell, 6
    aligning data in, **17–19**
    centering data across, 18

changing cells in scenarios, **375–376**
changing cells in Solver problems, 393, 394, 395
changing number formats, 164–165
copying, 361
deleting cell and range names, 354
deleting tracer arrows, 23
entering and editing data in, 56
inserting cell names in formulas, 354
moving, 361
naming cells and ranges, **352–353**
notes, **274–276**
replacing references with reference names, 354–355
selecting, **56**
target cells in Solver problems, 392–393
tracing cell dependents, **23**
tracing cell precedents, **25**
charts, **58–61**
  changing chart type, 61
  creating, 58–60
  editing, 60–61
clip art, **62–64**
columns
  centering data across, 18
  changing column widths, 460–461
  hiding, 462
  overview of, 7
  printing options, 296, 297
  unhiding, 462–463
cutting, copying, and pasting, **84–85**
databases (lists), **86–93**. *See also* fields
  creating, 88–89
  entering data, 89
  filtering with AutoFilter feature, 124–125
  filtering with comparison or calculated criteria, 125–127
  inserting in Word documents, **89–93**
  sorting, **403–406**
  updating databases inserted in Word documents, 92
drag-and-drop feature, **99**
Drawing tools. *See also specific Drawing tools entries*
  Create Button tool, 100
  displaying, **98**
  Drop Shadow tool, 101

477

INDEX

Text Box tool, 100
error values, 24
exiting, **109**
fields, **110–112**. *See also* databases
  defining types of, 111–112
  naming, 112
filtering databases, **123–127**. *See also* databases
  with AutoFilter feature, 124–125
  with comparison or calculated criteria, 125–127
Find File dialog box, **128–133**. *See also* Advanced Search dialog box
  defining search criteria, 128–131
  displaying found file information, 131–132
  managing found files, 132–133
Format Painter, **166**
forms, **154–155**
formula bar, 6
formulas, **168–170, 359–361**
  entering references in, 358, **359–361**
  hiding in protected worksheets, 343
  inserting range names in, 354
  moving and copying references and, 361–362
  overview of, **168–170**
Full Screen view, 448
functions, **174–176**. *See also* formulas
  AutoSum function, 175
  entering, 174–175
  Function Wizard, 175–176
Go To command (F5), **179–181**
Goal Seek feature, **177–178**. *See also* scenarios; Solver add-in
graphics, **182–187**
  clip art, **62–64**
  editing, 182–184
  inserting graphic files, 185–186
  linking graphic files, 186–187
headers and footers, **191–192**
inserting date and time, **94–95**
lists. *See* databases
macros, 220, **227–232**
  creating, 227–229
  editing, 230–232
  running, 230
managing windows, **454–456**
name box, 6
navigating, 7, **179–181**

notes, **274–276**
number formats, **164–165**
opening screens, **5–7**, 6
outlines, **282–284**
overview of, **5**
page breaks, **288–289**
page numbers, **291**
Page Setup options, 293–294, **295–297**
passwords, 301, **302–304**
  changing, 304
  creating, 302–304
  deleting, 304
  overview of, 301
pivot tables, **312–321**. *See also* queries
  creating, **312–315**
  creating in closed workbooks, 314
  customizing, **315–319**
  customizing display of, **319–321**
  grouping items, 319
  hiding items, 319–320
  sorting, 320–321
Print dialog box, **328–331**
Print Preview window, **335–336**, 448
protection, **341–346**
  hiding data in workbooks, 345
  hiding formulas in protected worksheets, 343
  passwords and, 342, 343, 344
  protecting forms, 341–343
  protecting workbooks, 344–346
  removing workbook protection, 346
  removing worksheet protection, 344
  for scenarios, 376
ranges, **352–355**. *See also* cells
  deleting range names, 354
  inserting range names in formulas, 354
  naming, 352–353
  replacing references with reference names, 354–355
  selecting named ranges, 354
references, **358–362**. *See also* cells
  3D references, **360–361**
  dollar sign ($) in, 359
  entering in formulas, 358, **359–361**
  moving and copying, **361–362**
  R1C1 reference style, 360
  reference operators (colon, comma, and space), 359

INDEX

relative versus absolute references, **358–359**
replacing references with reference names, **354–355**
repeating commands or actions, **366–367**
reports
  creating, **338–341**
  installing Report Manager add-in, 340
  scenario reports, 377–378
rows, 7
  changing row height, 461–462
  hiding, 462
  printing options, 296, 297
  unhiding, 462–463
Save Options dialog box, 121–122
scenarios. *See also* Goal Seek feature; Solver add-in
  creating, **375–378**
  saving Solver problems as, 395–396
series. *See* AutoFill feature
shortcut menus, 382, **385–386**
Solver add-in, **392–398**. *See also* Goal Seek feature; scenarios
  creating reports, 395
  saving problems as scenarios, 395–396, 398
  Solver Options dialog box, 396–398
  solving problems, 392–395
Spelling tool, **406–412**
  checking spelling, 407–409
  creating custom dictionaries, 410–412
  creating exclude dictionaries, 409–410
splitting windows, **455–456**
styles
  applying to worksheets, 413
  copying between workbooks, 415
  creating or changing, 417–418
  overview of, 412–413
summary information, **422–423**
switching between Microsoft Office applications, 1–2
toolbars
  Auditing toolbar, 22–25
  Formatting toolbar, 17–19, 42, 164–165
tracing, **22–25**
  cell dependents, 23
  cell precedents, 25
  deleting tracer arrows, 23
  errors in worksheets, 24
  overview of, 22–23
troubleshooting
  creating pivot tables in closed workbooks, 314
  disabling automatic formula recalculation, 168
  entering text values with custom lists, 383
  updating links, 219
Undo feature, **445–446**
View Manager add-in, **452–454**
views, **447–448, 452–454**
Wizards
  Function Wizard, 175–176
  Pivot Table Wizard, 312–319
workbooks, **457–460**
  adding worksheets to, **458–459**
  copying styles between, 415
  deleting worksheets, **459**
  hiding data, 345
  managing, **457–460**
  moving or copying worksheets between, **458**
  moving or copying worksheets in, **457–458**
  protecting, 344–346
  removing protection, 346
  renaming worksheets, **457**
  selecting worksheets in active workbook, **459–460**
worksheets, **7, 457–463**
  adding to workbooks, **458–459**
  applying styles to, **413**
  changing column width, **460–461**
  changing row height, **461–462**
  deleting, 459
  endpoint sheets, 361
  hiding, 345
  hiding columns or rows, **462**
  hiding formulas in protected worksheets, 343
  inserting in PowerPoint slides, 34–35
  margins, **251–252**
  moving or copying, **457–458**
  navigating, 7
  navigating with Go To command (F5), **179–181**
  protecting, 341–343
  removing protection, 344
  renaming, **457**

INDEX

saving, 121–122
selecting in active workbook, **459–460**
tracing errors in, 24
unhiding columns or rows, **462–463**
worksheet tabs, 7
Zoom options, **465–466**
exclude spelling dictionaries, 409–410
exiting
　applications, 109
　Microsoft Office, 110
exporting data from Access, **200–201**, 203–204. *See also* importing expressions in Access. *See also* formulas
　overview of, **167–168**
　in queries, 351
extensions. *See also* file formats
　.EXC in Word, 409–410

F

F4 key, Alt + F4 (Exit), 109
F5 key (Go To command), **178–181**. *See also* navigating
　in Access databases, 178–179
　in Excel worksheets, 179–181
　in Word documents, 181
faxes, sending Mail Merge documents via, 249
field codes, **112–115**. *See also* Word for Windows
　displaying in documents, 112–113
　inserting, 113–114
　navigating between fields, 115
　toggling between field codes and results, 114
　updating fields, 114–115
fields, **110–112**. *See also* Access; databases; Excel; records
　defining types of, 111–112
　inserting in Mail Merge data files, 247–248
　naming, 112
　records in Access and, 356
file extensions, .EXC in Word, 409–410
file formats
　changing file format of embedded objects, 280–281
　saving graphics in native formats in Word, 185
files, **115–123**. *See also* databases; documents; Find File dialog box; workbooks; worksheets
　closing, 116–117
　creating, 117–118
　embedding, **278–280**
　　existing files, 278–279
　　part of a file, 280
　graphic files, **185–187**
　　inserting, 185–186
　　linking, 186–187
　inserting in Word documents, 118–119
　linking, **216–217**
　in Mail
　　attaching to messages, 237, 241
　　backing up message files, 115–116
　　routing and sending files, **239–241**
　opening, 119–120
　saving, 120–123
　summary information, **422–423**
Fill Color tool, 100
fill patterns. *See* colors; shading
Filled Arc tool, 99
Filled Ellipse tool, 99
Filled Freeform tool, 99–100
Filled Rectangle tool, 99
filling in forms, in Word, 162–163
filtering
　Excel databases, **123–127**
　　with AutoFilter feature, 124–125
　　with comparison or calculated criteria, 125–127
　　overview of, 123
　Mail Merge data file records, 250
　tables in Microsoft Query table list box, 270
Find File dialog box, **128–133**. *See also* Advanced Search dialog box; finding
　defining search criteria, 128–131
　displaying found file information, 131–132
　managing found files, 132–133
Find and Replace features, **134–138**
　editing Word documents while finding or replacing data, 136
　finding data, 134–136
　finding formatting, 137
　replacing data, 137–138
finding
　clip art in ClipArt Gallery, 64
　data in records in Access, 358
　formatting, 137

480

INDEX

Mail messages, 263–264
First Page Number option, Excel Page Setup dialog box, 296
Flip Horizontal button, 102
Flip Vertical button, 102
folders, **138–141**. *See also* Mail
  changing attributes, 140
  copying, 141
  creating folders and subfolders, 139–140
  deleting, 140
  moving or copying private folders, 140–141
  promoting subfolders, 140
fonts, **141–145**. *See also* formatting
  applying, **142–144**
  bold style, 142
  changing
    character spacing (kerning), **144–145**
    default font, **145**
  coloring, 143
  copying formatting with Format Painter, **166**
  drop caps in Word, **103–104**
  embossed style, 144
  hidden text, 143
  italic style, 142
  selecting font size, 142–143
  shadow text style, 144
  small caps and all caps, 57, 144
  special effects, **143–144**
  strikethrough style, 143
  superscripts and subscripts, 143
  underline style, 143
footers, **188–195**
  in Access, **188–190**, 378–380
    for forms, 188–190, 378–380
    for reports, 188, 190, 378–380
  in Excel, **191–192**
  in Word, 79, **192–195**
    creating different headers and footers, 194–195
    creating or editing, 192–194
    page numbers and, 291, 293
    section and chapter cross-references in, 79
footnotes and endnotes, **146–151**. *See also* Word for Windows
  adding, 146–148
  converting, 148
  cross-references and, 146
  deleting, 150
  displaying, 148–149
  editing, 149
  editing note separators, 150–151
  formatting, 147–149
  printing endnotes, 299
Form view, in Access, 447
Form Wizard, in Access, 68
Format Callout tool, in Word, 100
Format Painter, **166**
formatting. *See also* fonts; styles; templates
  alignment in Excel, PowerPoint, and Word, **17–19**
  AutoFormat feature, **28–32**
    in Excel, 28–29
    in Word, 29–32
  copying with Format Painter, **166**
  finding, **137**
  numbers
    in Access, 164
    in Excel, 164–165
  PowerPoint slides with Slide Master, **260–262**
  in Word
    alignment, **17–19**
    AutoFormat feature, 29–32
    bullets and numbered lists, 50–52
    caption numbers, 55
    caption text, 55
    columns of text, 65–66, 67
    copying with Format Painter, **166**
    footnotes and endnotes, 147–149
    frames, 171–174
    page numbers, 292
    paragraphs, 300
    sections and, 298, 380, **381–382**
    text in frames, 172
Formatting toolbar
  in Excel, 17–19, 42, 164–165
  in PowerPoint and Word, 17–19
forms, **151–163**
  in Access. *See also* controls
    adding records in, 357
    attaching macros to, 220, 221, 226–227
    creating, **151–153**
    editing, **159–161**
    expressions (formulas) in, **167–168**
    functions in, 174–175
    headers and footers, 188–190, 378–380
    inserting date and time, **93–94**
    margins, **250–251**

481

INDEX

page breaks, **288**
page numbering, **290–291**
Print Setup options, **293–299**
sorting records, **399–400**
in Excel, **154–155**
in Word
creating, **155–158**
filling in, **162–163**
protecting, **161–162**, 347
formulas, **167–170**. *See also* functions
in Access, **167–168**
disabling automatic formula recalculation, 168
in Excel, **168–170**, **359–361**
entering references in, 358, **359–361**
hiding in protected worksheets, 343
inserting range names in, 354
overview of, **168–170**
in Word, 170
frames, 103, **170–174**. *See also* Word for Windows
adding to graphics, 183
creating, 103, **170–171**
deleting, 174
formatting, **171–174**
formatting text in, 172
Free Rotate tool, in PowerPoint, 102
Freeform tool, 99–100
Freehand tool, 100
Full Screen view, in Word or Excel, 448
functions, **174–176**. *See also* formulas
AutoSum function in Excel, 175
entering in Access, Excel, and Word, 174–175
Function Wizard in Excel, 175–176

G

global modules, in Access, 267
Go To command (F5), **178–181**. *See also* navigating
in Access databases, 178–179
in Excel worksheets, 179–181
in Word documents, 181
Goal Seek feature, in Excel, **177–178**. *See also* scenarios; Solver add-in
graphics, **182–187**. *See also* captions; Drawing tools
in Access, 186
adding to envelopes, 108–109

clip art, **62–64**
in columns of text in Word, 66
editing, **182–184**
adding borders, 183
adding frames, 183
adding shading, 183–184
copying, 183
cropping in Word, 184
moving, 182
resizing, 182
inserting graphic files, **185–186**
inserting in Word tables, 434
linking graphic files, **186–187**
placeholders
in PowerPoint slides, 34–35
in Word documents, 187
saving in native formats in Word, **185**
graphs, **58–61**
changing chart type, 61
creating, 58–60
editing, 60–61
gridlines
for charts, 59
guides in PowerPoint, 187–188
printing in Excel, 296
in Word tables, 424
group headers and footers, in Access reports, 379–380
Group button, 102
grouping data
in Access reports, 367, 401–403
in Excel pivot tables, 319
groups
in Access. *See also* user accounts; workgroups
creating, 306–307
deleting, 307, 309
naming, 306–307
printing security reports, 341
personal groups in Mail address book, 16–17
guides, in PowerPoint, **187–188**. *See also* gridlines

H

Handout Master, in PowerPoint, 262–263
hard page breaks
in Access, 288
in Excel, 288–289
in Word, 289
headers and footers, **188–195**

INDEX

in Access, **188–190**, 378–380
  for forms, 188–190, 378–380
  for reports, 188, 190, 378–380
in Excel, **191–192**
in Word, 79, **192–195**
  creating different headers and footers, 194–195
  creating or editing, 192–194
  page numbers and, 291, 293
  section and chapter cross-references in, 79
Help, **195–197**
  context-sensitive Help, 196–197
  Cue Cards, 3–4, 197
  Examples and Demos command, 197
  "How To" Help, 197
hidden text, 143
hiding. *See also* displaying
  columns or rows in Excel worksheets, 462
  Cue Cards, 3–4
  Excel worksheets, 345
  items in Excel pivot tables, 319–320
  slides in PowerPoint slide shows, 388
  Tip of the Day dialog box, 11

I

importing data into Access, **198–200**, **201–204**. *See also* exporting
  attaching tables from other applications, 198–200
  import/export specifications, 203–204
  importing data, **201–203**
indentation, in Word
  in columns of text, 67
  in paragraphs, **205–206**, 374
indirect cell dependents, **23**
indirect cell precedents, **25**
inner joins, in Access, **364**
Insert Frame button, in Word, 103, 171
inserting. *See also* adding; entering
  annotations in Word, 20–21
  AutoText entries in Word, 37
  cells, rows, or columns in Word tables, 428
  clip art, 62–64
  databases in Word documents, 89–93
  date and time, **93–96**
    in Access, 93–94
    in Excel, 94–95
    in PowerPoint, 95–96
    in Word, 96
  documents into Word master documents, 257–258
  fields in Mail Merge data files, 247–248
  files in Word documents, 118–119
  graphic files, 185–186
  graphics in Word tables, 434
  manual page breaks in Access, Excel, and Word, 288–289
  placeholders on PowerPoint slides for tables, worksheets, graphs, etc., 34–35
  range names in Excel formulas, 354
  slides in PowerPoint, 327
  subdocuments into master documents, 257–258
  tab characters in Word tables, 426
installing, Excel Report Manager add-in, 340
intersection operator, in Excel, 359
italic font style, 142
Item Layout option, Access Print Setup dialog box, 295
Item Size option, Access Print Setup dialog box, 295
Items Across option, Access Print Setup dialog box, 295
Iterations option, Excel Solver dialog box, 396

J

joining a different workgroup in Access, 464–465
joins, in Access, **364–365**
justification
  in Excel, 18–19
  in PowerPoint, 19
  in Word, 20

K

kerning, in Word, **144–145**

L

Label tool, in Access, 100
labels, **206–211**
  in Access, 100, 206–208
  in Word, 208–211

483

INDEX

leading, in Word, **212–213**
left outer joins, in Access, **364–365**
legends, for charts, 60
Line Color tool, 101
line spacing (leading), in Word, **212–213**
Line Style tool, in PowerPoint, 101
Line tool, 99
linear trends, in Excel, 384–385
lines. *See* borders
linking, 186–187, **213–219**. *See also* Object Linking and Embedding (OLE)
   in Access, 216
   data, **214–216**
   editing links, **217–219**
   in Excel, 214, 219
   files, **216–217**
   graphic files, **186–187**
   updating links in Excel and Word, 218, **219**
   in Word, 216, 218, 219
listening to sound annotations in Word, 21–22
lists. *See* databases
Load Model option, Excel Solver dialog box, 398
Location tab, Advanced Search dialog box, 129–130
locking. *See also* passwords; permissions; protection
   subdocuments in Word, 258
lowercase
   changing to uppercase in PowerPoint and Word, 57
   in passwords, 301
   and sorting in Word, 404

M

Macro view, in Access, 447
macros, **220–235**
   in Access, **220–227**, 447
     adding conditions, 220–221
     attaching to forms and reports, 220, 221, 226–227
     changing Macro window display, 225
     creating, 221–223
     creating macro groups, 225–226
     editing, 224–225
     overview of, 220
     renaming, 223
     running, 224
   in Excel, 220, **227–232**
     creating, 227–229
     editing, 230–232
     running, 230
   in Word, 220, **232–235**
     creating, 232–233
     editing, 233–235
     running, 233
magnification settings for Zoom views, **465–466**
Mail, 236–242
   address book, **15–17**
     adding names, 15–16
     creating personal groups, 16–17
     deleting names from groups, 17
   backing up message files, 115–116
   button bar, 8–9
   cutting, copying, and pasting, **84–85**
   exiting, **109**
   folder pane, **9**
   folders, **138–141**
     changing attributes, 140
     copying, 141
     creating folders and subfolders, 139–140
     deleting, 140
     moving or copying private folders, 140–141
     promoting subfolders, 140
   Mail Sign In dialog box, 8
   managing windows, **454–456**
   merging revisions to Word documents, **241–242**
   Message Finder, **263–264**
   message pane, **9**
   messages, 123, **236–239**, **263–264**
     answering, 238
     attaching files, 237, 241
     creating, 236–237
     deleting, 239
     finding, **263–264**
     receiving, 238–239
     saving, 123
   opening screens, **8–9**, *8*
   Postoffice Manager, **321–323**
   routing and sending files, **239–241**
   switching between Microsoft Office applications, 1–2
   workgroup post office (WGPO), 15, 321–323

INDEX

Mail Merge, **242–250**. *See also* Word for Windows
  creating main documents, 242–243
  designating data files, 243–245
  editing data files, 245–246
  editing main documents, 246–247
  filtering and sorting data file records, 250
  inserting fields in data files, 247–248
  linking Access databases with, 368
  merging data files and main documents, 248–250
  merging to e-mail or faxes, 249
mailing labels, **206–211**
  in Access, 100, 206–208
  in Word, 208–211
manual page breaks
  in Access, 288
  in Excel, 288–289
  in Word, 289
margins, **250–254**
  in Access forms and reports, 250–251
  in Excel worksheets, 251–252
  in Word documents, 252–254, 374–375
Master Document view, in Word, 448
master documents, **254–260**. *See also* cross-references; Word for Windows, 254–255
  converting documents to, 255–256
  creating, 256
  editing subdocuments, 257
  inserting subdocuments into, 257–258
  locking subdocuments, 258
  merging and splitting subdocuments, 259
  moving or renaming subdocument files, 259–260
Master views, **260–263**. *See also* PowerPoint
  Outline Master, Handout Master, and Notes Master, 262–263
  Slide Master, 260–262
Max Time Seconds option, Excel Solver dialog box, 396
memo fields in databases, **111**
menus, shortcut menus, **385–386**
merging. *See also* Mail Merge
  revisions in Word documents, 241–242, **372–373**
  scenarios in Excel, 377

  subdocuments in Word, 259
Message Finder, in Mail, **263–264**
messages, 123, **236–239**, **263–264**. *See also* Mail
  answering, 238
  attaching files, 237, 241
  creating, 236–237
  deleting, 239
  finding, **263–264**
  receiving, 238–239
  saving, 123
Microsoft Access. *See* **Access**
Microsoft Excel. *See* **Excel**
Microsoft Graph. *See* charts
Microsoft Mail. *See* **Mail**
Microsoft Office
  customizing, **264–266**
  exiting, **110**
  opening screens, 2–13
  switching between applications, 1–2
  Microsoft Office Manager toolbar, 1–2, 5, 8, **264–266**
Microsoft PowerPoint. *See* **PowerPoint**
Microsoft Query, **269–273**. *See also* queries
  creating queries, 269–272
  filtering tables in table list box, 270
  toolbar buttons, 272–273
Microsoft Windows, switching between open applications, 279
Microsoft Word for Windows. *See* Word for Windows
modifying. *See* changing; editing
Module view, in Word, 447
modules, in Access, **267–269**
mouse, drag-and-drop feature, 97
moving. *See also* cutting and pasting
  bookmarks in Word, 41
  buttons on toolbars, 444
  cells in Excel, 361
  controls in Access, 72–73
  with drag and drop, 97
  graphics, 182
  private Mail folders, 140–141
  references and formulas in Excel, 361–362
  subdocument files in Word, 259–260
  toolbars, 442
  worksheets in Excel, 457–458

INDEX

N

naming
  cells and ranges in Excel, 352–353
  fields in databases, 112
  groups and user accounts in Access, 306–307
navigating
  in Excel, 7, 179–181
  with Go To command, **178–181**
    in Access databases, 178–179
    in Excel worksheets, 179–181
    in Word documents, 181
  in PowerPoint, 11, 34
  in Word
    with bookmarks, 39
    with buttons and scroll bars, 13
    between fields, 115
    with Go To command, 181
nonprinting characters, displaying in Word, 299, 380–381, 435
Normal view, in Word, 447–448
notes. *See also* annotations; footnotes and endnotes
  creating speaker notes in PowerPoint, 327
  in Excel
    creating, **274–276**
    printing, 296
Notes Master, in PowerPoint, 262–263
Notes Pages view, in PowerPoint, 327, 449
number fields in databases, **111**
number formats
  in Access, 164
  in Excel, 164–165
number sign (#), for error values in Excel, 24
Number Slides From option, Excel Page Setup dialog box, 296
numbered lists
  in PowerPoint, 49
  in Word, **49–52**
numbering
  cells in Word tables, 434–435
  outline headings in Word, 287
  pages, **289–293**
    in Access, 290–291
    in Excel, 291
    in PowerPoint, 289
    in Word, 291–293

O

Object Linking and Embedding (OLE), **213–219**, **276–281**
  embedding, **277–281**
    in Access, 277, 281
    changing file format of embedded objects, 280–281
    creating and embedding new objects, 277–278
    editing embedded objects, 278
    embedding existing files, 278–279
    embedding part of a file, 280
  linking, 186–187, **213–219**
    in Access, 216
    data, **214–216**
    editing links, **217–219**
    in Excel, 214, 219
    files, **216–217**
    graphic files, **186–187**
    updating links in Excel and Word, 218, **219**
    in Word, 216, 218, 219
OLE object fields, **111**
one-to-one relationships, in Access, **364**
opening
  databases in Access, 4, 119–120
  documents
    documents in other file formats, 120
    as read-only, 304
  files, 119–120
opening screens, **2–13**. *See also* windows
  in Access, 3–5, *3*, *4*
  in Excel, 5–7, *6*
  in Mail, 8–9, *8*
  in PowerPoint, 9–11, *9*, *10*
  in Word, 11–13, *12*
operators
  comparison operators in Excel filters, 125–126
  in Excel formulas, 169
Organizer dialog box. *See also* Word for Windows
  copying macros, AutoText, and toolbars, 440
  copying styles, 416–417, 440
outer joins, in Access, **364–365**
Outline Master, in PowerPoint, 262–263

INDEX

Outline view
  in PowerPoint, 449
  in Word, 448
outlines, **282–287**
  in Excel, 282–284
  in PowerPoint, 282, 284–287, 326
  in Word
    creating, 282, 284–287
    numbering outline headings, 287

P

page breaks
  in Access, 288
  in Excel, 288–289
  in Word, 289
Page Layout view, in Word, 448
page numbers, **289–293**
  in Access, 290–291
  in Excel, 291
  in PowerPoint, 289
  in Word, 291–293
    chapter numbers, 292–293
    deleting, 293
    formatting, 292
    headers and footers and, 291, 293
    inserting, 291–292
    sections and, 293
Page Order option, Excel Page Setup dialog box, 297
page ranges, printing, 329–330
Page Setup options, **293–299**
  in Access (Print Setup dialog box), 293–295
  in Excel, 293–294, 295–297
  in Word, 293–294, 297–299
Paper Source option, Word Page Setup dialog box, 297
paragraph styles, in Word, 412–413
paragraphs, **205–206**, **299–300**. See also Word for Windows
  creating, 300
  creating a new line of text without creating a paragraph, 300
  displaying paragraph marks, 299
  formatting, 300
  indentation, **205–206**, 374
  line spacing (leading), 212–213
  spacing between, 300
  tab stops, **375**, **435–437**
pass-through queries, in Access, 348
passwords, **301–304**. See also locking; permissions; protection
  in Access, **301–302**
    clearing forgotten passwords, 302
    creating for user accounts, 301–302
  in Excel and Word, 301, **302–304**
    changing, 304
    creating, 302–304
    deleting, 304
    for protection in Excel, 342, 343, 344
    for protection in Word, 346, 347
Paste Special dialog box, 214–216
pasting, cutting, copying, and, **84–85**
patterns. See colors; shading
pen annotations, 20
percent number format style in Excel, 164
permissions, **305–312**. See also Access; passwords
  assigning, 309–312
  changing database ownership, 305–306
  creating groups, 306–307
  creating user accounts, 308–309
  deleting groups, 307, 309
  deleting user accounts, 308
  naming groups and user accounts, 306–307
personal groups in Mail address book, 16–17
Pick a Look Wizard, in PowerPoint, 323–324, 325
pivot tables, **312–321**. See also Excel; queries
  creating, **312–315**
  creating in closed workbooks, 314
  customizing, **315–319**
  customizing display of, **319–321**
  grouping items, 319
  hiding items, 319–320
  sorting, 320–321
placeholders. See also graphics
  in PowerPoint slides, 34–35
  in Word documents, 187
playing sound annotations in Word, 21–22
plot area, of charts, 59
point size, of fonts, 142–143
postal bar codes, 107
Postoffice Manager, in Mail, **321–323**
pound sign (#), for error values in Excel, 24
PowerPoint
  aligning
    objects with guides, **187–188**

487

INDEX

text, **17–19**
borders and shading, **44–47**
cells, **56**
changing case, **57**
charts, **58–61**
   changing chart type, 61
   creating, 58–60
   editing, 60–61
clip art, **62–64**
Cue Cards, 197
cutting, copying, and pasting, **84–85**
Drawing tools. *See also specific Drawing tools entries*
   Arrowheads tool, 101
   AutoShapes tool, 101
   displaying, **98**
   Edit Freeform Object command, 102
   Free Rotate tool, 102
   Line Style tool, 101
   Shadow Color tool, 101
   Shadow On/Off tool, 101
   Text tool, 100
Duplicate feature, **105–106**
embossed font style, 144
exiting, **109**
Find File dialog box, **128–133**.
   See also Advanced Search dialog box
   defining search criteria, 128–131
   displaying found file information, 131–132
   managing found files, 132–133
Format Painter, **166**
graphics, 34–35, 62–64, **182–187**
   clip art, **62–64**
   editing, 182–184
   inserting graphic files, 185–186
   linking graphic files, 186–187
   placeholders for, **34–35**
guides, **187–188**
inserting date and time, **95–96**
managing windows, **454–456**
Master views, **260–263**
   Outline Master, Handout Master, and Notes Master, 262–263
   Slide Master, 260–262
navigating, 11, 34
Notes Pages view, 327, 449
numbered lists, **49**
opening screens, **9–11**, *9*, *10*
Outline view, 449
outlines, 282, **284–287**, 326
overview of, **9–11**

page numbers, **289**
presentations, **117–118**, **323–327**.
   See also slide shows; slides
   changing slide layouts, 327
   changing templates, 327
   creating, **117–118**, **323–326**
   creating speaker notes, 327
   inserting slides, 327
   previewing, 327
   printing, 330
   saving, 120–121
   sorting slides, 326
Print dialog box, **328–331**
shortcut menus, **385–386**
Slide Setup options, **293–299**
Slide Show dialog box, 327, 387, 449
slide shows, **386–392**, **451–452**
   adding notes or drawings to slides, 387–388
   build effects, 390
   creating, **386–387**
   hiding slides, 388
   running with Viewer application, **451–452**
   setting slide timings, **391–392**
   transition effects, 389
Slide Sorter view, 326, 449
Slide view, 326, 449
slides, **32–35**, **324**
   adding notes or drawings to, 387–388
   changing slide layouts, 327
   creating with AutoLayout feature, 32–33
   editing layouts, 33–34
   formatting with Slide Master, **260–262**
   hiding in slide shows, 388
   inserting, 327
   inserting placeholders for tables, worksheets, graphs, etc., 34–35
   navigating, 34
   printing, 330
   setting slide timings in slide shows, **391–392**
   sorting, 326
Spelling tool, **406–412**
   checking spelling, 407–409
   creating custom dictionaries, 410–412
   creating exclude dictionaries, 409–410
summary information, **422–423**

INDEX

switching
  between Microsoft Office applications, 1–2
  between views, 11
templates, 323, 325, 327
Tip of the Day dialog box, 9, 324
toolbars, 10
  Formatting toolbar, 17–19
  Outlining toolbar, 285–287
  Standard toolbar, 34
Undo feature, **445–446**
Viewer application, **450–452**
  copying, 450–451
  running slide shows with, 451–452
views, **449**
Wizards
  AutoContent Wizard, 323–324
  Pick A Look Wizard, 323–324, 325
  Zoom options, **465–466**
precedent cells, in Excel, **25**
Precision option, Excel Solver dialog box, 397
presentations. *See* PowerPoint
previewing. *See also* Print Preview window
  presentations in PowerPoint, 327
Print Area option, Excel Page Setup dialog box, 296
Print dialog box, **328–331**
Print Preview window, **334–338**
  in Access, 334–335
  in Excel, 335–336, 448
  in Word, 336–338, 448
Print Quality option, Excel Page Setup dialog box, 295–296
Print Titles option, Excel Page Setup dialog box, 296
printer setup, **331–332**
printing, **328–334**
  endnotes, 299
  envelopes, 106–108, 110
  files, **328–331**
  to files, 330
  gridlines in Excel, 296
  notes in Excel, 296
  page ranges, 329–330
  revision marks in Word, 370
  row and column titles in Excel, 296
  Scale to Fit Paper option, 331
  sections in Word, 297–298
  security reports in Access, 341
  setting up printers, **331–332**
  slides in PowerPoint, 330

Word Print options, **332–333**
privileges. *See* passwords; permissions
procedures, in Access, **267–269**
promoting Mail subfolders, 140
protection. *See also* locking; passwords; permissions
  in Excel, **341–346**
    hiding data in workbooks, 345
    hiding formulas in protected worksheets, 343
    passwords and, 342, 343, 344
    protecting workbooks, 344–346
    protecting worksheets, 341–343
    removing workbook protection, 346
    removing worksheet protection, 344
    for scenarios, 376
  in Word
    locking subdocuments, 258
    passwords and, 346, 347
    protecting documents, **346–347**
    protecting forms, **161–162**, 347

Q

queries. *See also* Access; pivot tables
  in Access, **82–84**, **348–351**, 447
    action queries, 348
    crosstab queries, 82–84, 348
    data-definition queries, 348
    dynasets and, 349
    pass-through queries, 348
    select queries, 349–351
    sorting records, **399**
    types of, 348–349
    union queries, 348
  Microsoft Query, **269–273**
    creating queries, 269–272
    filtering tables in table list box, 270
    toolbar buttons, 272–273
Query view, in Access, 447
quitting. *See* exiting

R

R1C1 reference style, in Excel, 360
range operator (:), in Excel references, 359
ranges, **352–355**. *See also* cells; Excel
  deleting range names, 354

489

INDEX

inserting range names in formulas, 354
naming, 352–353
replacing references with reference names, 354–355
selecting named ranges, 354
Read-Only Recommended option, in Word, 304
receiving, Mail messages, 238–239
recording macros
  in Access, 221–223
  creating macro groups in Access, 225–226
  in Excel, 227–229
  in Word, 232–233
records
  in Access, **356–358**. *See also* databases; fields
    adding in datasheets, 356
    adding in forms, 357
    adding to databases, 179, 356–357
    editing, 357
    fields and, 356
    finding data in, 358
    sorting, **399–403**
    sorting in forms and tables, 399–400
    sorting in queries, 399
    sorting in reports, 401–403
    filtering and sorting Mail Merge data file records, 250
Rectangle tool, 99
references, **358–362**. *See also* cells; Excel
  3D references, 360–361
  dollar sign ($) in, 359
  entering in formulas, 358, **359–361**
  moving and copying, **361–362**
  R1C1 reference style, 360
  reference operators (colon, comma, and space), 359
  relative versus absolute references, **358–359**
  replacing references with reference names, **354–355**
referential integrity in Access, 363, 364
relationships, **362–366**. *See also* Access; databases
  between attached tables, 363
  deleting, 366
  displaying, 365
  editing, 365
  enforcing referential integrity, 363, 364
  equi-joins (inner joins) and, 364
  left outer joins and, 364–365
  one-to-one relationships, 364
  right outer joins and, 365
relative references in Excel, **358–359**
Remove User option, Mail Postoffice Manager, 322
renaming
  AutoText entries in Word, 37–38
  macros and database objects in Access, 223
  subdocument files in Word, 259–260
  worksheets in Excel, 457
Replace dialog box, **137–138**. *See also* Find and Replace features
replacing cell references with reference names in Excel, 354–355
Report view, in Access, 447
reports. *See also* Access; controls
  in Access
    attaching macros to, 220, 221, 226–227
    creating, **367–369**
    grouping data, **401–403**
    headers and footers, 188, 190, 378–380
    inserting date and time, **93–94**
    margins, **250–251**
    page breaks, **288**
    page numbering, **290–291**
    Print Setup options, **293–299**
    security reports, 341
    sorting records, **401–403**
    types of, **367–368**
  in Excel
    creating, **338–341**
    Report Manager add-in, 340
    scenario reports, 377–378
    Solver reports, 395
Reshape button, in Word, 102
resizing
  controls in Access, 74–75
  graphics, 182
Review AutoFormat Changes dialog box, in Word, 31–32
revisions, **241–242**, **369–373**. *See also* Word for Windows
  changing format of revision marks, 371
  comparing versions of a document, **369–370**

INDEX

disabling revision marking, 371
displaying revision marks, 370
merging, 241–242, **372–373**
printing revision marks, 370
protection and, 346
reviewing, accepting, or rejecting, 371–372
right outer joins, in Access, **365**
rights. *See* passwords; permissions
Rotate Right button, 102
routing and sending files via Mail, **239–241**
Row and Column Headings option, Excel Page Setup dialog box, 297
Row Spacing option, Access Print Setup dialog box, 295
rows
  in Excel
    changing row height, 461–462
    hiding, 462
    overview of, 7
    printing options, 296, 297
    unhiding, 462–463
  in Word tables
    adding, 428–429
    changing row height, 430–433
    deleting, 427–428
    inserting, 428
    selecting, 432
rulers
  in Access, 373
  in Word, 12, **373–375**, **435–436**
running
  macros
    in Access, 224
    in Excel, 230
    in Word, 233
  slide shows with Viewer application, 451–452

S

Save Model option, Excel Solver dialog box, 398
Save Options, in Excel and Word, 121–122
saving
  files, 120–123
  Mail messages, 123
  Solver problems as Excel scenarios, 395–396, 398
Scale to Fit Paper option, Print dialog box, 331

Scaling option, Excel Page Setup dialog box, 295
scenarios. *See also* Excel; Goal Seek feature; Solver add-in
  creating, **375–378**
  saving Solver problems as, 395–396
screens, **2–13**. *See also* windows
  in Access, 3–5, *3, 4*
  in Excel, 5–7, *6*
  in Mail, 8–9, *8*
  in PowerPoint, 9–11, *9, 10*
  in Word, 11–13, *12*
Search option, Excel Solver dialog box, 398
searches. *See* Find File dialog box; finding
Section Start option, Word Page Setup dialog box, 297–298
sections, **378–382**. *See also* breaks
  in Access forms and reports (headers and footers), **378–380**
  in Word, **380–382**
    adding, 381
    deleting section breaks, 381–382
    displaying section marks, 380–381
    formatting and, 298, 380, 381–382
    page numbers and, 293
    printing, 297–298
security. *See also* locking; passwords; permissions; protection
security information reports in Access, 341
select queries, in Access, **349–351**
Select button, 101
selecting
  cells, rows, columns, or data in Word tables, 432
  columns of text for sorting in Word, 405
  controls in Access, 73–74
  font size, 142–143
  named ranges in Excel, 354
  worksheets in active Excel workbook, 459–460
Send to Back tool, 101–102
Send Behind Text button, in Word, 102
sending
  files via Mail, 239–241
  Mail Merge documents via fax or e-mail, 249
sentences, capitalizing first word of, 57
separators, for footnotes and endnotes, 150–151

491

INDEX

series
  for charts, 59
  entering in Excel, 382–384
shading, **42–48**. *See also* colors
  adding to graphics, 183–184
  in Excel, 42–43, 101
  in PowerPoint, 44–47
  in Word, 47–48
Shadow Color tool, in PowerPoint, 101
Shadow On/Off button, in PowerPoint, 101
shadow text font style, 144
Shared Folders option, Mail Postoffice Manager, 322
shortcut keys, for Word styles, 414–415
shortcut menus, 382, **385–386**
Show Iteration Results option, Excel Solver dialog box, 397
showing. *See* displaying; hiding
single-column reports, in Access, 367
sizing
  controls in Access, 74–75
  graphics, 182
Slide Show dialog box, in PowerPoint, 327, 387, 449
slide shows, **386–392**, **451–452**. *See also* PowerPoint
  adding notes or drawings to slides, 387–388
  build effects, 390
  creating, **386–387**
  hiding slides, 388
  running with Viewer application, **451–452**
  setting slide timings, **391–392**
  transition effects, 389
Slide Sorter view, in PowerPoint, 326, 449
Slide view, in PowerPoint, 326, 449
slides, **32–35, 324**. *See also* PowerPoint
  adding notes or drawings to, 387–388
  changing slide layouts, 327
  creating with AutoLayout feature, 32–33
  editing layouts, 33–34
  formatting with Slide Master, **260–262**
  hiding in slide shows, 388
  inserting, 327
  inserting placeholders for tables, worksheets, graphs, etc., 34–35
  navigating, 34
  printing, 330
  setting slide timings in slide shows, **391–392**
  Slide Setup options, **293–299**
  sorting, 326
small caps option, 57, 144
Snap to Grid tool, in Word, 102–103
Solver add-in, **392–398**. *See also* Excel; Goal Seek feature; scenarios
  creating reports, 395
  saving problems as scenarios, 395–396, 398
  Solver Options dialog box, 396–398
  solving problems, 392–395
sorting, **399–406**
  Access records, **399–403**
    in forms and tables, 399–400
    in queries, 399
    in reports, 401–403
  in Excel
    databases (lists), **403–406**
    pivot tables, 320–321
  PowerPoint slides, 326
  in Word, **403–406**
    Mail Merge data file records, 250, 403
    selecting columns of text, 405
    undoing, 406
sound annotations, in Word, 21
sound notes, in Excel, **274–276**
space, as intersection operator in Excel, 359
Spacebar, Alt + Spacebar (Control menu), 109
spacing in Word
  character spacing (kerning), 144–145
  line spacing (leading), 212–213
  paragraph spacing, 300
speaker notes, in PowerPoint, 327
special effects
  with fonts, 143–144
  in PowerPoint slide shows, 389–390
Spelling tool, **406–412**
  checking spelling, 407–409
  creating custom dictionaries, 410–412
  creating exclude dictionaries, 409–410
splitting
  subdocuments in Word, 259
  windows in Excel and Word, 455–456
spreadsheets. *See* Excel

INDEX

strikethrough font style, 143
styles, **412–420**. *See also* formatting; templates
  in Excel
    applying to worksheets, 413
    copying between workbooks, 415
    creating or changing, 417–418
  in Word
    applying to documents, 413–415
    copying, 415–417, 440
    copying with Style Gallery, 421–422
    creating or changing, 418–419
    deleting, 420
    displaying, 414, 420
    paragraph styles versus character styles, 412–413
    shortcut keys, 414–415
    updating in templates, 440
subdocuments. *See also* master documents; Word for Windows
  editing, 257
  inserting into master documents, 257–258
  locking, 258
  merging and splitting, 259
  moving or renaming subdocument files, 259–260
summary information, **422–423**
Summary tab, Advanced Search dialog box, 130
summary totals reports, in Access, 367
superscript and subscript font style, 143
Suppress Endnotes option, Word Page Setup dialog box, 299
switching
  between Microsoft Office applications, 1–2
  between open applications in Windows, 279

T

3D references, in Excel, 360–361
tab characters
  displaying, 435
  inserting in Word tables, 426
tab stops, in Word, **375**, **435–437**
table reports, in Access, 368
Table view, in Access, 446–447
tables in Word, **424–435**. *See also* databases; pivot tables
  adding cells, rows, or columns, 428–429
  changing
    column widths, 429–430
    row height, 430–433
    table format, **433–434**
  converting to documents, 434
  creating, **424–426**
  creating headings, 426–427
  deleting cells, rows, or columns, 427–428
  editing, **427–433**
  gridlines, 424
  inserting
    cells, rows, or columns in, 428
    graphics in, 434
    in PowerPoint slides, **34–35**
    tab characters in, 426
  numbering cells, **434–435**
  overview of, 424
  selecting cells, rows, columns, or data, 432
  Table AutoFormat feature, 433
target cells, in Excel Solver problems, 392–393
templates. *See also* formatting; styles
  in PowerPoint, 323, 325, 327
  in Word, **437–440**
    attaching to documents, 420, 440
    copying AutoText entries between, 38, 440
    copying styles from, 415–417, 421–422, 440
    creating documents from, **437–438**
    creating new templates, **438–439**
    Templates and Add-ins dialog box, 439–440
    updating styles in, 440
text. *See also* columns of text
  aligning
    overview of, **17–19**
    for printing in Word, 298
  centering text in Excel cells, 17
  Drawing tools in Word
    Bring in Front of Text button, 102
    Send Behind Text button, 102
    Text Box tool, 100
  entering text values in Excel, 383
  formatting
    caption text in Word, 55
    text in Word frames, 172
  hidden text in Word, 143
Text Box tool, in Access, Excel, and Word, 100

INDEX

text fields in databases, **111**
Text tool, in PowerPoint, 100
Thesaurus, in Word, **441–442**
three-dimensional references, in Excel, 360–361
time fields in databases, **111**
time, inserting, **93–96**
 in Access, 93–94
 in Excel, 94–95
 in PowerPoint, 95–96
 in Word, 96
Timestamp tab, Advanced Search dialog box, 131
titles, capitalizing each word in, 57
toggling, between field codes and results in Word, 114
Tolerance option, Excel Solver dialog box, 397
toolbars, **442–445**
 in Access, 5
 adding, deleting, moving, copying, or customizing buttons, **444–445**
 creating or editing, **443–444**
 in Excel
  Auditing toolbar, 22–25
  Formatting toolbar, 17–19, 42, 164–165
  Microsoft Query toolbar, 272–273
  moving, **442**
  Outlining toolbar in PowerPoint and Word, 285–287
 in PowerPoint, 10
  Formatting toolbar, 17–19
  Outlining toolbar, 285–287
  Standard toolbar, 34
 in Word
  Formatting toolbar, 17–19
  Outlining toolbar, 285–287
tracing in Excel, **22–25**
 cell dependents, 23
 cell precedents, 25
 deleting tracer arrows, 23
 errors in worksheets, 24
transition effects, in PowerPoint slide shows, 389
trends, in Excel, 384–385
trial-and-error analysis, in Excel, **177–178**
troubleshooting
 Access
  changing Macro window display in Access, 225
  forgotten passwords, 302
  renaming database objects, 223
  searching for data in records, 358
 Excel
  creating pivot tables in closed workbooks, 314
  disabling automatic formula recalculation, 168
  entering text values with custom lists, 383
  updating links, 219
 filtering tables in Microsoft Query table list box, 270
 finding formatting, 137
 Word for Windows
  annotations, 20
  AutoFormat feature, 30
  AutoText entries, 38
  editing in Word Print Preview window, 338
  formatting text in frames, 172
  merging revisions into original document, 373
  printing envelopes, 110
  section or chapter cross-references in headers and footers, 79
  sections and formatting, 298
  selecting cells, rows, columns, or data in tables, 432
  selecting columns of text for sorting, 405
  updating links, 219
turning off
 AutoCorrect feature in Word, 27
 automatic formula recalculation, 168
 revision marking in Word, 371

U

unbound controls, **68**. *See also* Access; controls
 creating, 70–71
underline font style, 143
Undo feature
 overview of, **445–446**
 undoing sorting in Word, 406
Ungroup button, 102
union operator (,) in Excel references, 359
union queries, in Access, 348
updating
 caption numbers in Word, 54
 databases inserted in Word documents, 92

INDEX

fields in Word, 114–115
links in Excel and Word, 218, 219
styles in Word templates, 440
uppercase
  changing to lowercase in PowerPoint and Word, 57
  in passwords, 301
  and sorting in Word, 404
Use Automatic Scaling option, Excel Solver dialog box, 397
user accounts. *See also* Access; workgroups
  creating, 308–309
  deleting, 308
  naming, 306–307
  passwords, **301–302**
  printing security reports, 341

V

Vertical Alignment option, Word Page Setup dialog box, 298
View Manager add-in, in Excel, **452–454**
Viewer application, **450–452**. *See also* PowerPoint
  copying, 450–451
  running slide shows with, 451–452
viewing. *See* displaying; hiding
views, **446–450**, **452–454**
  in Access, 446–447
  in Excel, 448, 452–454
  in PowerPoint, 449
  in Word, 447–448
voice annotations, 21

W

windows, **454–456**. *See also* opening screens
Wizards. *See also* charts; crosstab queries
  in Access
    Form Wizard, 68
    Mailing Label Wizard, 206–208
    Report Wizards, 367–369
  in Excel
    Function Wizard, 175–176
    Pivot Table Wizard, 312–319
  in PowerPoint
    AutoContent Wizard, 323–324
    Pick A Look Wizard, 323–324, 325

Word for Windows
  aligning text
    overview of, **17–19**
    for printing, 298
  all caps option, 57
  annotations, **19–22**
    deleting, 21
    displaying, 20
    inserting, 20–21
    pen annotations, 20
    protection and, 347
    viewing or listening to, 21–22
    voice annotations, 21
  AutoCaption feature, **53–55**
  AutoCorrect entries, **25–28**
    changing, 26
    creating, 26–28
    disabling, 27
  AutoFormat feature, **29–32**
    Table AutoFormat feature, 433
  AutoText entries, **35–38**
    copying between templates, 38, 440
    creating, 35–36
    deleting, 36
    editing, 36
    inserting, 37
    renaming, 37–38
  bookmarks, **38–41**
    copying or moving, 41
    creating, 39–40
    deleting, 39, 40
    displaying, 40
    editing, 40–41
    navigating, 39
  borders and shading, **47–48**
  bullets, **49–52**
  captions, **52–55**
    adding to graphics, 52–53
    AutoCaption feature, 53–55
    changing numbering format, 55
    deleting, 53
    editing, 53
    formatting, 55
    updating caption numbers, 54
  cells, **56**
  changing case, **57**
  charts, **58–61**
    changing chart type, 61
    creating, 58–60
    editing, 60–61
  clip art, **62–64**
  columns of text, **65–67**. *See also* tables
    changing layout, 67
    creating, 65–66

495

INDEX

graphics in, 66
cross-references, **79–82**. *See also* master documents
  changing or deleting, 81
  creating, 79–81
  footnotes, endnotes and, 146
  section or chapter cross-references in headers and footers, 79
cutting, copying, and pasting, **84–85**
displaying nonprinting characters, 299, 380–381, 435
documents. *See also* master documents
  attaching templates to, 420, 440
  converting tables to, 434
  converting to master documents, **255–256**
  creating, 118
  creating from templates, **437–438**
  displaying field codes in, 112–113
  editing in Print Preview window, **338**
  editing while finding or replacing data, 136
  inserting databases in, **89–93**
  inserting date and time in, **96**
  inserting field codes, **113–114**
  inserting files in, 118–119
  inserting into master documents, **257–258**
  linking with Access databases, 368
  margins, **252–254**, 374–375
  merging revisions to, **241–242**
  navigating, 13, 39
  navigating with Go To command (F5), **181**
  opening documents in other file formats, 120
  opening as read-only, 304
  password-protecting, 301, **302–304**
  saving, 121–122, 123
  summary information, **422–423**
drag-and-drop feature, **99**
Drawing tools. *See also specific Drawing tools entries*
  Align Drawing Objects tool, 103
  Bring in Front of Text button, 102
  Callout tool, 100
  Create Picture tool, 103
  displaying, **98**
  Format Callout tool, 100
  Insert Frame tool, 103
  Reshape tool, 102
  Send Behind Text button, 102
  Snap to Grid tool, 102–103
  Text Box tool, 100
drop caps, **103–104**
envelopes, **106–109**
  adding graphics to, 108–109
  addressing and printing, 106–108, 110
  postal bar codes, 107
  troubleshooting, **110**
exiting, **109**
field codes, **112–115**
  displaying in documents, 112–113
  inserting, 113–114
  navigating between fields, 115
  toggling between field codes and results, 114
  updating fields, 114–115
Find File dialog box, **128–133**. *See also* Advanced Search dialog box
  defining search criteria, 128–131
  displaying found file information, 131–132
  managing found files, 132–133
footnotes and endnotes, **146–151**
  adding, 146–148
  converting, 148
  cross-references and, 146
  deleting, 150
  displaying, 148–149
  editing, 149
  editing note separators, 150–151
  formatting, 147–149
Format Painter, **166**
formatting
  alignment, **17–19**
  AutoFormat feature, 29–32
  bullets and numbered lists, 50–52
  caption numbers, 55
  caption text, 55
  columns of text, 65–66, 67
  copying with Format Painter, **166**
  footnotes and endnotes, 147–149
  frames, 171–174
  page numbers, 292
  paragraphs, 300
  sections and, 298, 380, **381–382**
  text in frames, 172
forms
  creating, **155–158**
  filling in, **162–163**

INDEX

protecting, **161–162**, 347
formulas, **170**
frames, 103, **170–174**. *See also* graphics
  adding to graphics, 183
  creating, 103, **170–171**
  deleting, 174
  formatting, **171–174**
  formatting text in, 172
Full Screen view, 448
functions, **174–175**. *See also* formulas
Go To command (F5), **181**
graphics, **182–187**. *See also* frames
  adding frames, 183
  adding to envelopes, 108–109
  clip art, **62–64**
  in columns of text, 66
  cropping, 184
  editing, **182–184**
  inserting graphic files, **185–186**
  linking graphic files, **186–187**
  placeholders for, 187
  saving in native formats, **185**
headers and footers, 79, **192–195**
  creating different headers and footers, 194–195
  creating or editing, 192–194
  page numbers and, 291, 293
  section and chapter cross-references in, 79
indentation
  in columns of text, 67
  in paragraphs, **205–206**, 374
insertion point, 12
line spacing (leading), **212–213**
macros, 220, **232–235**
  creating, 232–233
  editing, 233–235
  running, 233
Mail Merge, **242–250**
  creating main documents, 242–243
  designating data files, 243–245
  editing data files, 245–246
  editing main documents, 246–247
  filtering and sorting data file records, 250
  inserting fields in data files, 247–248
  linking Access databases with, 368
  merging data files and main documents, 248–250
  merging to e-mail or faxes, 249
mailing labels, **208–211**

managing windows, **454–456**
Master Document view, 448
master documents, **254–260**. *See also* cross-references, 254–255
  converting documents to, 255–256
  creating, 256
  editing subdocuments, 257
  inserting subdocuments into, 257–258
  locking subdocuments, 258
  merging and splitting subdocuments, 259
  moving or renaming subdocument files, 259–260
navigating
  with bookmarks, 39
  with buttons and scroll bars, 13
  between fields, 115
  with Go To command, 181
Normal view, 447–448
numbered lists, **49–52**
opening screens, **11–13**, *12*
Organizer dialog box
  copying macros, AutoText, and toolbars, 440
  copying styles, 416–417, 440
Outline view, 448
outlines, 282, **284–287**
page breaks, **288–289**
Page Layout view, 448
page numbers, **291–293**
  chapter numbers, 292–293
  deleting, 293
  formatting, 292
  headers and footers and, 291, 293
  inserting, 291–292
  sections and, 293
Page Setup options, 293–294, **297–299**
paragraphs, **299–300**
  creating, 300
  creating a new line of text without creating a paragraph, 300
  displaying paragraph marks, 299
  formatting, 300
  indentation, **205–206**, 374
  line spacing (leading), 212–213
  spacing between, 300
  tab stops, **375**, **435–437**
passwords, 301, **302–304**. *See also* protection
  changing, 304
  creating, 302–304

497

INDEX

deleting, 304
for protection, 346, 347
Print dialog box, **328–331**
Print Preview window, **336–338**, 448
Print tab, Options dialog box, **332–333**
protection. *See also* passwords
  locking subdocuments, 258
  passwords and, 346, 347
  protecting documents, **346–347**
  protecting forms, **161–162**, 347
repeating commands or actions, **366–367**
Review AutoFormat Changes dialog box, 31–32
revisions, **241–242**, **369–373**
  changing format of revision marks, 371
  comparing versions of a document, **369–370**
  disabling revision marking, 371
  displaying revision marks, 370
  merging, 241–242, **372–373**
  printing revision marks, 370
  protection and, 346
  reviewing, accepting, or rejecting, **371–372**
rows. *See* tables
rulers, 12, **373–375**, **435–436**
Save tab, Options dialog box, 121–122
sections, **380–382**
  adding, 381
  deleting section breaks, 381–382
  displaying section marks, 380–381
  formatting and, 298, 380, 381–382
  page numbers and, 293
  printing, 297–298
shortcut menus, **385–386**
small caps option, 57
sorting, **403–406**
  Mail Merge data file records, 250, 403
  selecting columns of text for, 405
  undoing, 406
spacing
  character spacing (kerning), 144–145
  line spacing (leading), 212–213
  paragraph spacing, 300
Spelling tool, **406–412**
  checking spelling, 407–409

creating custom dictionaries, 410–412
creating exclude dictionaries, 409–410
splitting windows, **455–456**
Style Gallery, **420–422**
styles, 412–413. *See also* templates
  applying to documents, 413–415
  copying, 415–417, 440
  copying with Style Gallery, 421–422
  creating or changing, 418–419
  deleting, 420
  displaying, 414, 420
  paragraph styles versus character styles, 412–413
  shortcut keys, 414–415
  updating in templates, 440
summary information, **422–423**
switching between Microsoft Office applications, 1–2
tab characters
  displaying, 435
  inserting in tables, 426
tab stops, **375**, **435–437**
tables, **424–435**
  adding cells, rows, or columns, 428–429
  changing column widths, 429–430
  changing row height, 430–433
  changing table format, **433–434**
  converting to documents, 434
  creating, **424–426**
  creating headings, 426–427
  deleting cells, rows, or columns, 427–428
  editing, **427–433**
  gridlines, 424
  inserting cells, rows, or columns, 428
  inserting graphics, 434
  inserting in PowerPoint slides, 34–35
  inserting tab characters, 426
  numbering cells, **434–435**
  selecting cells, rows, columns, or data, 432
  Table AutoFormat feature, 433
templates, **437–440**. *See also* styles
  attaching to documents, 420, 440
  copying AutoText entries between, 38, 440
  copying styles from, 415–417, 421–422, 440

INDEX

creating documents from, **437–438**
creating new templates, **438–439**
Templates and Add-ins dialog box, 439–440
updating styles in, 440
Thesaurus, **441–442**
Tip of the Day dialog box, 11
toolbars
  Formatting toolbar, 17–19
  Outlining toolbar, 285–287
troubleshooting
  annotations, 20
  AutoFormat feature, 30
  AutoText entries, 38
  editing in Word Print Preview window, 338
  formatting text in frames, 172
  merging revisions into original document, 373
  printing envelopes, 110
  section or chapter cross-references in headers and footers, 79
  sections and formatting, 298
  selecting cells, rows, columns, or data in tables, 432
  selecting columns of text for sorting, 405
  updating links, 219
Undo feature, 406, **445–446**
views, **447–448**
Zoom options, **465–466**
workgroup post office (WGPO), in Mail, 15, 321–323
workbooks, **457–460**. *See also* Excel
  adding worksheets to, **458–459**
  copying styles between, 415
  deleting worksheets, **459**
  hiding data in, 345
  managing, **457–460**
  moving or copying worksheets between, **458**
  moving or copying worksheets in, **457–458**
  protecting, 344–346
  removing protection, 346
  renaming worksheets, **457**
  selecting worksheets in active workbook, **459–460**
workgroups, **463–465**. *See also* Access; user accounts
  creating unique workgroups, 463–464
  joining a different workgroup, 464–465
worksheets, **7, 457–463**. *See also* Excel
  adding to workbooks, **458–459**
  applying styles to, **413**
  changing column width, **460–461**
  changing row height, **461–462**
  deleting, 459
  endpoint sheets, 361
  hiding, 345
  hiding columns or rows, **462**
  hiding formulas in protected worksheets, 343
  margins, **251–252**
  moving or copying, **457–458**
  navigating, 7
    with Go To command (F5), **179–181**
  protecting, 341–343
  removing protection, 344
  renaming, **457**
  saving, 121–122
  selecting in active workbook, **459–460**
  tracing errors in, 24
  unhiding columns or rows, **462–463**
worksheet tabs, 7

Y

Yes/No fields in databases, **111**

Z

Zoom options, **465–466**

499

Everything you need to star using the Internet today!

FREE SOFTWARE

Windows, a modem and this comprehensive book/software package. That's everything you need to start using the Intern now. Includes economical, full-featured, direct Internet connection. Point and click interface. Gopher, World Wide E-mail, Usenet Newsgroups, FTP, Telnet and much more.

Now available wherever computer books are sold.
250 pages.
ISBN 1529-2

SYBEX
Shortcuts to Understanding.

SYBEX, Inc.
2021 Challenger
Alameda, CA 945
1-800-227-2346
1-510-523-8233

Now available wherever computer books are sold.

Ready to be on-line?

Here's a beginner's guide that provides a clear, step-by-step path to hooking up to the outside world. Find out what to look for when shopping for a modem, what to do with it when you've bought it, and which online service will serve you best.

FREE disk Includes NetCruiser on disk with everything you need to access the Internet instantly.

Your First Modem
SECOND EDITION
The Essential How-To Guide for Beginners

Sharon Crawford

- Learn to Shop for and Install Your First Modem
- Compare Popular Online Services
- Access the Internet with NetCruiser Software Included with This Book and Save the Usual $25 Registration Fee

300 pages   ISBN 1683-3

SYBEX

SYBEX Inc. • 2021 Challenger Dr., Alameda, CA 94501 • 800-227-2346 • 510-523-8233

Outlining Toolbar Buttons

⬅	Promote	All	Show All
➡	Demote	=	Show First Line Only
➡	Demote to Body Text	A̲A̲	Show Formatting
⬆	Move Up		Master Document View
⬇	Move Down		Show Titles
➕	Expand		Show All
➖	Collapse		

View Buttons

	Slide View		Page Layout View
	Outline View		Full Screen
	Slide Sorter View		Design View
	Notes Pages View		Datasheet View
	Slide Show		Form View
	Normal View		